Abelard

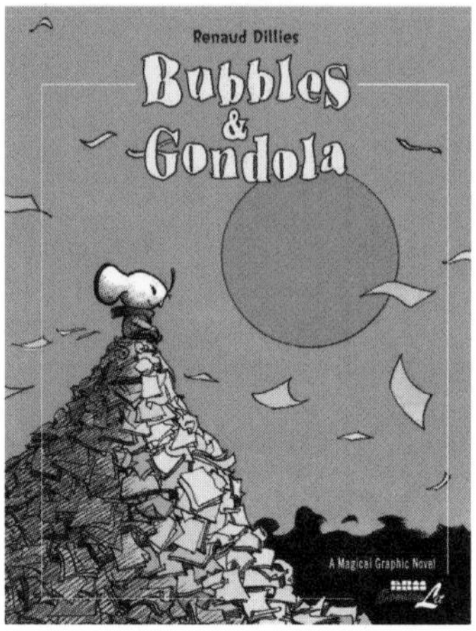
Renaud Dillies
Bubbles
&
Gondola
A Magical Graphic Novel

Dillies ~ Hautière

Abelard

Colors: Christophe Bouchard

[redacted]

NBM ComicsLit

To Eugène Hütz.
To my children, Adèle and Gilles, from whom
Abelard and Gaston have borrowed some of their retorts.
Believe in your dreams, don't let life break you down.
Régis

To Marie, to Carl…to the stars!
Renaud

This story is fiction.
But, do let's agree that
just because everything's false
doesn't mean that nothing's true.

ISBN: 978-1-56163-701-0
Library of Congress Control Number: 2012944123
© 2011 Dillies – Hautière- Dargaud Benelux
(Dargaud-Lombard s.a.)
© 2012 NBM for the English Translation
Translation by Joe Johnson
Lettering by Ortho
Printed in China

1st printing September 2012

Comicslit is an imprint
and trademark of

NANTIER · BEALL · MINOUSTCHINE
Publishing inc.
new york

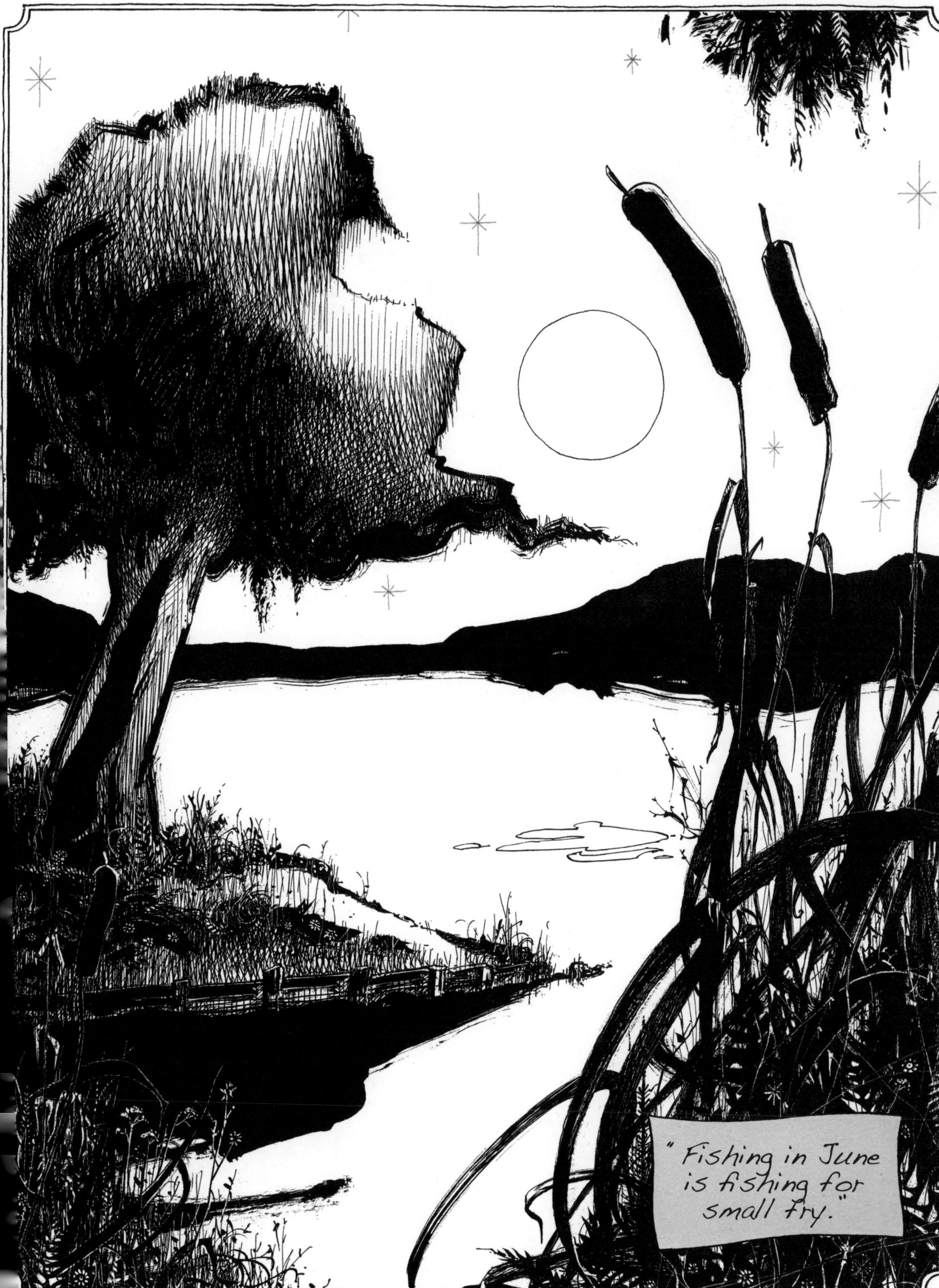
" Fishing in June is fishing for small fry."

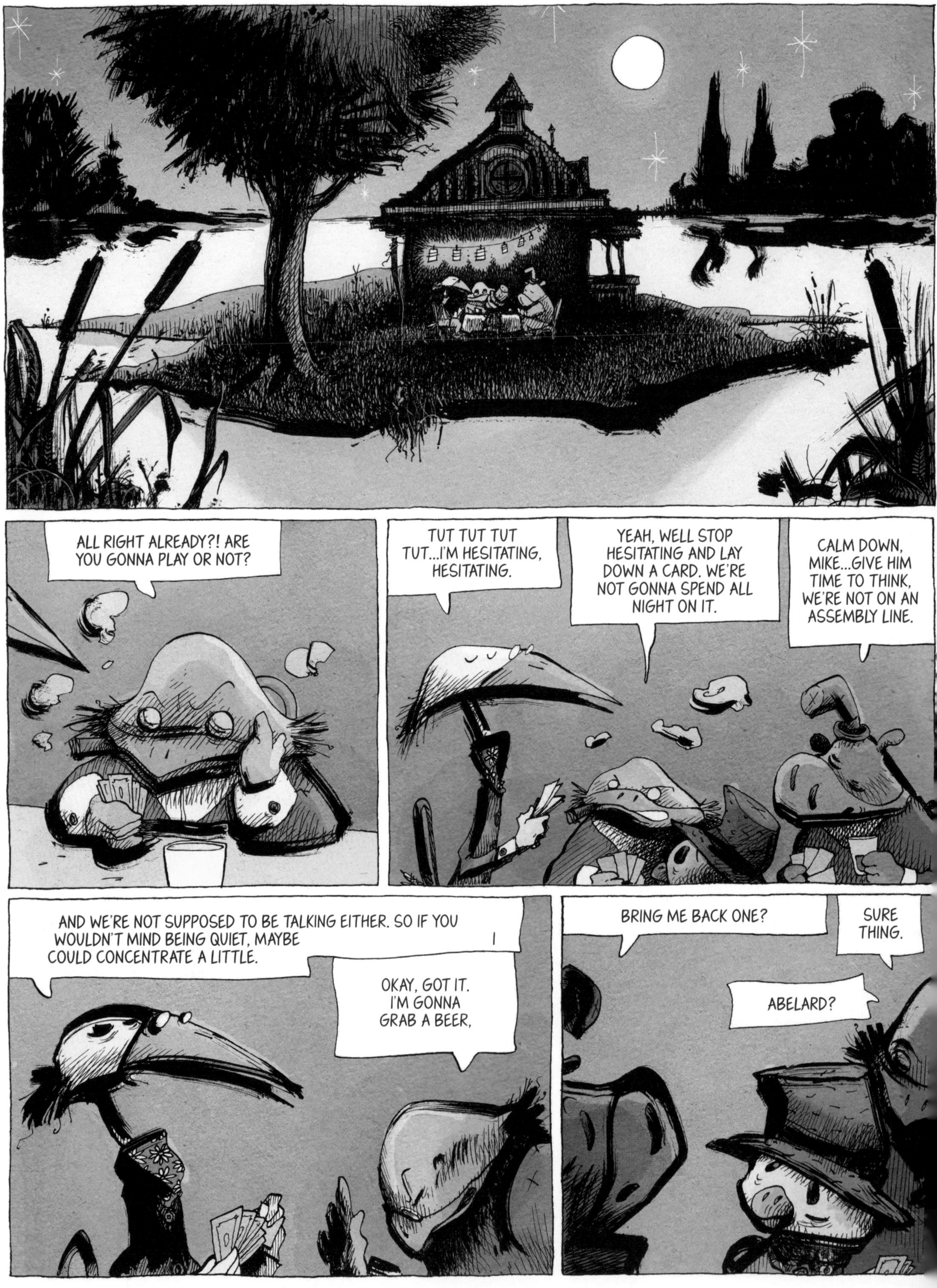
ALL RIGHT ALREADY?! ARE YOU GONNA PLAY OR NOT?
TUT TUT TUT TUT...I'M HESITATING, HESITATING.
YEAH, WELL STOP HESITATING AND LAY DOWN A CARD. WE'RE NOT GONNA SPEND ALL NIGHT ON IT.
CALM DOWN, MIKE...GIVE HIM TIME TO THINK, WE'RE NOT ON AN ASSEMBLY LINE.
AND WE'RE NOT SUPPOSED TO BE TALKING EITHER. SO IF YOU WOULDN'T MIND BEING QUIET, MAYBE I COULD CONCENTRATE A LITTLE.
OKAY, GOT IT. I'M GONNA GRAB A BEER,
BRING ME BACK ONE?
SURE THING.
ABELARD?

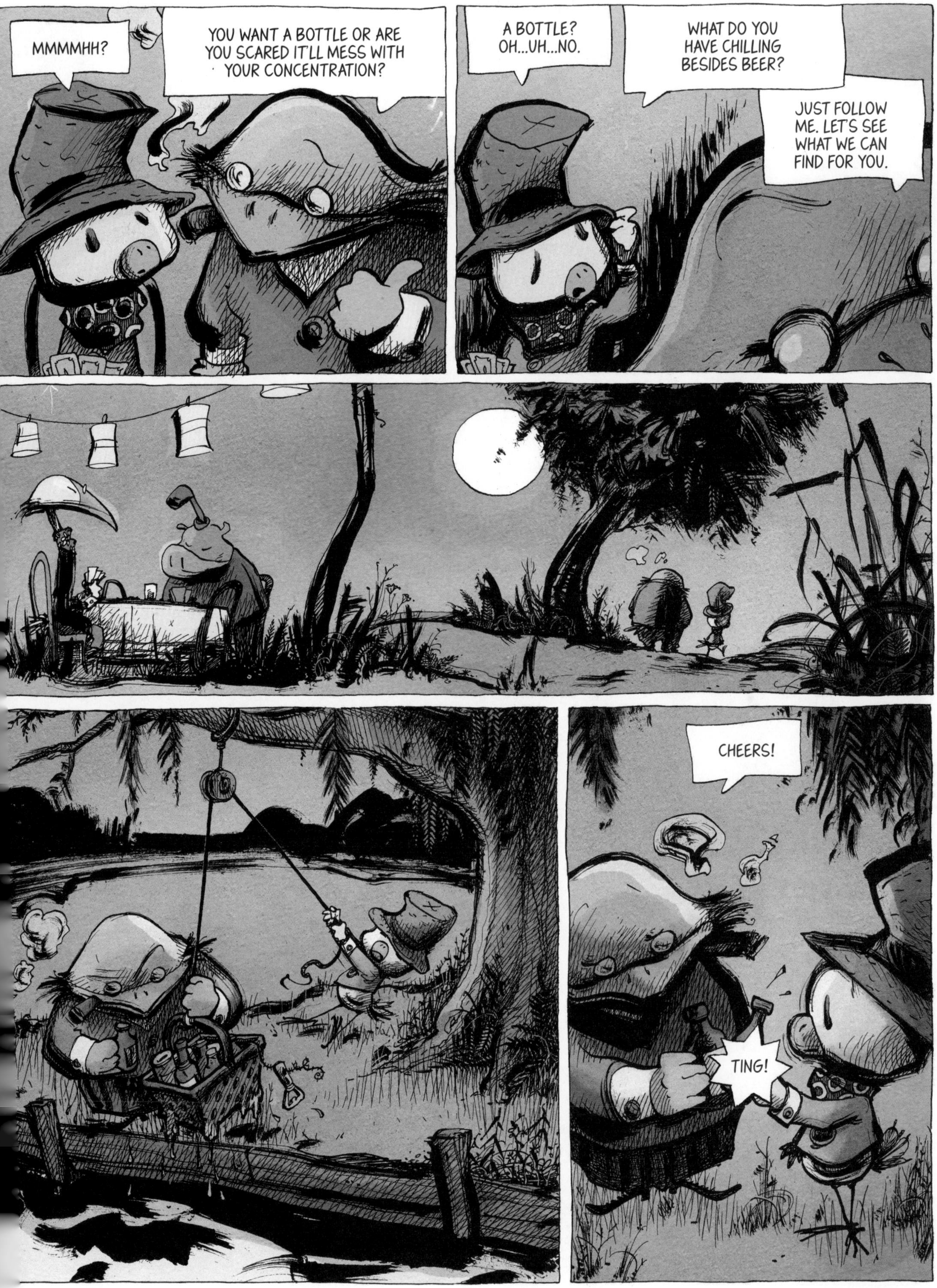
MMMMHH?
YOU WANT A BOTTLE OR ARE YOU SCARED IT'LL MESS WITH YOUR CONCENTRATION?
A BOTTLE? OH...UH...NO.
WHAT DO YOU HAVE CHILLING BESIDES BEER?
JUST FOLLOW ME. LET'S SEE WHAT WE CAN FIND FOR YOU.
CHEERS!
TING!

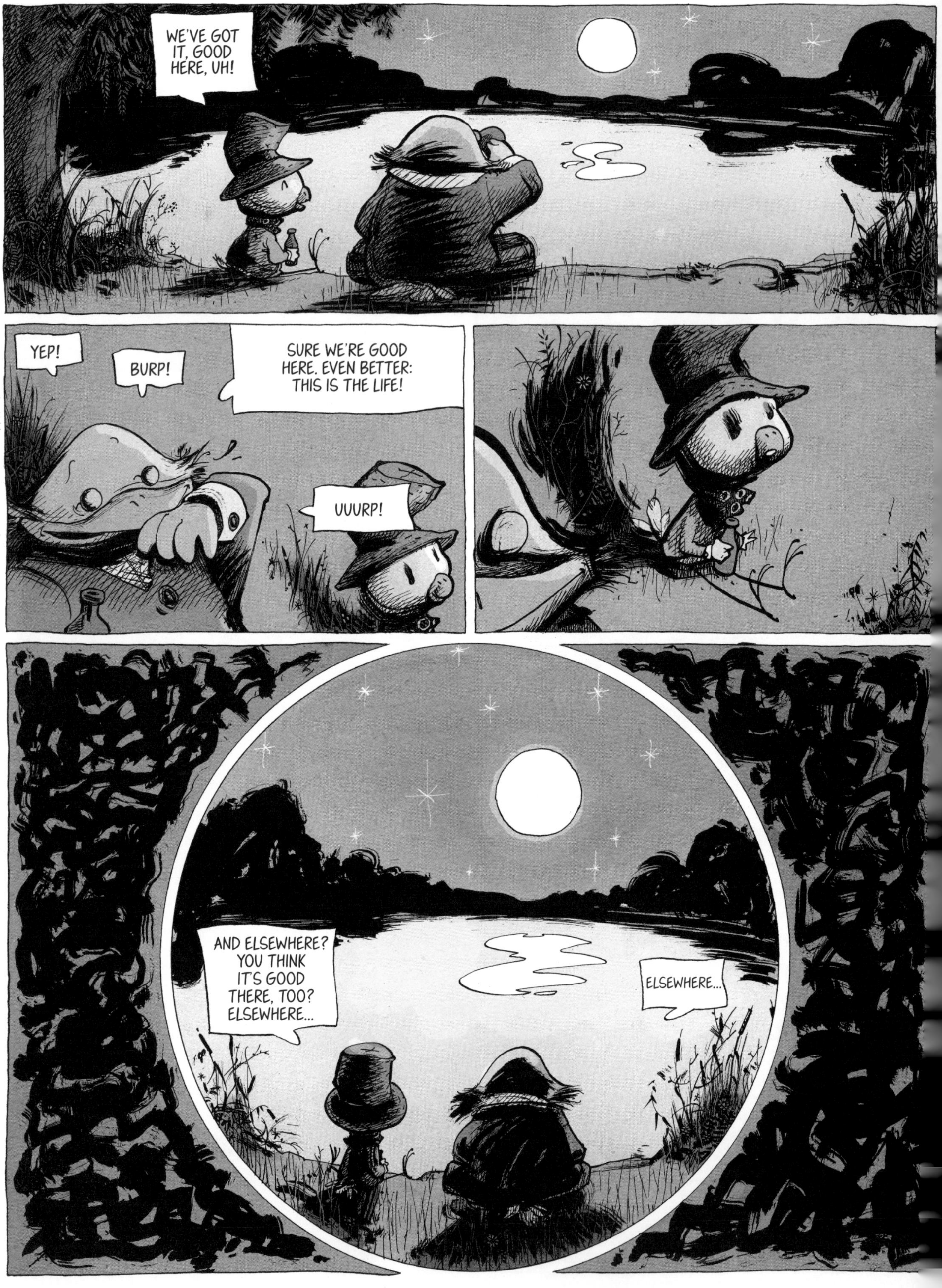
WE'VE GOT IT, GOOD HERE, UH!
YEP!
BURP!
SURE WE'RE GOOD HERE. EVEN BETTER: THIS IS THE LIFE!
UUURP!
AND ELSEWHERE? YOU THINK IT'S GOOD THERE, TOO? ELSEWHERE...
ELSEWHERE...

LISTEN CLOSELY, KID. I TRAVELED A LOT BEFORE WINDING UP HERE.

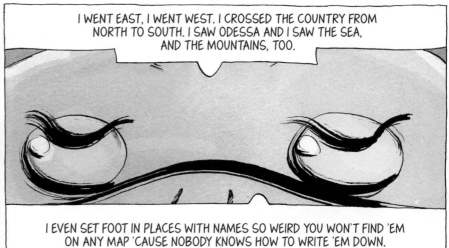

I WENT EAST, I WENT WEST. I CROSSED THE COUNTRY FROM NORTH TO SOUTH. I SAW ODESSA AND I SAW THE SEA, AND THE MOUNTAINS, TOO.

I EVEN SET FOOT IN PLACES WITH NAMES SO WEIRD YOU WON'T FIND 'EM ON ANY MAP 'CAUSE NOBODY KNOWS HOW TO WRITE 'EM DOWN.

SO, IF I TELL YOU I'VE FOUND NOTHING BETTER THAN THIS MARSH TO SET DOWN ROOTS, YOU CAN BELIEVE ME THERE'S NOTHING BETTER.

I'VE ALWAYS LIVED HERE.

WELL, YOU CAN SAY YOU'RE LUCKY.

COME ON, LET'S GO FINISH THAT HAND OF CARDS.

IF EUGENE'S DECIDED TO PLAY, MAYBE WE CAN GET TO BED BEFORE THE MOON SETS.

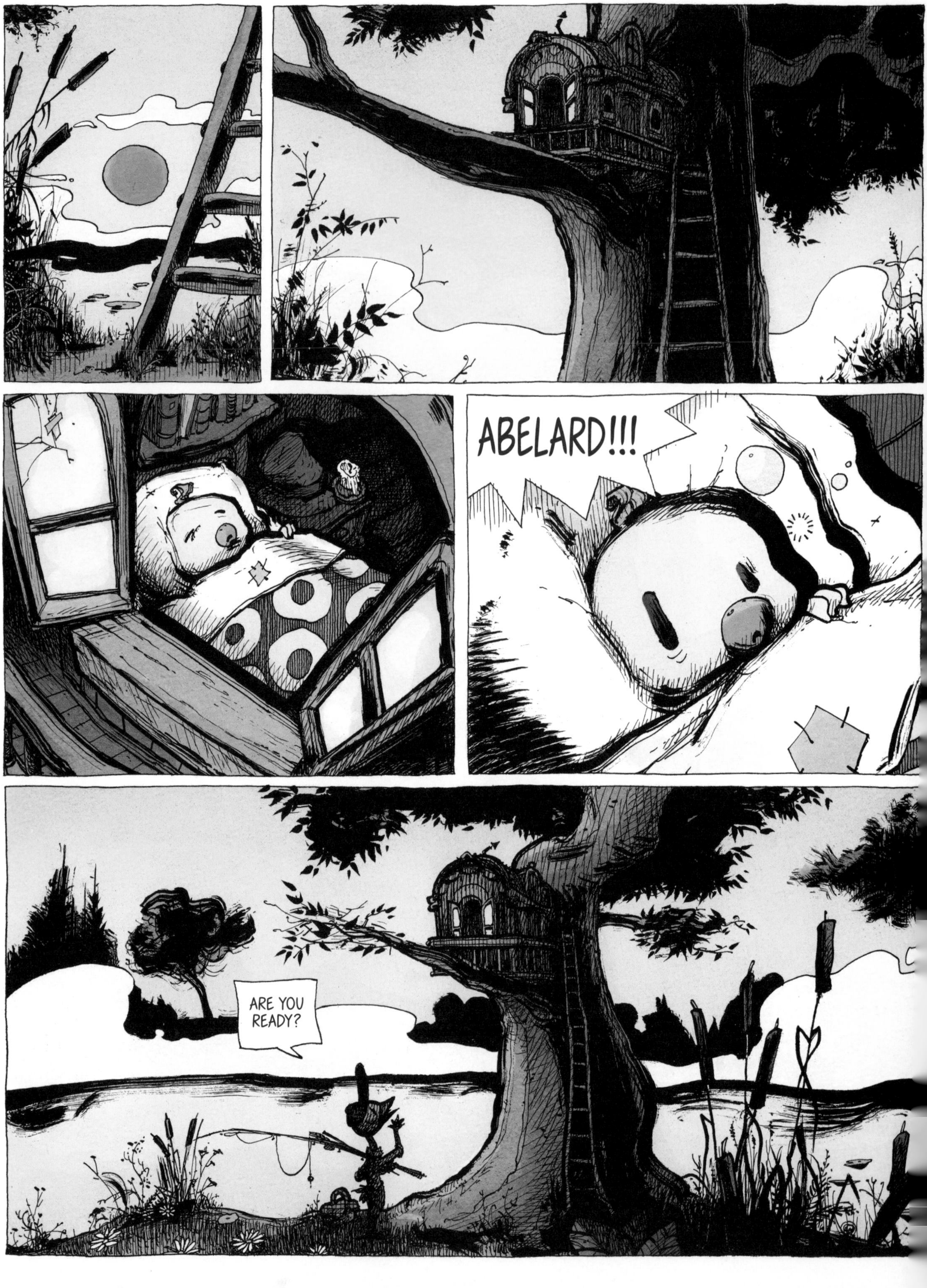
ABELARD!!!
ARE YOU READY?

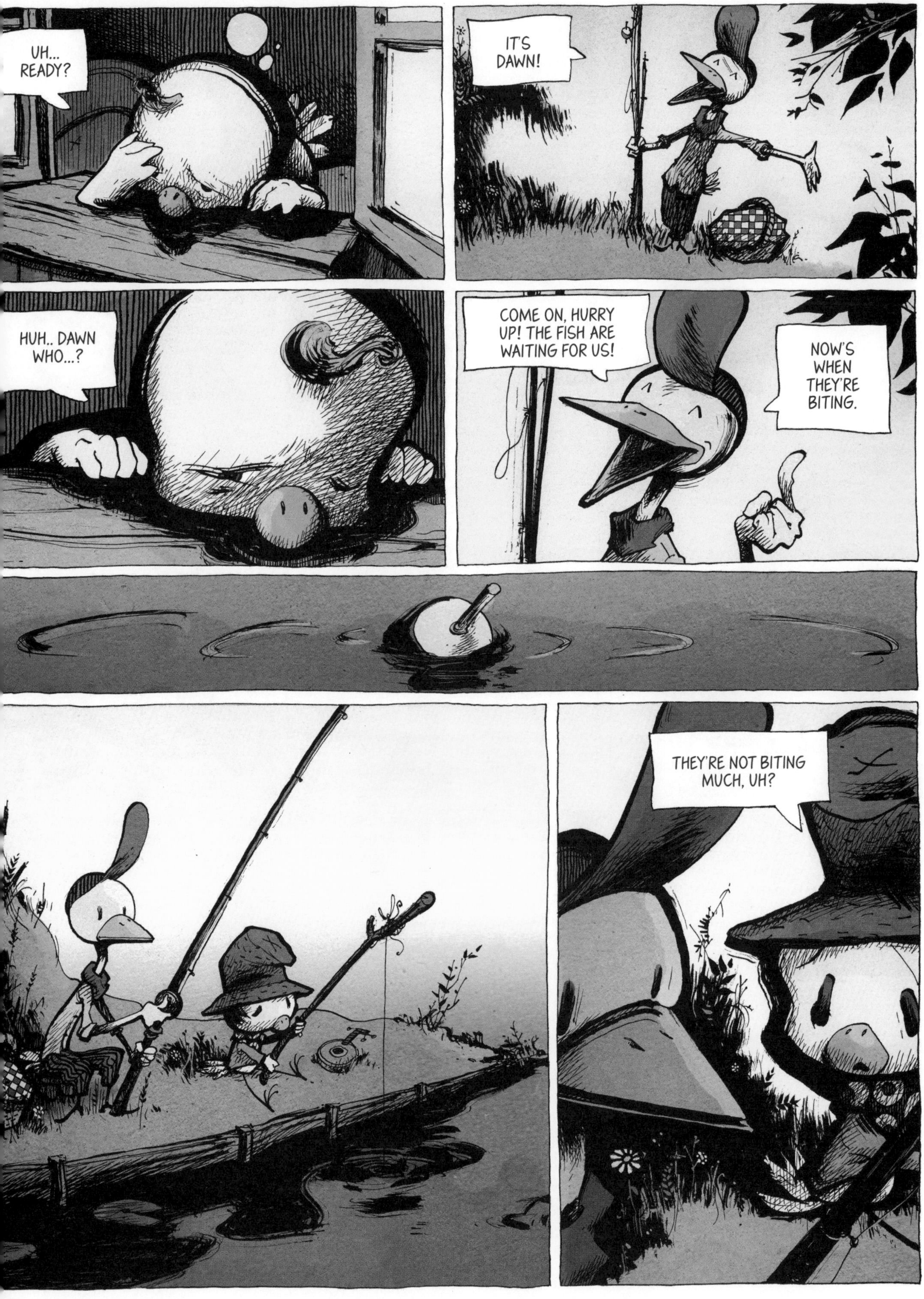
UH... READY?
IT'S DAWN!
HUH.. DAWN WHO...?
COME ON, HURRY UP! THE FISH ARE WAITING FOR US!
NOW'S WHEN THEY'RE BITING.
THEY'RE NOT BITING MUCH, UH?

NO, NOT VERY MUCH.

OOOOWHAAAAAAA

YOU PLAYED CARDS WITH PAVEL AND MIKHAIL AGAIN LAST NIGHT.

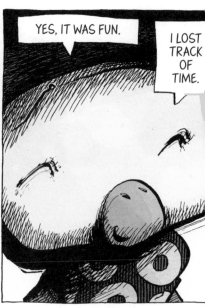

YES, IT WAS FUN.

I LOST TRACK OF TIME.

HAVE YOU EVER NOTICED THAT WHEN YOU PLAY CARDS, TIME REALLY FLIES BY?

OH?

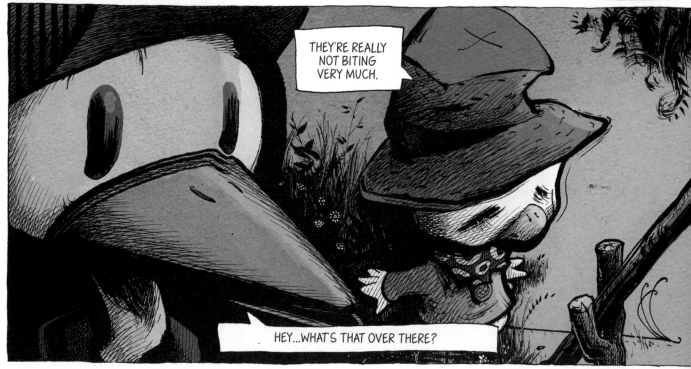

THEY'RE REALLY NOT BITING VERY MUCH.

HEY...WHAT'S THAT OVER THERE?

IT LOOKS LIKE A HAT.

IT'S PROBABLY FROM THE BIG ELM HOUSE.

THE FOLKS YONDER AREN'T THE SORT TO KEEP AN EYE ON THEIR THINGS.

SOMEONE'S STAYING IN THE BIG ELM HOUSE?

FOR A FEW DAYS. A SMALL GROUP OF YOUNG FOLK ARRIVED YESTERDAY.

THEY PARTIED ALL NIGHT LONG. THAT MUST BE WHAT SCARED OFF THE FISH.

TSSS...THOSE CITY FOLK.

THE CITY. IT MUST BE NICE THERE, NO?

YES, IT'S PEACEFUL.

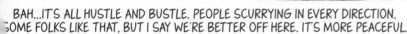

BAH...IT'S ALL HUSTLE AND BUSTLE. PEOPLE SCURRYING IN EVERY DIRECTION. SOME FOLKS LIKE THAT, BUT I SAY WE'RE BETTER OFF HERE. IT'S MORE PEACEFUL.

BY THE WAY, WHAT'S YOUR HAT TOLD YOU TODAY?

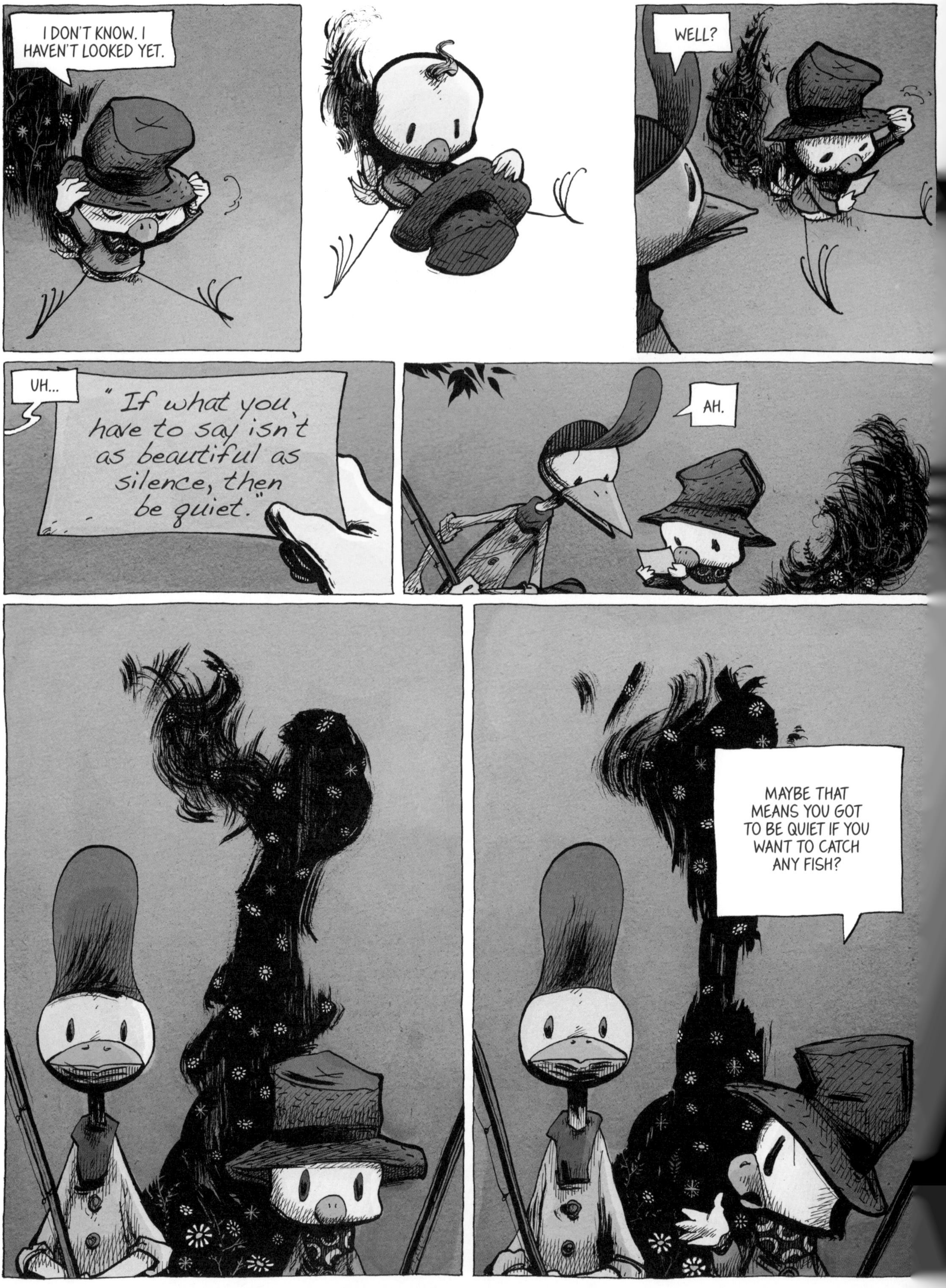
I DON'T KNOW. I HAVEN'T LOOKED YET.
WELL?
UH...
"If what you have to say isn't as beautiful as silence, then be quiet."
AH.
MAYBE THAT MEANS YOU GOT TO BE QUIET IF YOU WANT TO CATCH ANY FISH?

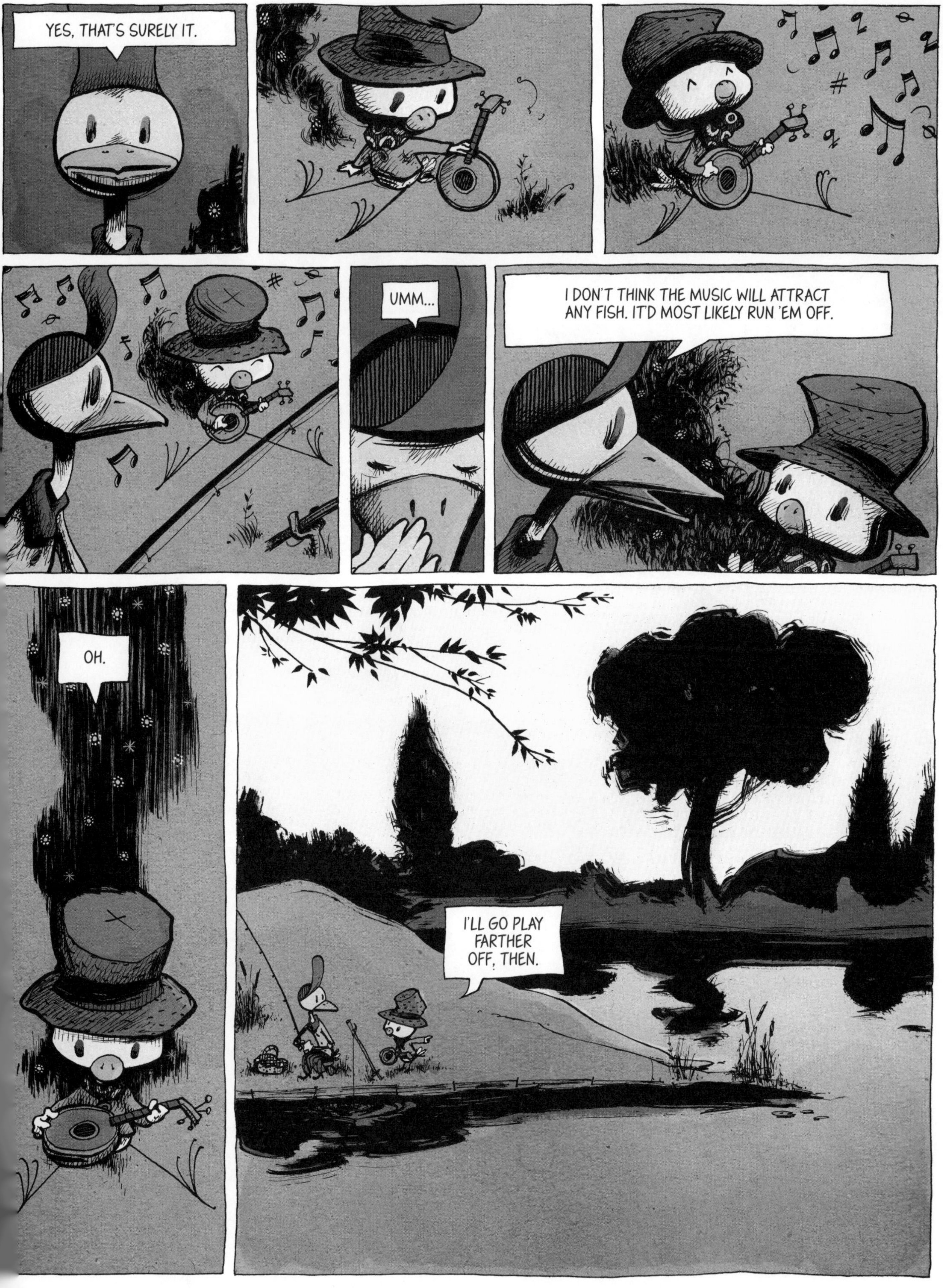
YES, THAT'S SURELY IT.
UMM...
I DON'T THINK THE MUSIC WILL ATTRACT ANY FISH. IT'D MOST LIKELY RUN 'EM OFF.
OH.
I'LL GO PLAY FARTHER OFF, THEN.

PLASH!

HA HA HA!

GO ON, EPPILY! YOUR TURN!

YOU'LL SEE. IT'S NICE ONCE YOU GET IN!

YES, THAT'S WHAT PEOPLE ALWAYS SAY.

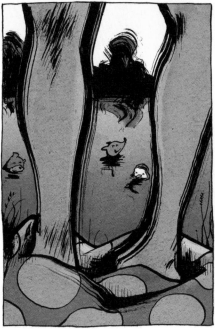

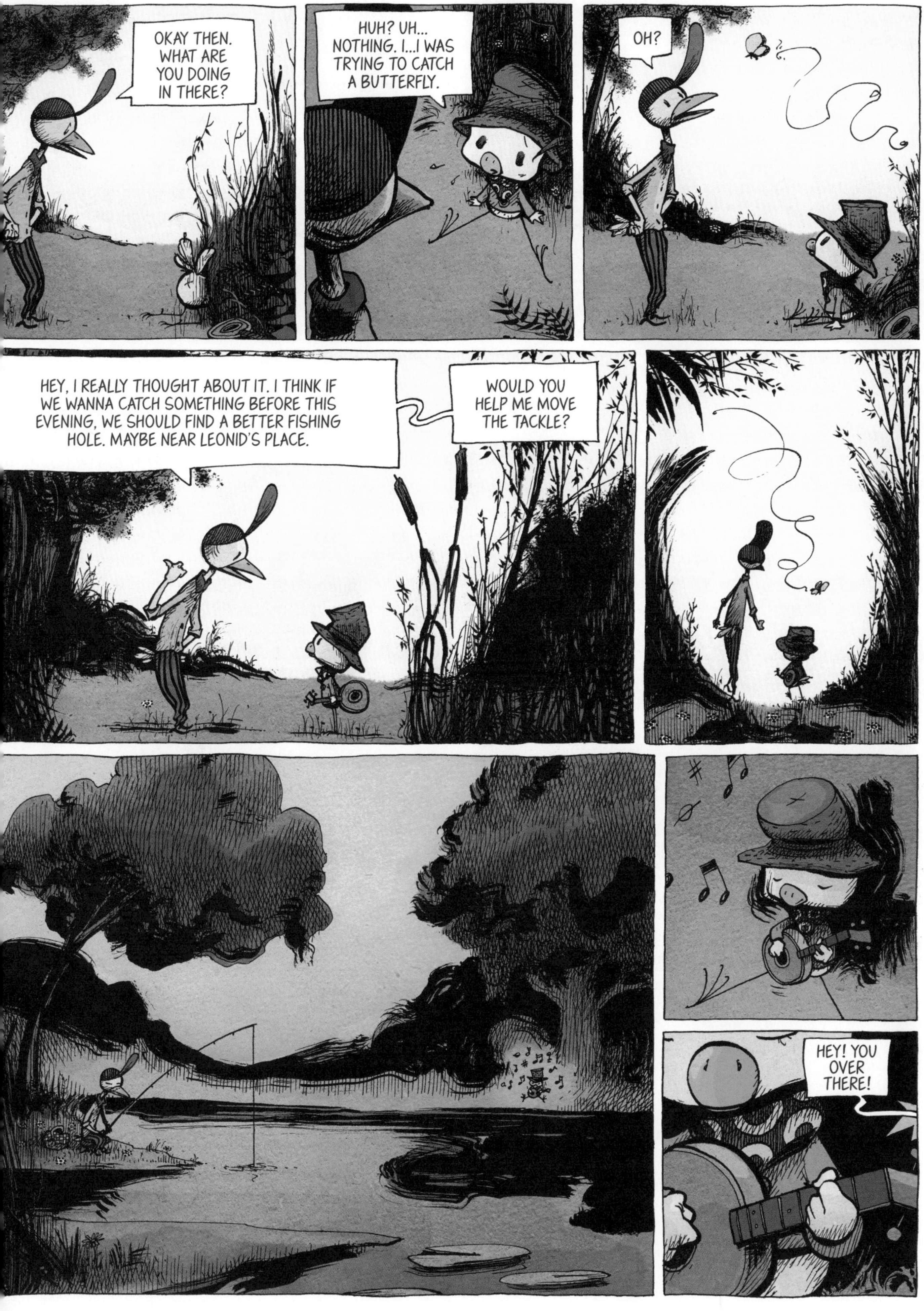
OKAY THEN. WHAT ARE YOU DOING IN THERE?
HUH? UH... NOTHING. I...I WAS TRYING TO CATCH A BUTTERFLY.
OH?
HEY, I REALLY THOUGHT ABOUT IT. I THINK IF WE WANNA CATCH SOMETHING BEFORE THIS EVENING, WE SHOULD FIND A BETTER FISHING HOLE. MAYBE NEAR LEONID'S PLACE.
WOULD YOU HELP ME MOVE THE TACKLE?
HEY! YOU OVER THERE!

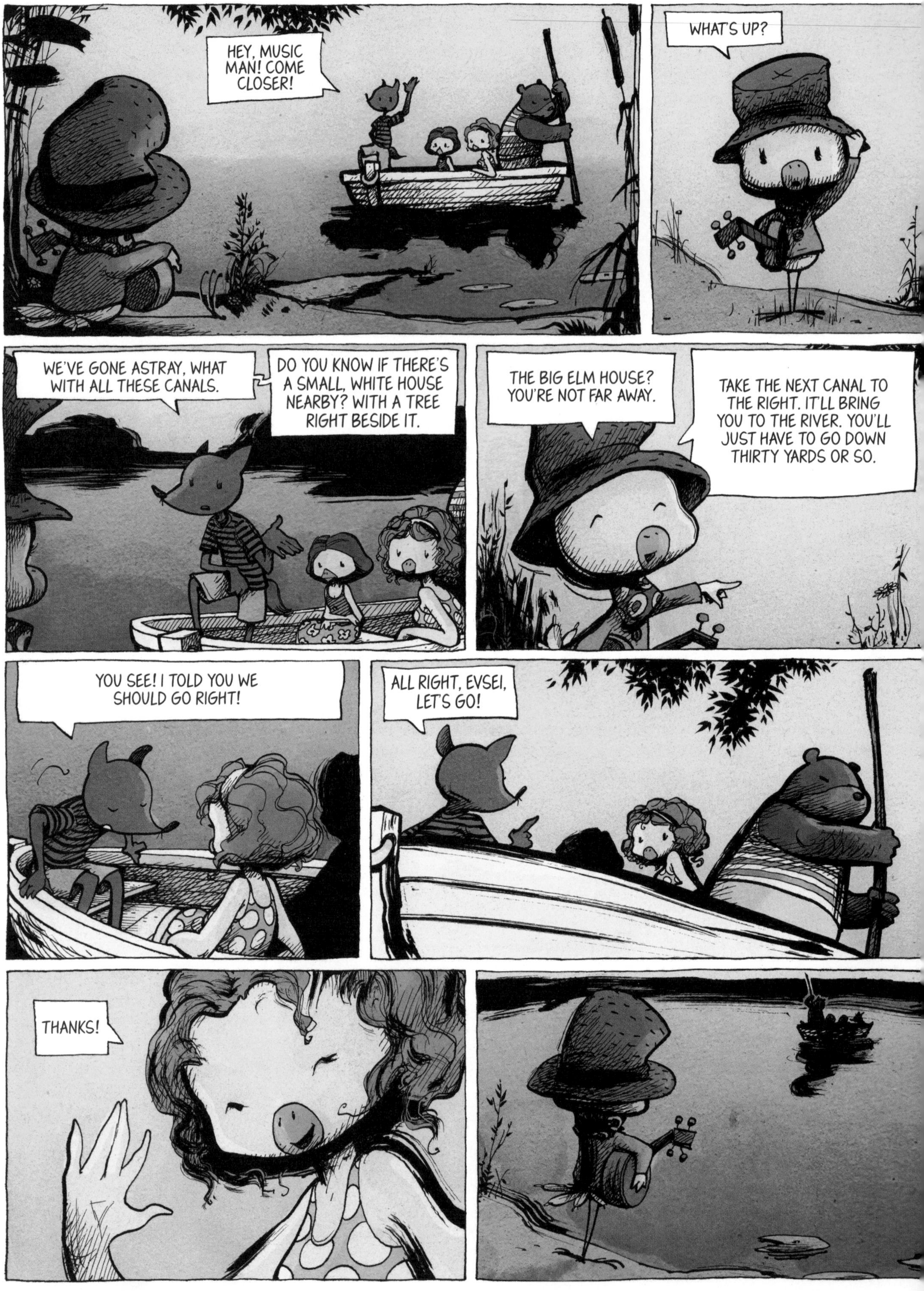
HEY, MUSIC MAN! COME CLOSER!
WHAT'S UP?
WE'VE GONE ASTRAY, WHAT WITH ALL THESE CANALS.
DO YOU KNOW IF THERE'S A SMALL, WHITE HOUSE NEARBY? WITH A TREE RIGHT BESIDE IT.
THE BIG ELM HOUSE? YOU'RE NOT FAR AWAY.
TAKE THE NEXT CANAL TO THE RIGHT. IT'LL BRING YOU TO THE RIVER. YOU'LL JUST HAVE TO GO DOWN THIRTY YARDS OR SO.
YOU SEE! I TOLD YOU WE SHOULD GO RIGHT!
ALL RIGHT, EVSEI, LET'S GO!
THANKS!

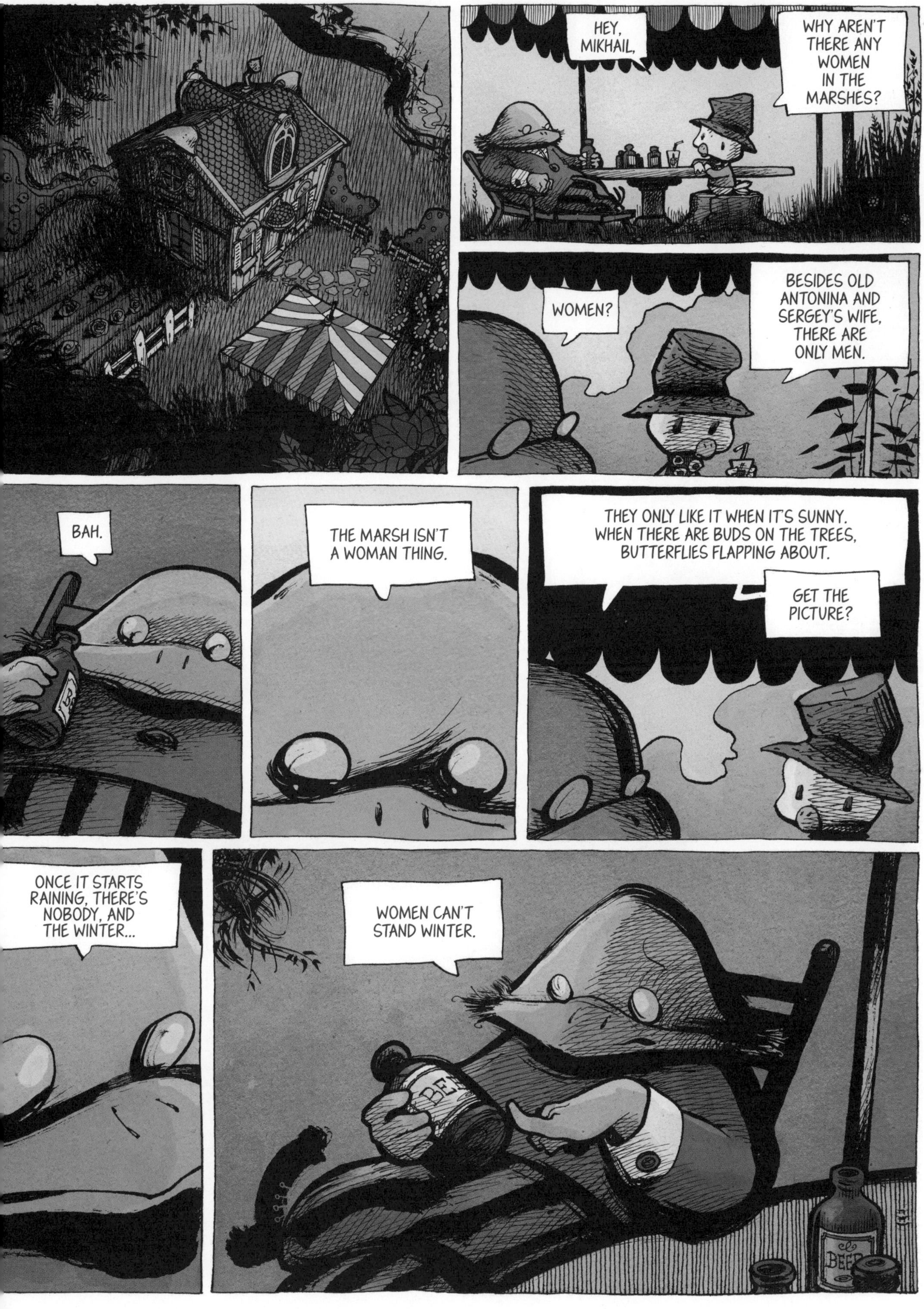
HEY, MIKHAIL,
WHY AREN'T THERE ANY WOMEN IN THE MARSHES?
WOMEN?
BESIDES OLD ANTONINA AND SERGEY'S WIFE, THERE ARE ONLY MEN.
BAH.
THE MARSH ISN'T A WOMAN THING.
THEY ONLY LIKE IT WHEN IT'S SUNNY. WHEN THERE ARE BUDS ON THE TREES, BUTTERFLIES FLAPPING ABOUT.
GET THE PICTURE?
ONCE IT STARTS RAINING, THERE'S NOBODY, AND THE WINTER...
WOMEN CAN'T STAND WINTER.
BEER

THEY'RE LIKE FLOWERS THEN?

YEAH, THAT'S IT. WOMEN ARE LIKE FLOWERS. THEY'RE PRETTY, THEY SMELL GOOD, BUT THEY MAKE ME SNEEZE.

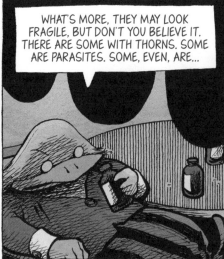

WHAT'S MORE, THEY MAY LOOK FRAGILE, BUT DON'T YOU BELIEVE IT. THERE ARE SOME WITH THORNS. SOME ARE PARASITES. SOME, EVEN, ARE...

...CARNIVORES.

UUURP

BELIEVE ME, WE'RE BETTER OFF WITH MEN ONLY.

WOMEN DO NOTHING BUT CAUSE PROBLEMS.

AND THEY'RE NEVER SATISFIED.

It's not because things are difficult that we dare not venture. It's because we dare not venture that they are difficult.

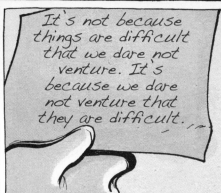

SCRATCH
SCRATCH

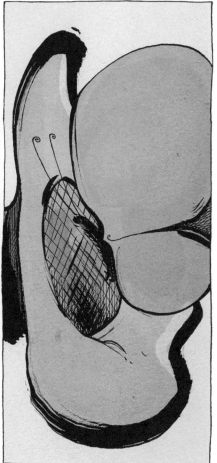

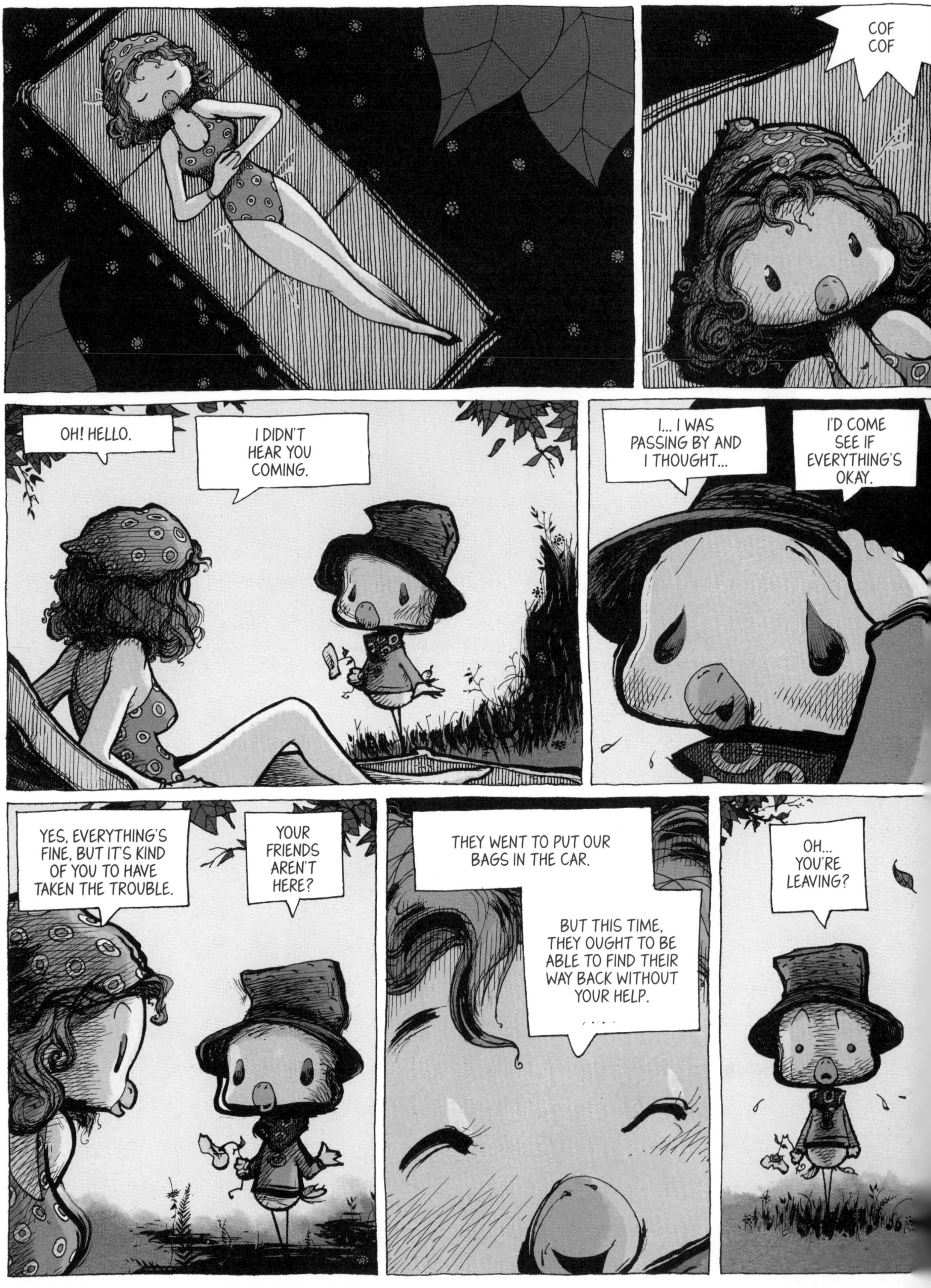
COF
COF
OH! HELLO.
I DIDN'T HEAR YOU COMING.
I... I WAS PASSING BY AND I THOUGHT...
I'D COME SEE IF EVERYTHING'S OKAY.
YES, EVERYTHING'S FINE, BUT IT'S KIND OF YOU TO HAVE TAKEN THE TROUBLE.
YOUR FRIENDS AREN'T HERE?
THEY WENT TO PUT OUR BAGS IN THE CAR.
BUT THIS TIME, THEY OUGHT TO BE ABLE TO FIND THEIR WAY BACK WITHOUT YOUR HELP.
OH... YOU'RE LEAVING?

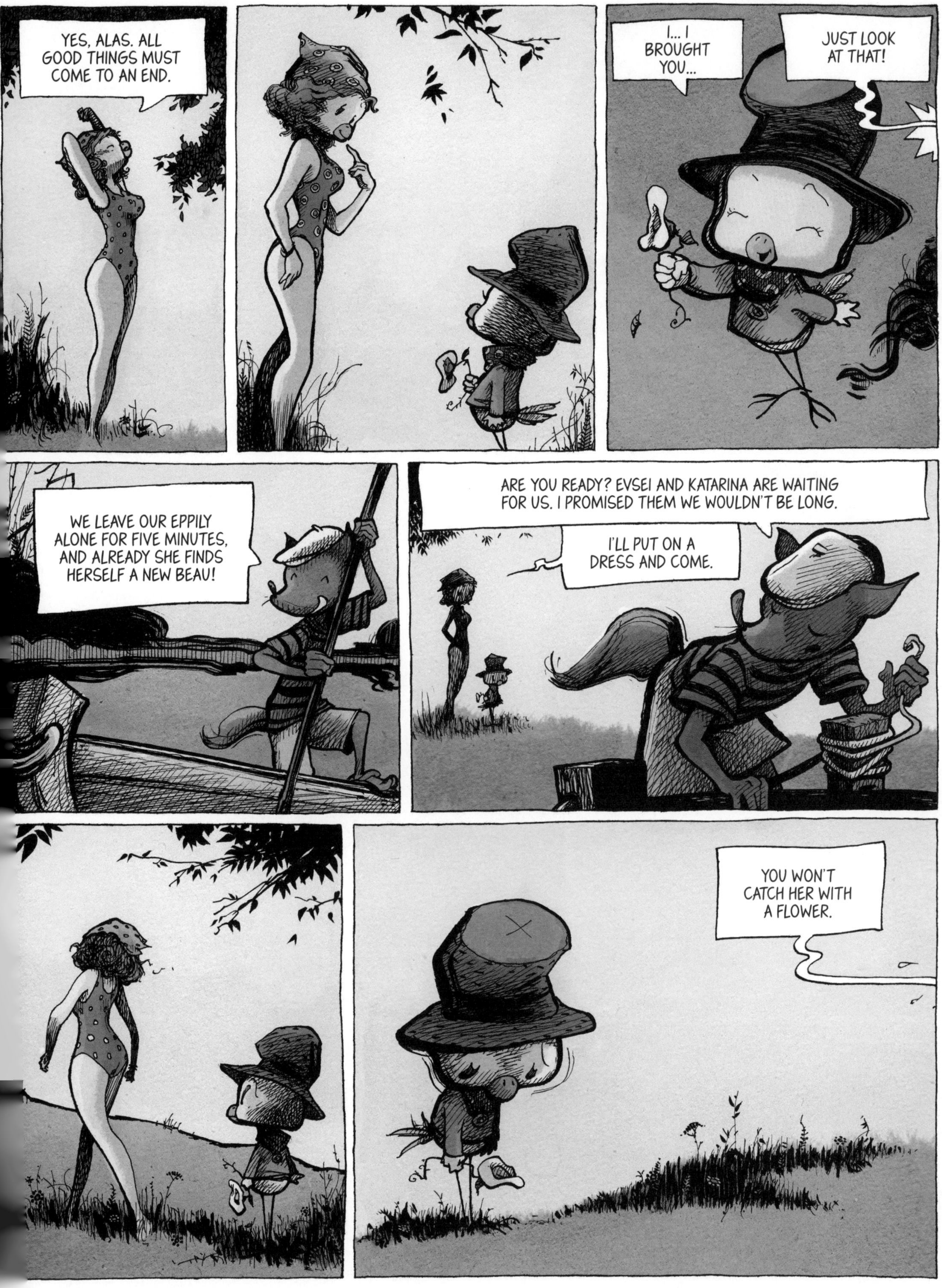
YES, ALAS. ALL GOOD THINGS MUST COME TO AN END.
I... I BROUGHT YOU...
JUST LOOK AT THAT!
WE LEAVE OUR EPPILY ALONE FOR FIVE MINUTES, AND ALREADY SHE FINDS HERSELF A NEW BEAU!
ARE YOU READY? EVSEI AND KATARINA ARE WAITING FOR US. I PROMISED THEM WE WOULDN'T BE LONG.
I'LL PUT ON A DRESS AND COME.
YOU WON'T CATCH HER WITH A FLOWER.

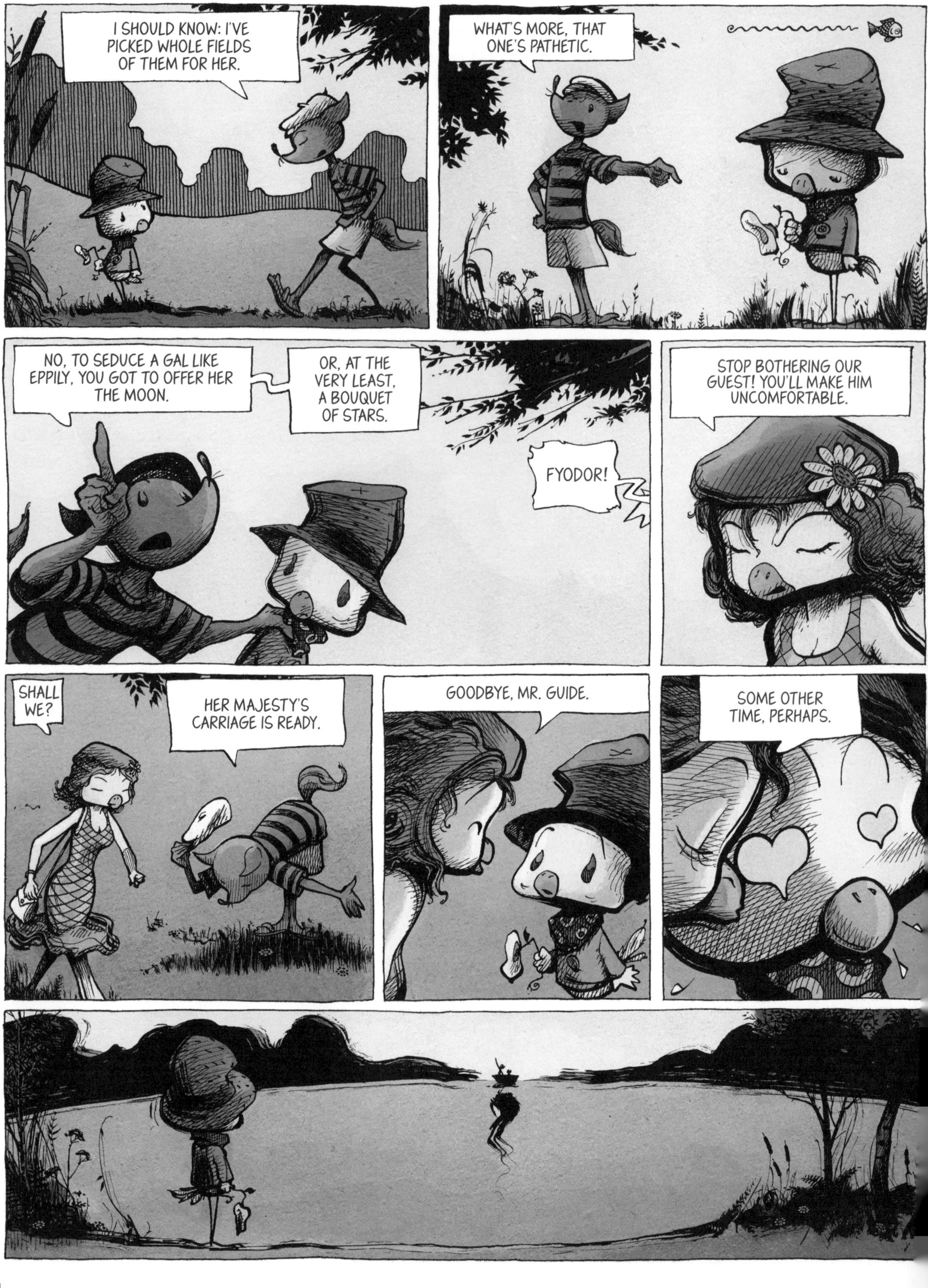
I SHOULD KNOW: I'VE PICKED WHOLE FIELDS OF THEM FOR HER.
WHAT'S MORE, THAT ONE'S PATHETIC.
NO, TO SEDUCE A GAL LIKE EPPILY, YOU GOT TO OFFER HER THE MOON.
OR, AT THE VERY LEAST, A BOUQUET OF STARS.
FYODOR!
STOP BOTHERING OUR GUEST! YOU'LL MAKE HIM UNCOMFORTABLE.
SHALL WE?
HER MAJESTY'S CARRIAGE IS READY.
GOODBYE, MR. GUIDE.
SOME OTHER TIME, PERHAPS.

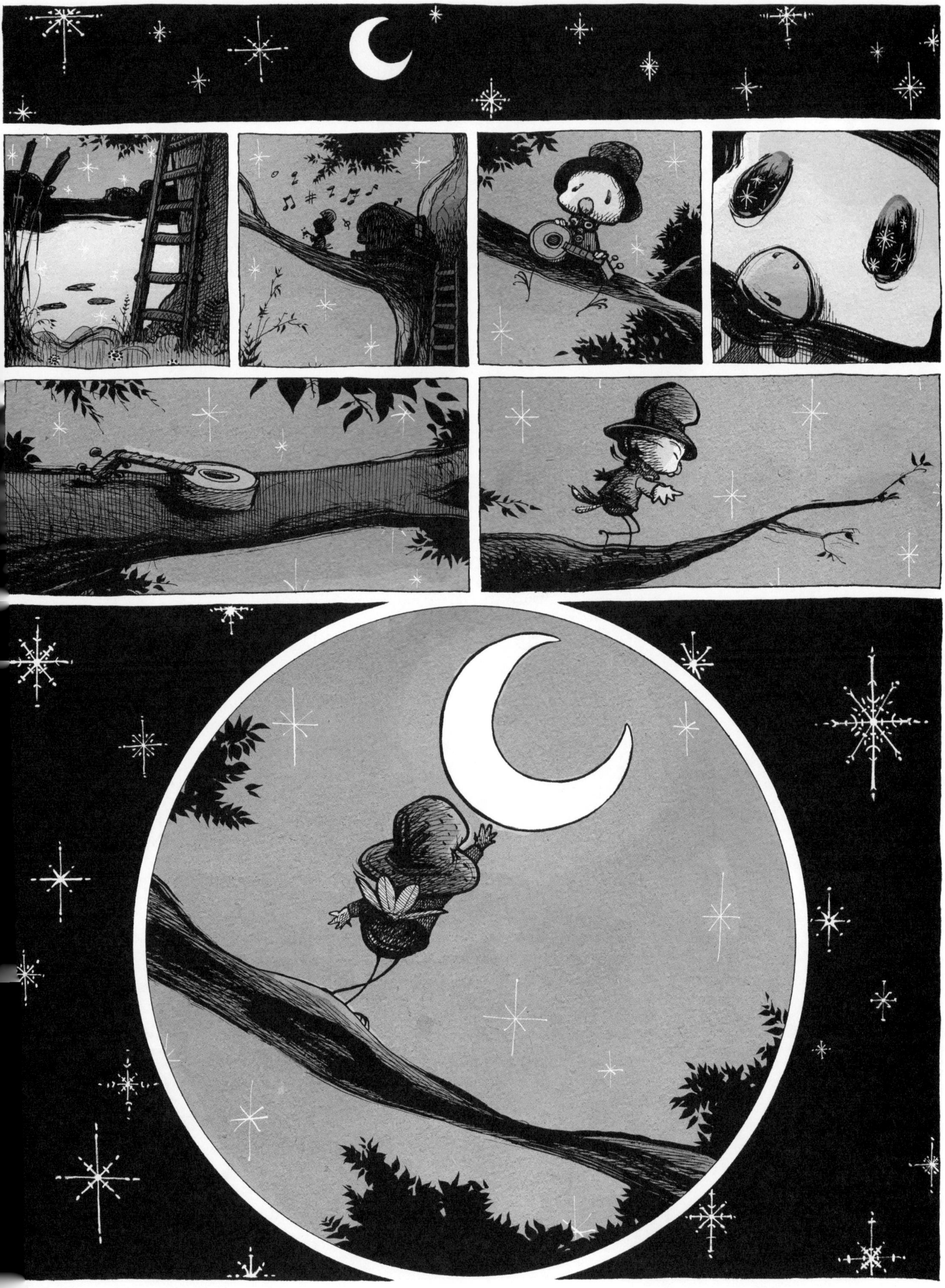

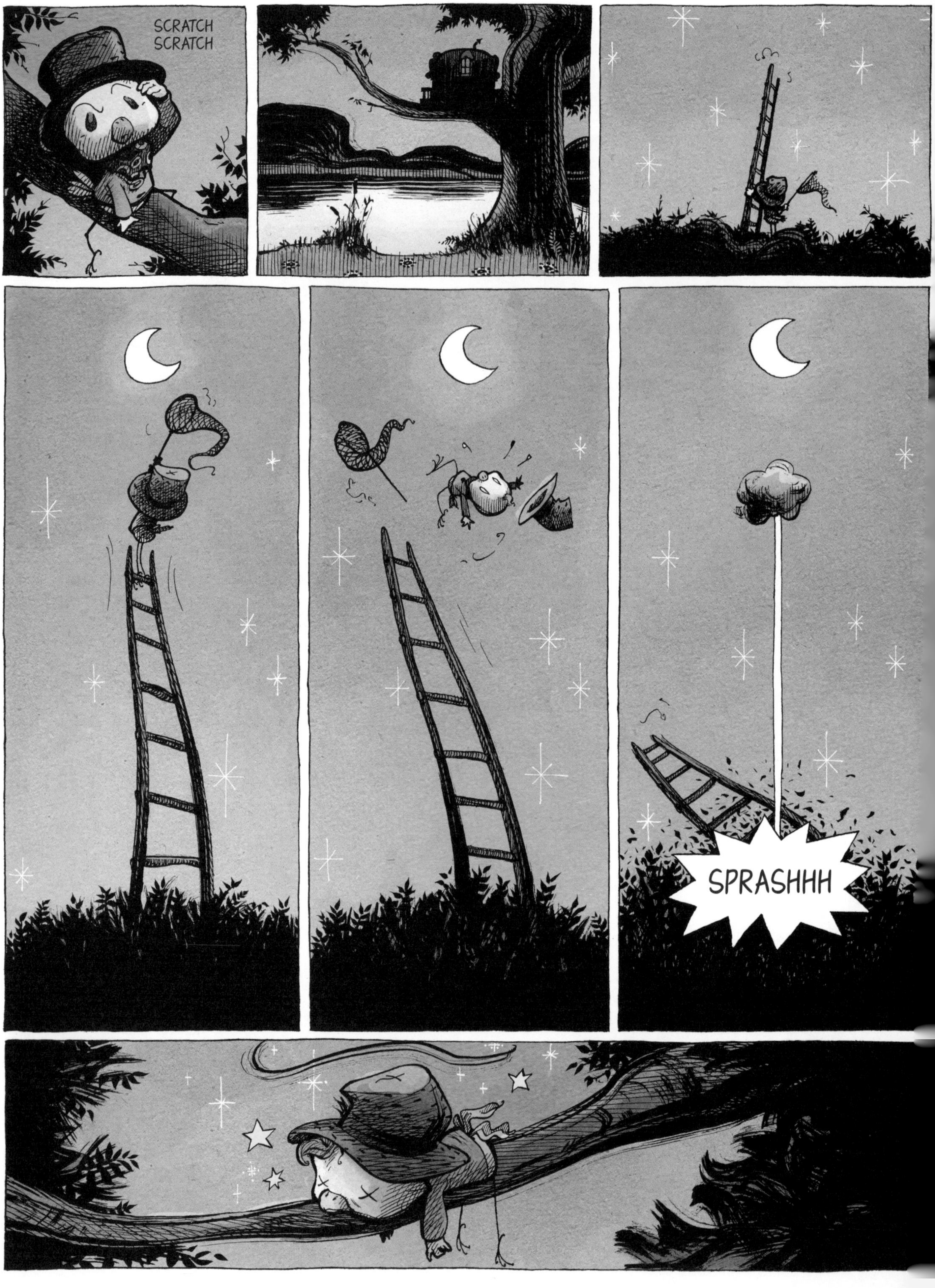
SCRATCH
SCRATCH
SPRASHHH

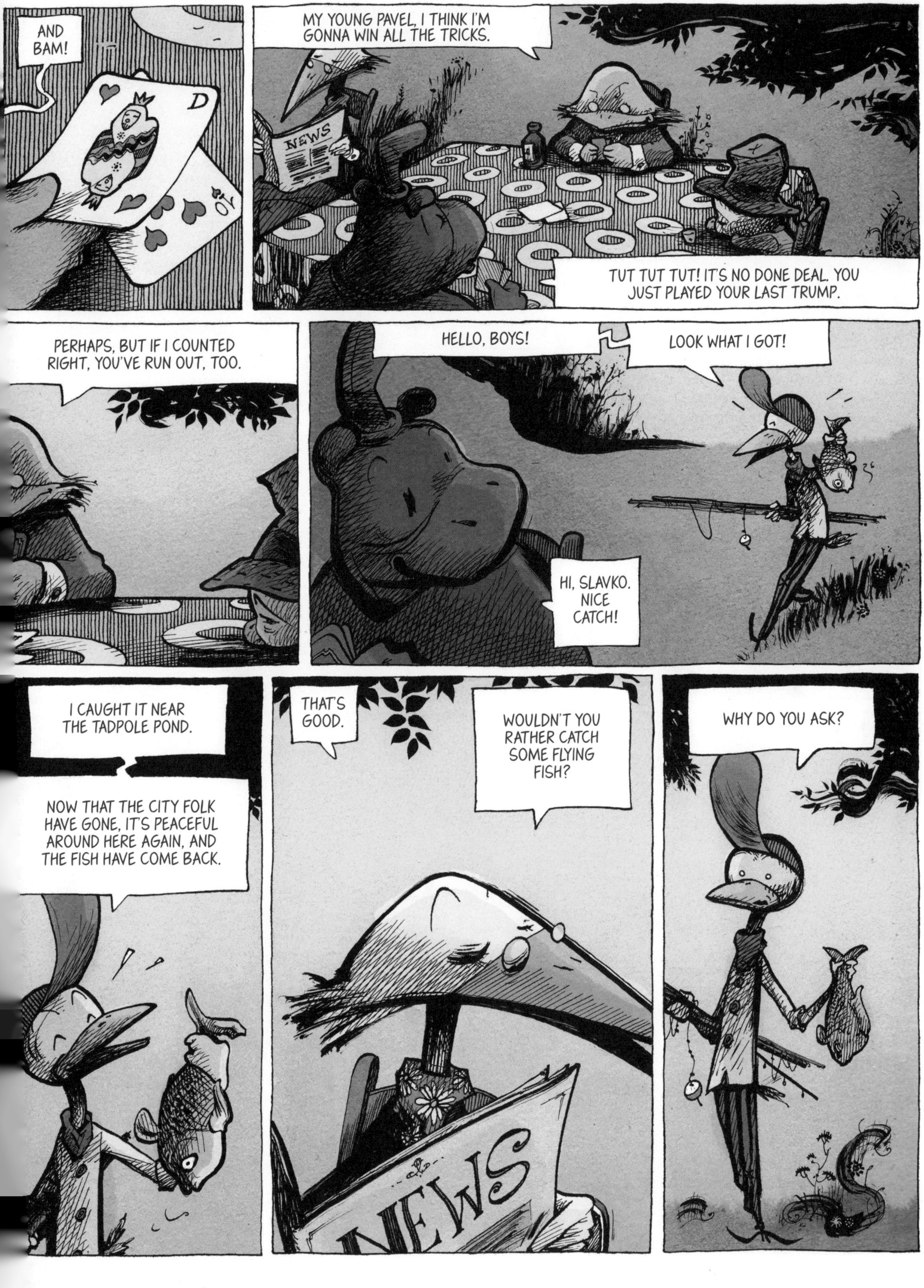

AND BAM!
MY YOUNG PAVEL, I THINK I'M GONNA WIN ALL THE TRICKS.
NEWS
TUT TUT TUT! IT'S NO DONE DEAL. YOU JUST PLAYED YOUR LAST TRUMP.
PERHAPS, BUT IF I COUNTED RIGHT, YOU'VE RUN OUT, TOO.
HELLO, BOYS!
LOOK WHAT I GOT!
HI, SLAVKO. NICE CATCH!
I CAUGHT IT NEAR THE TADPOLE POND.
NOW THAT THE CITY FOLK HAVE GONE, IT'S PEACEFUL AROUND HERE AGAIN, AND THE FISH HAVE COME BACK.
THAT'S GOOD.
WOULDN'T YOU RATHER CATCH SOME FLYING FISH?
NEWS
WHY DO YOU ASK?

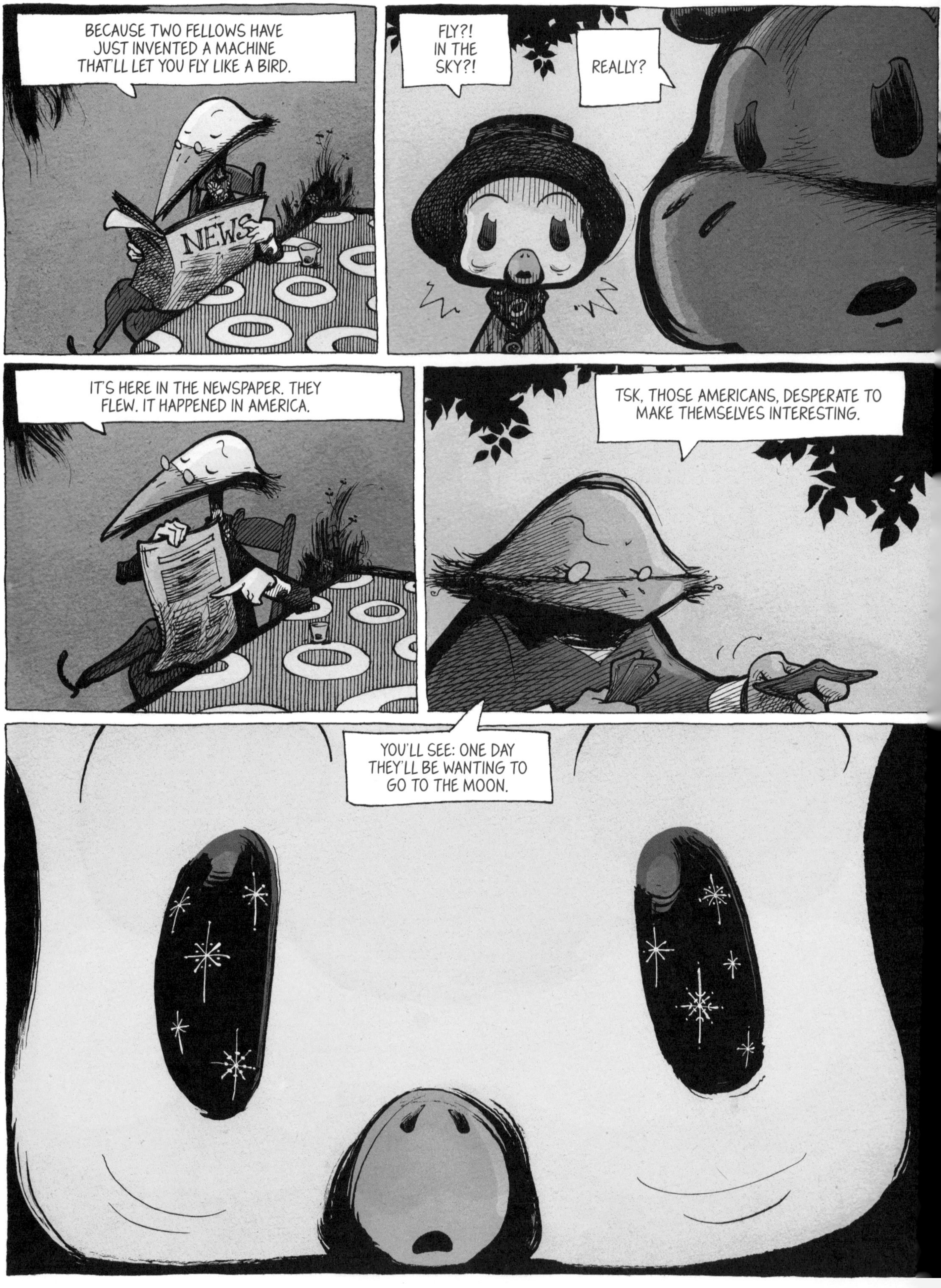
BECAUSE TWO FELLOWS HAVE JUST INVENTED A MACHINE THAT'LL LET YOU FLY LIKE A BIRD.
NEWS
FLY?! IN THE SKY?!
REALLY?
IT'S HERE IN THE NEWSPAPER. THEY FLEW. IT HAPPENED IN AMERICA.
TSK, THOSE AMERICANS, DESPERATE TO MAKE THEMSELVES INTERESTING.
YOU'LL SEE: ONE DAY THEY'LL BE WANTING TO GO TO THE MOON.

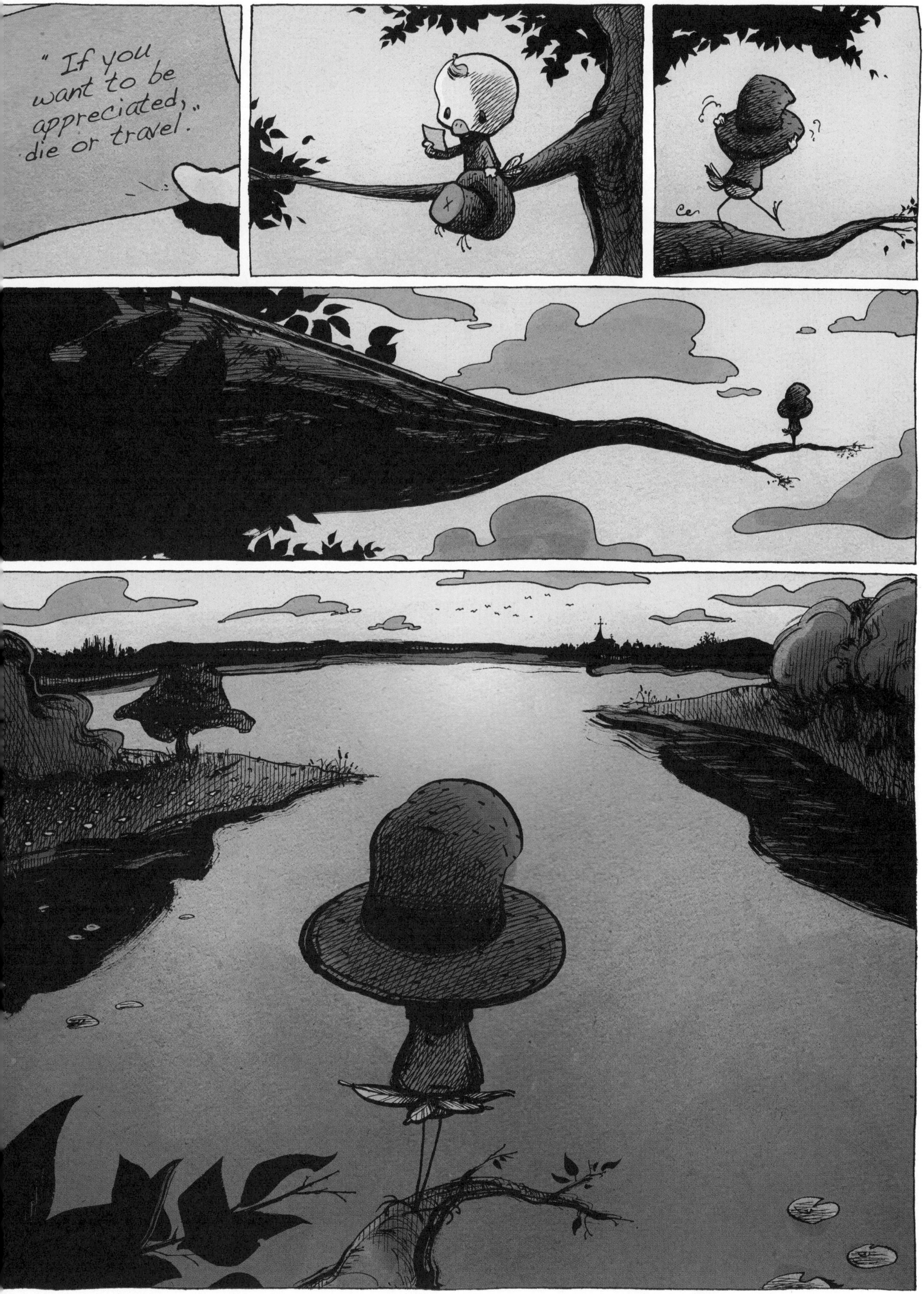
"If you want to be appreciated," die or travel.

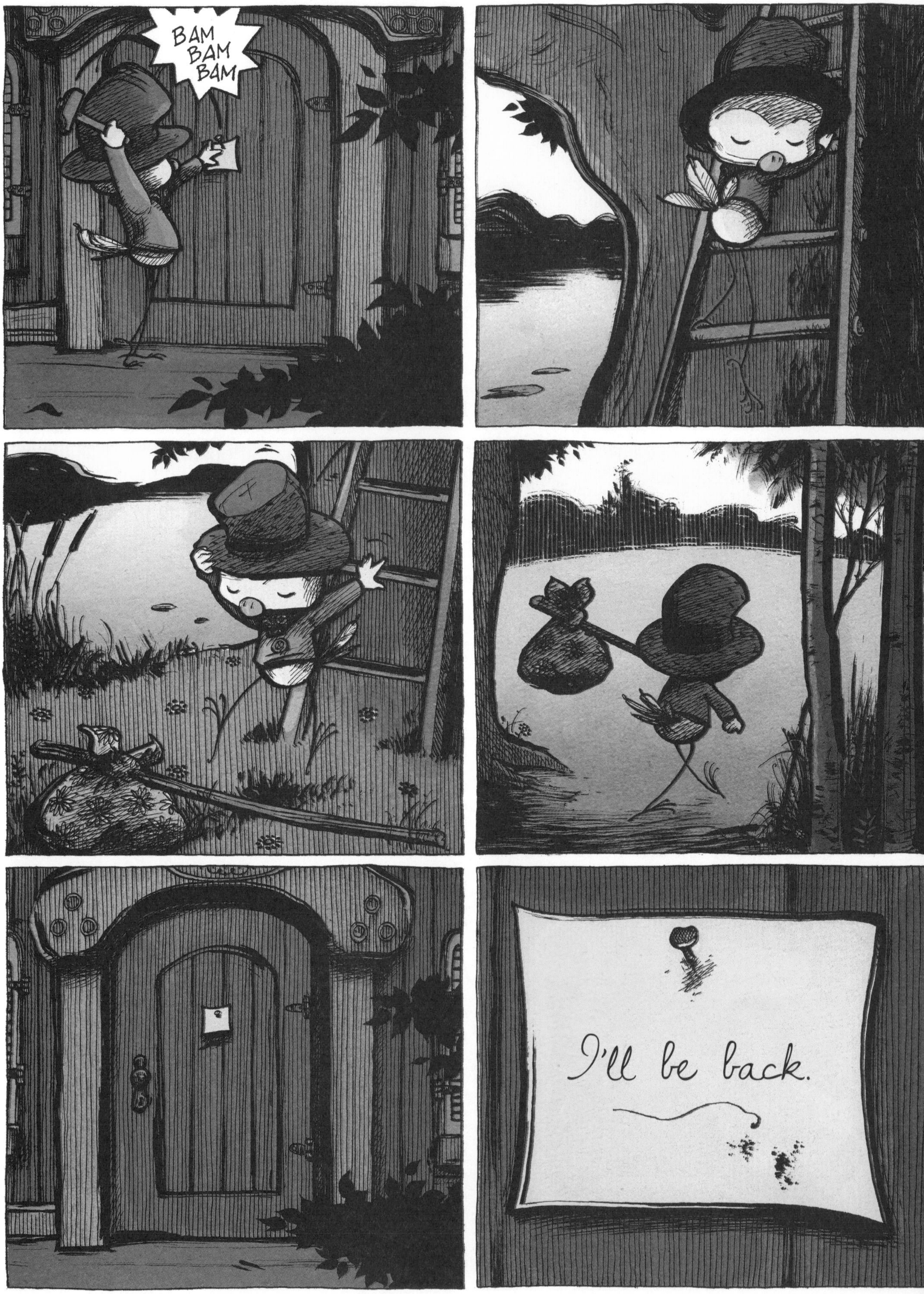
BAM BAM BAM
I'll be back.

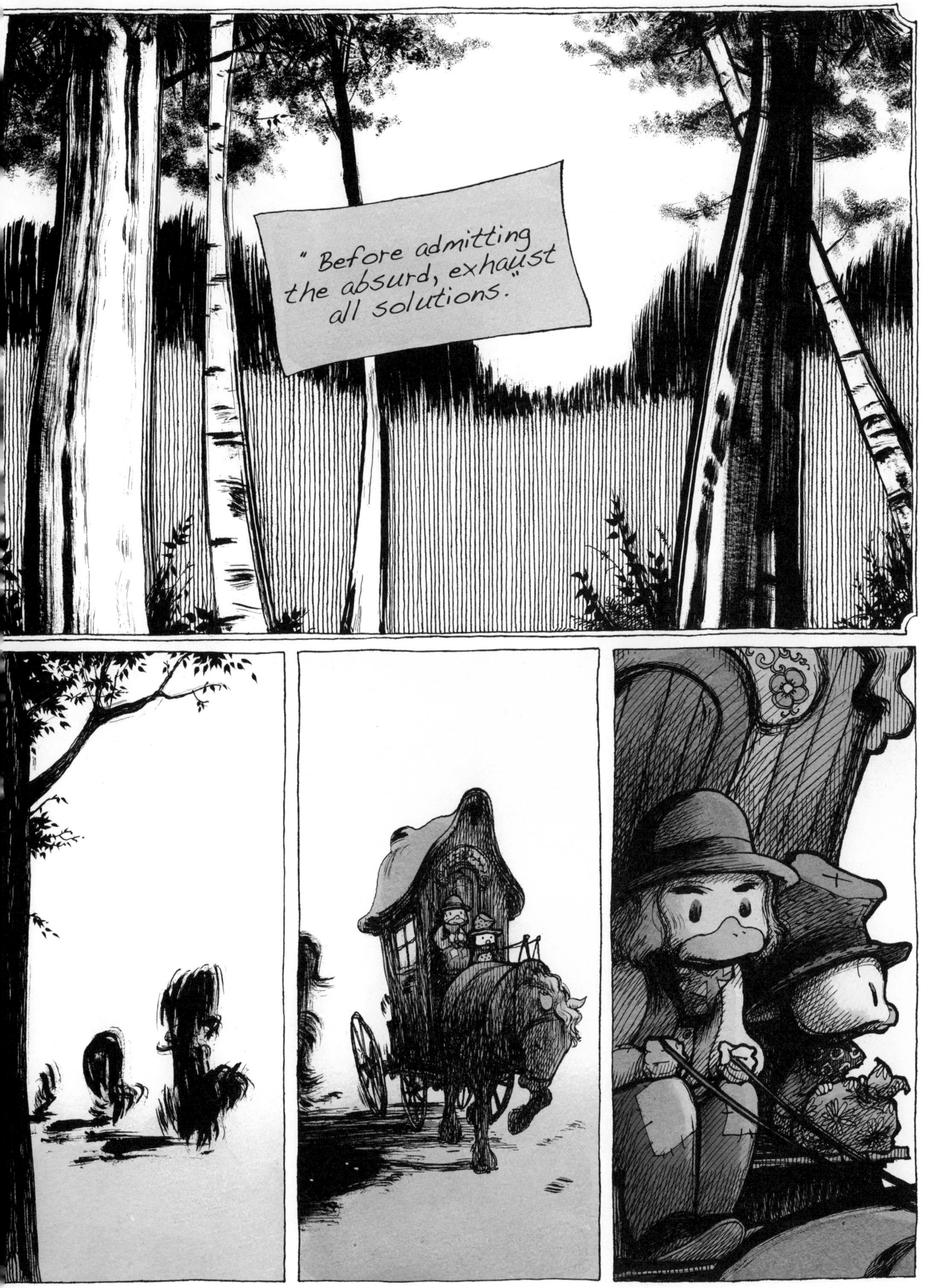
"Before admitting the absurd, exhaust all solutions."

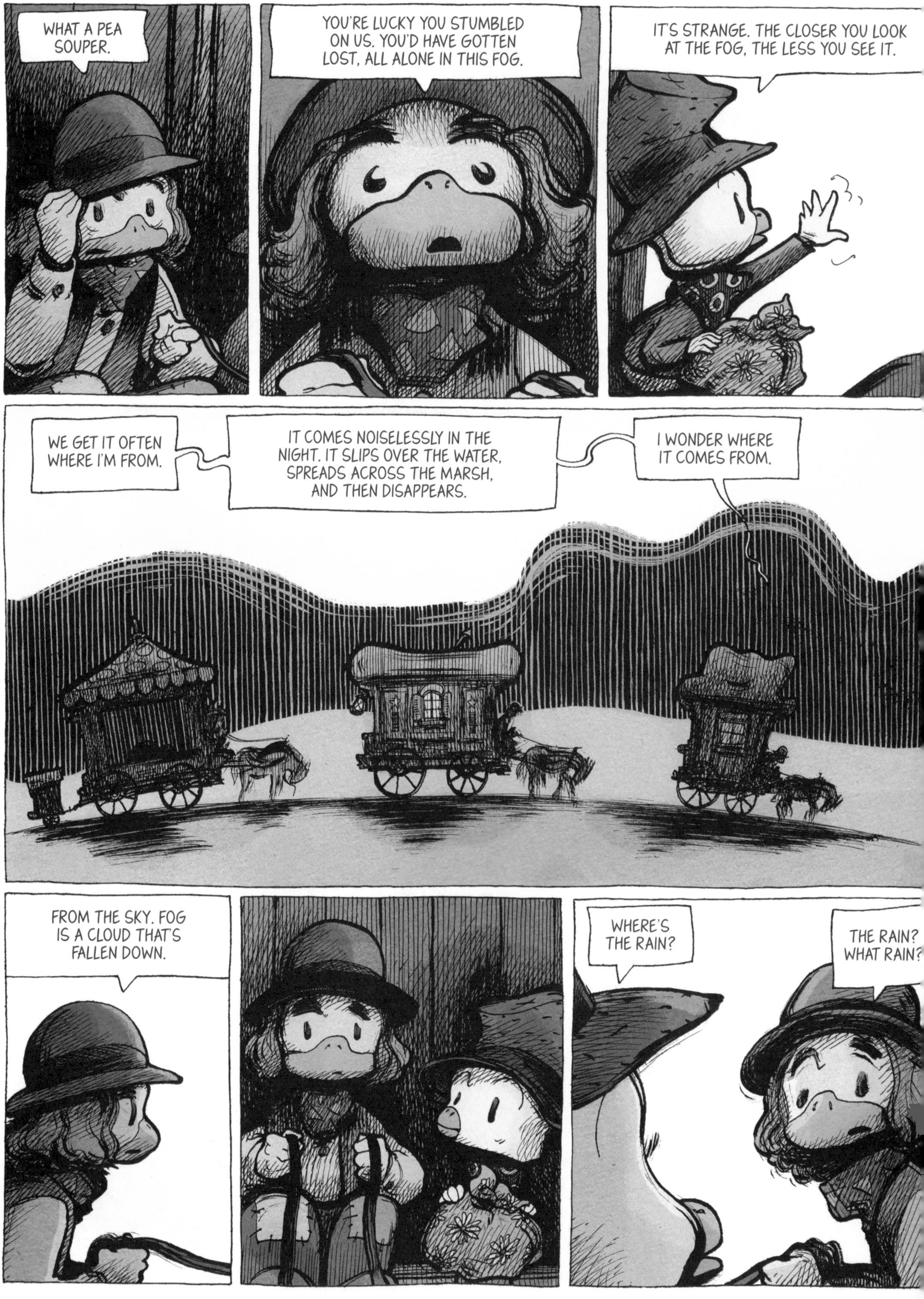
WHAT A PEA SOUPER.
YOU'RE LUCKY YOU STUMBLED ON US. YOU'D HAVE GOTTEN LOST, ALL ALONE IN THIS FOG.
IT'S STRANGE. THE CLOSER YOU LOOK AT THE FOG, THE LESS YOU SEE IT.
WE GET IT OFTEN WHERE I'M FROM.
IT COMES NOISELESSLY IN THE NIGHT. IT SLIPS OVER THE WATER, SPREADS ACROSS THE MARSH, AND THEN DISAPPEARS.
I WONDER WHERE IT COMES FROM.
FROM THE SKY. FOG IS A CLOUD THAT'S FALLEN DOWN.
WHERE'S THE RAIN?
THE RAIN? WHAT RAIN?

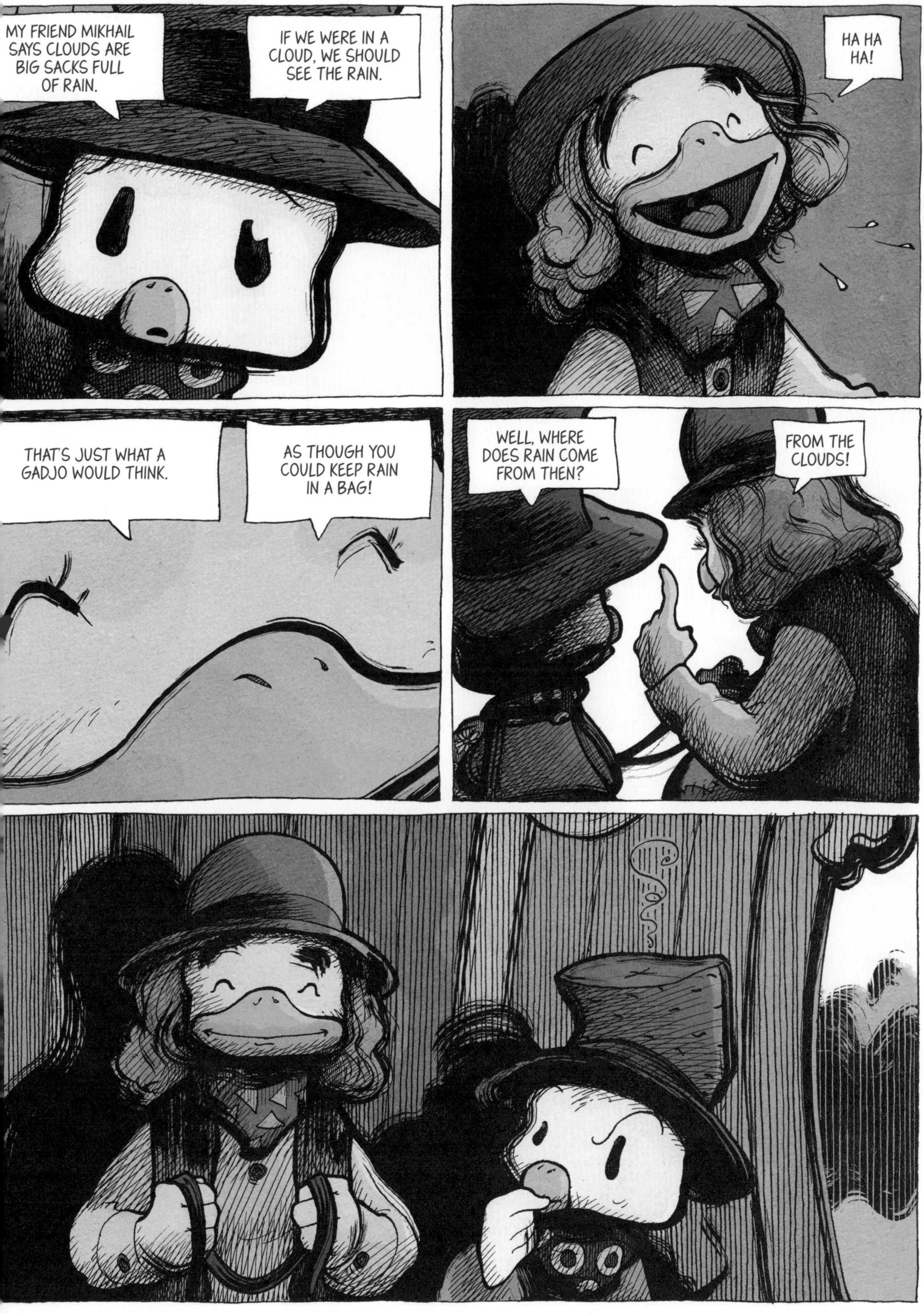
MY FRIEND MIKHAIL SAYS CLOUDS ARE BIG SACKS FULL OF RAIN.
IF WE WERE IN A CLOUD, WE SHOULD SEE THE RAIN.
HA HA HA!
THAT'S JUST WHAT A GADJO WOULD THINK.
AS THOUGH YOU COULD KEEP RAIN IN A BAG!
WELL, WHERE DOES RAIN COME FROM THEN?
FROM THE CLOUDS!

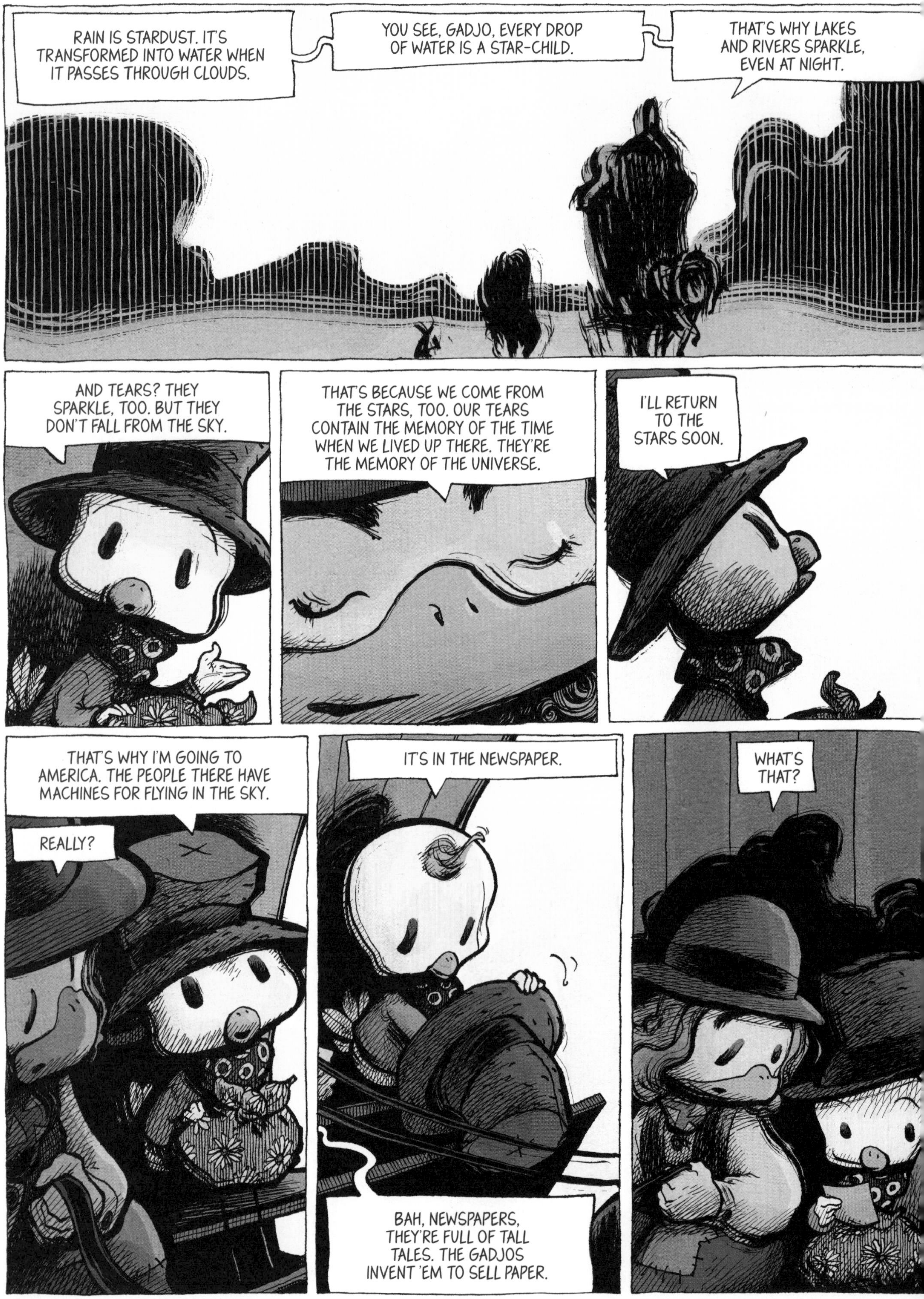
RAIN IS STARDUST. IT'S TRANSFORMED INTO WATER WHEN IT PASSES THROUGH CLOUDS.
YOU SEE, GADJO, EVERY DROP OF WATER IS A STAR-CHILD.
THAT'S WHY LAKES AND RIVERS SPARKLE, EVEN AT NIGHT.
AND TEARS? THEY SPARKLE, TOO. BUT THEY DON'T FALL FROM THE SKY.
THAT'S BECAUSE WE COME FROM THE STARS, TOO. OUR TEARS CONTAIN THE MEMORY OF THE TIME WHEN WE LIVED UP THERE. THEY'RE THE MEMORY OF THE UNIVERSE.
I'LL RETURN TO THE STARS SOON.
THAT'S WHY I'M GOING TO AMERICA. THE PEOPLE THERE HAVE MACHINES FOR FLYING IN THE SKY.
REALLY?
IT'S IN THE NEWSPAPER.
BAH, NEWSPAPERS, THEY'RE FULL OF TALL TALES. THE GADJOS INVENT 'EM TO SELL PAPER.
WHAT'S THAT?

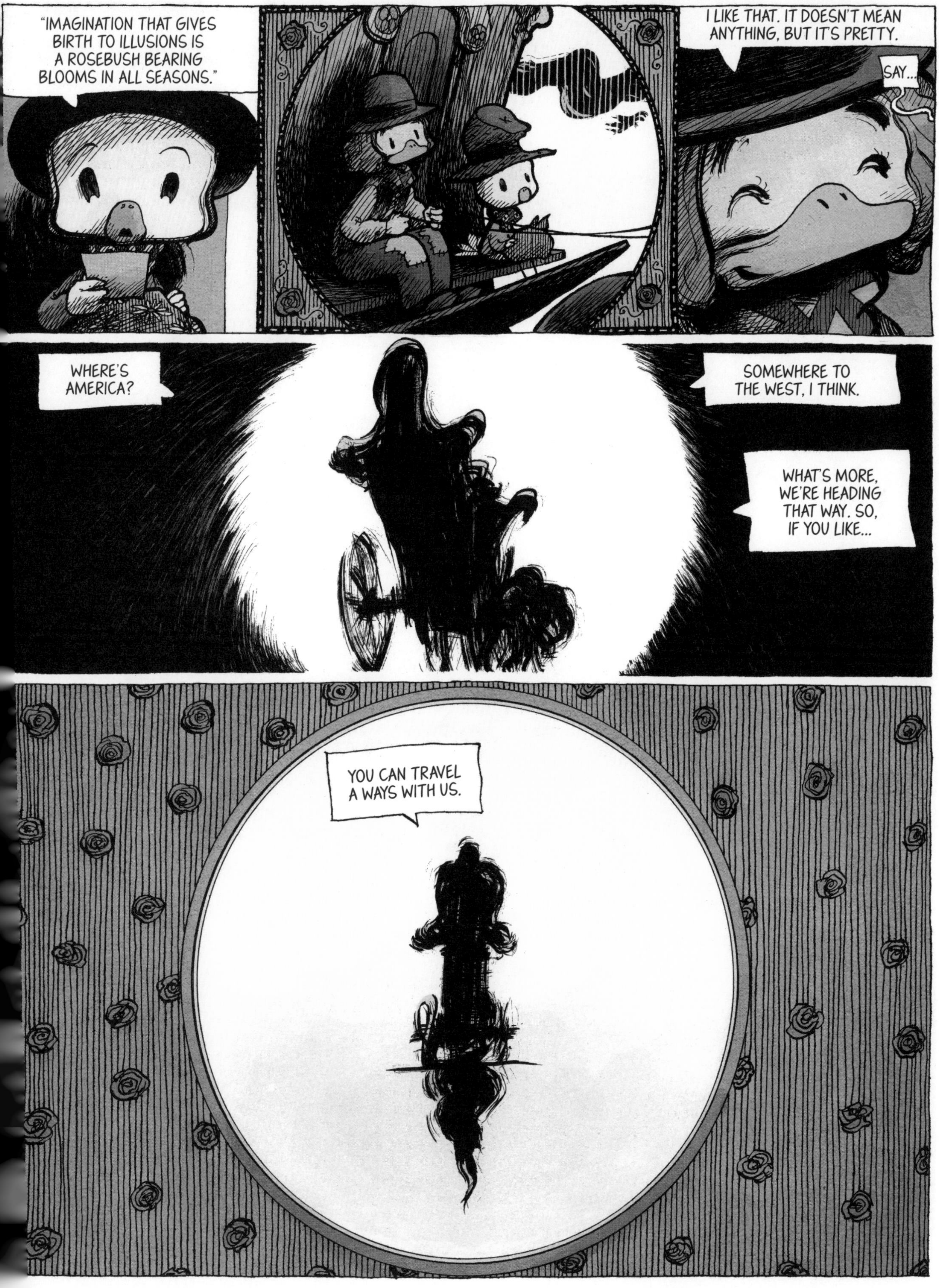
"IMAGINATION THAT GIVES BIRTH TO ILLUSIONS IS A ROSEBUSH BEARING BLOOMS IN ALL SEASONS."
I LIKE THAT. IT DOESN'T MEAN ANYTHING, BUT IT'S PRETTY.
SAY...
WHERE'S AMERICA?
SOMEWHERE TO THE WEST, I THINK.
WHAT'S MORE, WE'RE HEADING THAT WAY. SO, IF YOU LIKE...
YOU CAN TRAVEL A WAYS WITH US.

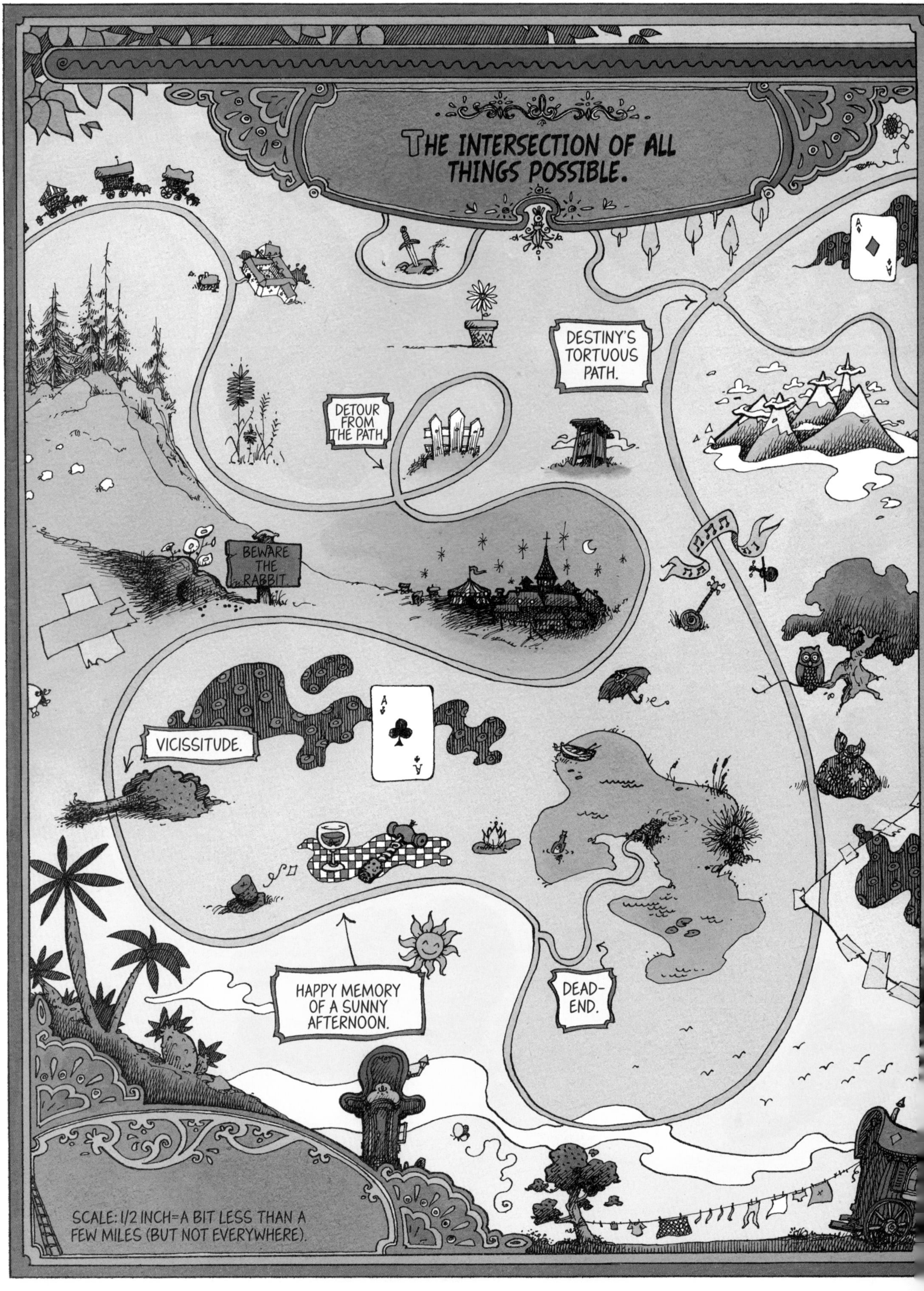
THE INTERSECTION OF ALL THINGS POSSIBLE.
DESTINY'S TORTUOUS PATH.
DETOUR FROM THE PATH
BEWARE THE RABBIT
VICISSITUDE.
HAPPY MEMORY OF A SUNNY AFTERNOON.
DEAD-END.
SCALE: 1/2 INCH=A BIT LESS THAN A FEW MILES (BUT NOT EVERYWHERE).

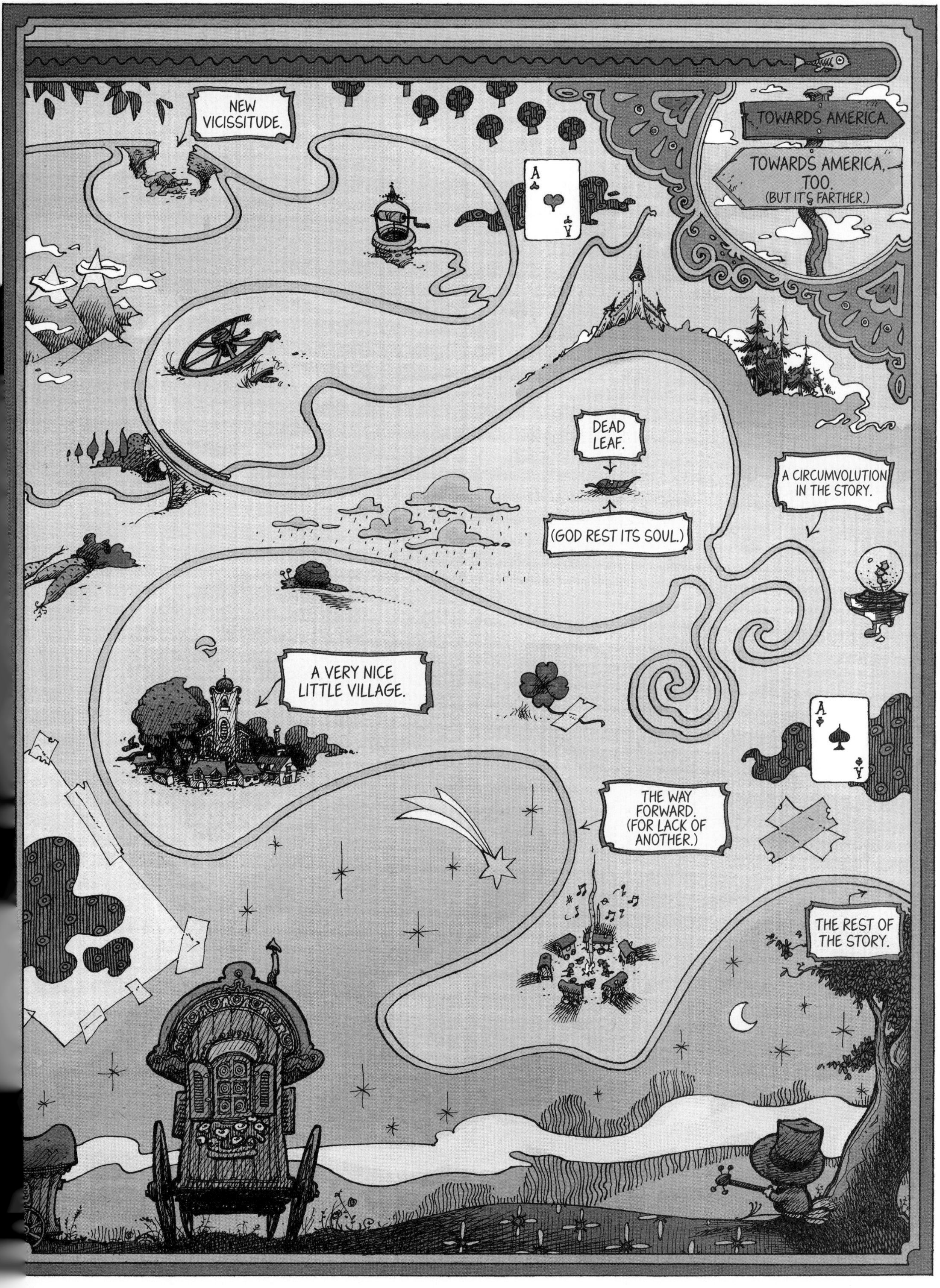
NEW VICISSITUDE.
TOWARDS AMERICA.
TOWARDS AMERICA, TOO. (BUT IT'S FARTHER.)
DEAD LEAF.
(GOD REST ITS SOUL.)
A CIRCUMVOLUTION IN THE STORY.
A VERY NICE LITTLE VILLAGE.
THE WAY FORWARD. (FOR LACK OF ANOTHER.)
THE REST OF THE STORY.

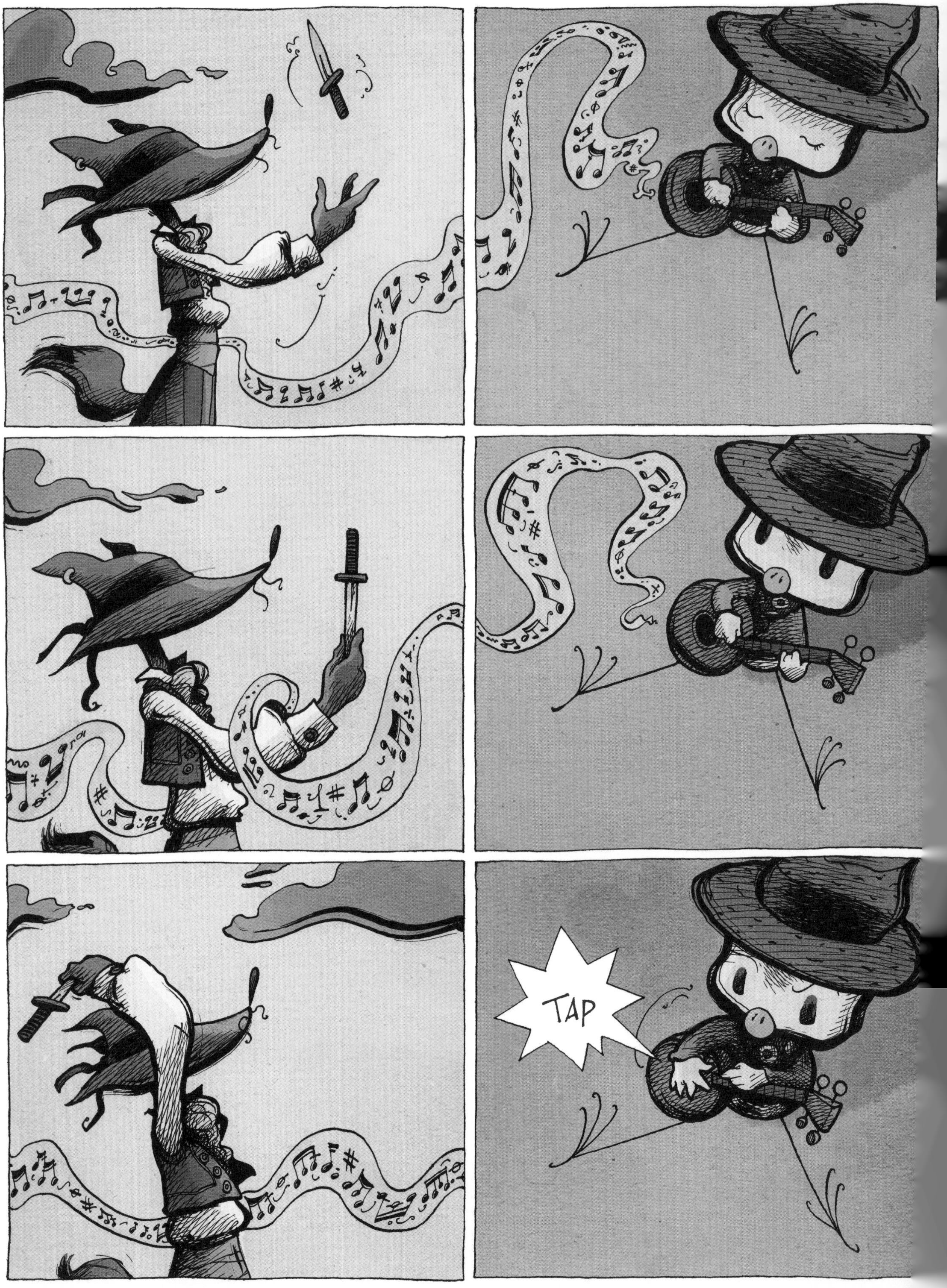
TAP

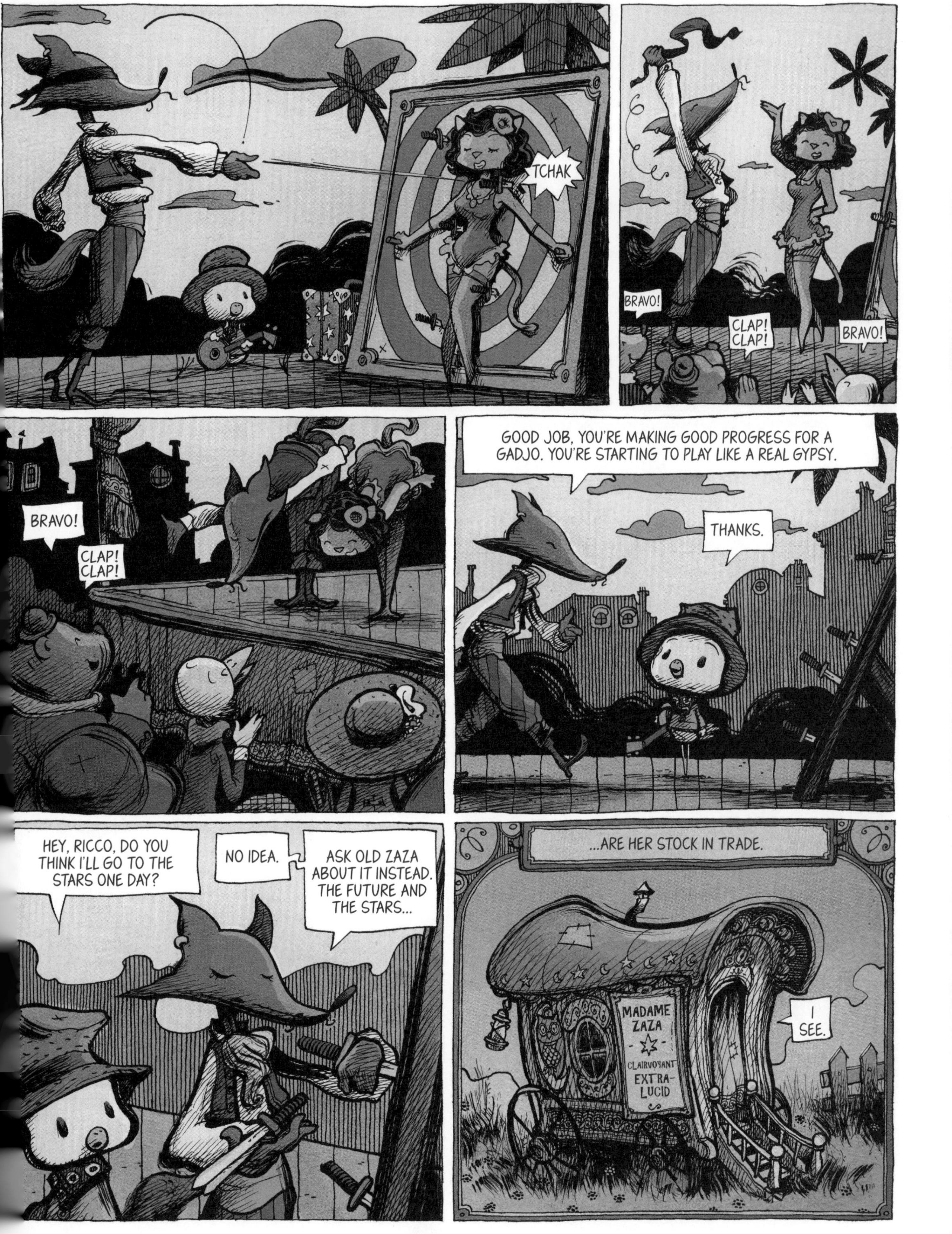
TCHAK
BRAVO!
CLAP! CLAP!
BRAVO!
BRAVO!
CLAP! CLAP!
GOOD JOB, YOU'RE MAKING GOOD PROGRESS FOR A GADJO. YOU'RE STARTING TO PLAY LIKE A REAL GYPSY.
THANKS.
HEY, RICCO, DO YOU THINK I'LL GO TO THE STARS ONE DAY?
NO IDEA.
ASK OLD ZAZA ABOUT IT INSTEAD. THE FUTURE AND THE STARS...
...ARE HER STOCK IN TRADE.
MADAME ZAZA
CLAIRVOYANT
EXTRA-LUCID
I SEE.

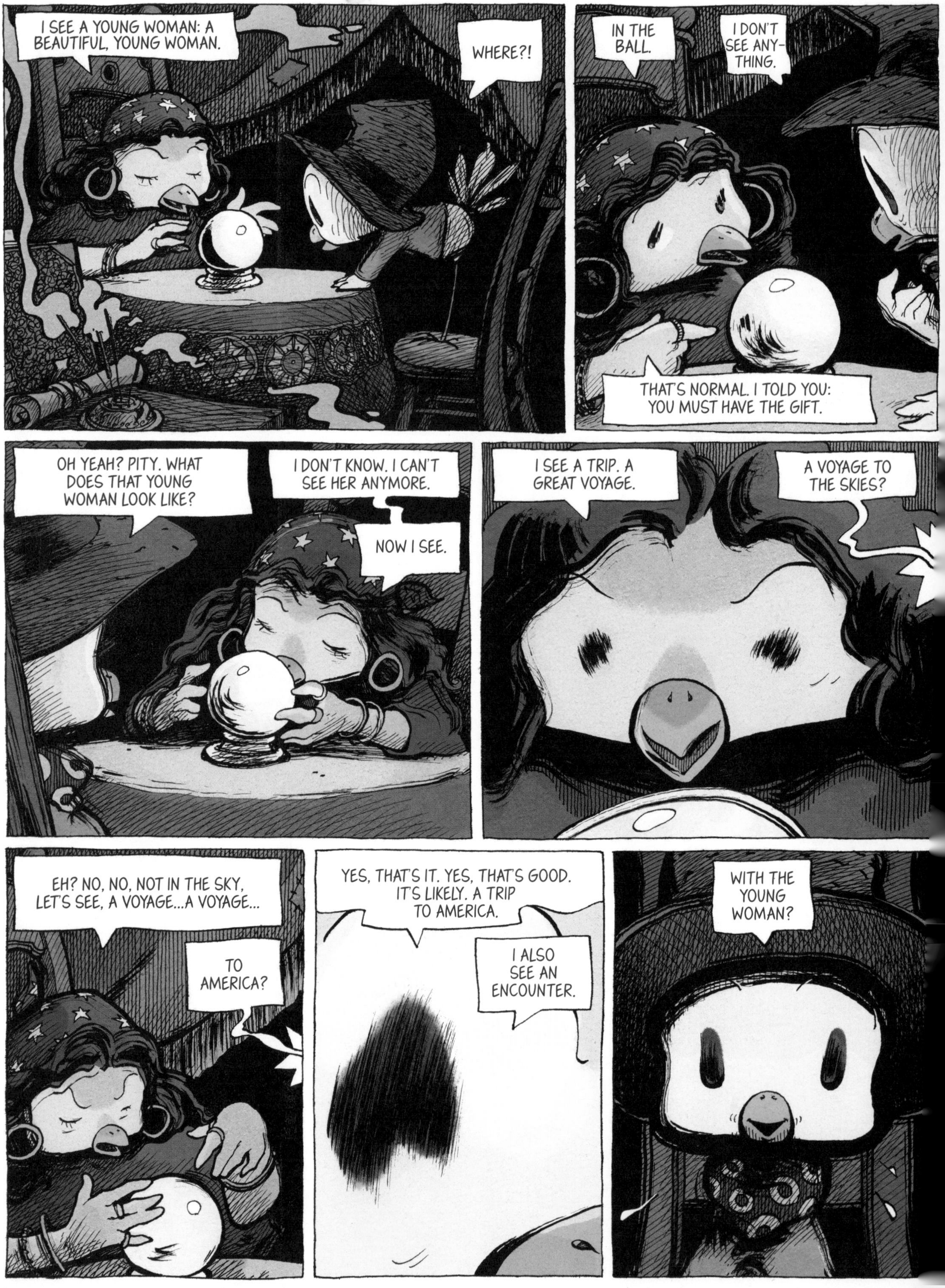
I SEE A YOUNG WOMAN: A BEAUTIFUL, YOUNG WOMAN.
WHERE?!
IN THE BALL.
I DON'T SEE ANYTHING.
THAT'S NORMAL. I TOLD YOU: YOU MUST HAVE THE GIFT.
OH YEAH? PITY. WHAT DOES THAT YOUNG WOMAN LOOK LIKE?
I DON'T KNOW. I CAN'T SEE HER ANYMORE.
NOW I SEE.
I SEE A TRIP. A GREAT VOYAGE.
A VOYAGE TO THE SKIES?
EH? NO, NO, NOT IN THE SKY, LET'S SEE, A VOYAGE...A VOYAGE...
TO AMERICA?
YES, THAT'S IT. YES, THAT'S GOOD. IT'S LIKELY. A TRIP TO AMERICA.
I ALSO SEE AN ENCOUNTER.
WITH THE YOUNG WOMAN?

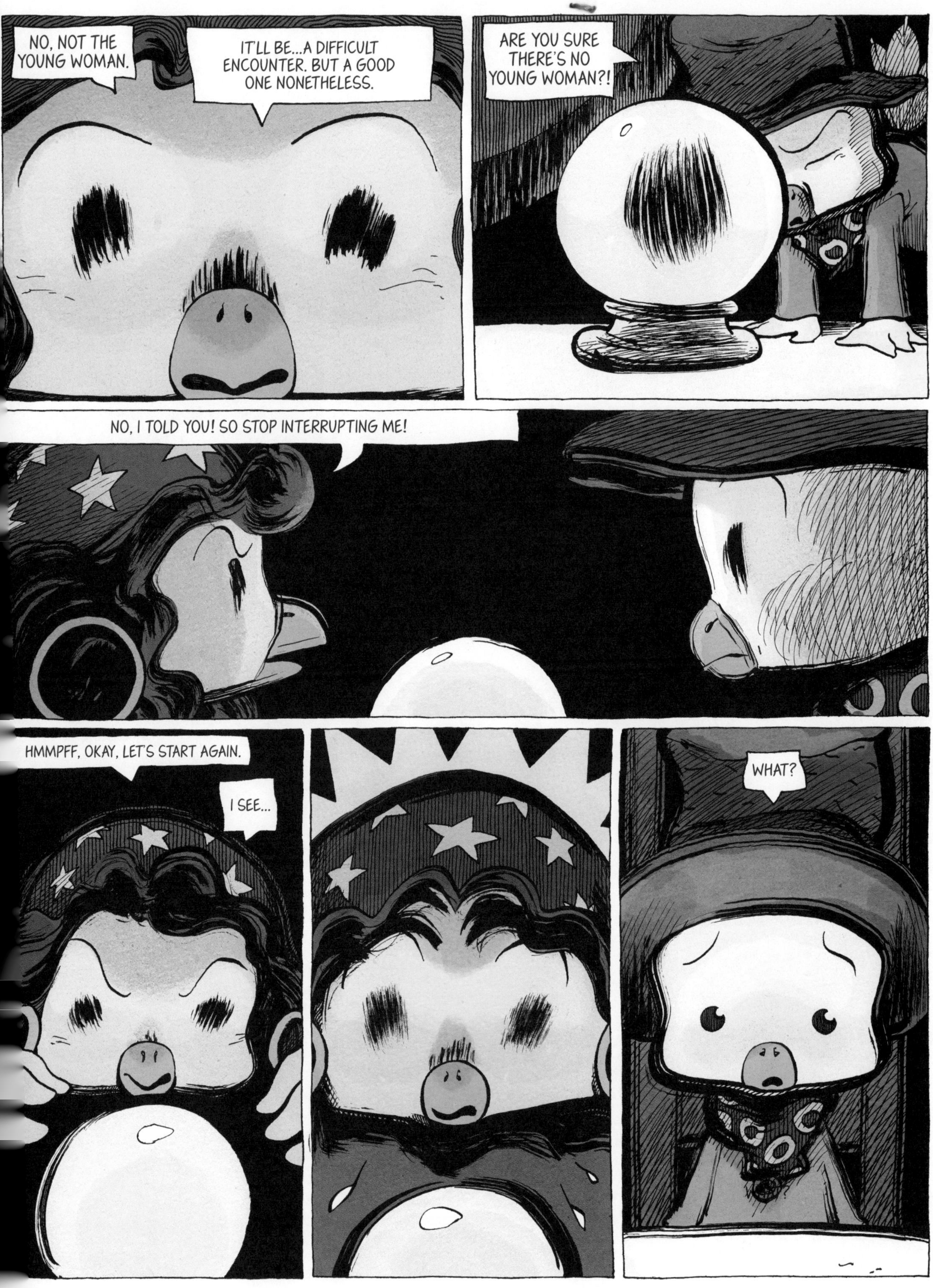

NO, NOT THE YOUNG WOMAN.
IT'LL BE...A DIFFICULT ENCOUNTER. BUT A GOOD ONE NONETHELESS.
ARE YOU SURE THERE'S NO YOUNG WOMAN?!
NO, I TOLD YOU! SO STOP INTERRUPTING ME!
HMMPFF, OKAY, LET'S START AGAIN.
I SEE...
WHAT?

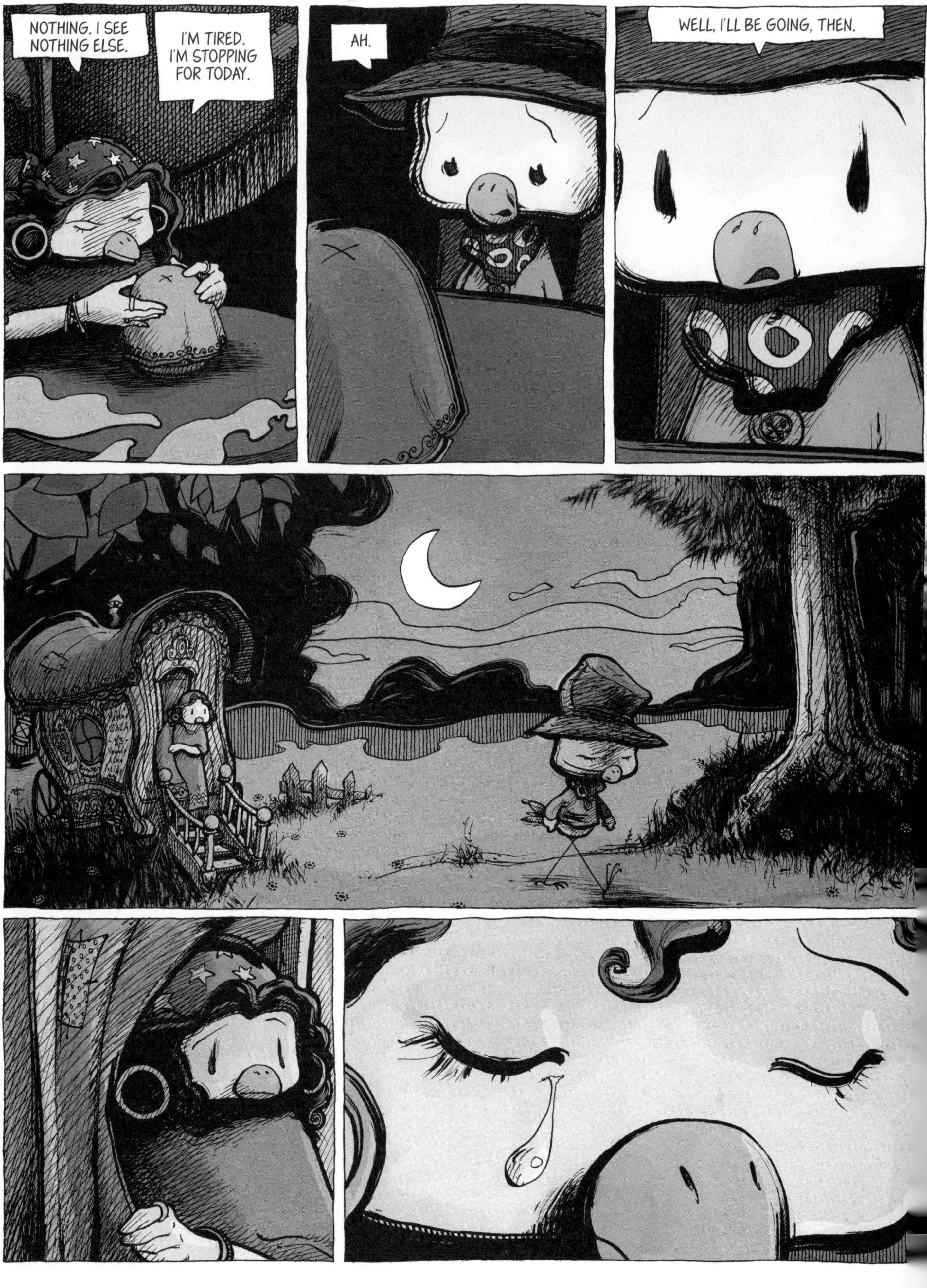
NOTHING. I SEE NOTHING ELSE.
I'M TIRED. I'M STOPPING FOR TODAY.
AH.
WELL, I'LL BE GOING, THEN.

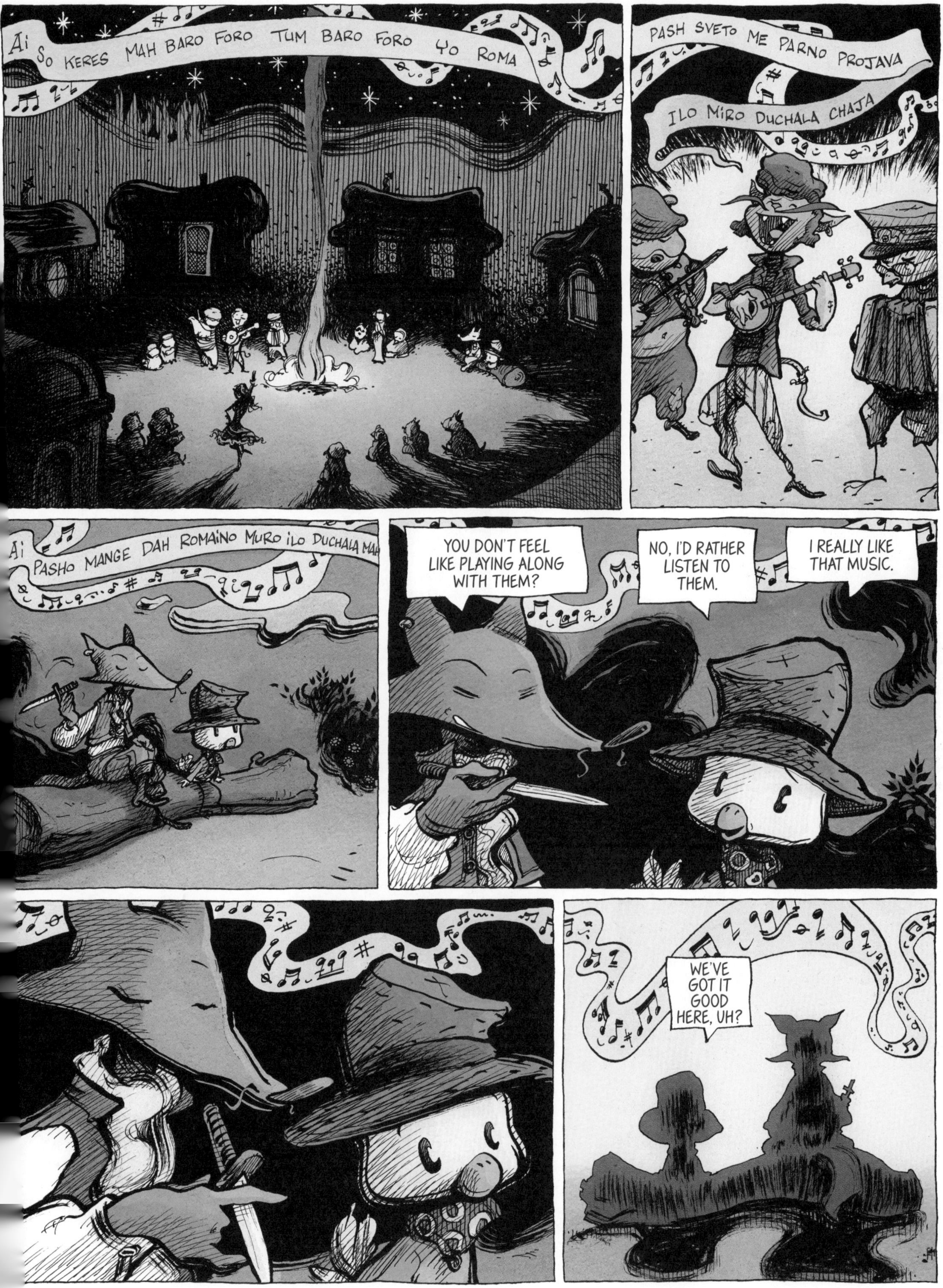
AI SO KERES MAH BARO FORO TUM BARO FORO YO ROMA
PASH SVETO ME PARNO PROJAVA
ILO MIRO DUCHALA CHAJA
AI PASHO MANGE DAH ROMAINO MURO ILO DUCHALA MAH
YOU DON'T FEEL LIKE PLAYING ALONG WITH THEM?
NO, I'D RATHER LISTEN TO THEM.
I REALLY LIKE THAT MUSIC.
WE'VE GOT IT GOOD HERE, UH?

YOU SAID IT, GADJO. ALMOST AS NICE AS BEING IN A GIRL'S ARMS!

I KNOW A GIRL. SHE HAS LONG ARMS. HER NAME'S EPPILY.

AH?

I KNEW AN EPPILY. ONE HELLUVA PRETTY GIRL. AND NO PRUDE EITHER. THE KIND OF GAL WHO CAN HAVE A GOOD TIME, IF YOU KNOW WHAT I MEAN.

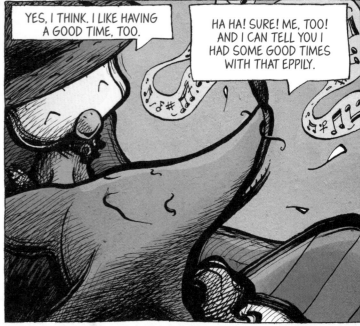

YES, I THINK. I LIKE HAVING A GOOD TIME, TOO.

HA HA! SURE! ME, TOO! AND I CAN TELL YOU I HAD SOME GOOD TIMES WITH THAT EPPILY.

BUT SHE WAS A STRANGE GIRL.

ONE MOMENT SHE'D BE AS HAPPY AS ALL GET OUT AND, FIVE MINUTES LATER, SHE'D BURST INTO TEARS.

SHE HAD A SORROW IN HER, YOU SEE, SOMETHING SHE'D NOT COME TO TERMS WITH.

REALLY?

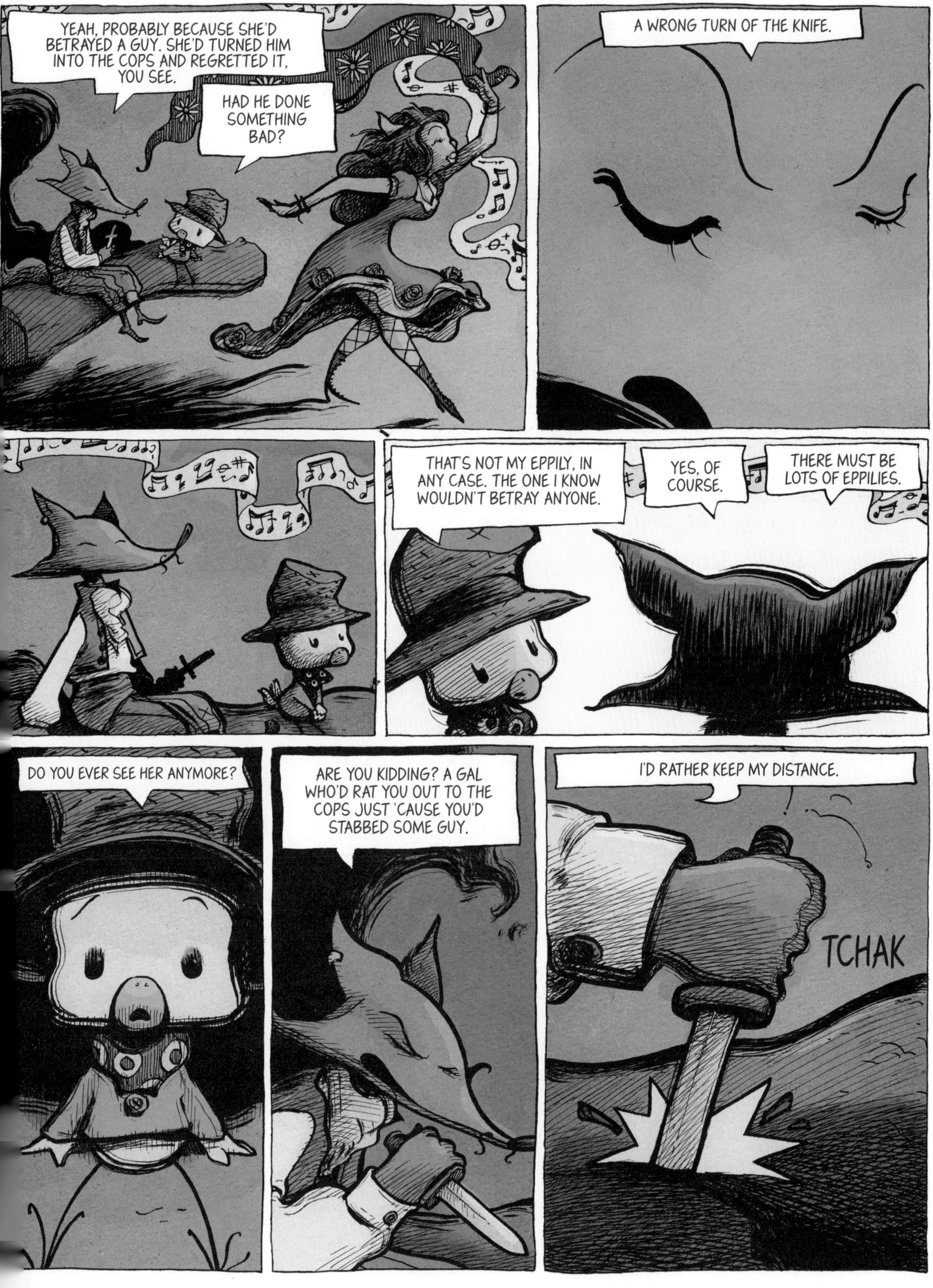
YEAH, PROBABLY BECAUSE SHE'D BETRAYED A GUY. SHE'D TURNED HIM INTO THE COPS AND REGRETTED IT, YOU SEE.
HAD HE DONE SOMETHING BAD?
A WRONG TURN OF THE KNIFE.
THAT'S NOT MY EPPILY, IN ANY CASE. THE ONE I KNOW WOULDN'T BETRAY ANYONE.
YES, OF COURSE.
THERE MUST BE LOTS OF EPPILIES.
DO YOU EVER SEE HER ANYMORE?
ARE YOU KIDDING? A GAL WHO'D RAT YOU OUT TO THE COPS JUST 'CAUSE YOU'D STABBED SOME GUY.
I'D RATHER KEEP MY DISTANCE.
TCHAK

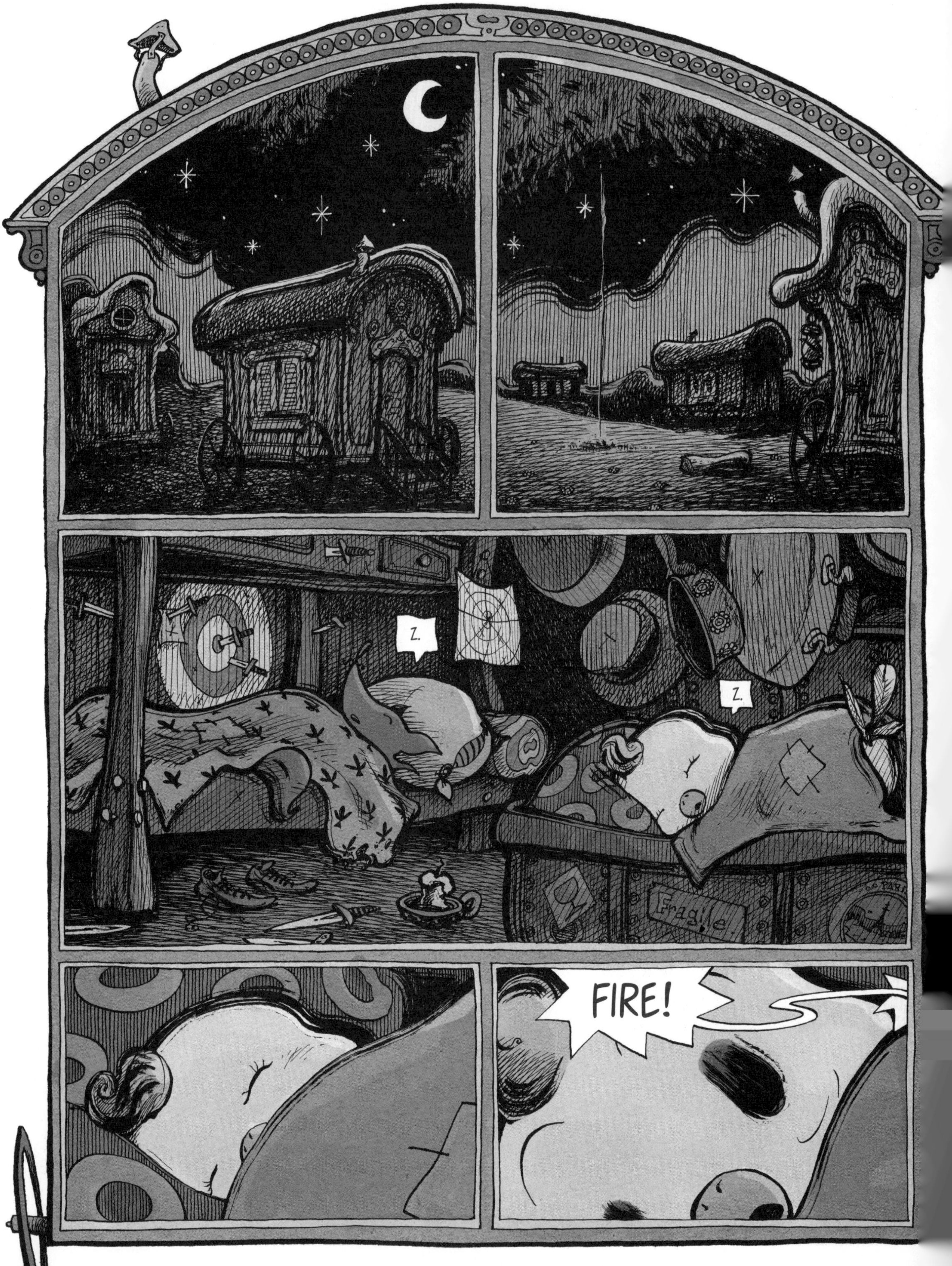
Z.
Z.
Fragile
FIRE!

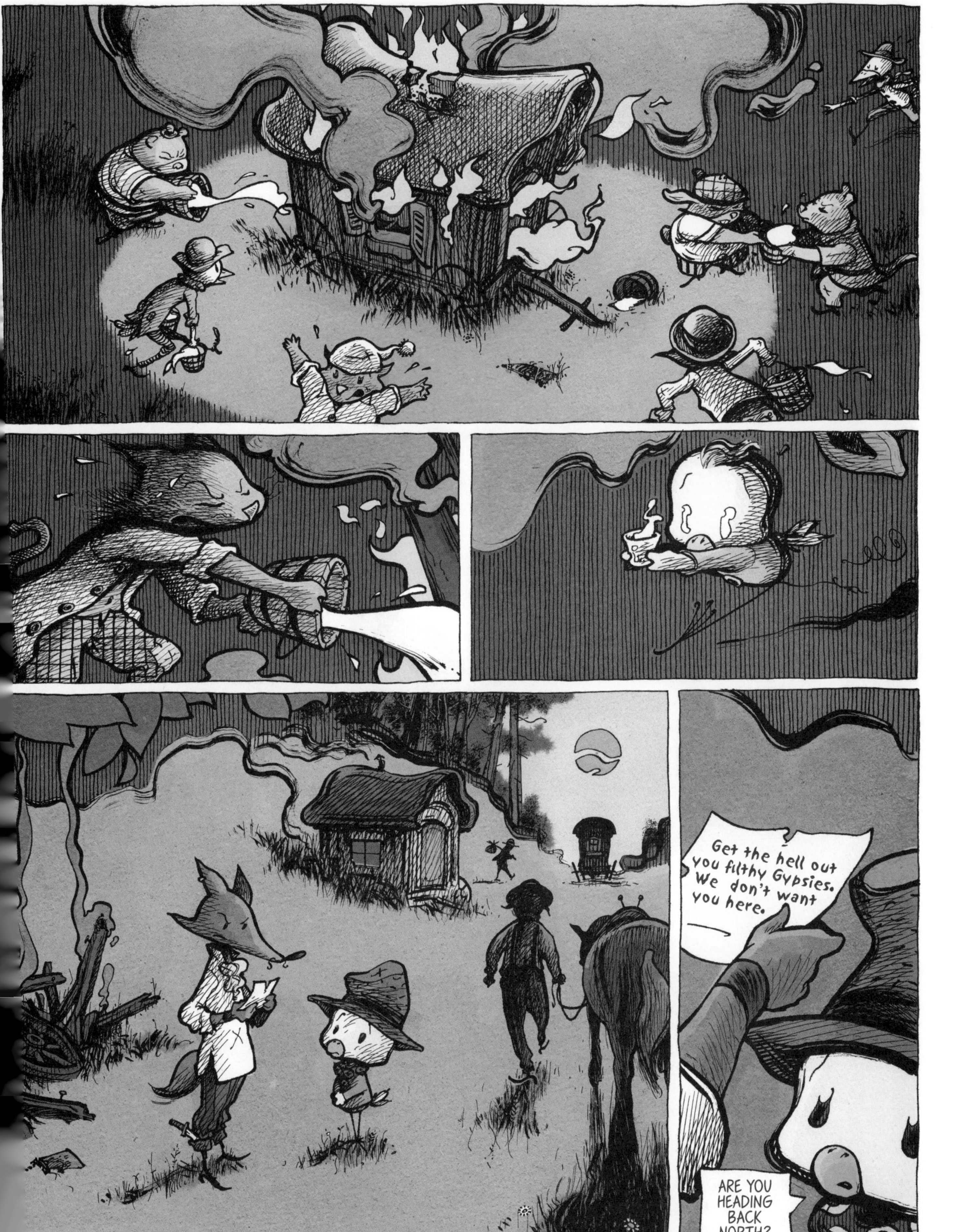
Get the hell out you filthy Gypsies. We don't want you here.
ARE YOU HEADING BACK NORTH?

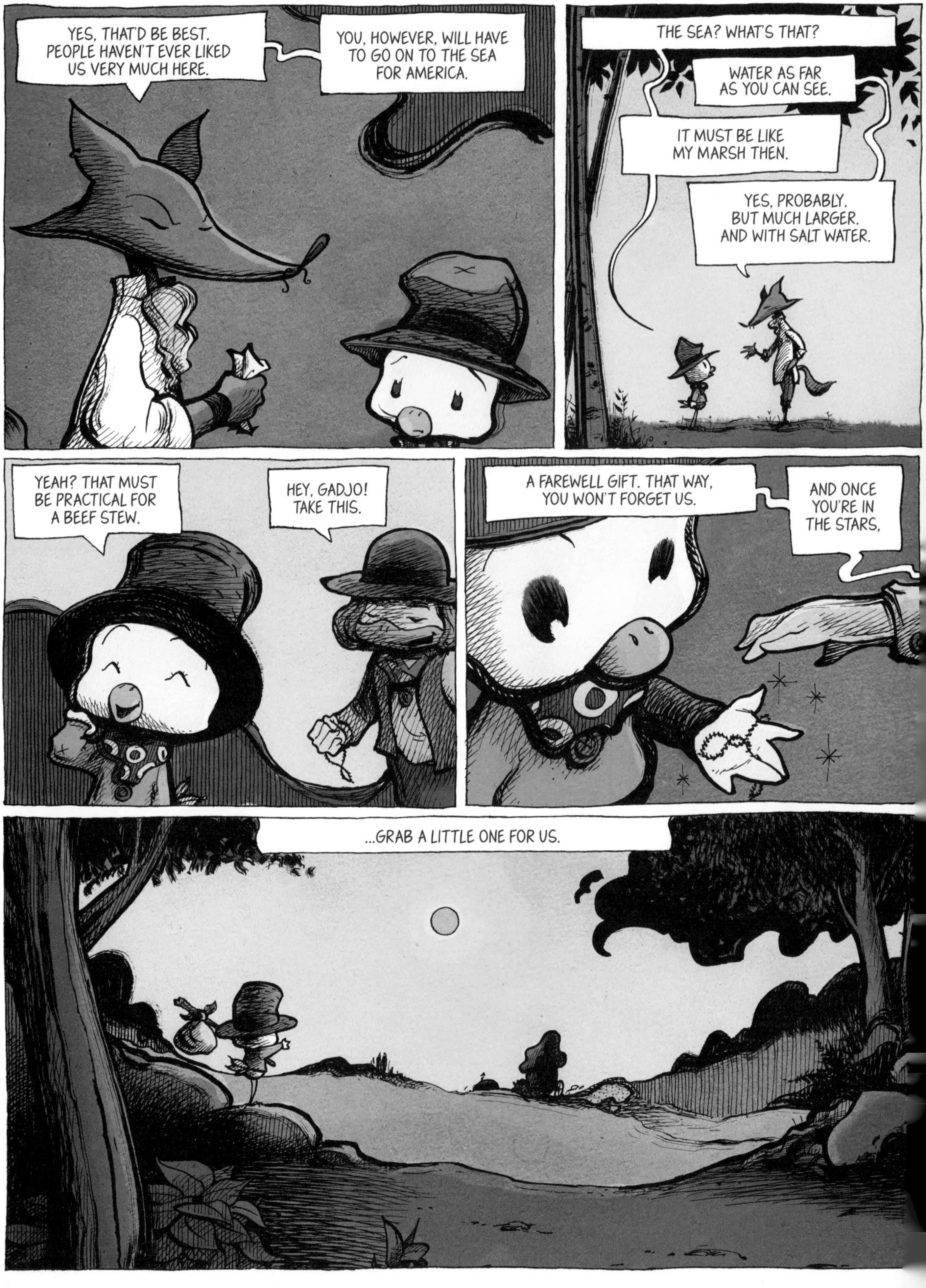

YES, THAT'D BE BEST. PEOPLE HAVEN'T EVER LIKED US VERY MUCH HERE.
YOU, HOWEVER, WILL HAVE TO GO ON TO THE SEA FOR AMERICA.
THE SEA? WHAT'S THAT?
WATER AS FAR AS YOU CAN SEE.
IT MUST BE LIKE MY MARSH THEN.
YES, PROBABLY. BUT MUCH LARGER. AND WITH SALT WATER.
YEAH? THAT MUST BE PRACTICAL FOR A BEEF STEW.
HEY, GADJO! TAKE THIS.
A FAREWELL GIFT. THAT WAY, YOU WON'T FORGET US.
AND ONCE YOU'RE IN THE STARS,
...GRAB A LITTLE ONE FOR US.

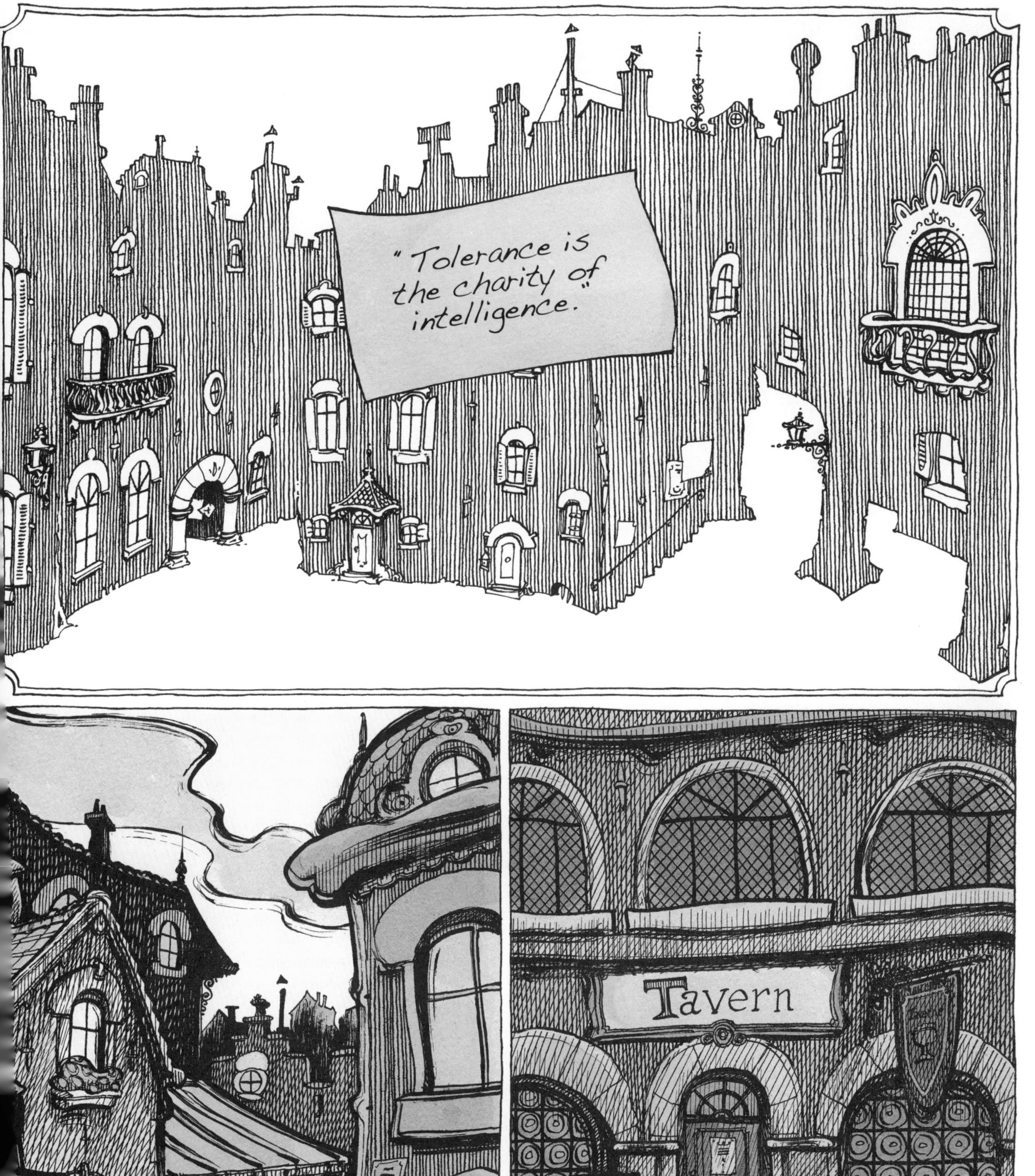
"Tolerance is the charity of intelligence."
Tavern

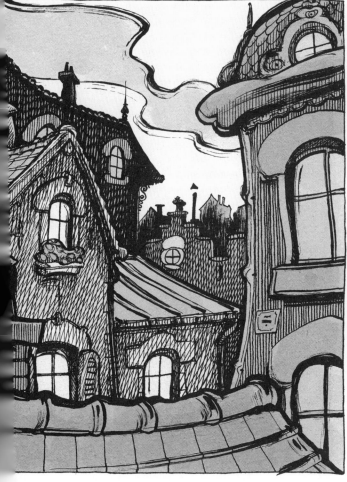

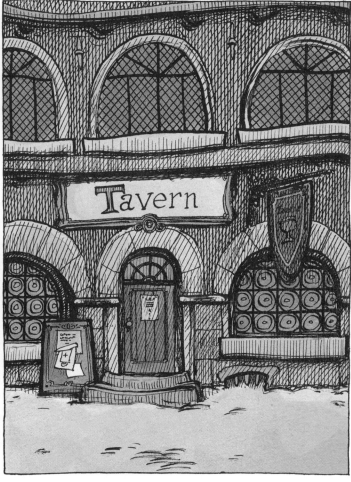

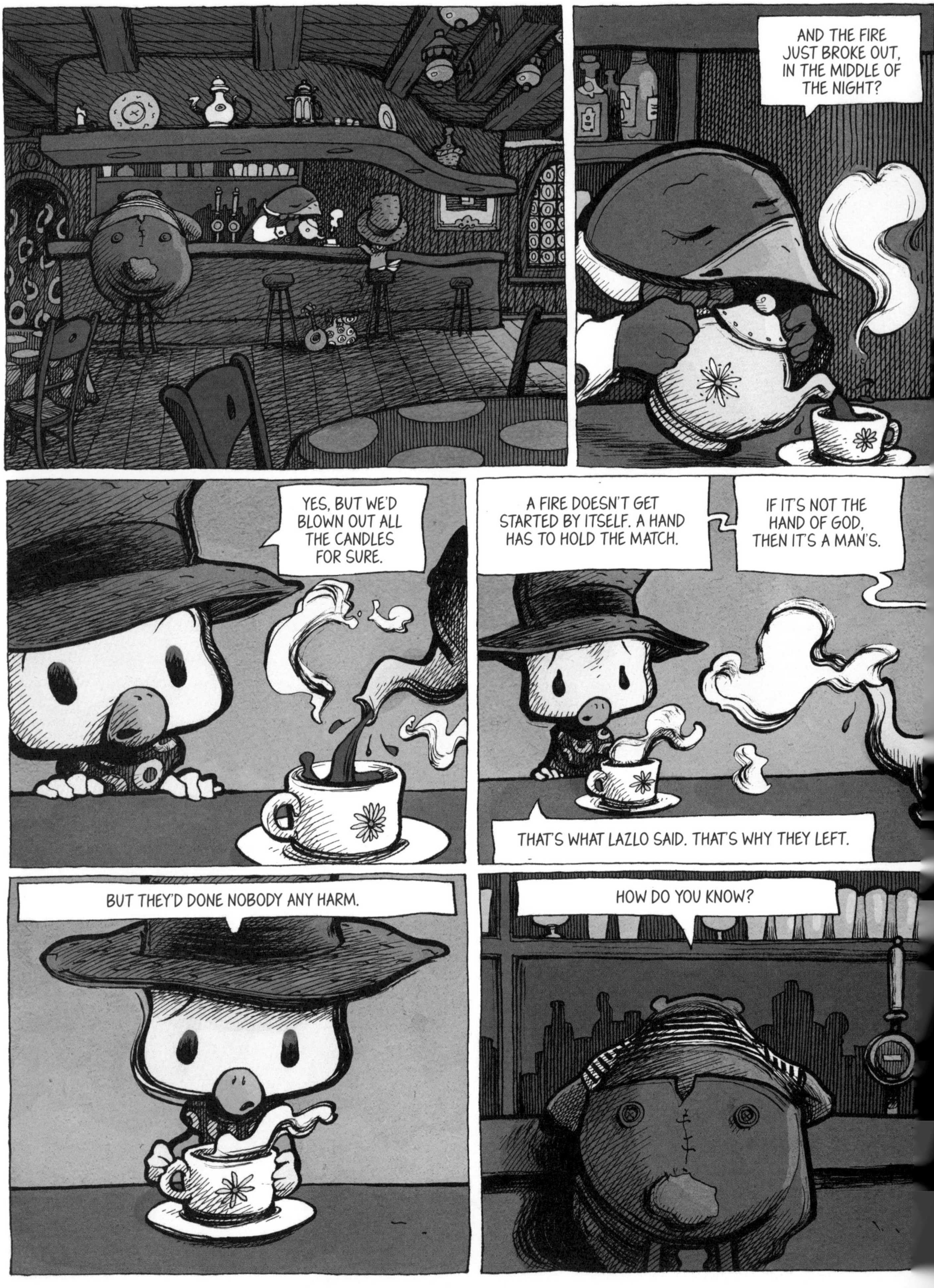
AND THE FIRE JUST BROKE OUT, IN THE MIDDLE OF THE NIGHT?
YES, BUT WE'D BLOWN OUT ALL THE CANDLES FOR SURE.
A FIRE DOESN'T GET STARTED BY ITSELF. A HAND HAS TO HOLD THE MATCH.
IF IT'S NOT THE HAND OF GOD, THEN IT'S A MAN'S.
THAT'S WHAT LAZLO SAID. THAT'S WHY THEY LEFT.
BUT THEY'D DONE NOBODY ANY HARM.
HOW DO YOU KNOW?

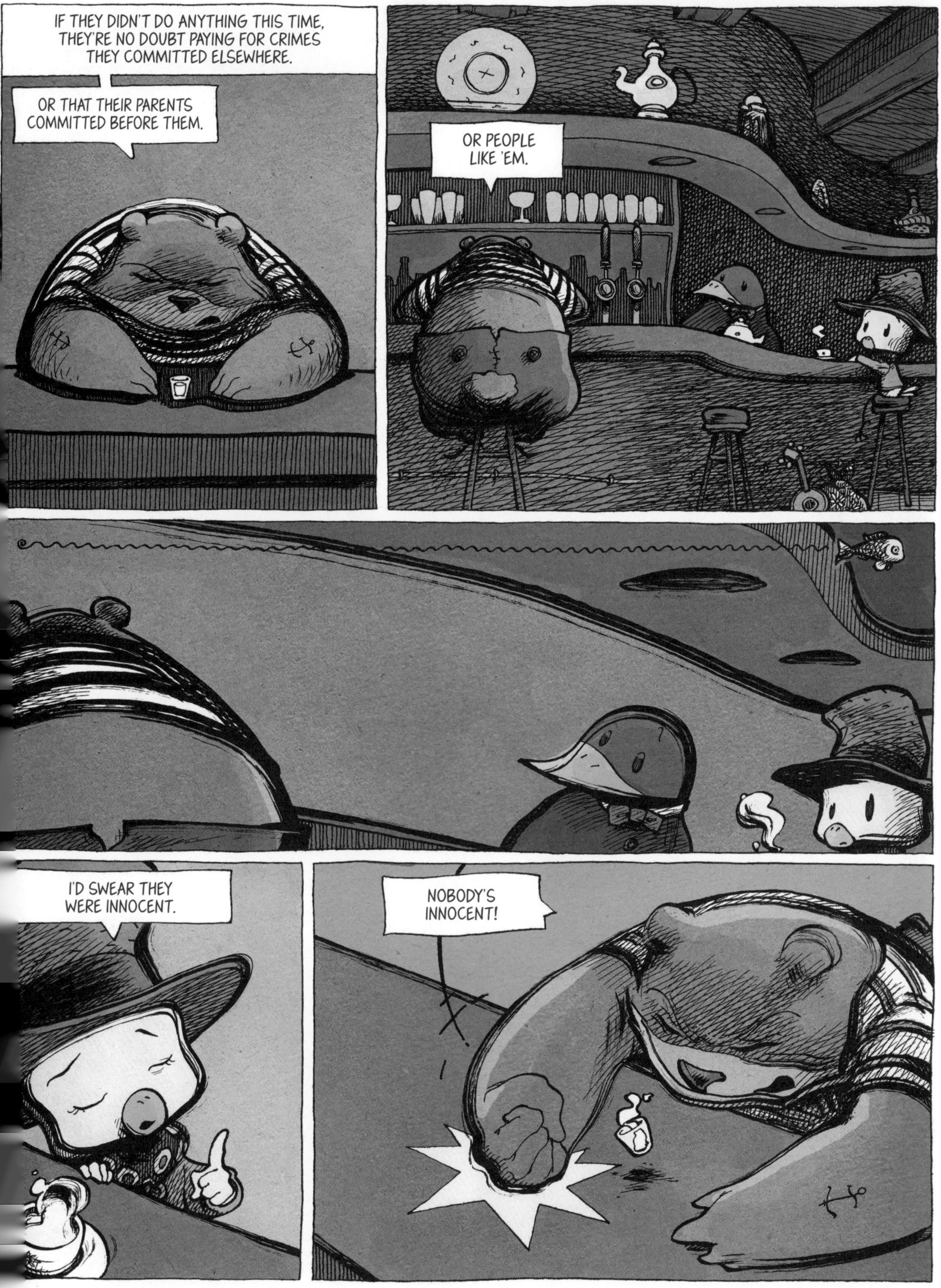
IF THEY DIDN'T DO ANYTHING THIS TIME, THEY'RE NO DOUBT PAYING FOR CRIMES THEY COMMITTED ELSEWHERE.
OR THAT THEIR PARENTS COMMITTED BEFORE THEM.
OR PEOPLE LIKE 'EM.
I'D SWEAR THEY WERE INNOCENT.
NOBODY'S INNOCENT!

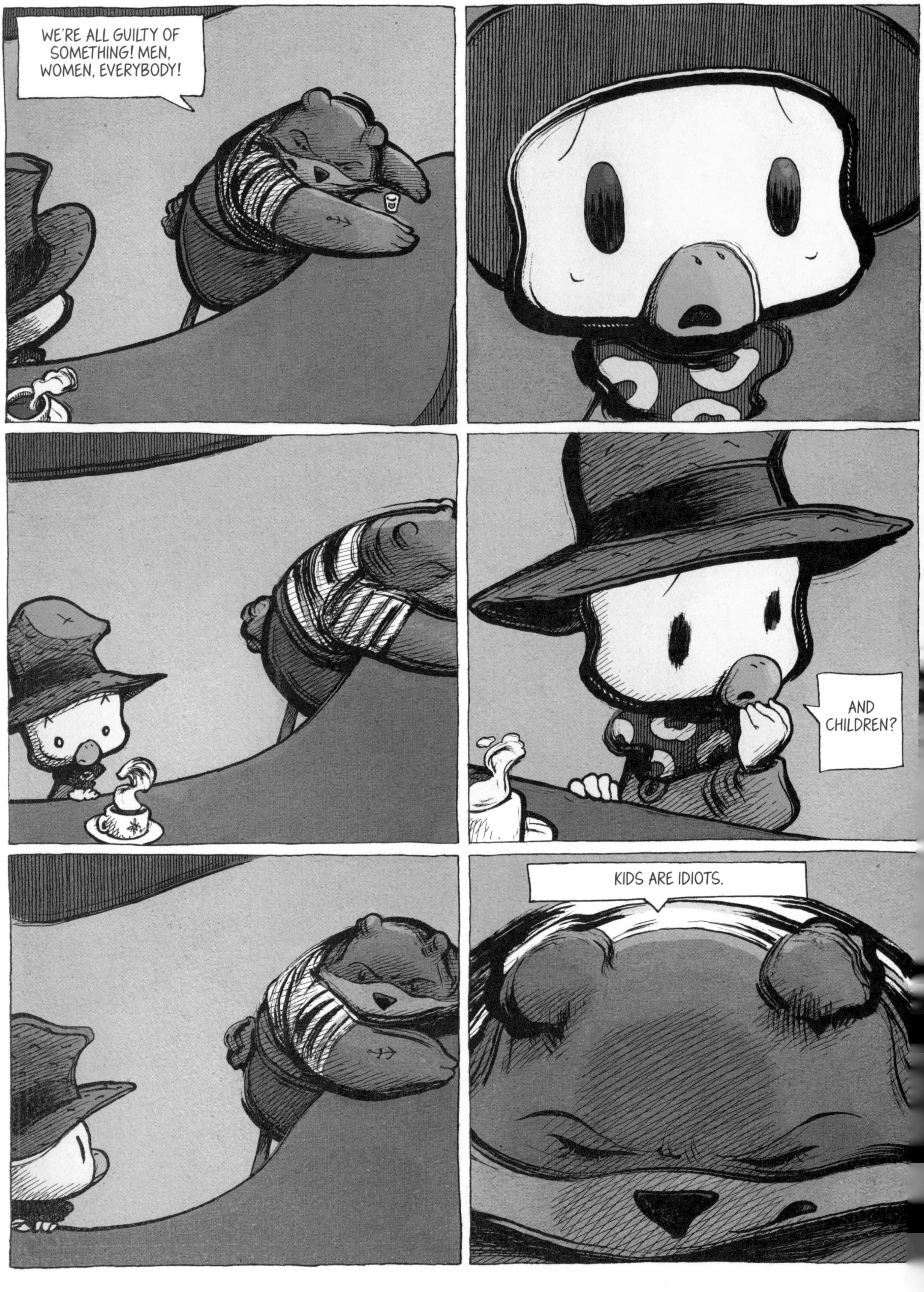
WE'RE ALL GUILTY OF SOMETHING! MEN, WOMEN, EVERYBODY!
AND CHILDREN?
KIDS ARE IDIOTS.

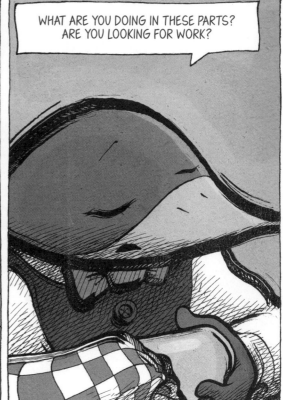

WHAT ARE YOU DOING IN THESE PARTS? ARE YOU LOOKING FOR WORK?

ME? NO, I'M JUST PASSING THROUGH. I'M GOING TO AMERICA.

I WANT TO GIVE EPPILY A GIFT WORTHY OF HER.

AND FOR THAT, I MUST...

EPPILY?

THAT'S NOT A COMMON NAME. WHERE ARE YOU FROM EXACTLY?

FROM OVER THAT WAY, BUT VERY FAR OFF.

I LIVE IN THE MARSH NEAR KANANIVKA.

KANANIVKA...

I KNOW YOUR EPPILY, THEN. FORGET HER.

WHY?

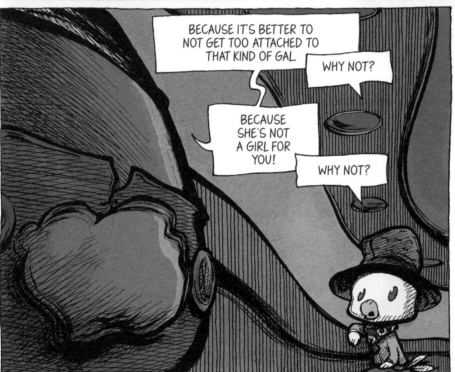

BECAUSE IT'S BETTER TO NOT GET TOO ATTACHED TO THAT KIND OF GAL.

WHY NOT?

BECAUSE SHE'S NOT A GIRL FOR YOU!

WHY NOT?

'CAUSE SHE'S A WHORE.

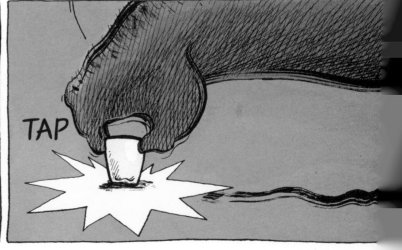

TAP

54

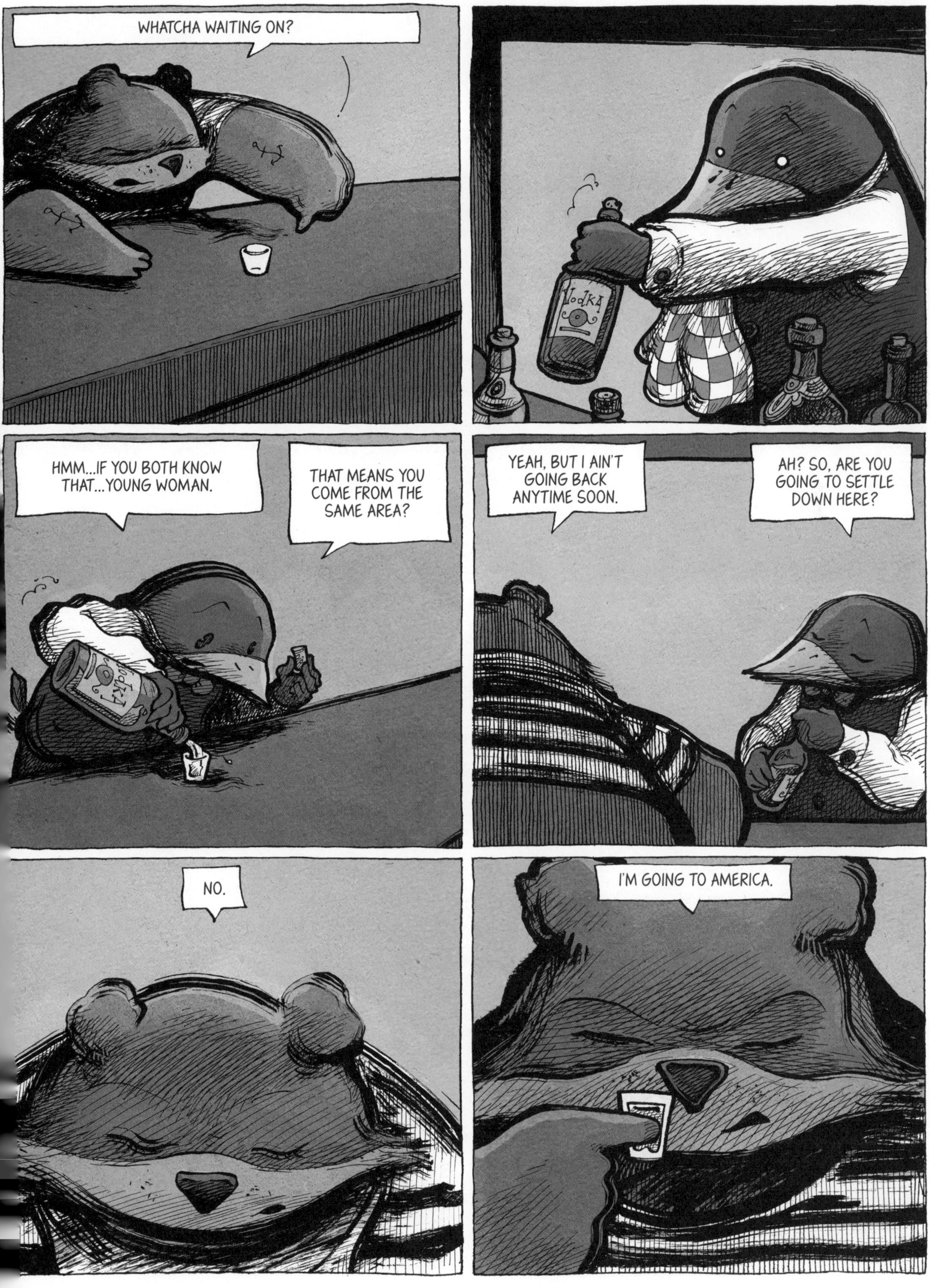
WHATCHA WAITING ON?
VodKA
HMM...IF YOU BOTH KNOW THAT...YOUNG WOMAN.
THAT MEANS YOU COME FROM THE SAME AREA?
YEAH, BUT I AIN'T GOING BACK ANYTIME SOON.
AH? SO, ARE YOU GOING TO SETTLE DOWN HERE?
NO.
I'M GOING TO AMERICA.

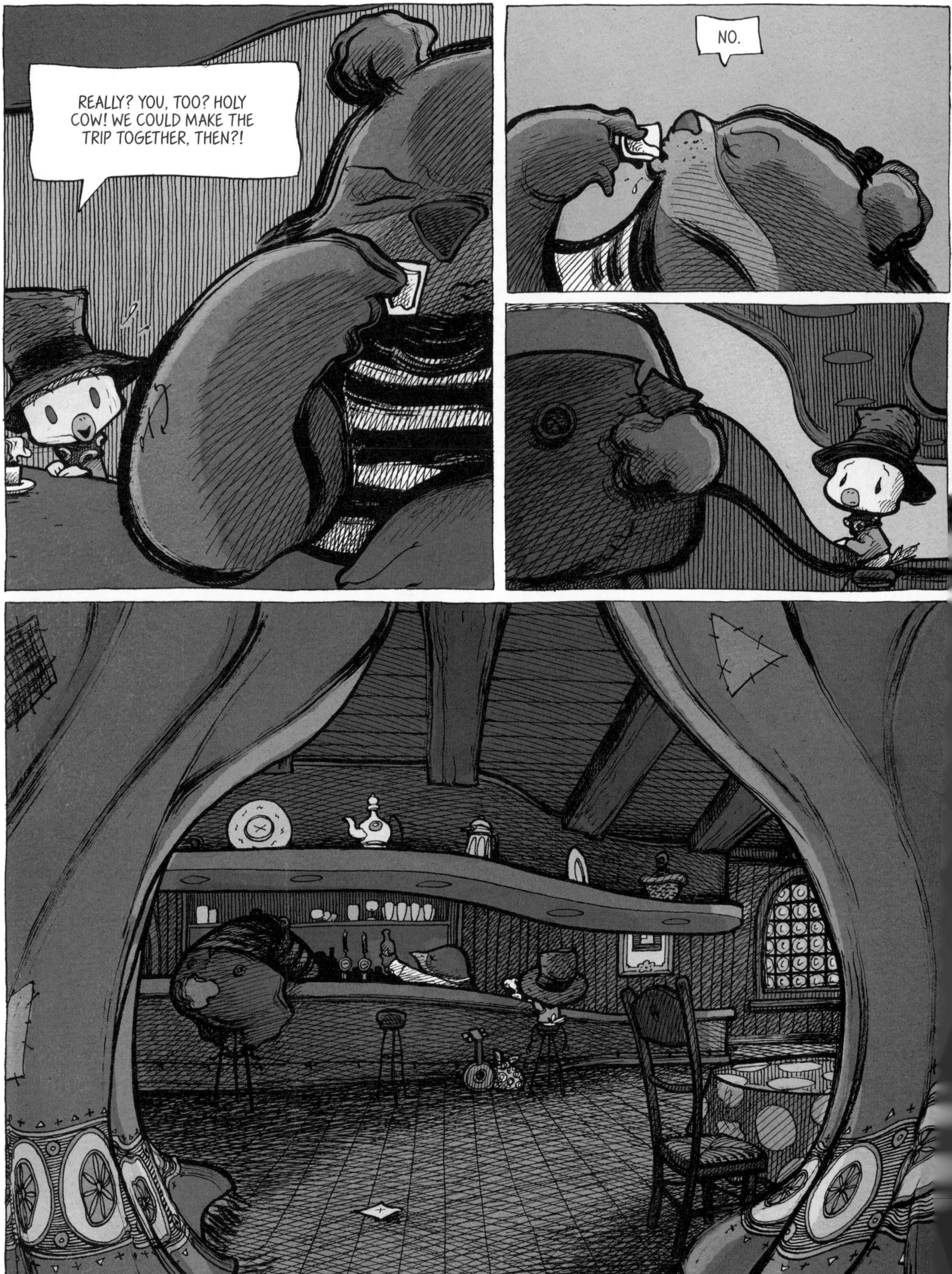
REALLY? YOU, TOO? HOLY COW! WE COULD MAKE THE TRIP TOGETHER, THEN?!
NO.

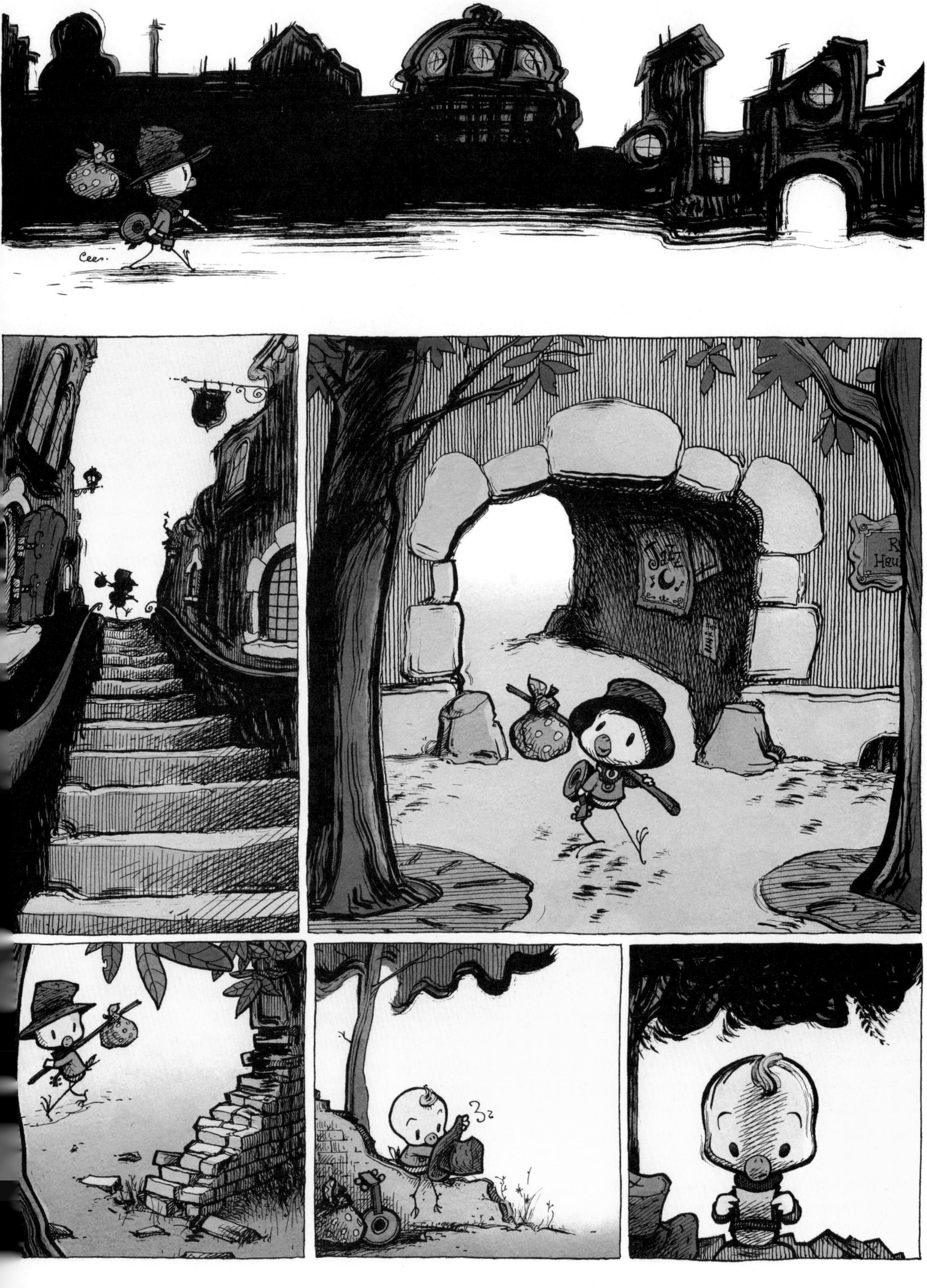
Cees.

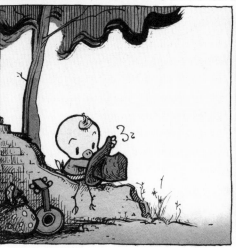

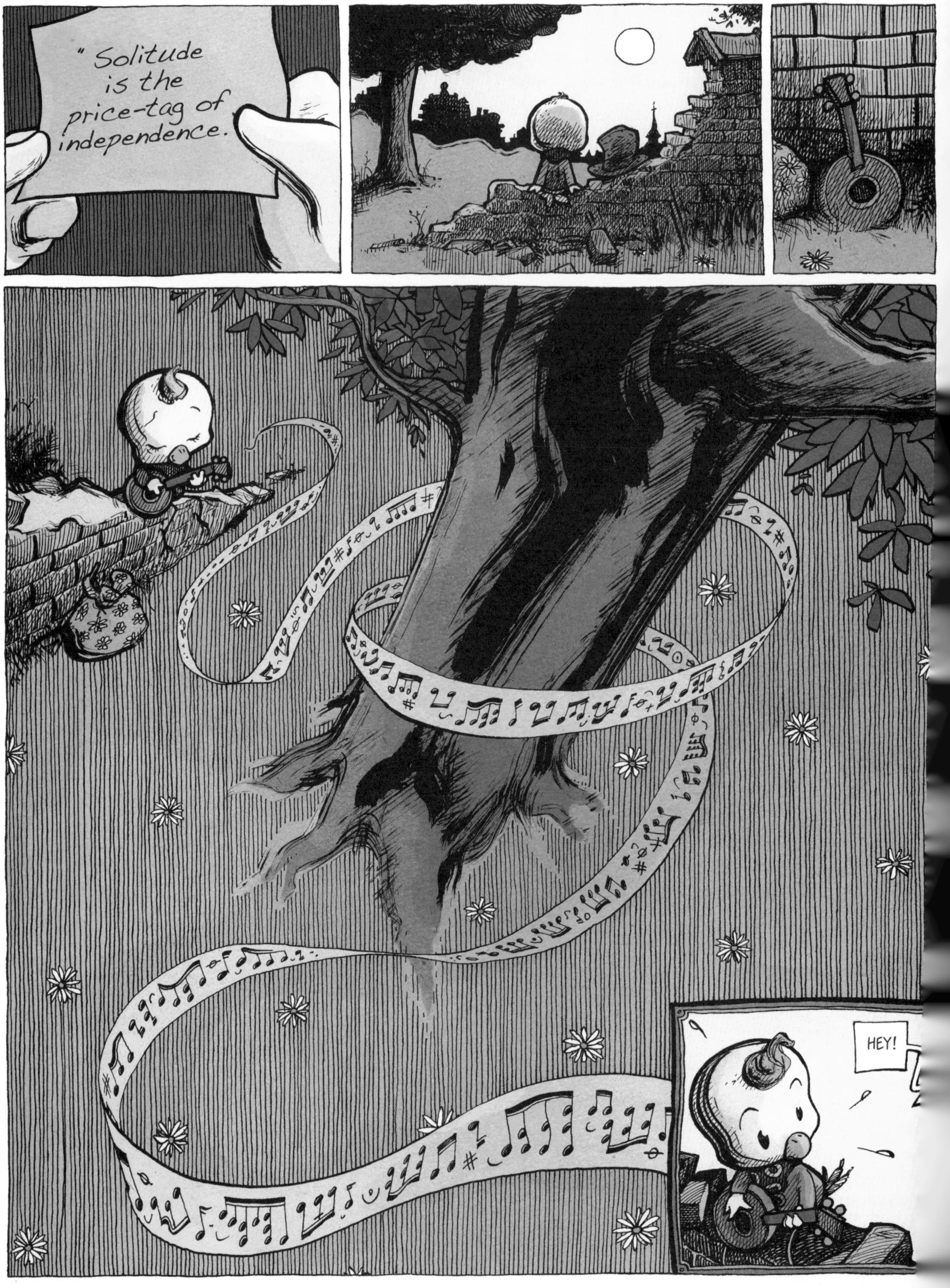
" Solitude is the price-tag of independence.
HEY!

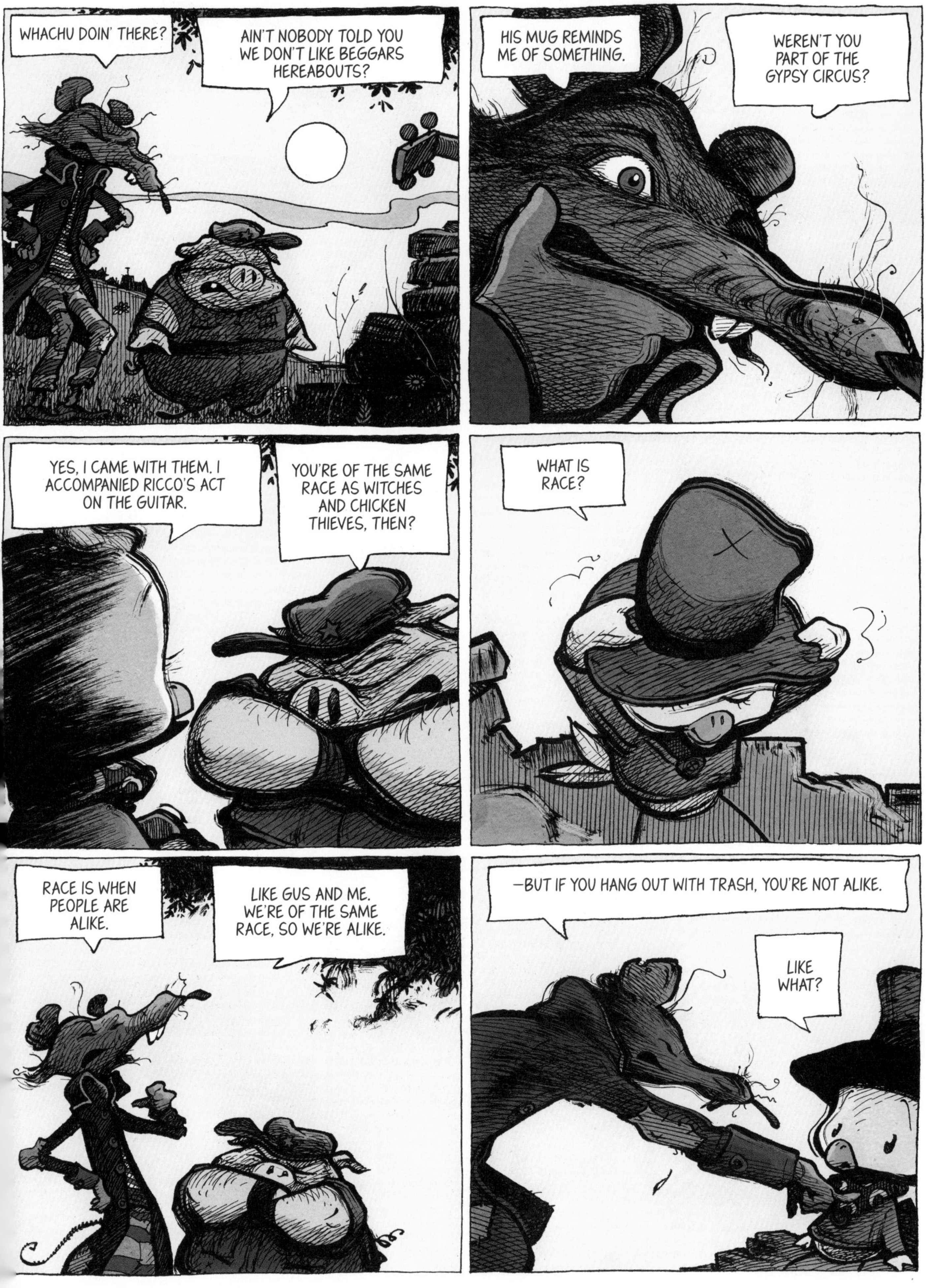
WHACHU DOIN' THERE?
AIN'T NOBODY TOLD YOU WE DON'T LIKE BEGGARS HEREABOUTS?
HIS MUG REMINDS ME OF SOMETHING.
WEREN'T YOU PART OF THE GYPSY CIRCUS?
YES, I CAME WITH THEM. I ACCOMPANIED RICCO'S ACT ON THE GUITAR.
YOU'RE OF THE SAME RACE AS WITCHES AND CHICKEN THIEVES, THEN?
WHAT IS RACE?
RACE IS WHEN PEOPLE ARE ALIKE.
LIKE GUS AND ME. WE'RE OF THE SAME RACE, SO WE'RE ALIKE.
—BUT IF YOU HANG OUT WITH TRASH, YOU'RE NOT ALIKE.
LIKE WHAT?

LIKE US, THAT'S WHAT!

HE'S LIKE ME AND I'M LIKE HIM!

OH? YOU LOOK A LOT TALLER.

AND SKINNIER.

YOU LOOK LIKE RICCO. HE MUST BE MORE OF YOUR RACE THAN YOUR FRIEND IS.

HUH?! ARE YOU TRYING TO CONFUSE ME?! RACE ISN'T ABOUT HEIGHT OR SIZE.

AH, SO RACE IS WHEN YOU'RE ALIKE EVEN IF YOU'RE TALLER?

OR FATTER.

WITH DIFFERENT EYES.

AND A DIFFERENT NOSE.

RACE IS WHEN YOU'RE ALIKE, BUT COMPLETELY DIFFERENT, IS THAT IT?

GUS, EXPLAIN WHAT RACE IS TO HIM.
IT'S EASY: RACE IS THE DIFFERENCE BETWEEN US AND THEM.
THERE ARE TWO KINDS OF PEOPLE IN THE WORLD. THERE ARE THOSE WHO ARE LIKE US, WHO TALK LIKE US, WHO EAT LIKE US, WHO WALK LIKE US.
THOSE PEOPLE ARE OUR RACE. THE SUPERIOR RACE.
THEN THERE ARE THE OTHERS: FOREIGNERS, BEGGARS, MUSICIANS.
VERMIN.
THE FILTHY RACE.
LEAVE HIM THE HELL ALONE!

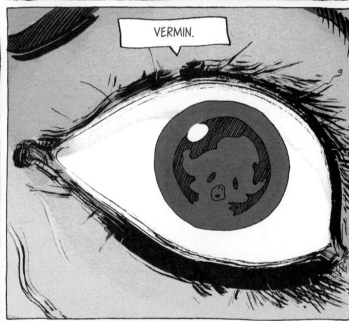

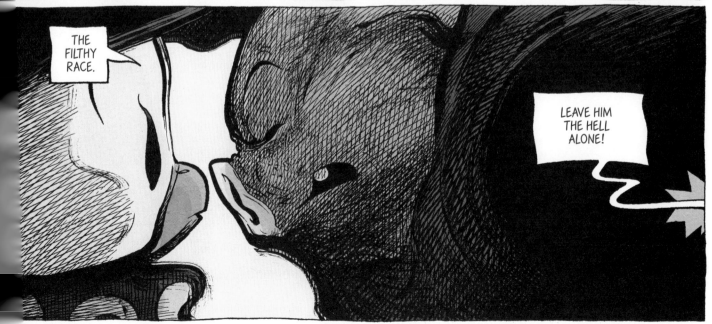

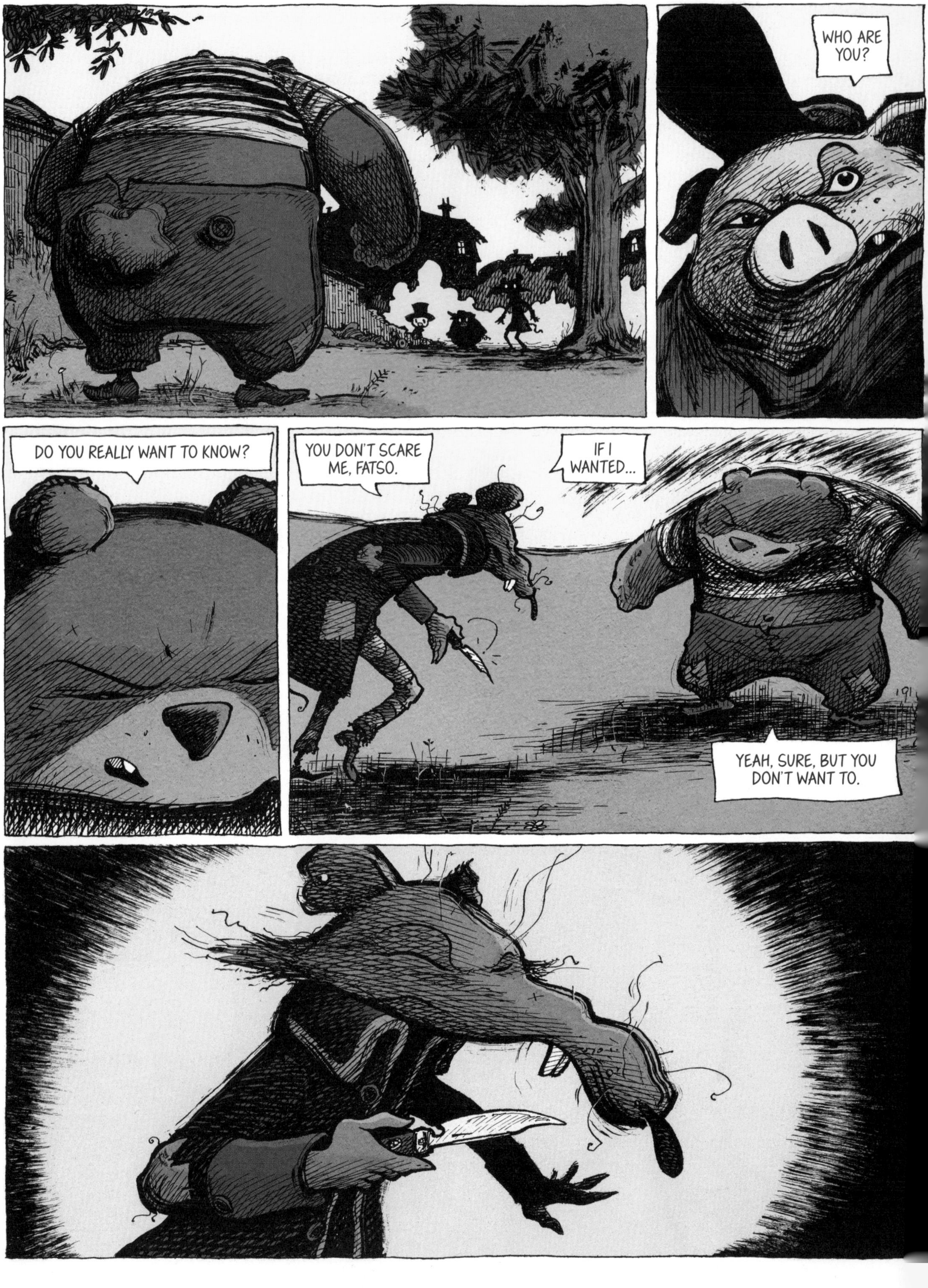
WHO ARE YOU?
DO YOU REALLY WANT TO KNOW?
YOU DON'T SCARE ME, FATSO.
IF I WANTED...
YEAH, SURE, BUT YOU DON'T WANT TO.

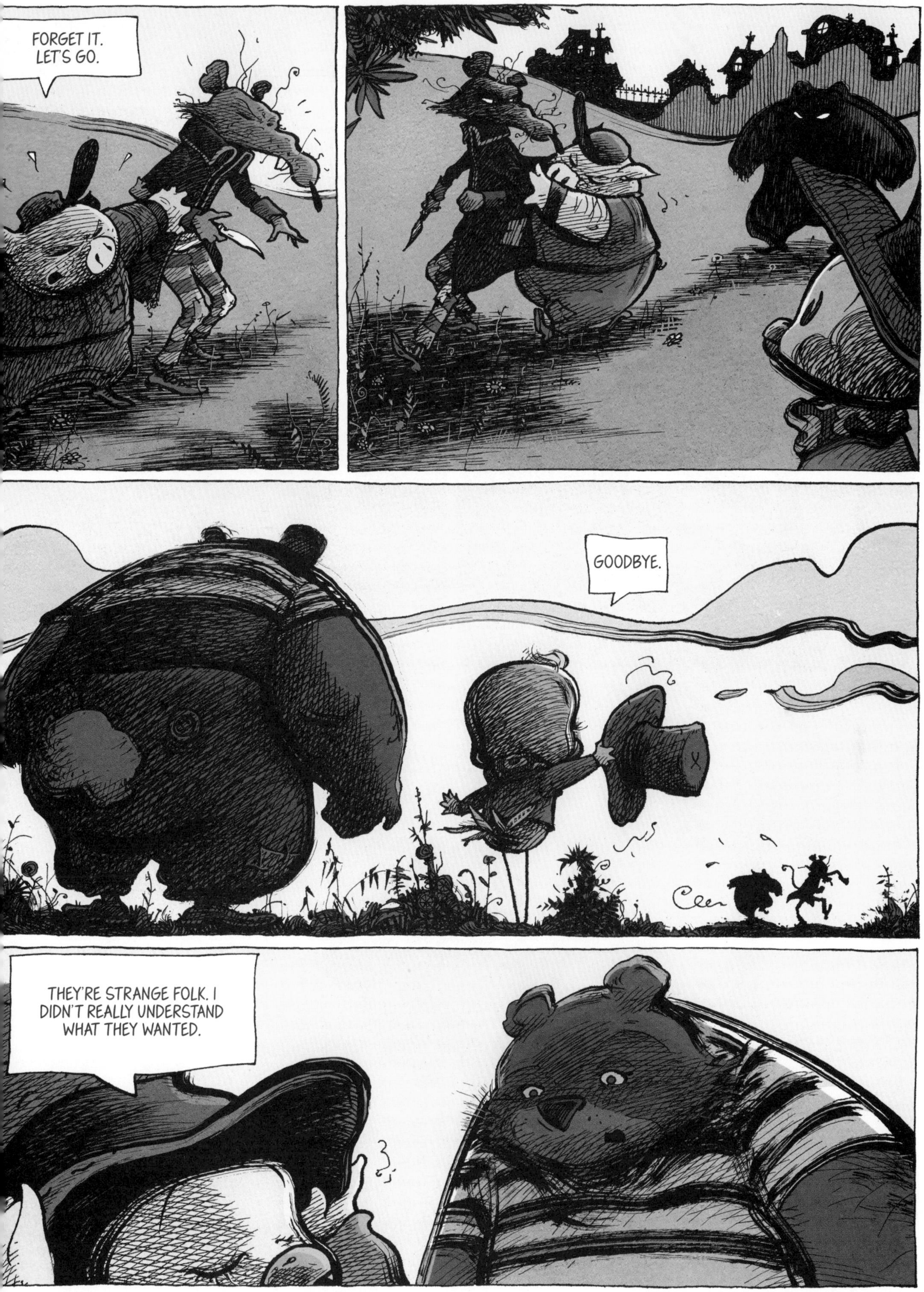
FORGET IT. LET'S GO.
GOODBYE.
THEY'RE STRANGE FOLK. I DIDN'T REALLY UNDERSTAND WHAT THEY WANTED.

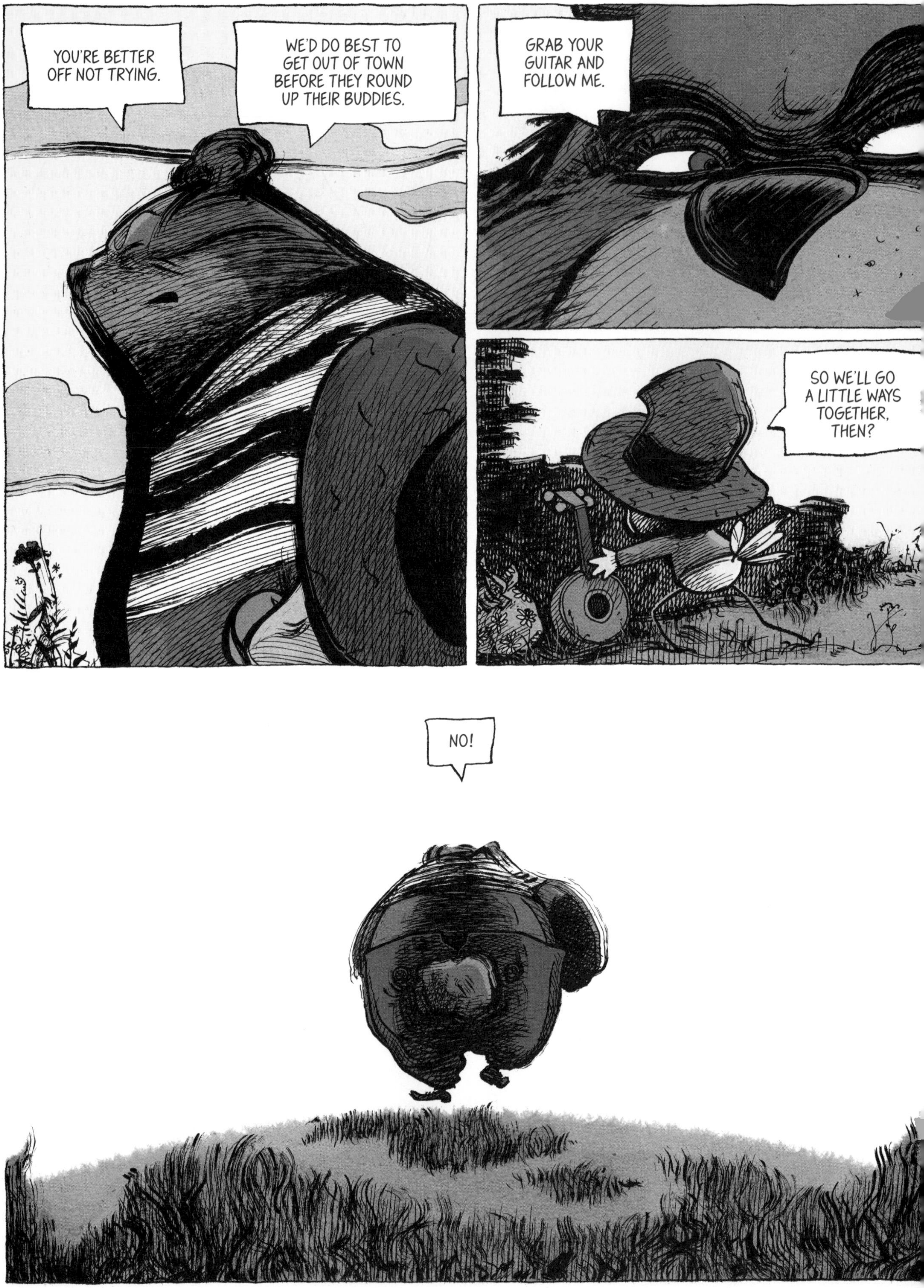
YOU'RE BETTER OFF NOT TRYING.
WE'D DO BEST TO GET OUT OF TOWN BEFORE THEY ROUND UP THEIR BUDDIES.
GRAB YOUR GUITAR AND FOLLOW ME.
SO WE'LL GO A LITTLE WAYS TOGETHER, THEN?
NO!

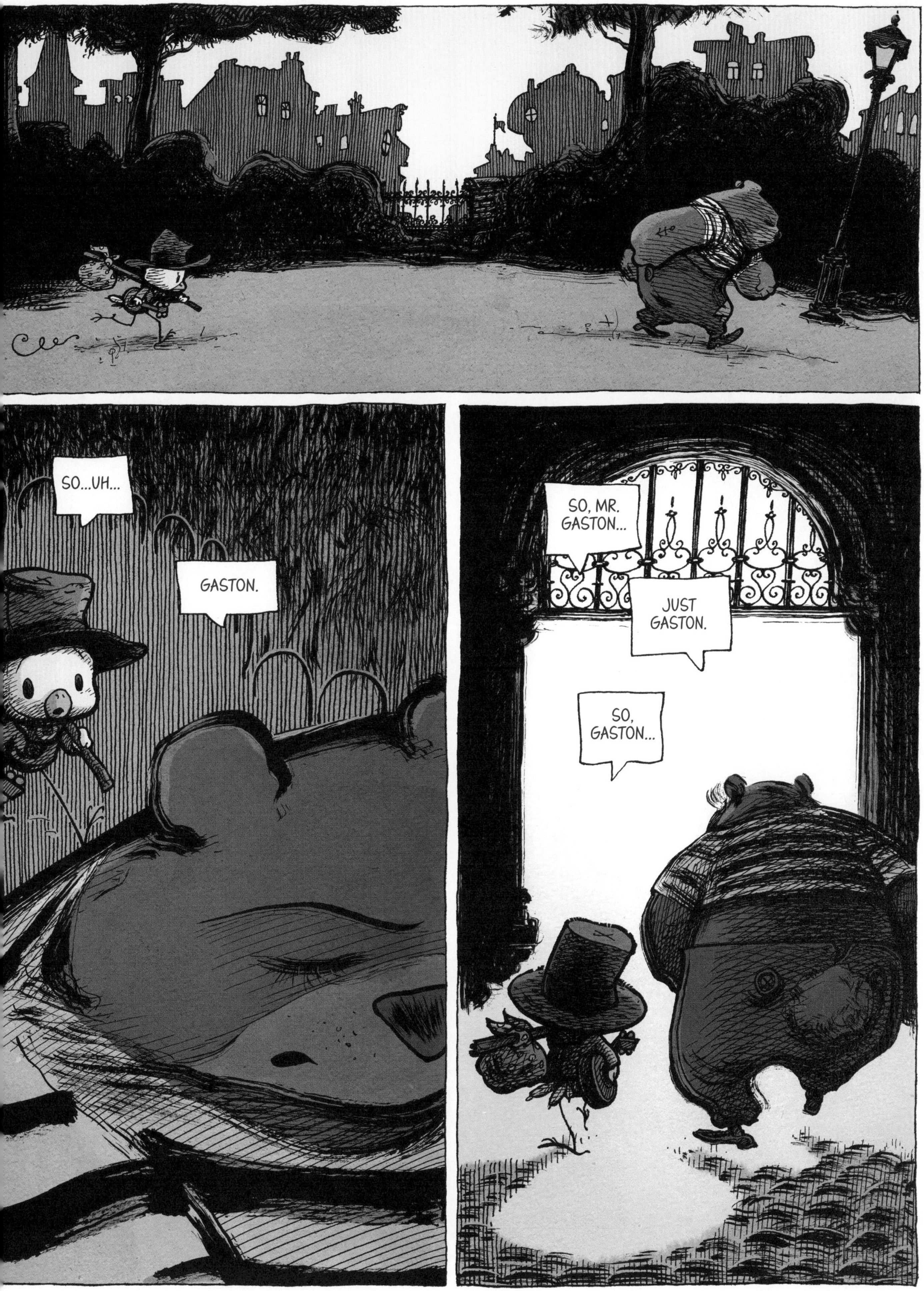
SO...UH...
GASTON.
SO, MR. GASTON...
JUST GASTON.
SO, GASTON...

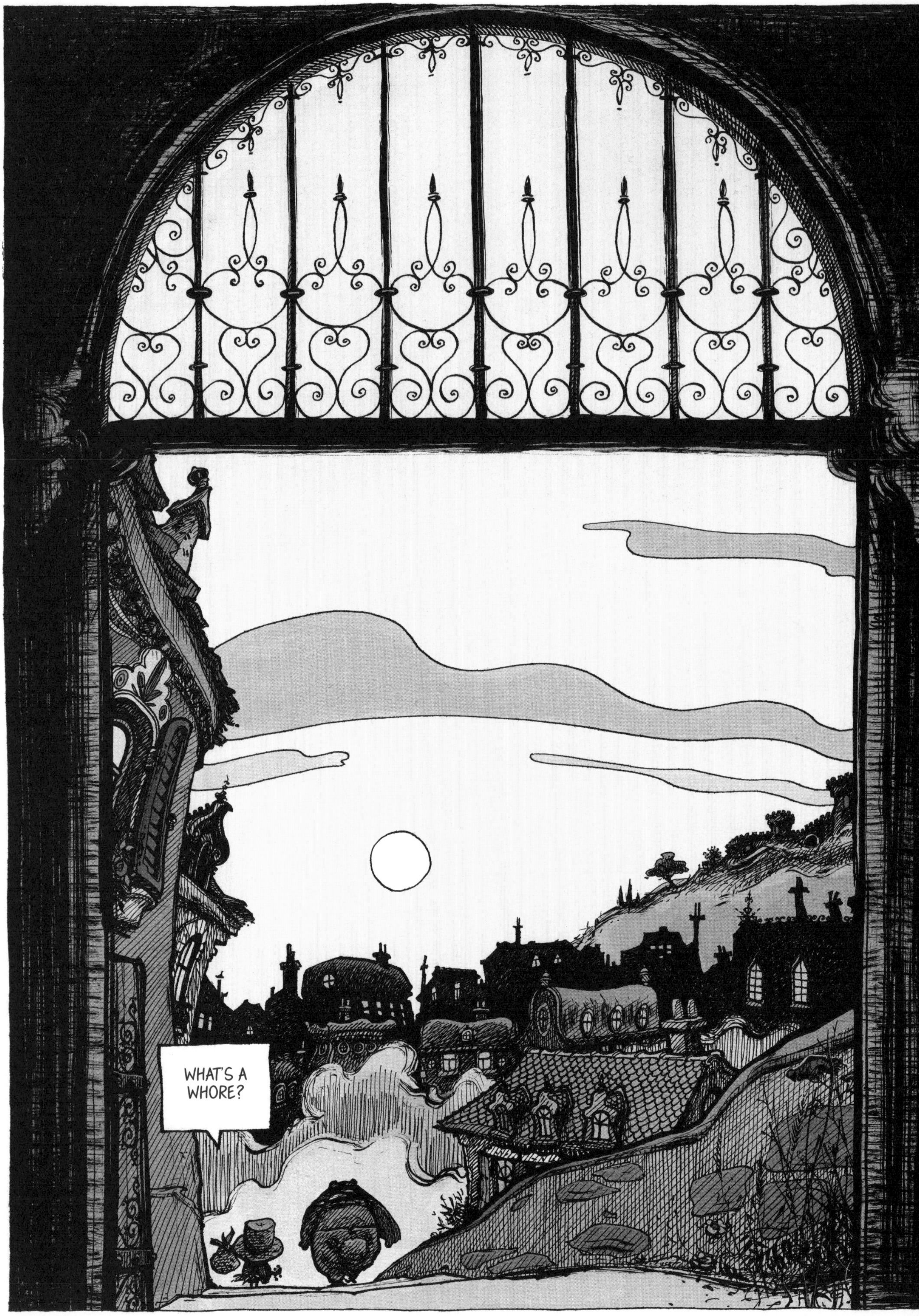
WHAT'S A WHORE?

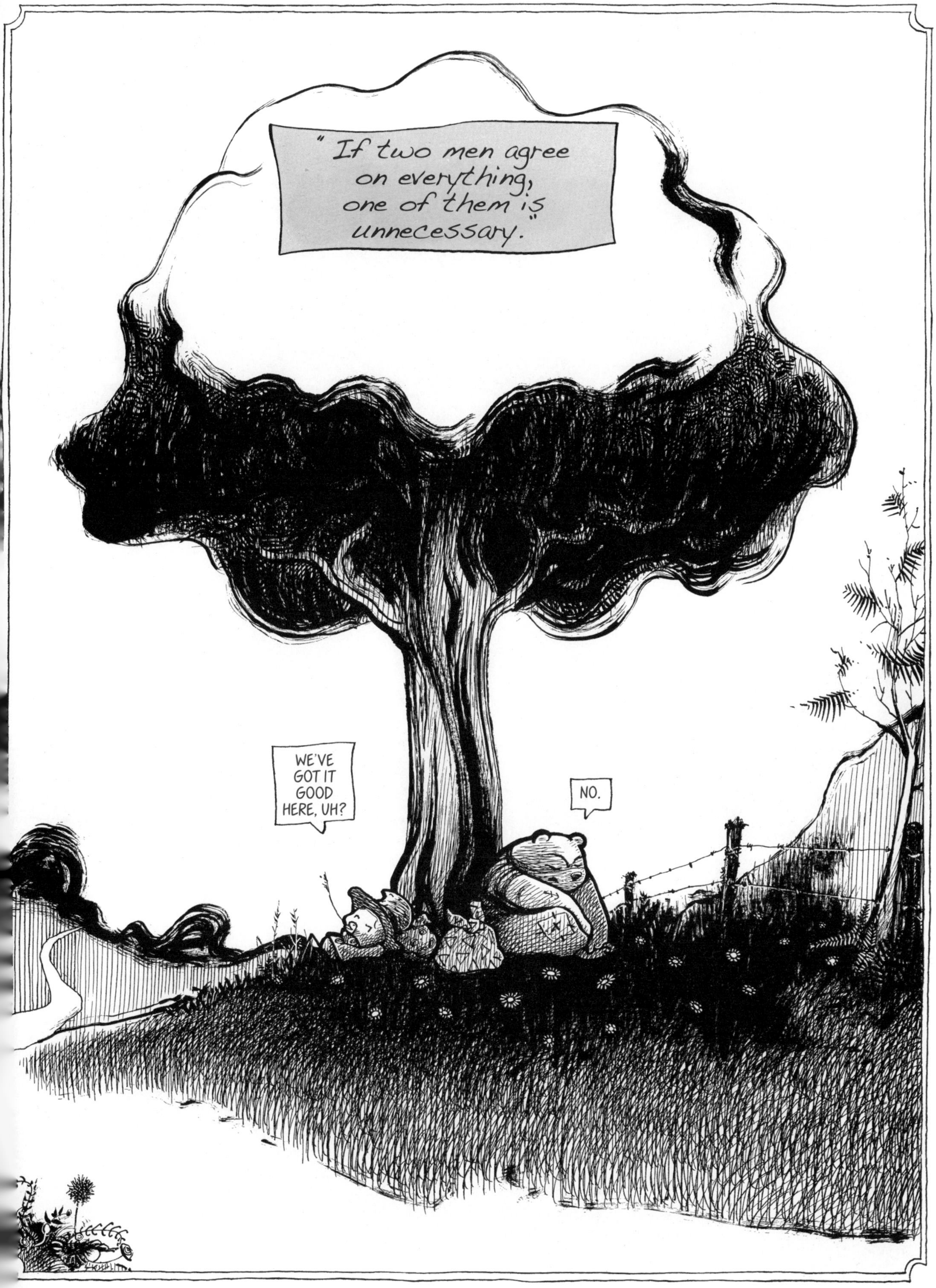
"If two men agree on everything, one of them is unnecessary."
WE'VE GOT IT GOOD HERE, UH?
NO.

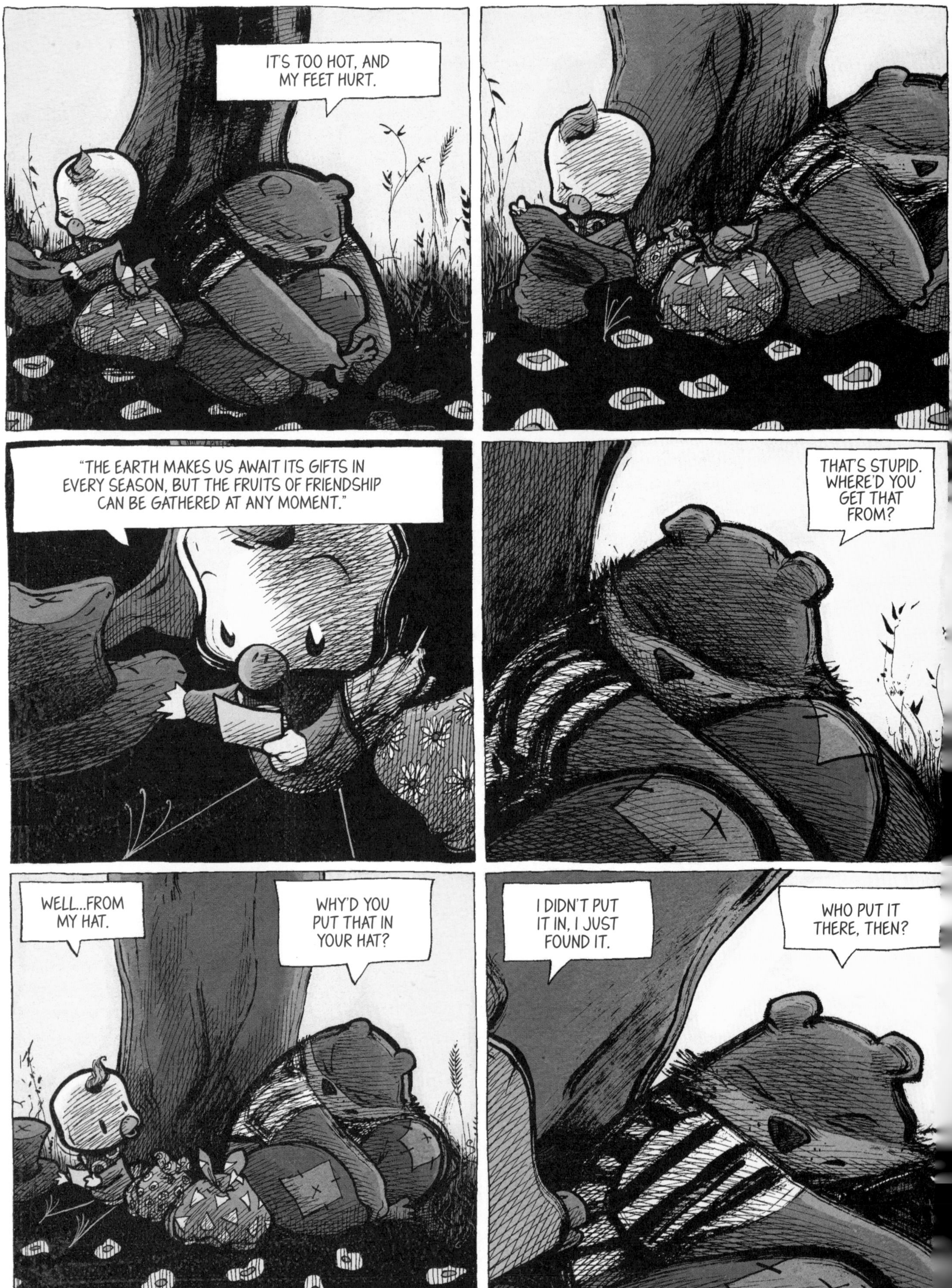
IT'S TOO HOT, AND MY FEET HURT.
"THE EARTH MAKES US AWAIT ITS GIFTS IN EVERY SEASON, BUT THE FRUITS OF FRIENDSHIP CAN BE GATHERED AT ANY MOMENT."
THAT'S STUPID. WHERE'D YOU GET THAT FROM?
WELL...FROM MY HAT.
WHY'D YOU PUT THAT IN YOUR HAT?
I DIDN'T PUT IT IN, I JUST FOUND IT.
WHO PUT IT THERE, THEN?

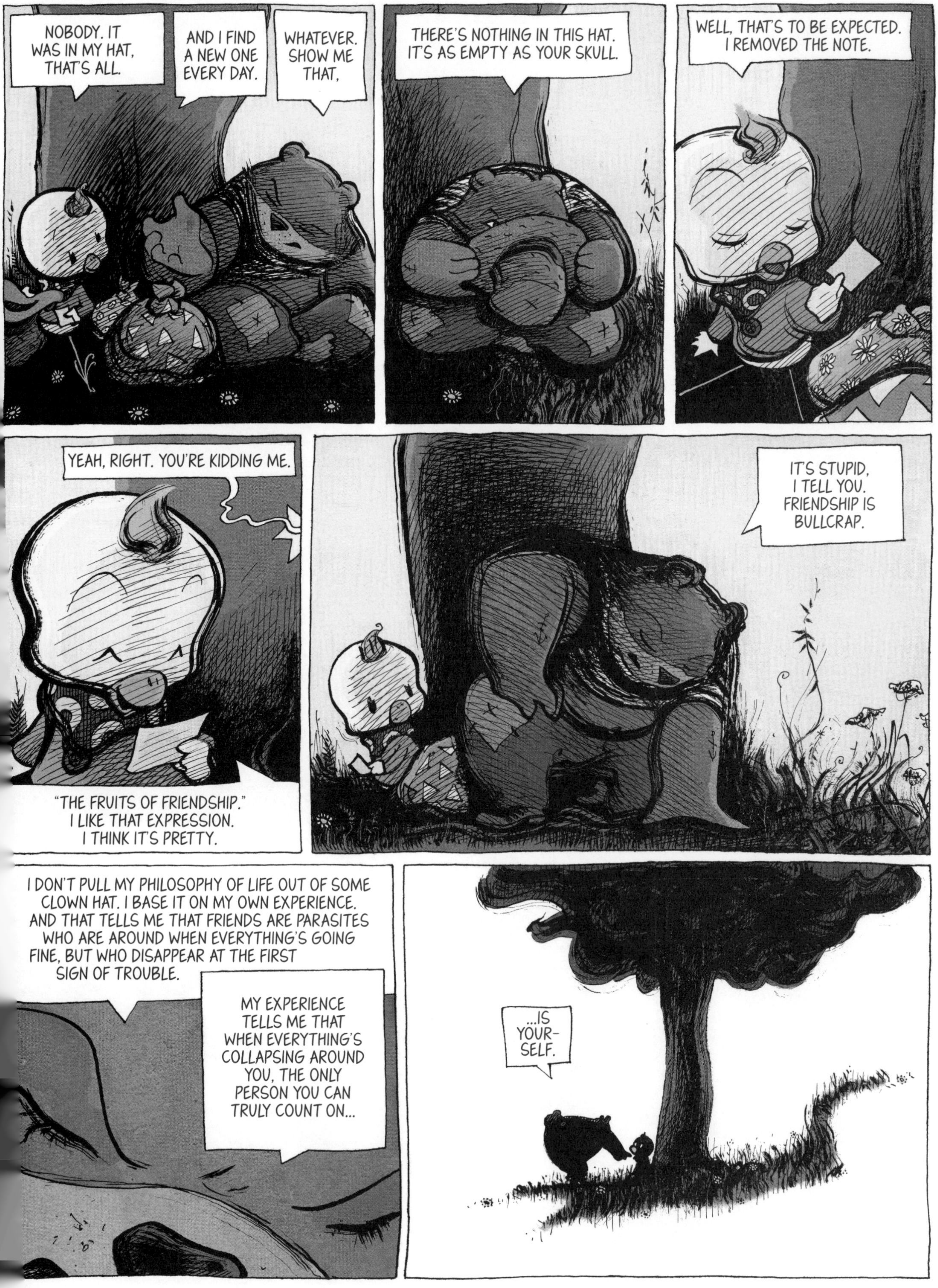
NOBODY. IT WAS IN MY HAT, THAT'S ALL.
AND I FIND A NEW ONE EVERY DAY.
WHATEVER. SHOW ME THAT,
THERE'S NOTHING IN THIS HAT. IT'S AS EMPTY AS YOUR SKULL.
WELL, THAT'S TO BE EXPECTED. I REMOVED THE NOTE.
YEAH, RIGHT. YOU'RE KIDDING ME.
"THE FRUITS OF FRIENDSHIP." I LIKE THAT EXPRESSION. I THINK IT'S PRETTY.
IT'S STUPID, I TELL YOU. FRIENDSHIP IS BULLCRAP.
I DON'T PULL MY PHILOSOPHY OF LIFE OUT OF SOME CLOWN HAT. I BASE IT ON MY OWN EXPERIENCE. AND THAT TELLS ME THAT FRIENDS ARE PARASITES WHO ARE AROUND WHEN EVERYTHING'S GOING FINE, BUT WHO DISAPPEAR AT THE FIRST SIGN OF TROUBLE.
MY EXPERIENCE TELLS ME THAT WHEN EVERYTHING'S COLLAPSING AROUND YOU, THE ONLY PERSON YOU CAN TRULY COUNT ON...
...IS YOUR-SELF.
3

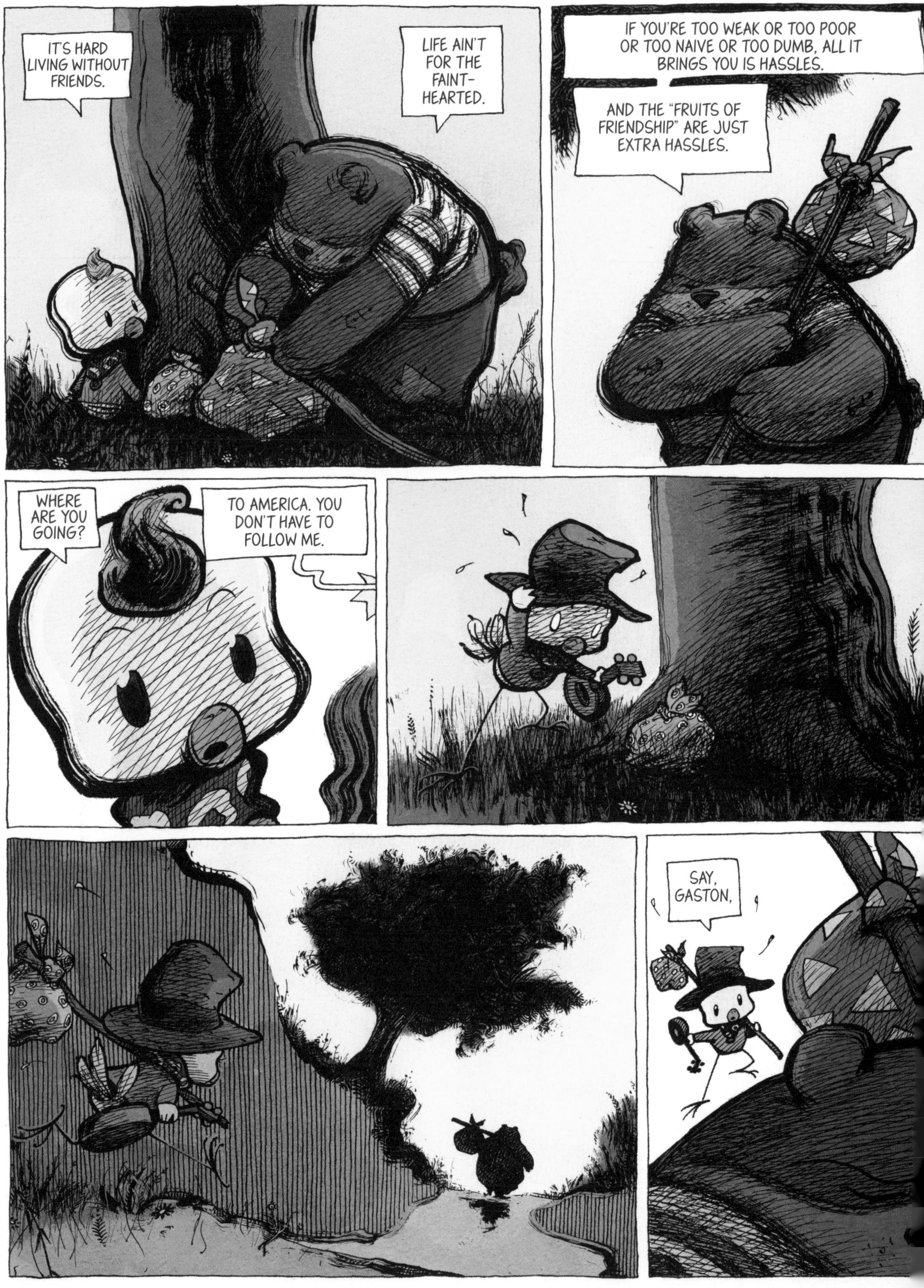

IT'S HARD LIVING WITHOUT FRIENDS.
LIFE AIN'T FOR THE FAINT-HEARTED.
IF YOU'RE TOO WEAK OR TOO POOR OR TOO NAIVE OR TOO DUMB, ALL IT BRINGS YOU IS HASSLES.
AND THE "FRUITS OF FRIENDSHIP" ARE JUST EXTRA HASSLES.
WHERE ARE YOU GOING?
TO AMERICA. YOU DON'T HAVE TO FOLLOW ME.
SAY, GASTON,

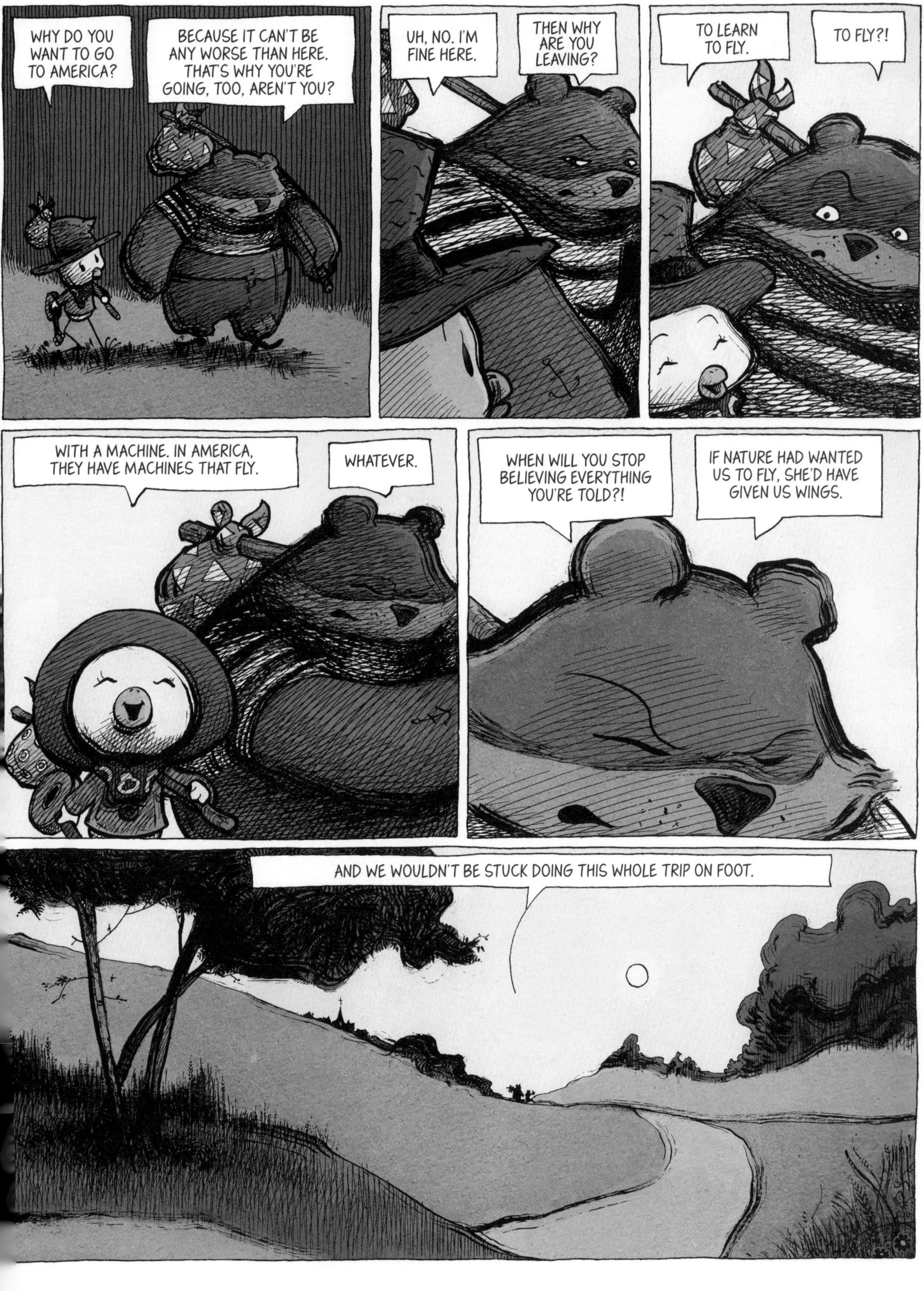
WHY DO YOU WANT TO GO TO AMERICA?
BECAUSE IT CAN'T BE ANY WORSE THAN HERE. THAT'S WHY YOU'RE GOING, TOO, AREN'T YOU?
UH, NO. I'M FINE HERE.
THEN WHY ARE YOU LEAVING?
TO LEARN TO FLY.
TO FLY?!
WITH A MACHINE. IN AMERICA, THEY HAVE MACHINES THAT FLY.
WHATEVER.
WHEN WILL YOU STOP BELIEVING EVERYTHING YOU'RE TOLD?!
IF NATURE HAD WANTED US TO FLY, SHE'D HAVE GIVEN US WINGS.
AND WE WOULDN'T BE STUCK DOING THIS WHOLE TRIP ON FOOT.
5

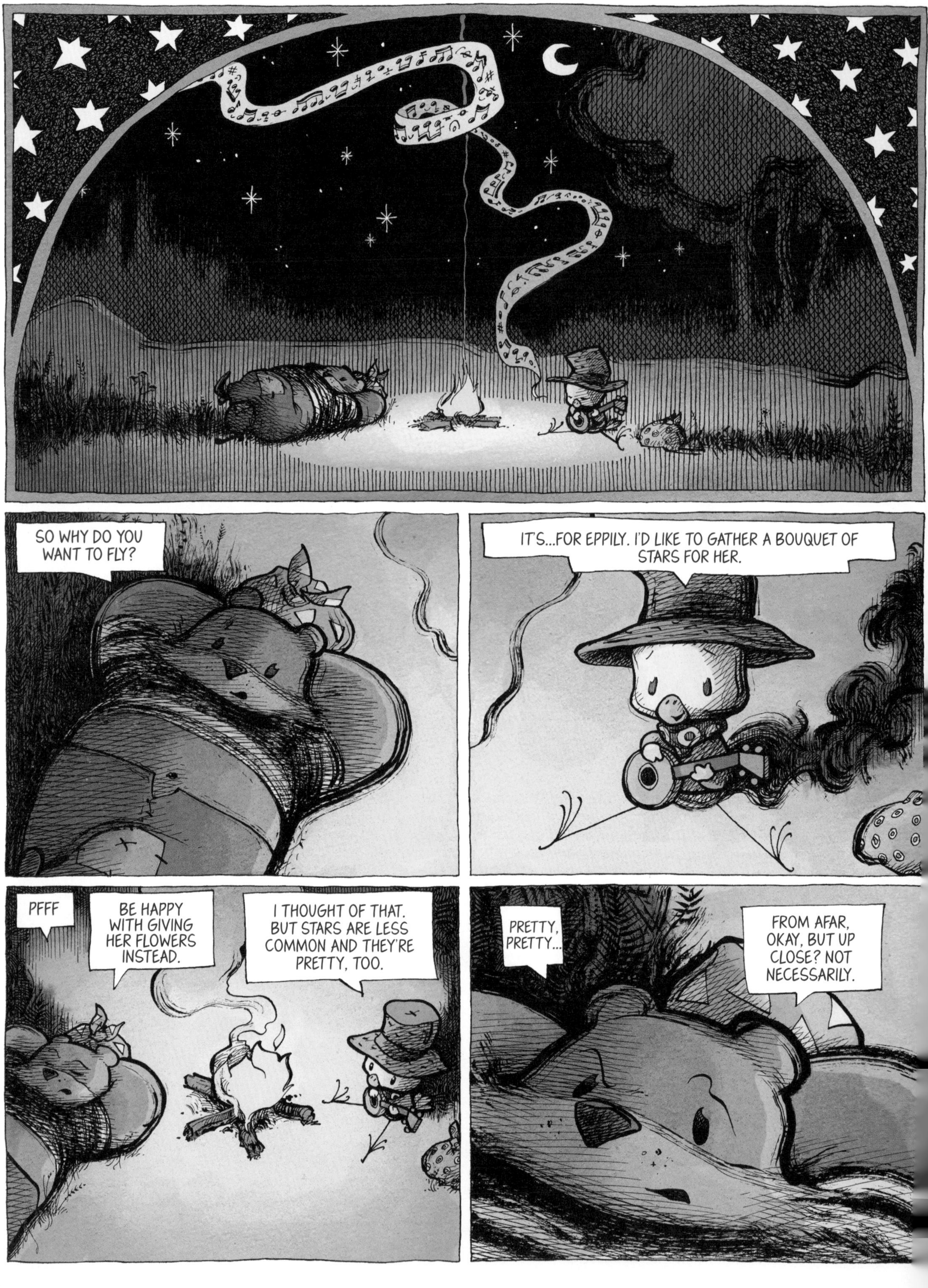
SO WHY DO YOU WANT TO FLY?
IT'S...FOR EPPILY. I'D LIKE TO GATHER A BOUQUET OF STARS FOR HER.
PFFF
BE HAPPY WITH GIVING HER FLOWERS INSTEAD.
I THOUGHT OF THAT. BUT STARS ARE LESS COMMON AND THEY'RE PRETTY, TOO.
PRETTY, PRETTY...
FROM AFAR, OKAY, BUT UP CLOSE? NOT NECESSARILY.

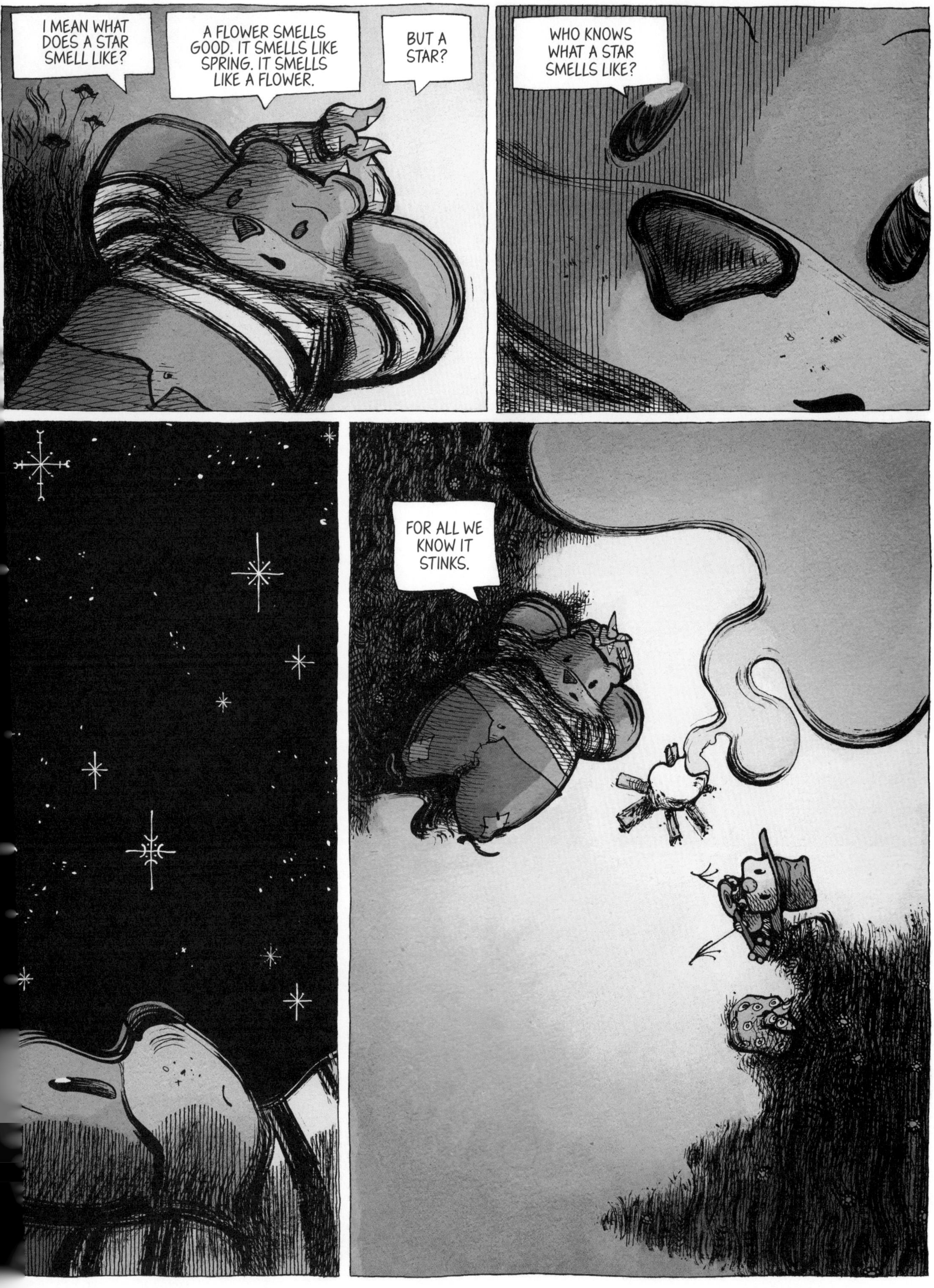
I MEAN WHAT DOES A STAR SMELL LIKE?
A FLOWER SMELLS GOOD. IT SMELLS LIKE SPRING. IT SMELLS LIKE A FLOWER.
BUT A STAR?
WHO KNOWS WHAT A STAR SMELLS LIKE?
FOR ALL WE KNOW IT STINKS.

"Write your troubles in the sand, Carve your blessings in stone."

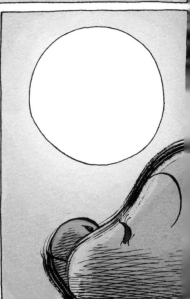

I LIKE THE SUN.

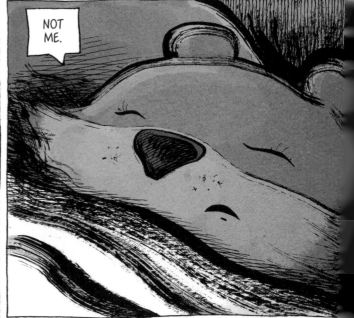

NOT ME.

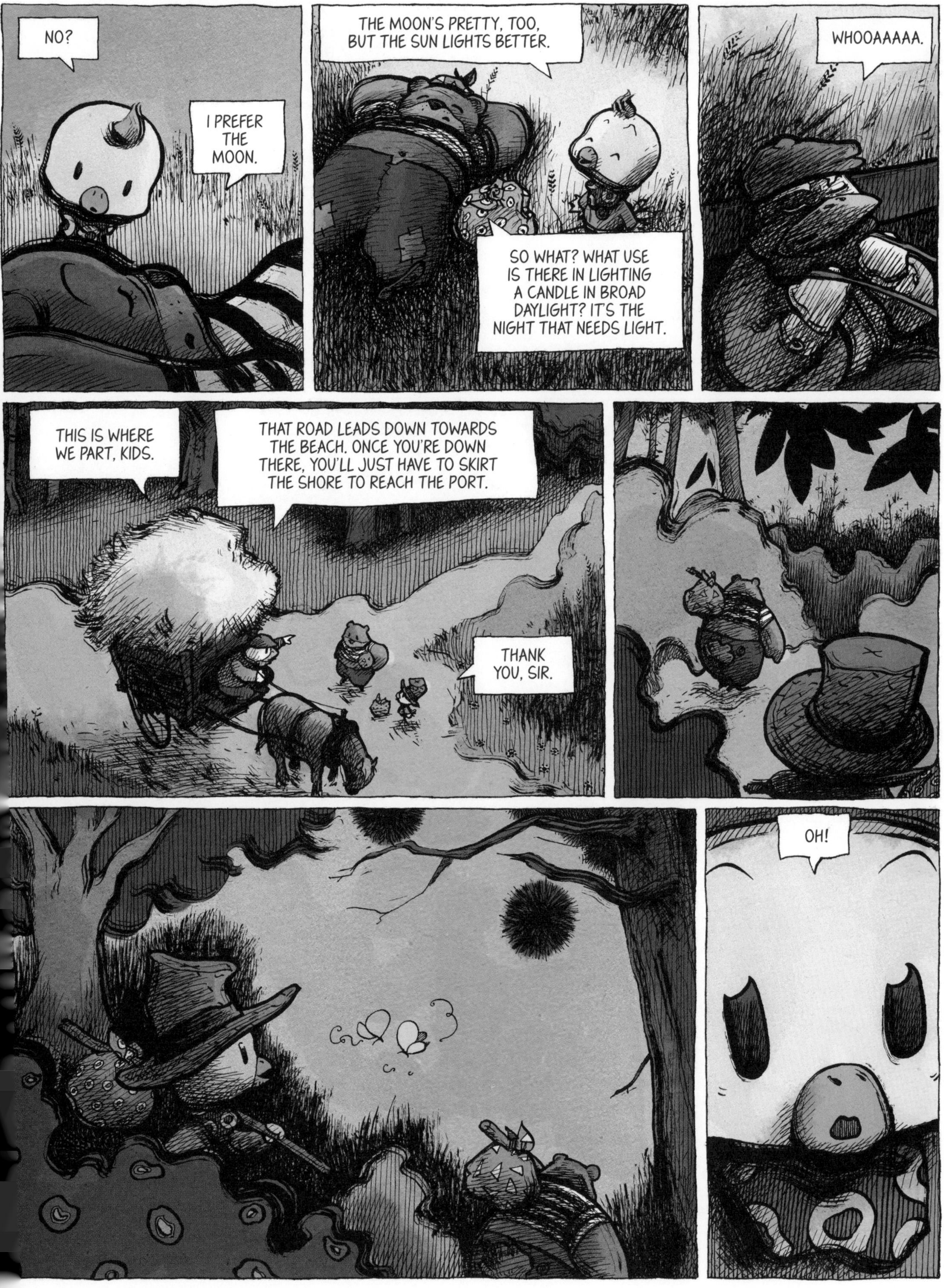
NO?
I PREFER THE MOON.
THE MOON'S PRETTY, TOO, BUT THE SUN LIGHTS BETTER.
SO WHAT? WHAT USE IS THERE IN LIGHTING A CANDLE IN BROAD DAYLIGHT? IT'S THE NIGHT THAT NEEDS LIGHT.
WHOOAAAAA.
THIS IS WHERE WE PART, KIDS.
THAT ROAD LEADS DOWN TOWARDS THE BEACH. ONCE YOU'RE DOWN THERE, YOU'LL JUST HAVE TO SKIRT THE SHORE TO REACH THE PORT.
THANK YOU, SIR.
OH!

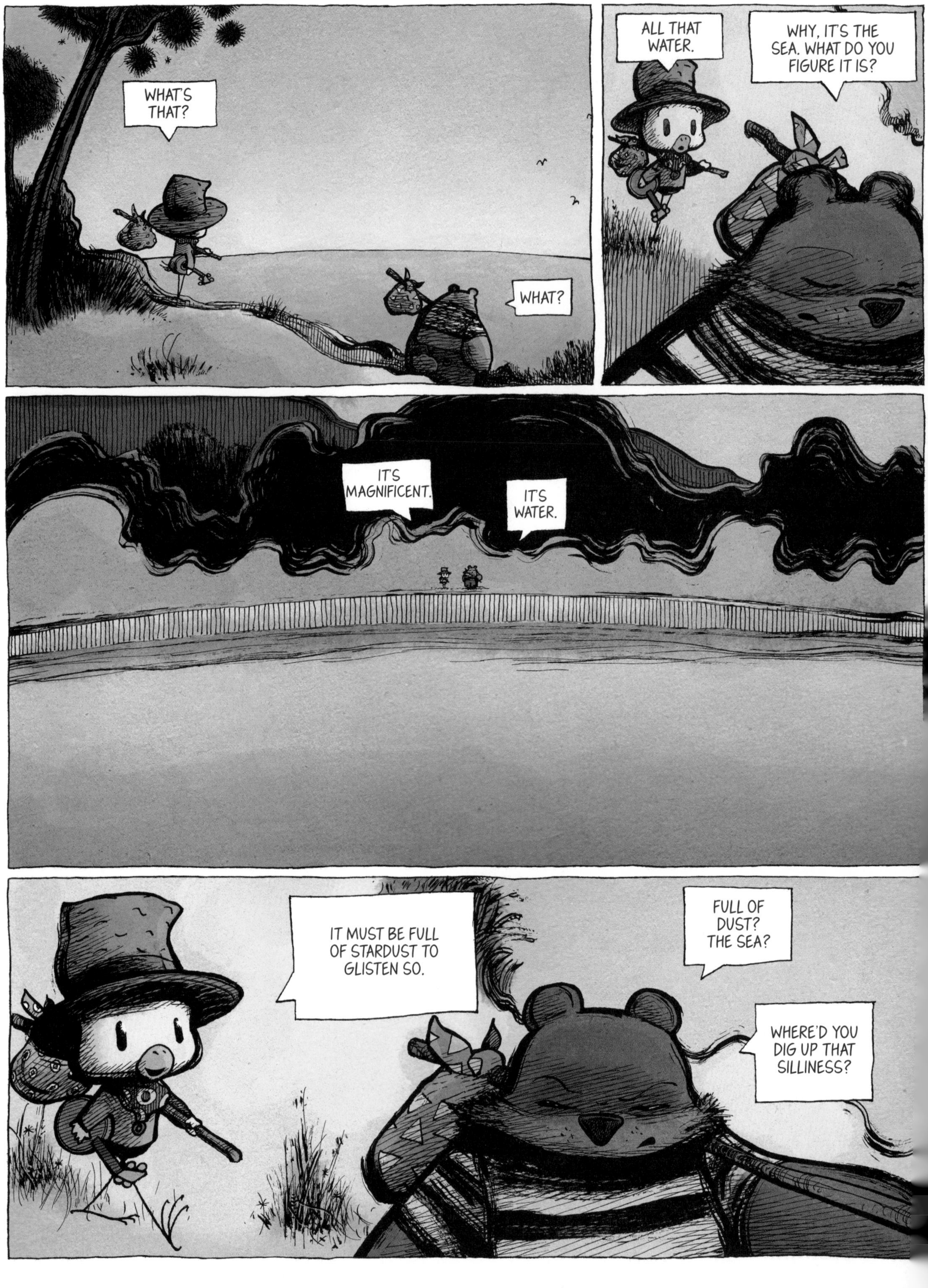
WHAT'S THAT?
WHAT?
ALL THAT WATER.
WHY, IT'S THE SEA. WHAT DO YOU FIGURE IT IS?
IT'S MAGNIFICENT.
IT'S WATER.
IT MUST BE FULL OF STARDUST TO GLISTEN SO.
FULL OF DUST? THE SEA?
WHERE'D YOU DIG UP THAT SILLINESS?

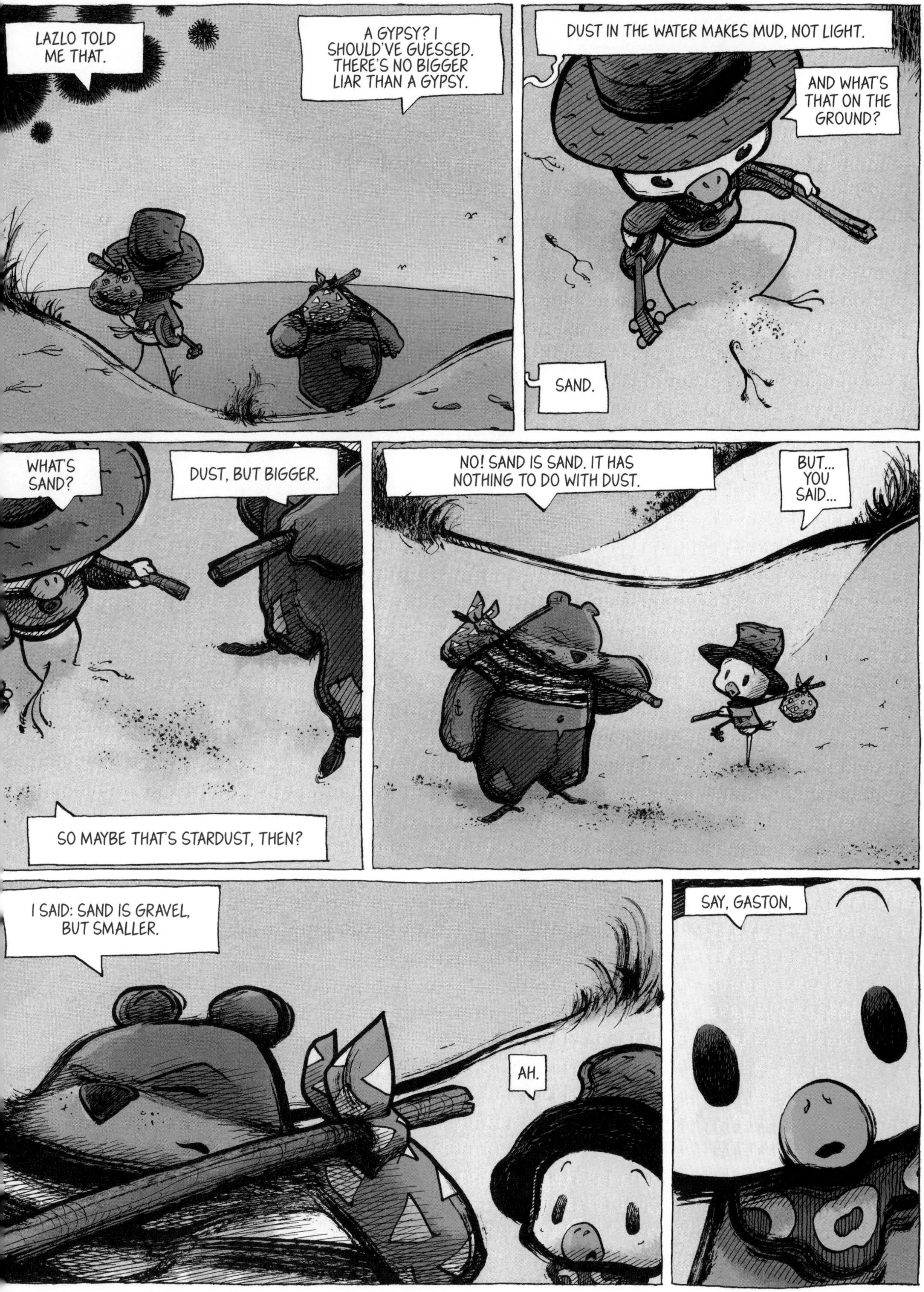

LAZLO TOLD ME THAT.
A GYPSY? I SHOULD'VE GUESSED. THERE'S NO BIGGER LIAR THAN A GYPSY.
DUST IN THE WATER MAKES MUD, NOT LIGHT.
AND WHAT'S THAT ON THE GROUND?
SAND.
WHAT'S SAND?
DUST, BUT BIGGER.
SO MAYBE THAT'S STARDUST, THEN?
NO! SAND IS SAND. IT HAS NOTHING TO DO WITH DUST.
BUT... YOU SAID...
I SAID: SAND IS GRAVEL, BUT SMALLER.
AH.
SAY, GASTON,

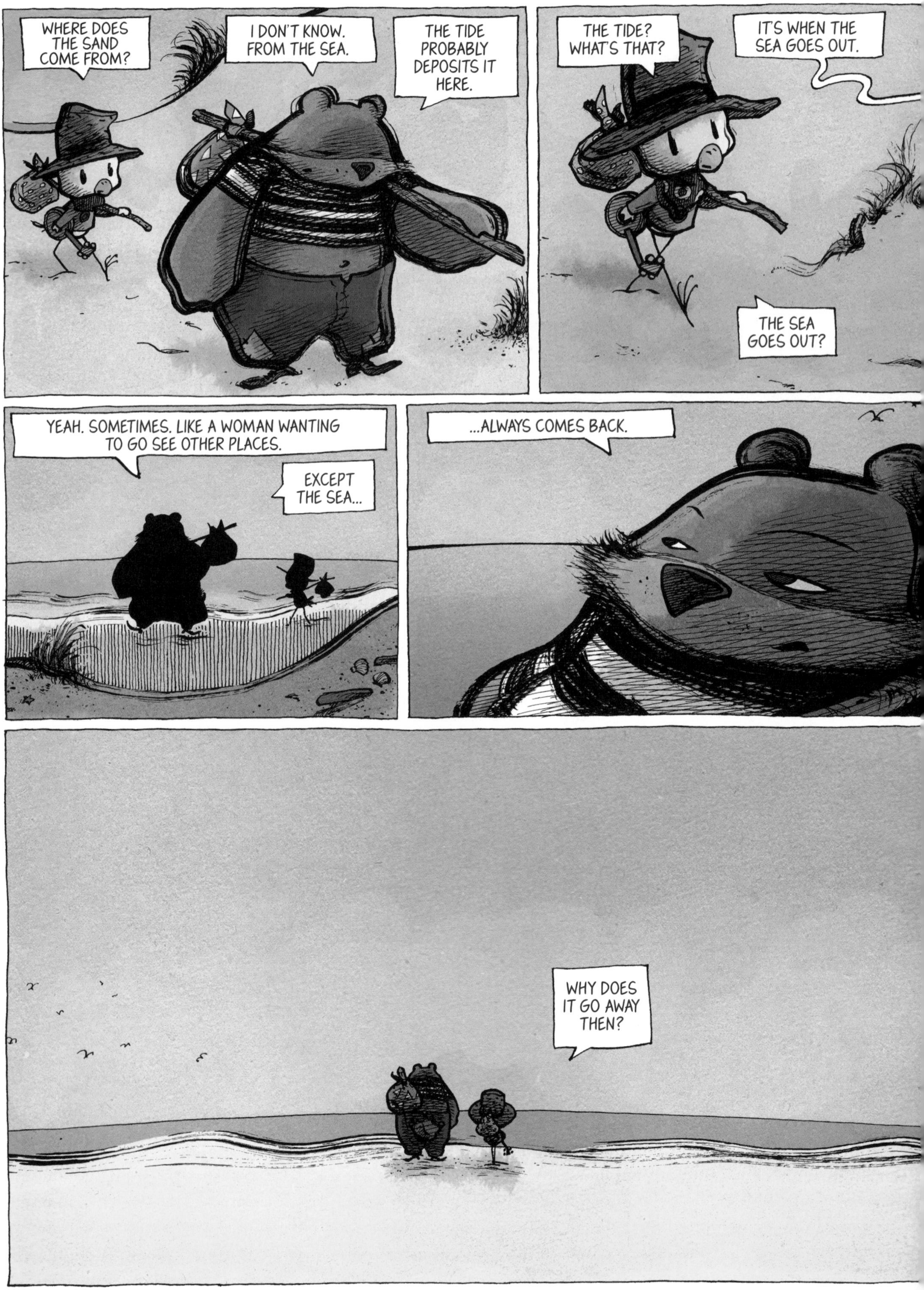
WHERE DOES THE SAND COME FROM?
I DON'T KNOW. FROM THE SEA.
THE TIDE PROBABLY DEPOSITS IT HERE.
THE TIDE? WHAT'S THAT?
IT'S WHEN THE SEA GOES OUT.
THE SEA GOES OUT?
YEAH. SOMETIMES. LIKE A WOMAN WANTING TO GO SEE OTHER PLACES.
EXCEPT THE SEA...
...ALWAYS COMES BACK.
WHY DOES IT GO AWAY THEN?

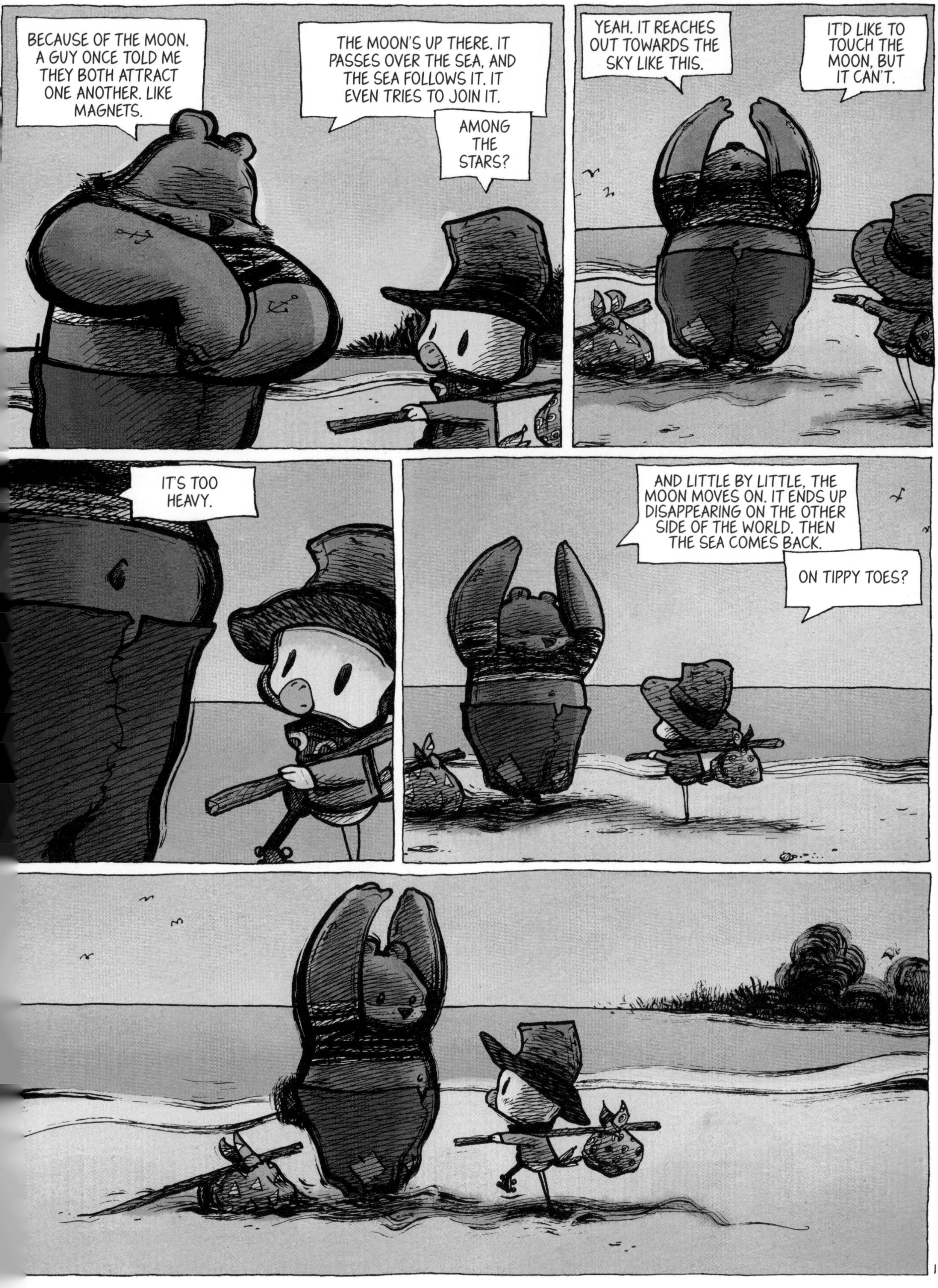
BECAUSE OF THE MOON. A GUY ONCE TOLD ME THEY BOTH ATTRACT ONE ANOTHER. LIKE MAGNETS.
THE MOON'S UP THERE. IT PASSES OVER THE SEA, AND THE SEA FOLLOWS IT. IT EVEN TRIES TO JOIN IT.
AMONG THE STARS?
YEAH. IT REACHES OUT TOWARDS THE SKY LIKE THIS.
IT'D LIKE TO TOUCH THE MOON, BUT IT CAN'T.
IT'S TOO HEAVY.
AND LITTLE BY LITTLE, THE MOON MOVES ON. IT ENDS UP DISAPPEARING ON THE OTHER SIDE OF THE WORLD. THEN THE SEA COMES BACK.
ON TIPPY TOES?
13

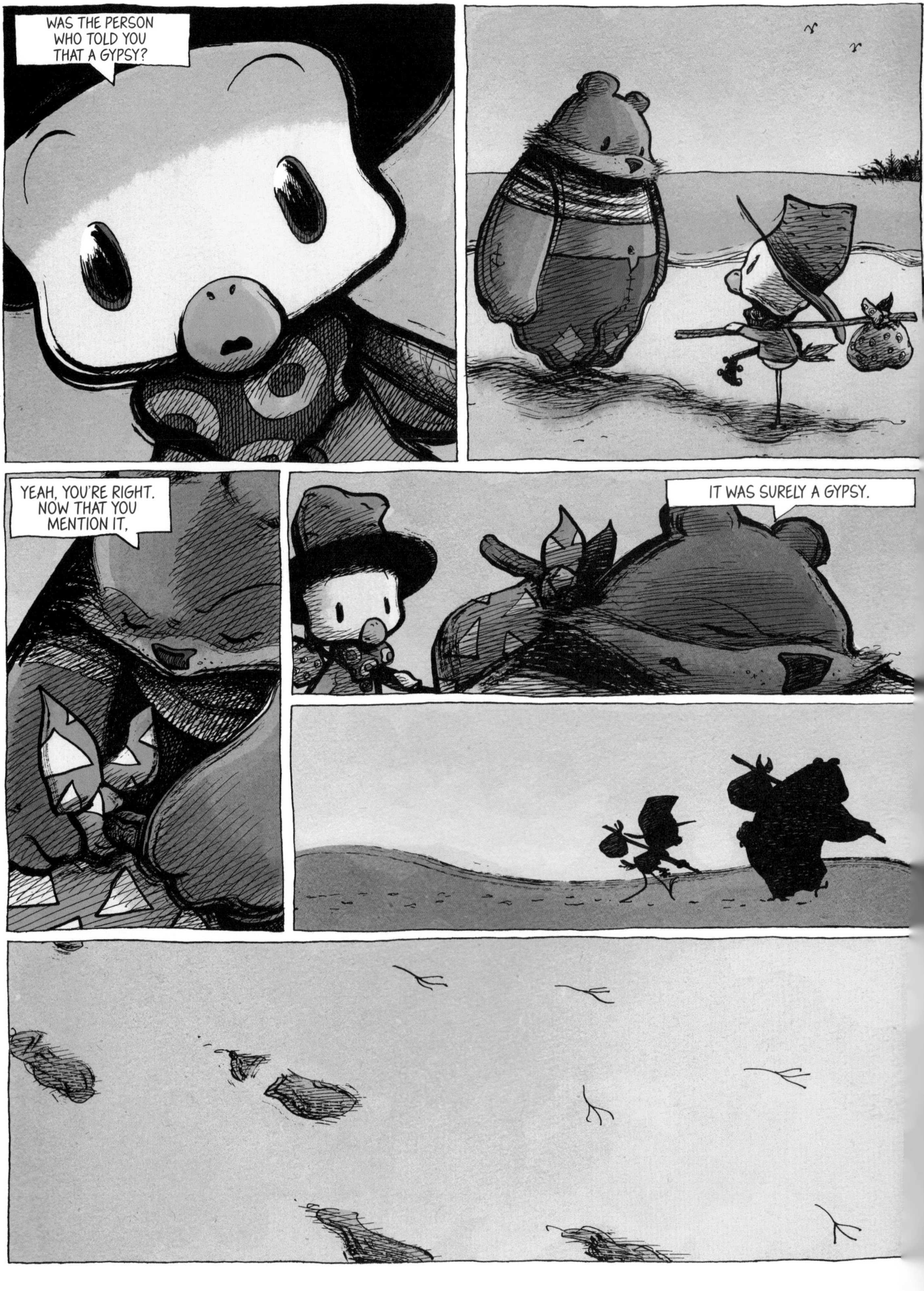
WAS THE PERSON WHO TOLD YOU THAT A GYPSY?
YEAH, YOU'RE RIGHT. NOW THAT YOU MENTION IT,
IT WAS SURELY A GYPSY.

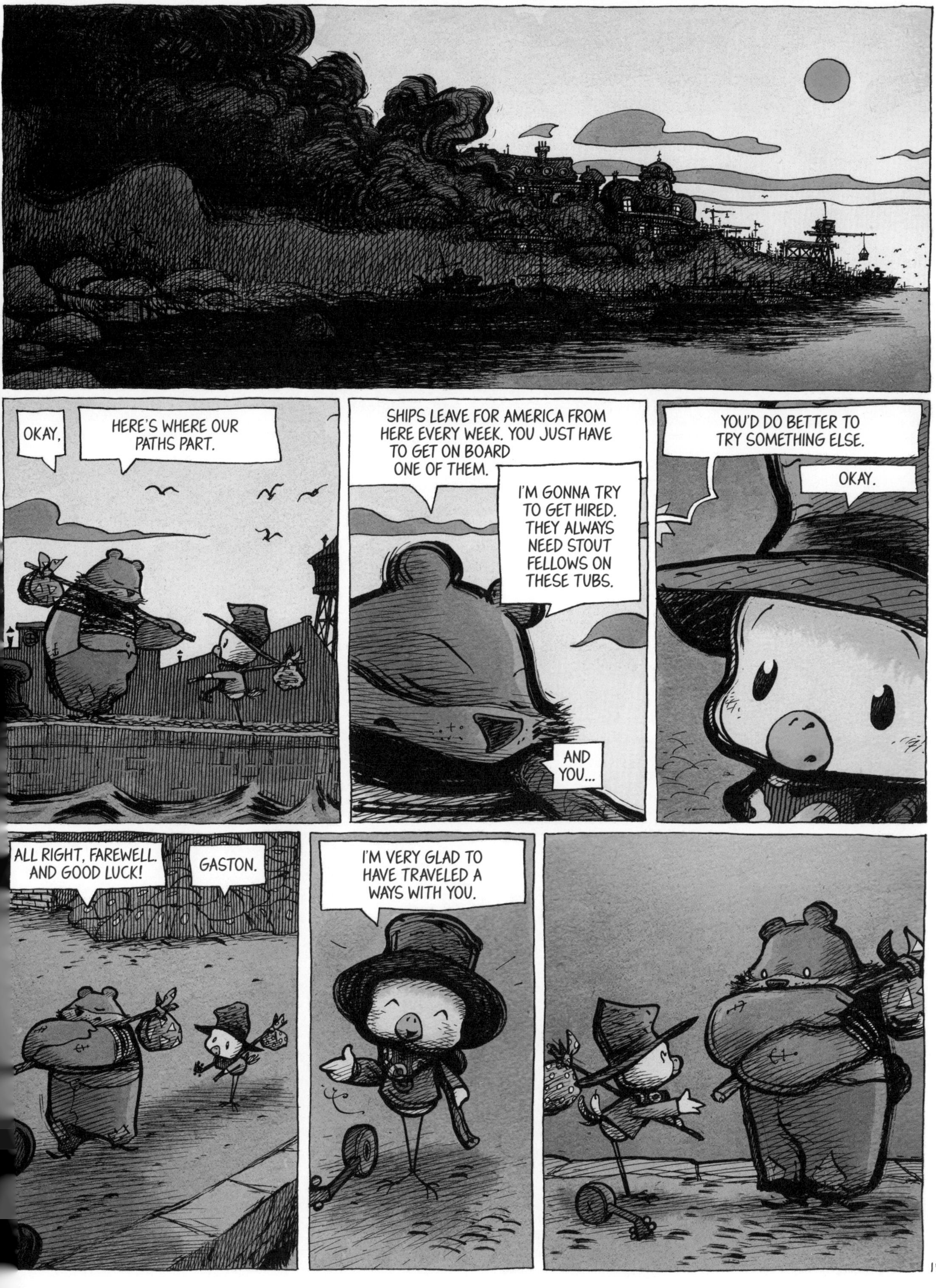

OKAY,
HERE'S WHERE OUR PATHS PART.
SHIPS LEAVE FOR AMERICA FROM HERE EVERY WEEK. YOU JUST HAVE TO GET ON BOARD ONE OF THEM.
I'M GONNA TRY TO GET HIRED. THEY ALWAYS NEED STOUT FELLOWS ON THESE TUBS.
AND YOU...
YOU'D DO BETTER TO TRY SOMETHING ELSE.
OKAY.
ALL RIGHT, FAREWELL. AND GOOD LUCK!
GASTON.
I'M VERY GLAD TO HAVE TRAVELED A WAYS WITH YOU.

15

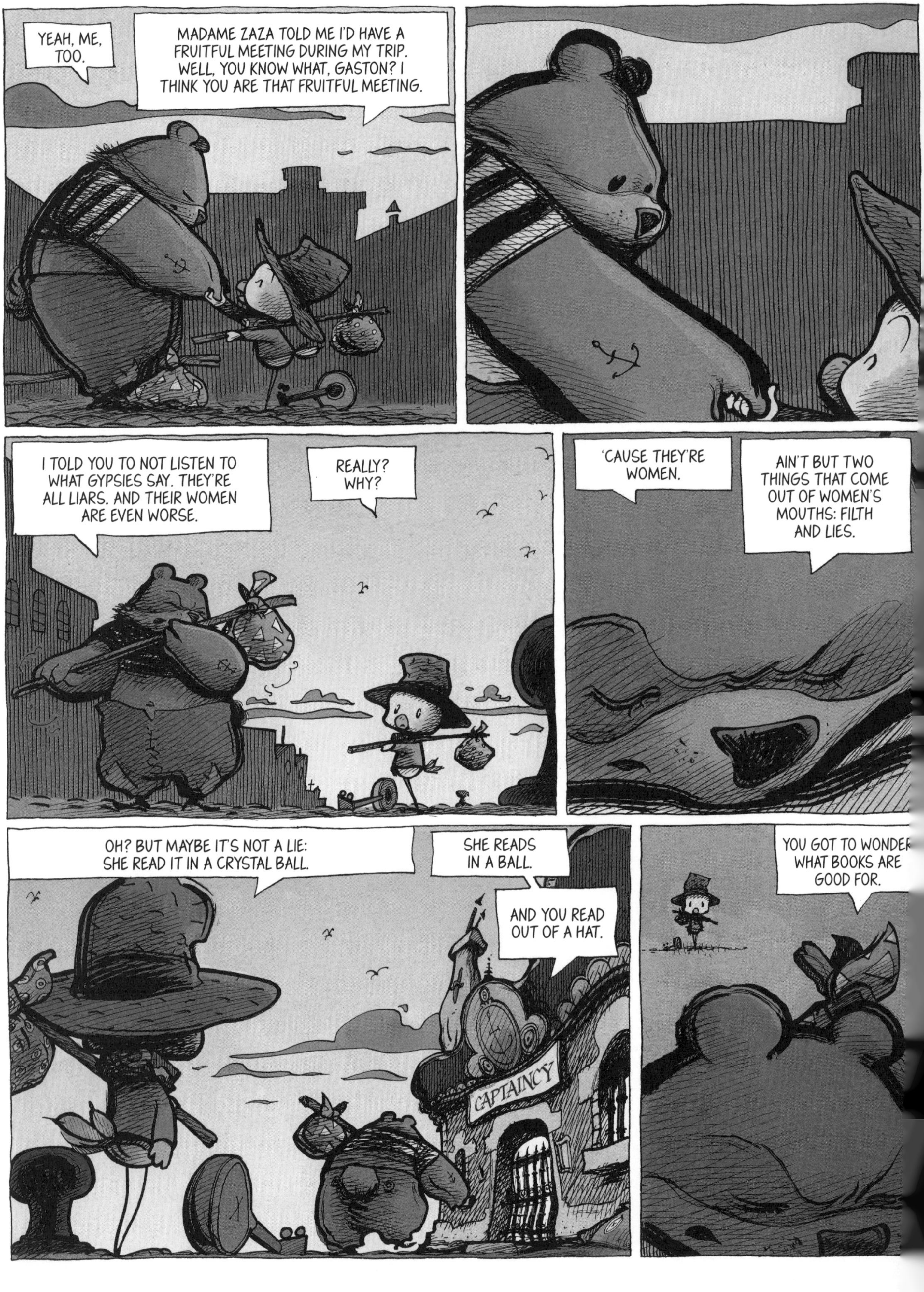
YEAH, ME, TOO.
MADAME ZAZA TOLD ME I'D HAVE A FRUITFUL MEETING DURING MY TRIP. WELL, YOU KNOW WHAT, GASTON? I THINK YOU ARE THAT FRUITFUL MEETING.
I TOLD YOU TO NOT LISTEN TO WHAT GYPSIES SAY. THEY'RE ALL LIARS. AND THEIR WOMEN ARE EVEN WORSE.
REALLY? WHY?
'CAUSE THEY'RE WOMEN.
AIN'T BUT TWO THINGS THAT COME OUT OF WOMEN'S MOUTHS: FILTH AND LIES.
OH? BUT MAYBE IT'S NOT A LIE: SHE READ IT IN A CRYSTAL BALL.
SHE READS IN A BALL.
AND YOU READ OUT OF A HAT.
CAPTAINCY
YOU GOT TO WONDER WHAT BOOKS ARE GOOD FOR.

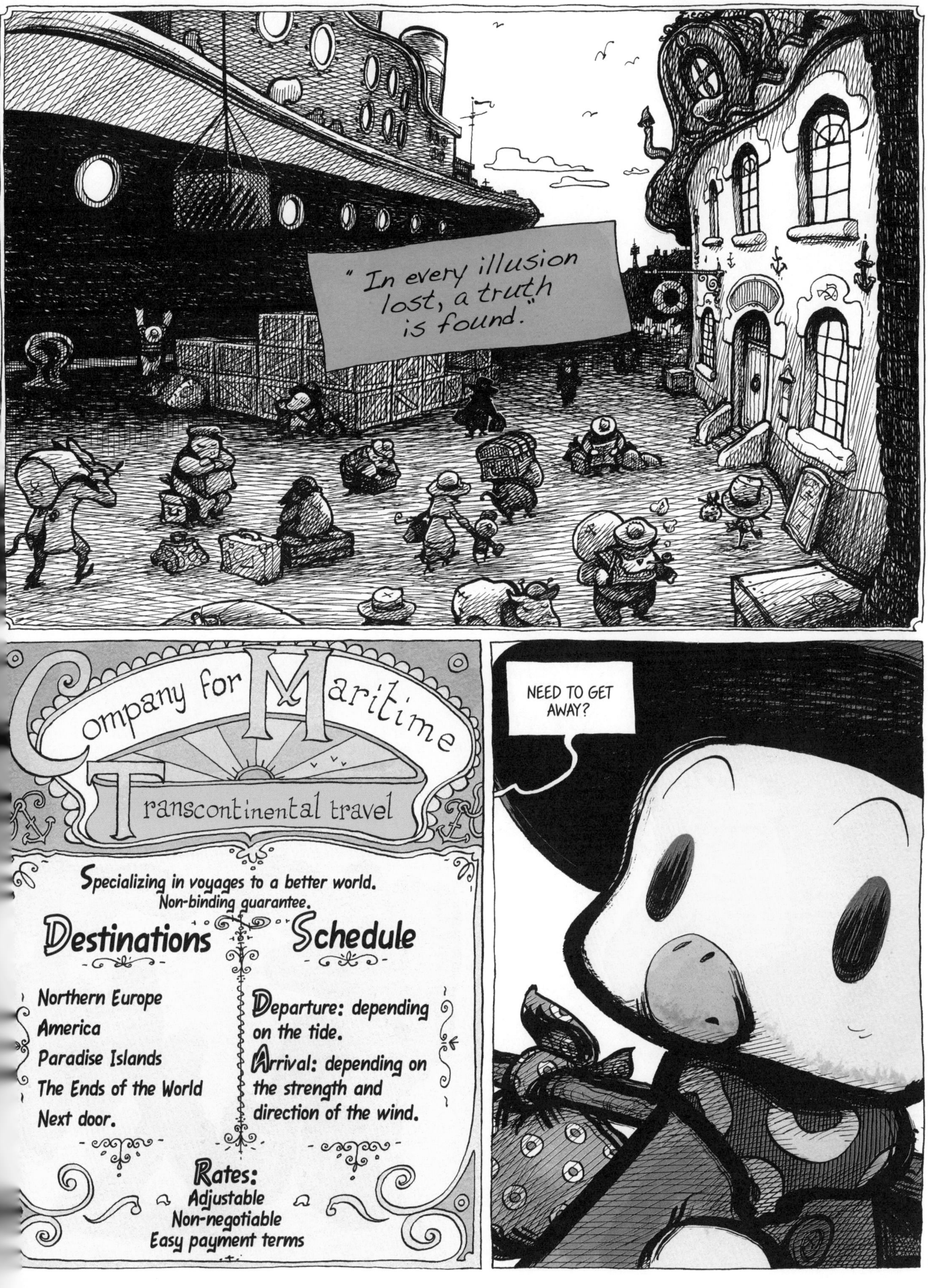
"In every illusion lost, a truth is found."
Company for Maritime Transcontinental travel
Specializing in voyages to a better world.
Non-binding guarantee.
Destinations
Northern Europe
America
Paradise Islands
The Ends of the World
Next door.
Schedule
Departure: depending on the tide.
Arrival: depending on the strength and direction of the wind.
Rates:
Adjustable
Non-negotiable
Easy payment terms
NEED TO GET AWAY?
17

UH, NO. I JUST WANT TO GO TO AMERICA.

I KNEW IT! AMERICA! ADVENTURE, WIDE OPEN SPACES, FREEDOM.

I SAW RIGHT OFF YOU HAVE THE PIONEERING SPIRIT!

YOU'RE TIRED OF THE OLD CONTINENT, OF ITS LITTLE TOWNS WITH DIRTY, NARROW STREETS. ENOUGH OF THIS MISERABLE LIFE AND THAT AWFUL HAT.

NO, I'M FINE HERE.

COME, COME NOW. OF COURSE WE'RE FINE HERE.

BUT THERE, YOU'RE NOT "FINE," YOU'RE BETTER!

EVERYTHING'S BIGGER IN AMERICA AND MORE BEAUTIFUL. EVERYTHING'S FASTER.

YOU EAT IN TWO MINUTES, MAKE A FORTUNE IN THREE. IT'S TRULY A LAND OF PLENTY!

WHATEVER YOU'RE SEEKING, YOU JUST GOTTA BEND DOWN AND PICK IT UP.

THE FIELDS ARE FLUSH WITH OIL, THE STREETS FILLED WITH MONEY, AND THE BROOKS FULL OF GOLD.

ANY STARS?

FLAGS FULL OF 'EM!

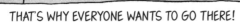

THAT'S WHY EVERYONE WANTS TO GO THERE!

AND THAT'S THE PROBLEM, TOO.

REALLY? WHY?

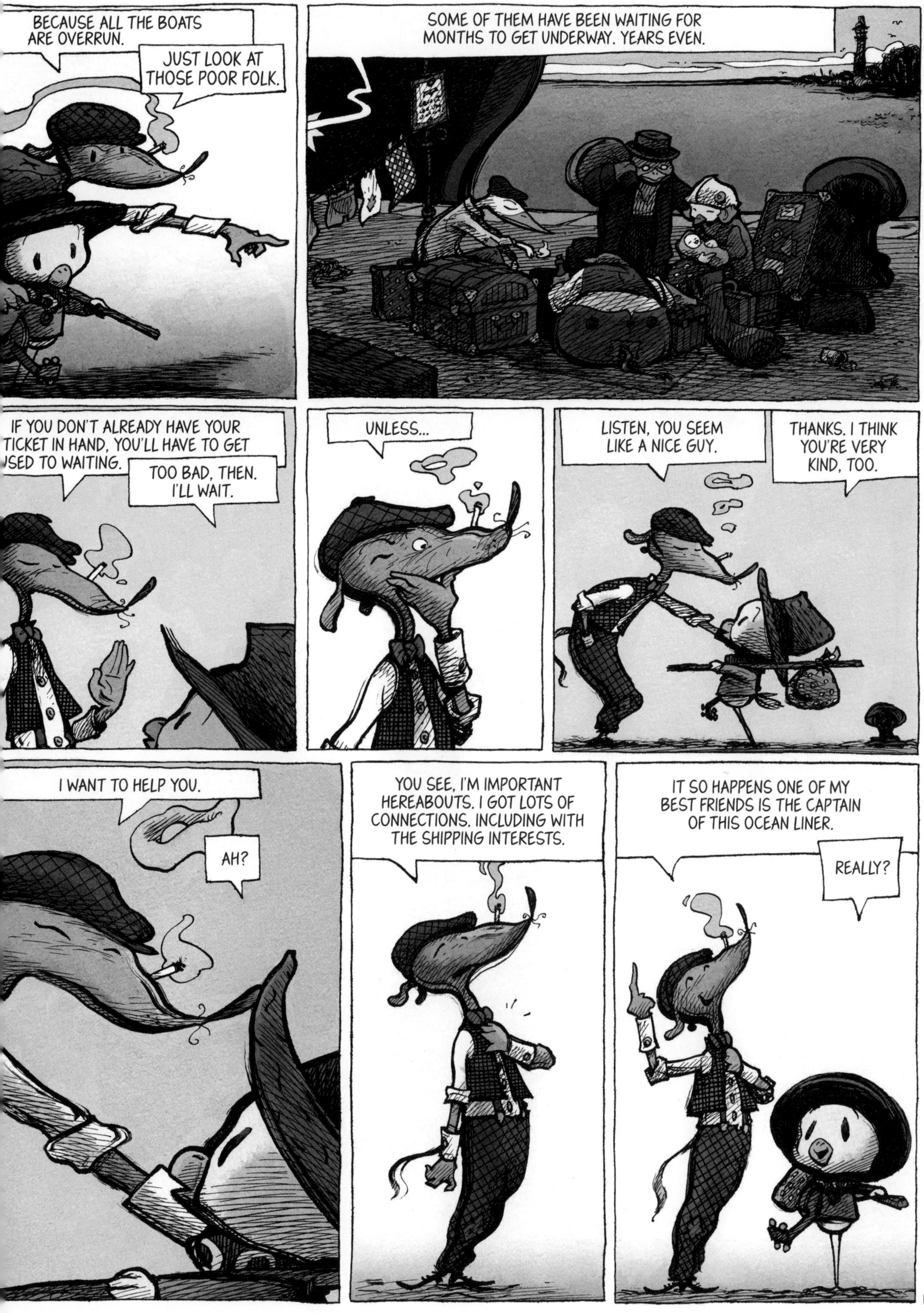
BECAUSE ALL THE BOATS ARE OVERRUN.
JUST LOOK AT THOSE POOR FOLK.
SOME OF THEM HAVE BEEN WAITING FOR MONTHS TO GET UNDERWAY. YEARS EVEN.
IF YOU DON'T ALREADY HAVE YOUR TICKET IN HAND, YOU'LL HAVE TO GET USED TO WAITING.
TOO BAD, THEN. I'LL WAIT.
UNLESS...
LISTEN, YOU SEEM LIKE A NICE GUY.
THANKS. I THINK YOU'RE VERY KIND, TOO.
I WANT TO HELP YOU.
AH?
YOU SEE, I'M IMPORTANT HEREABOUTS. I GOT LOTS OF CONNECTIONS. INCLUDING WITH THE SHIPPING INTERESTS.
IT SO HAPPENS ONE OF MY BEST FRIENDS IS THE CAPTAIN OF THIS OCEAN LINER.
REALLY?
19

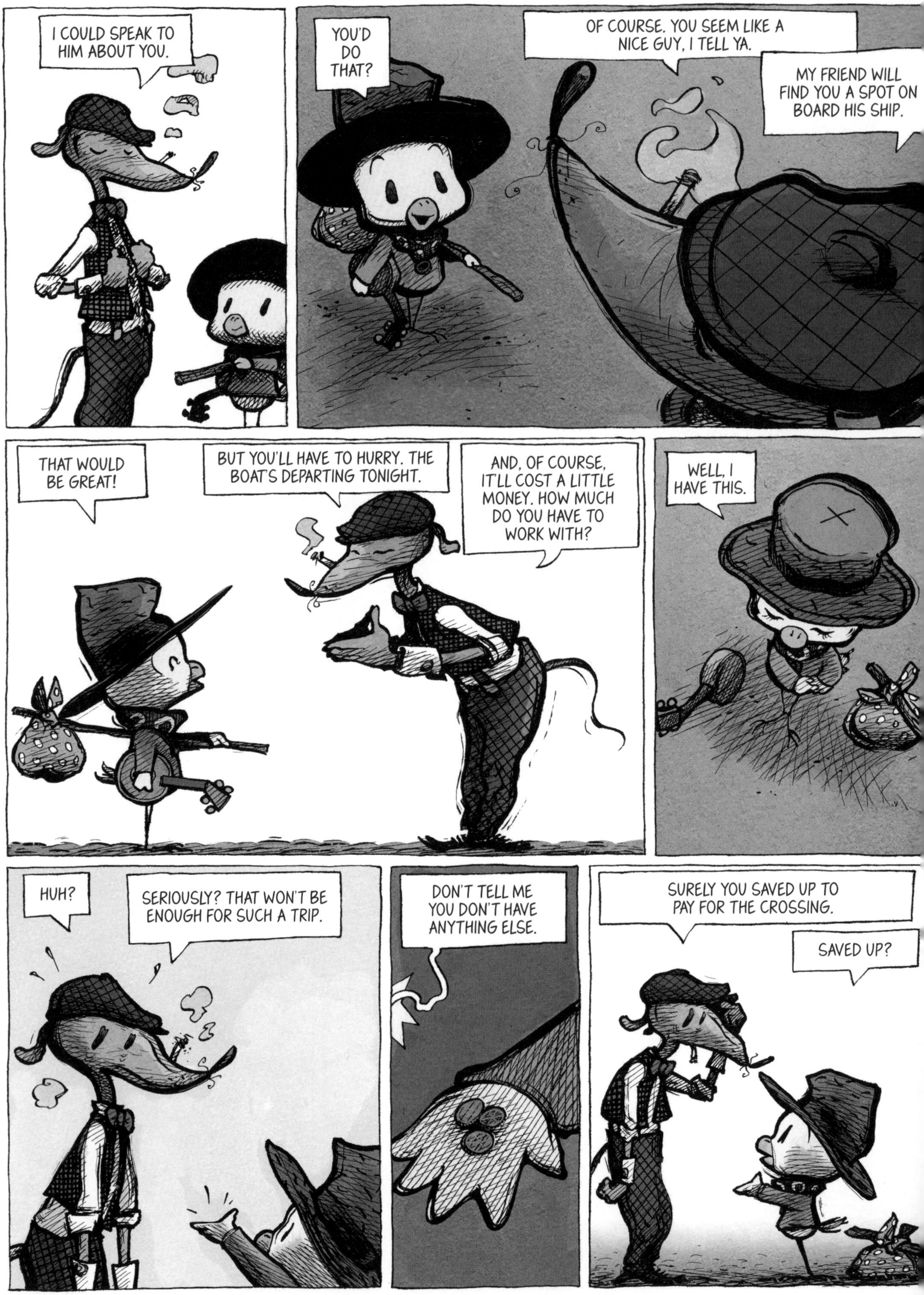
I COULD SPEAK TO HIM ABOUT YOU.
YOU'D DO THAT?
OF COURSE. YOU SEEM LIKE A NICE GUY, I TELL YA.
MY FRIEND WILL FIND YOU A SPOT ON BOARD HIS SHIP.
THAT WOULD BE GREAT!
BUT YOU'LL HAVE TO HURRY. THE BOAT'S DEPARTING TONIGHT.
AND, OF COURSE, IT'LL COST A LITTLE MONEY. HOW MUCH DO YOU HAVE TO WORK WITH?
WELL, I HAVE THIS.
HUH?
SERIOUSLY? THAT WON'T BE ENOUGH FOR SUCH A TRIP.
DON'T TELL ME YOU DON'T HAVE ANYTHING ELSE.
SURELY YOU SAVED UP TO PAY FOR THE CROSSING.
SAVED UP?

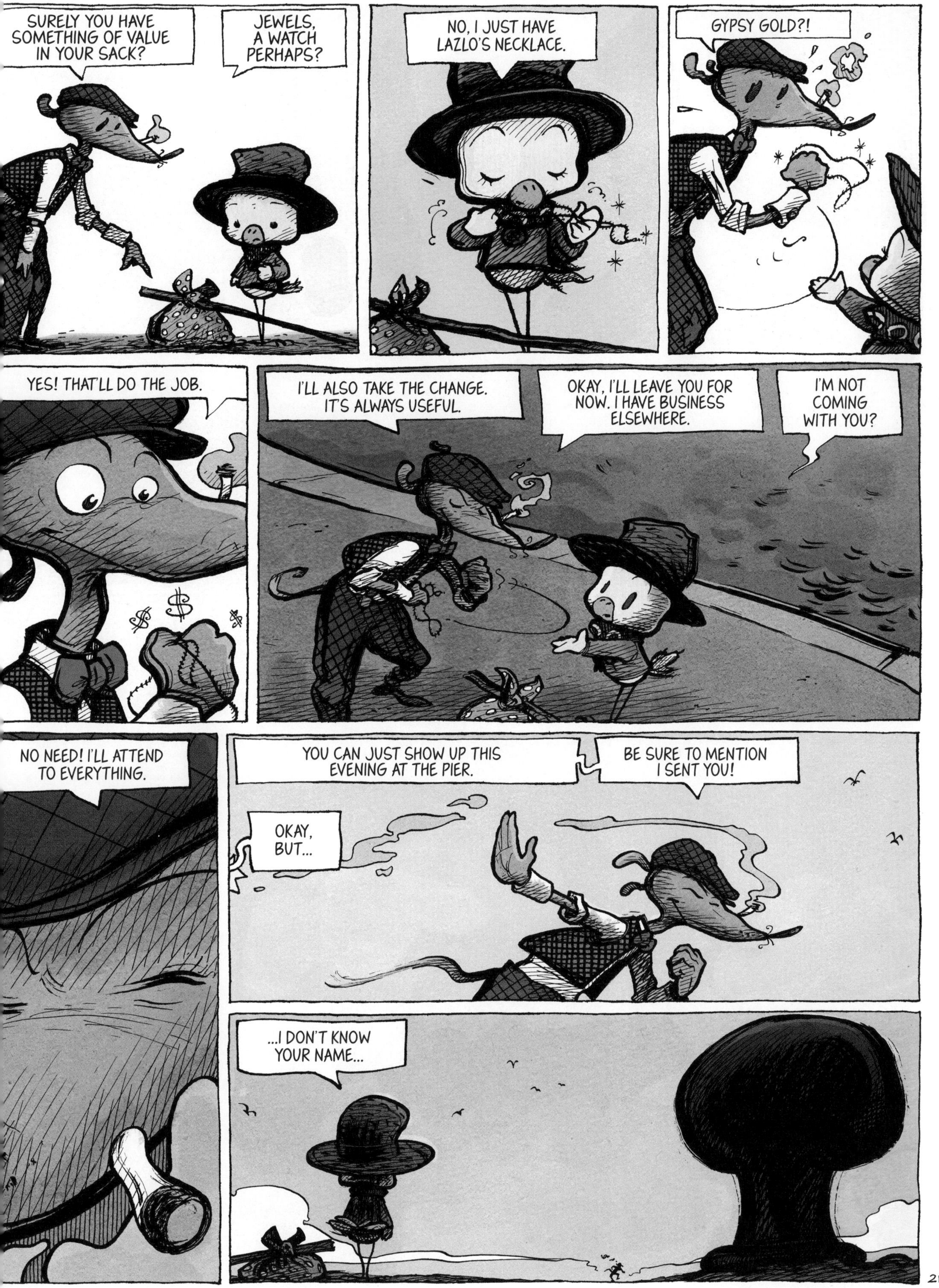
SURELY YOU HAVE SOMETHING OF VALUE IN YOUR SACK?
JEWELS, A WATCH PERHAPS?
NO, I JUST HAVE LAZLO'S NECKLACE.
GYPSY GOLD?!
YES! THAT'LL DO THE JOB.
I'LL ALSO TAKE THE CHANGE. IT'S ALWAYS USEFUL.
OKAY, I'LL LEAVE YOU FOR NOW. I HAVE BUSINESS ELSEWHERE.
I'M NOT COMING WITH YOU?
NO NEED! I'LL ATTEND TO EVERYTHING.
YOU CAN JUST SHOW UP THIS EVENING AT THE PIER.
BE SURE TO MENTION I SENT YOU!
OKAY, BUT...
...I DON'T KNOW YOUR NAME...
21

A TALL SKINNY FELLOW, WITH PLAID PANTS, AND A BOWTIE?
L'Atlantic Princesse
DOES THAT REMIND YOU OF ANYONE?
THAT COULD BE ANASZTAZ.
SO YOU KNOW HIM?
I'VE HEARD TELL OF HIM. HE'S A SMALL-TIME CON MAN WHO SCAMS NAIVE TOURISTS.
WHAT DID YOU HAVE TO DO WITH HIM?

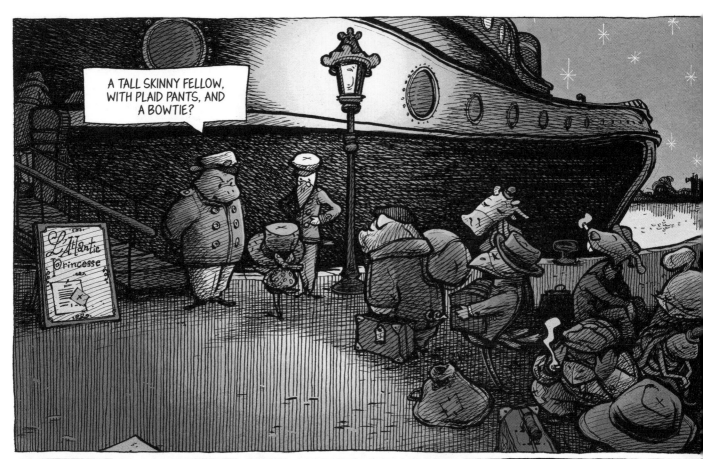

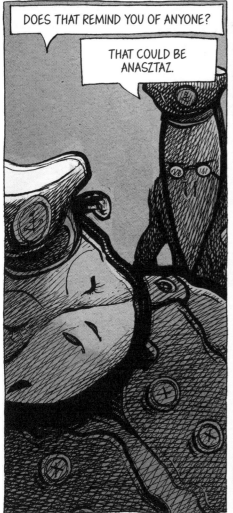

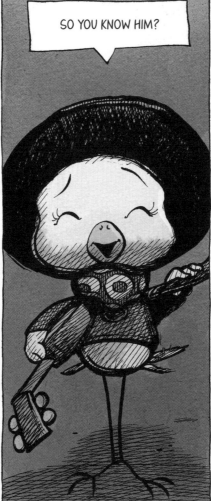

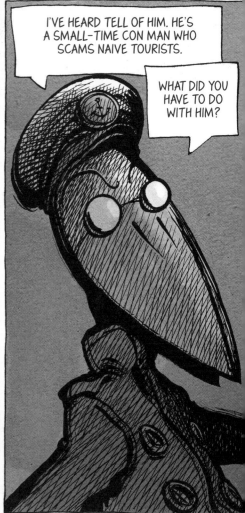

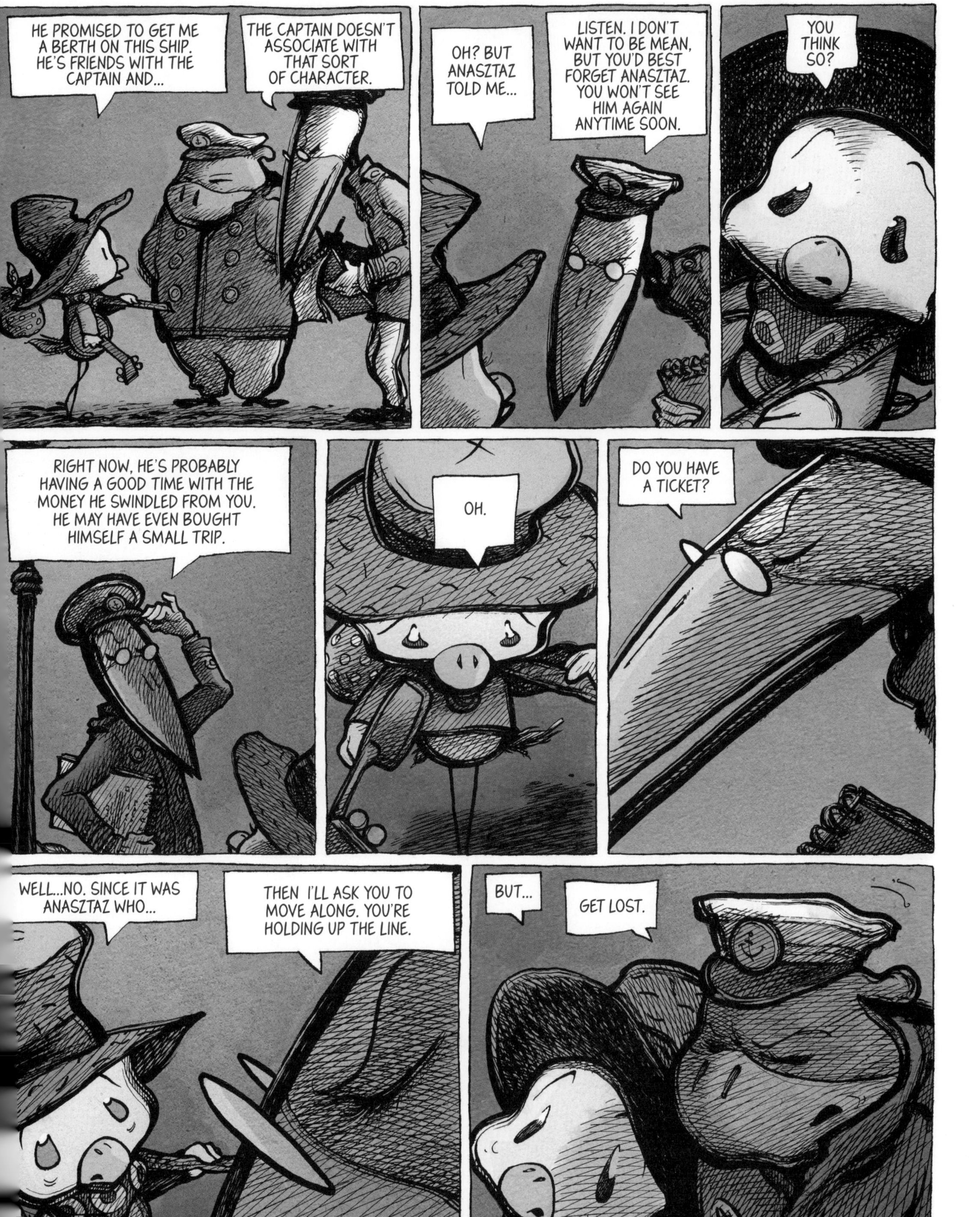
HE PROMISED TO GET ME A BERTH ON THIS SHIP. HE'S FRIENDS WITH THE CAPTAIN AND...
THE CAPTAIN DOESN'T ASSOCIATE WITH THAT SORT OF CHARACTER.
OH? BUT ANASZTAZ TOLD ME...
LISTEN. I DON'T WANT TO BE MEAN, BUT YOU'D BEST FORGET ANASZTAZ. YOU WON'T SEE HIM AGAIN ANYTIME SOON.
YOU THINK SO?
RIGHT NOW, HE'S PROBABLY HAVING A GOOD TIME WITH THE MONEY HE SWINDLED FROM YOU. HE MAY HAVE EVEN BOUGHT HIMSELF A SMALL TRIP.
OH.
DO YOU HAVE A TICKET?
WELL...NO. SINCE IT WAS ANASZTAZ WHO...
THEN I'LL ASK YOU TO MOVE ALONG. YOU'RE HOLDING UP THE LINE.
BUT...
GET LOST.

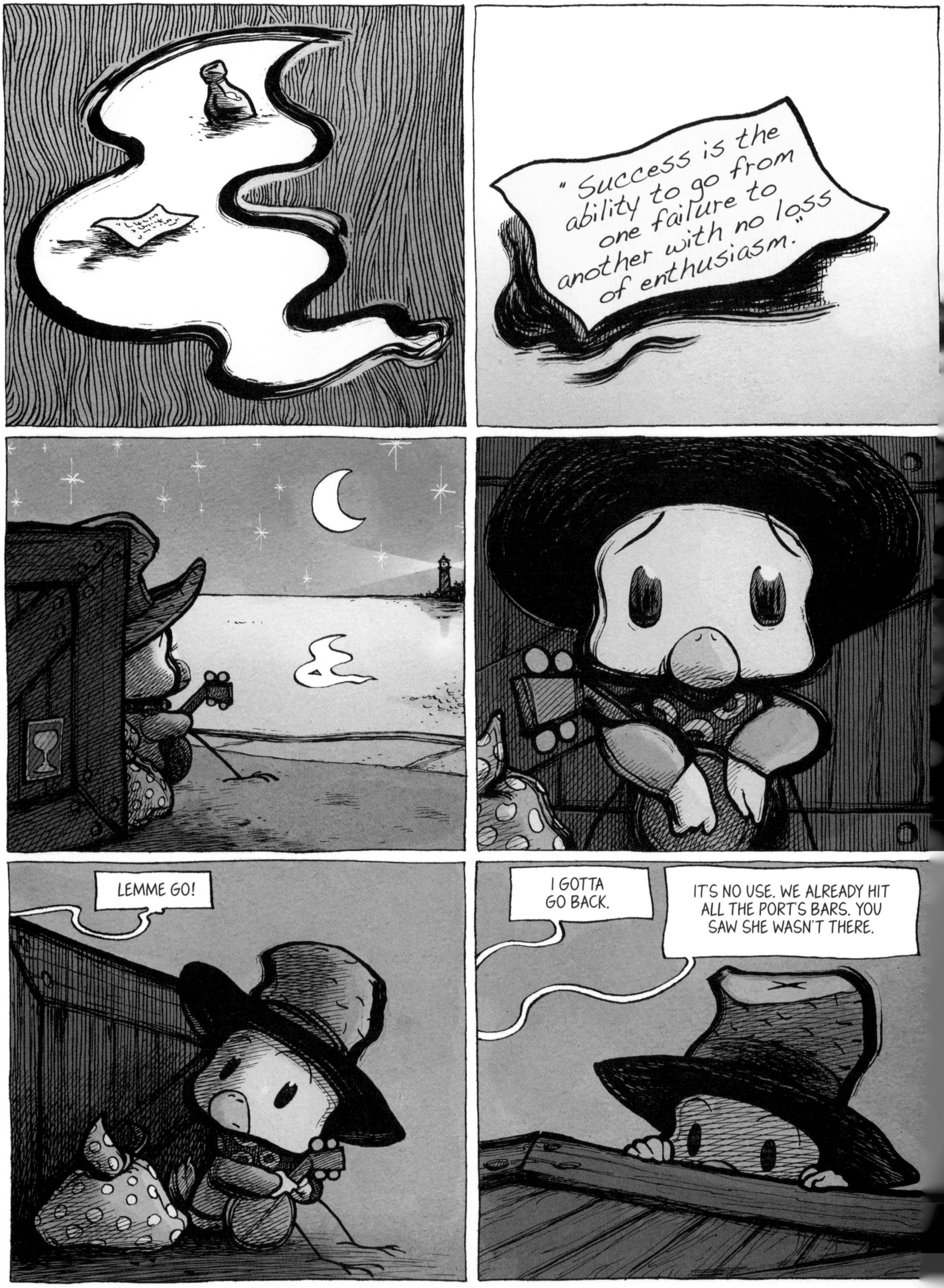
"Success is the ability to go from one failure to another with no loss of enthusiasm."
LEMME GO!
I GOTTA GO BACK.
IT'S NO USE. WE ALREADY HIT ALL THE PORT'S BARS. YOU SAW SHE WASN'T THERE.

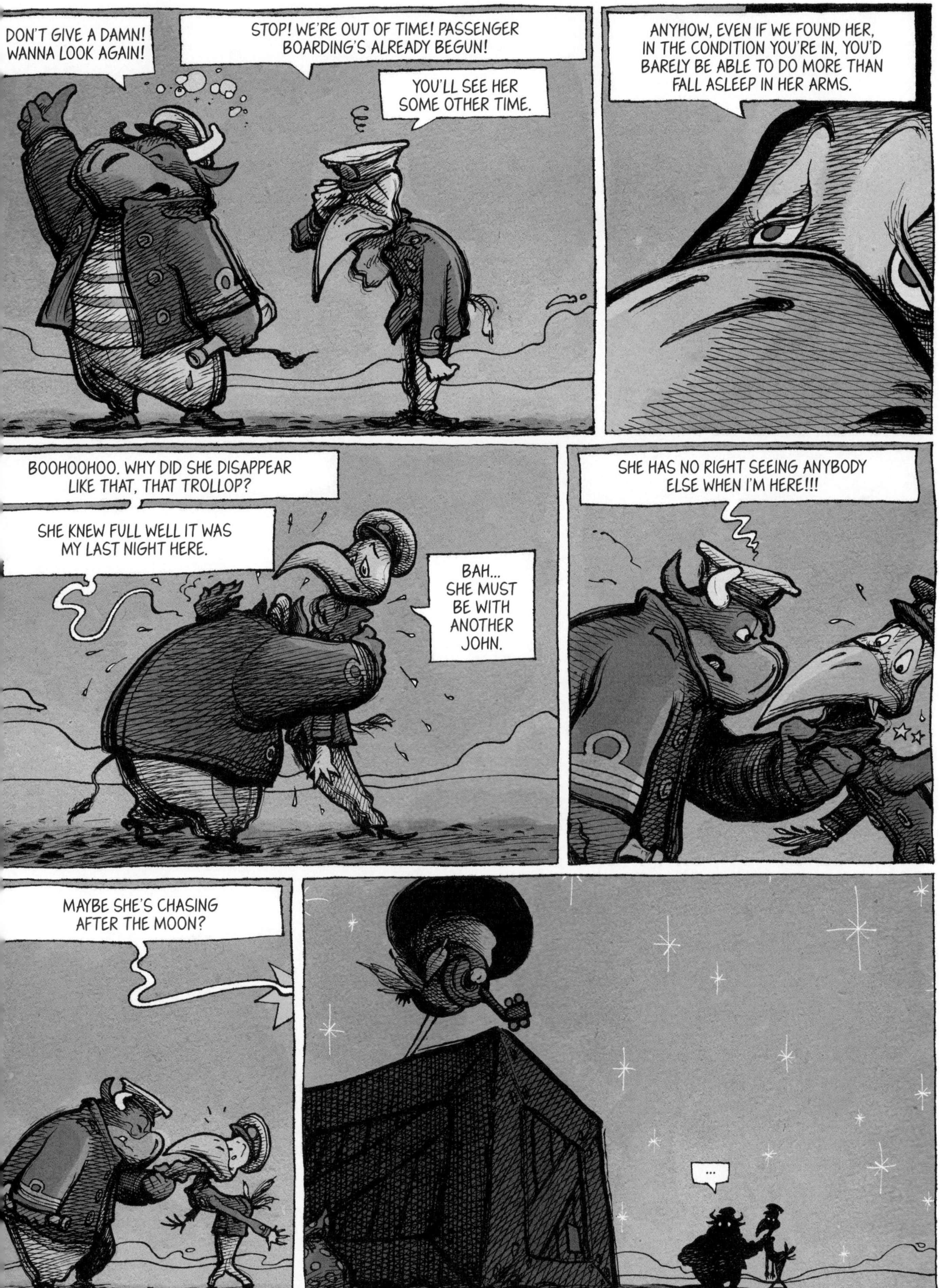
DON'T GIVE A DAMN! WANNA LOOK AGAIN!
STOP! WE'RE OUT OF TIME! PASSENGER BOARDING'S ALREADY BEGUN!
YOU'LL SEE HER SOME OTHER TIME.
ANYHOW, EVEN IF WE FOUND HER, IN THE CONDITION YOU'RE IN, YOU'D BARELY BE ABLE TO DO MORE THAN FALL ASLEEP IN HER ARMS.
BOOHOOHOO. WHY DID SHE DISAPPEAR LIKE THAT, THAT TROLLOP?
SHE KNEW FULL WELL IT WAS MY LAST NIGHT HERE.
BAH... SHE MUST BE WITH ANOTHER JOHN.
SHE HAS NO RIGHT SEEING ANYBODY ELSE WHEN I'M HERE!!!
MAYBE SHE'S CHASING AFTER THE MOON?
...
25

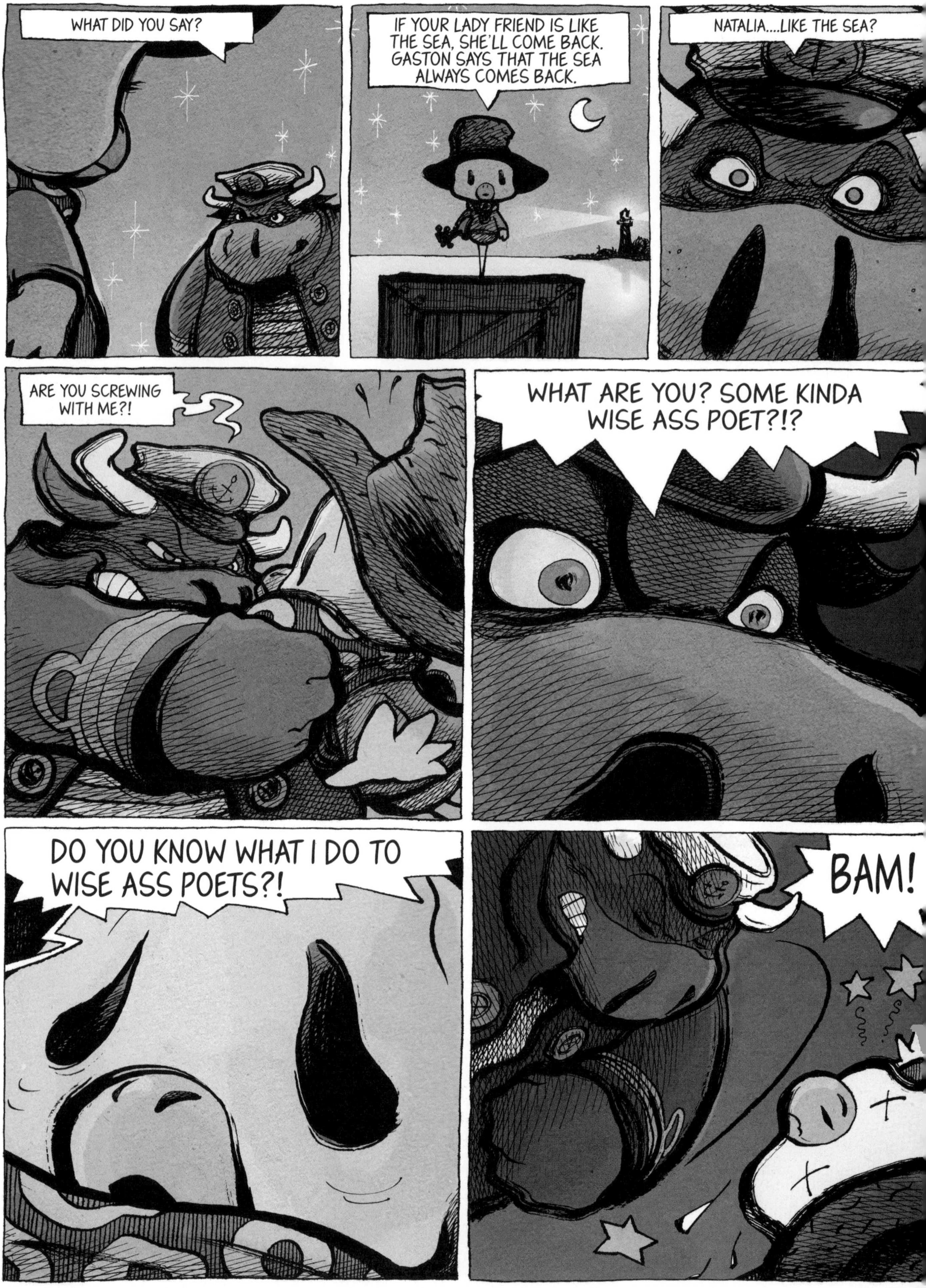
WHAT DID YOU SAY?
IF YOUR LADY FRIEND IS LIKE THE SEA, SHE'LL COME BACK. GASTON SAYS THAT THE SEA ALWAYS COMES BACK.
NATALIA....LIKE THE SEA?
ARE YOU SCREWING WITH ME?!
WHAT ARE YOU? SOME KINDA WISE ASS POET?!?
DO YOU KNOW WHAT I DO TO WISE ASS POETS?!
BAM!

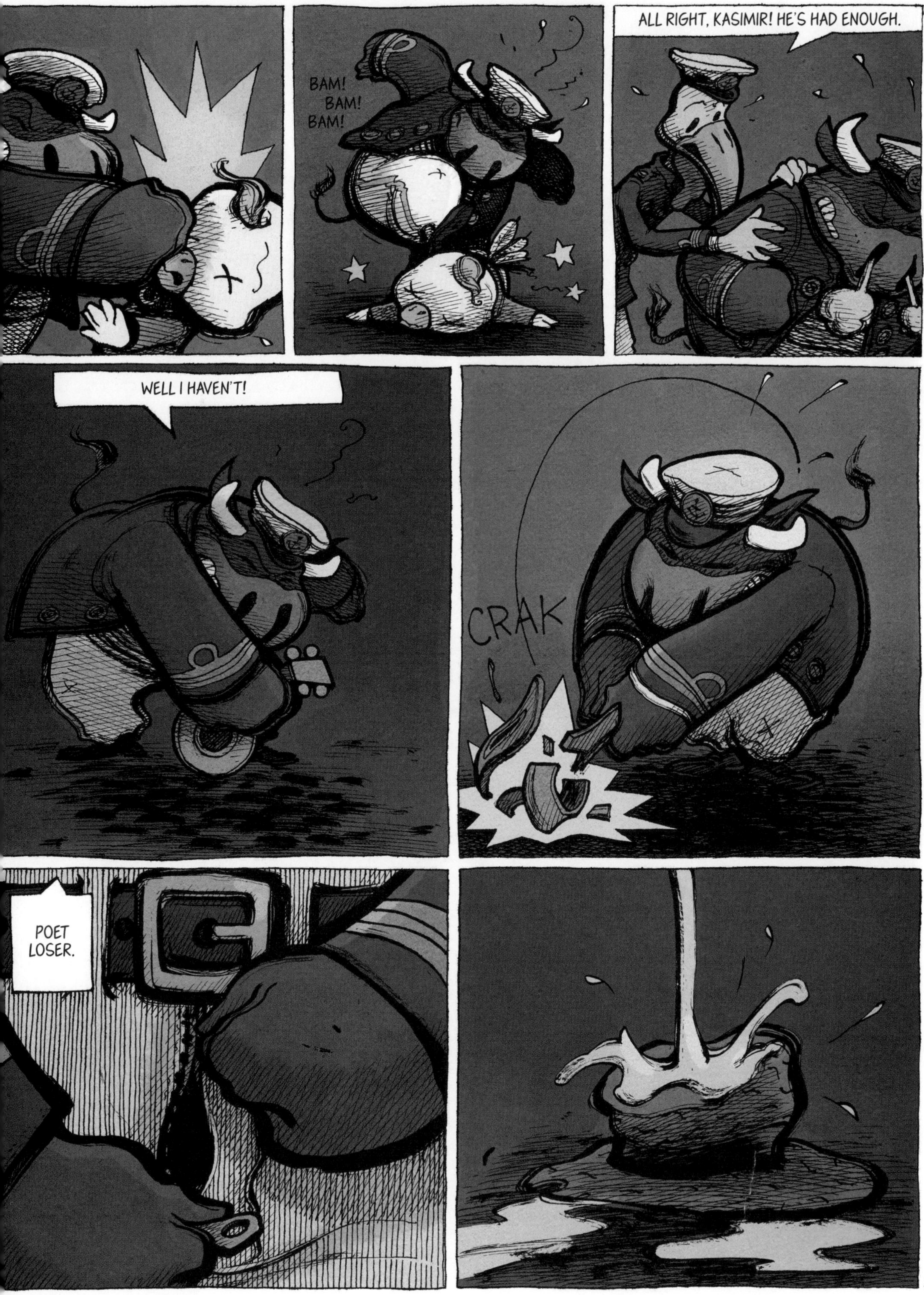
BAM!
BAM!
BAM!
ALL RIGHT, KASIMIR! HE'S HAD ENOUGH.
WELL I HAVEN'T!
CRAK
POET
LOSER.

27

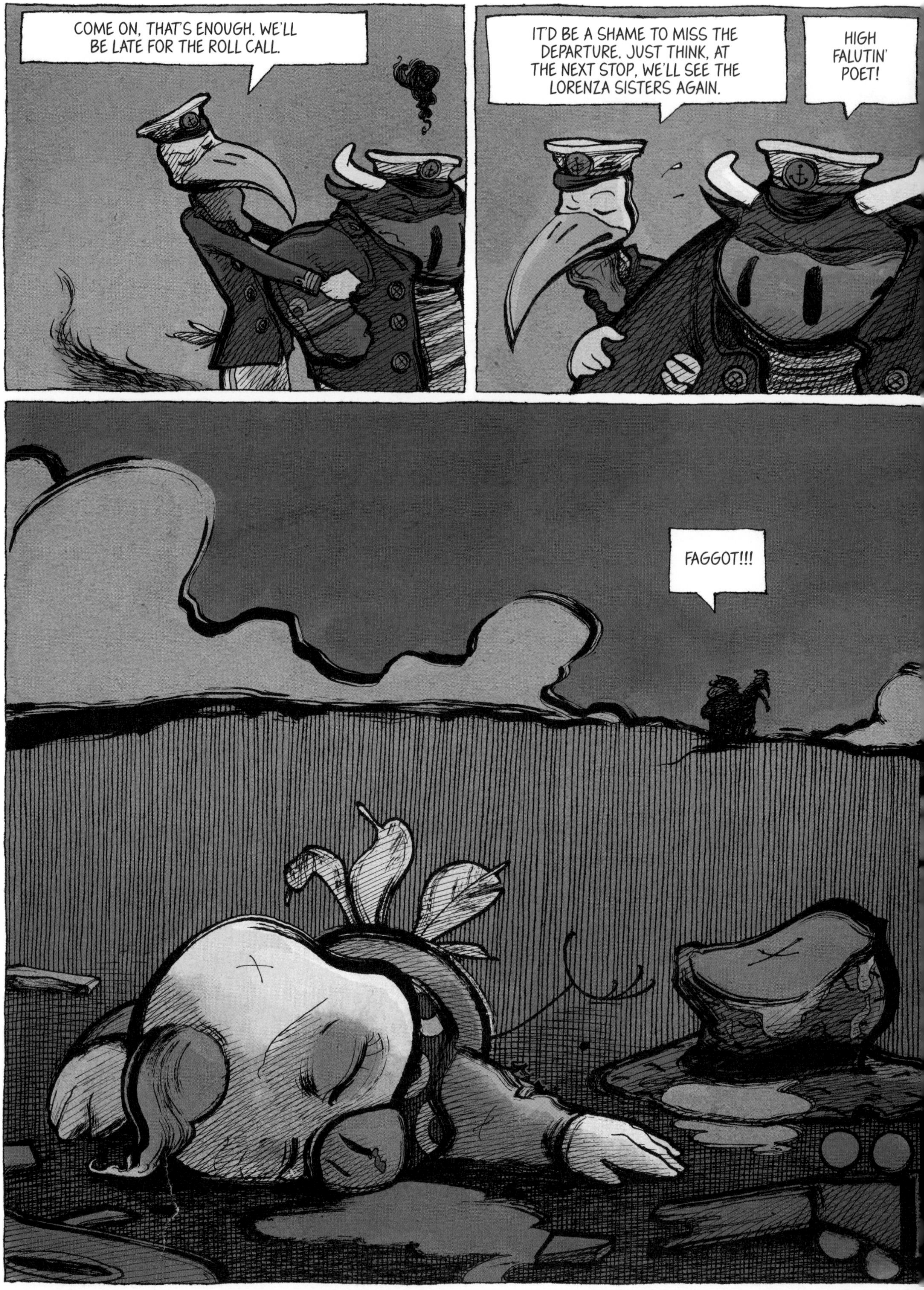
COME ON, THAT'S ENOUGH. WE'LL BE LATE FOR THE ROLL CALL.
IT'D BE A SHAME TO MISS THE DEPARTURE. JUST THINK, AT THE NEXT STOP, WE'LL SEE THE LORENZA SISTERS AGAIN.
HIGH FALUTIN' POET!
FAGGOT!!!

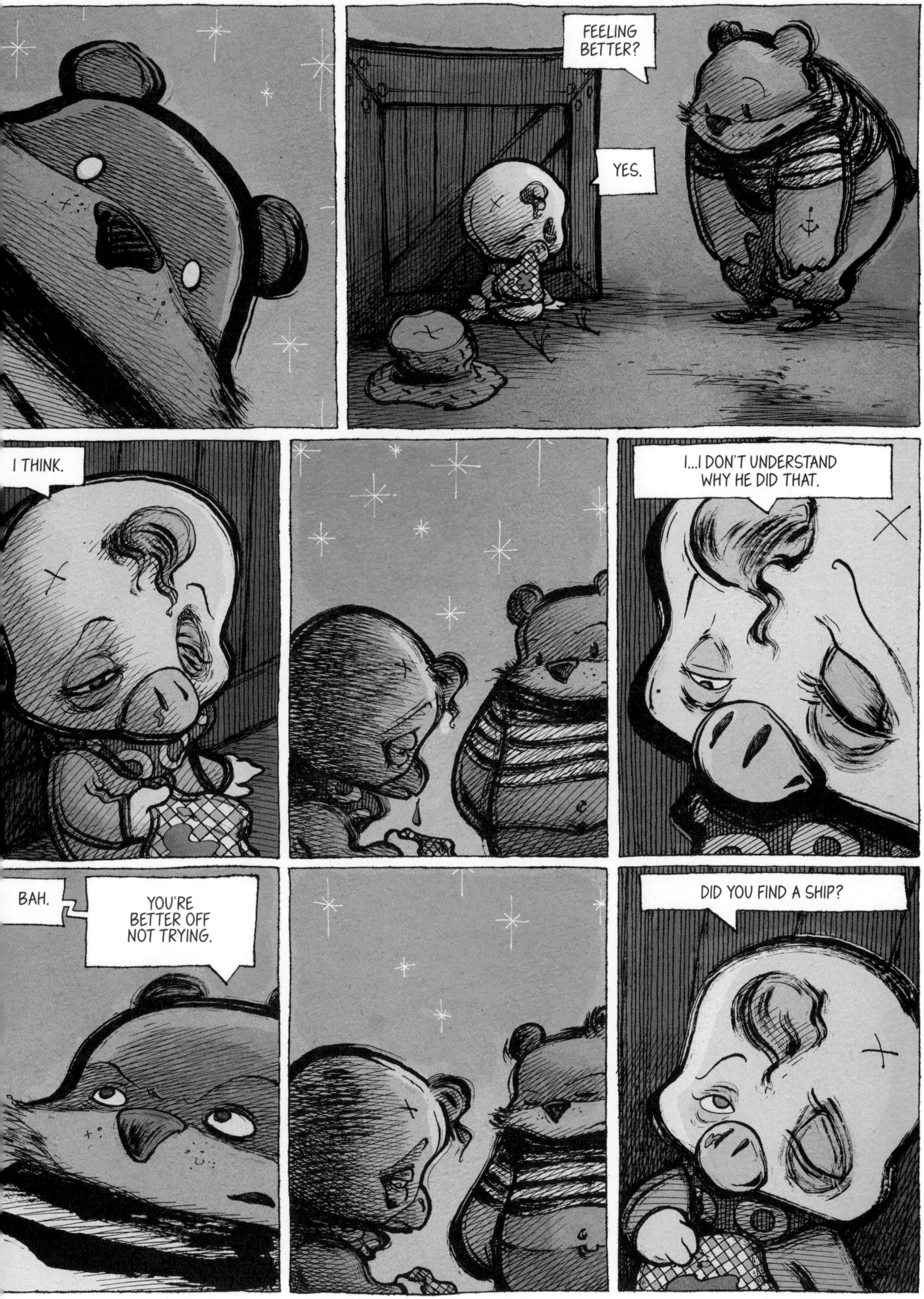
FEELING BETTER?
YES.
I THINK.
I...I DON'T UNDERSTAND WHY HE DID THAT.
BAH.
YOU'RE BETTER OFF NOT TRYING.
DID YOU FIND A SHIP?
29

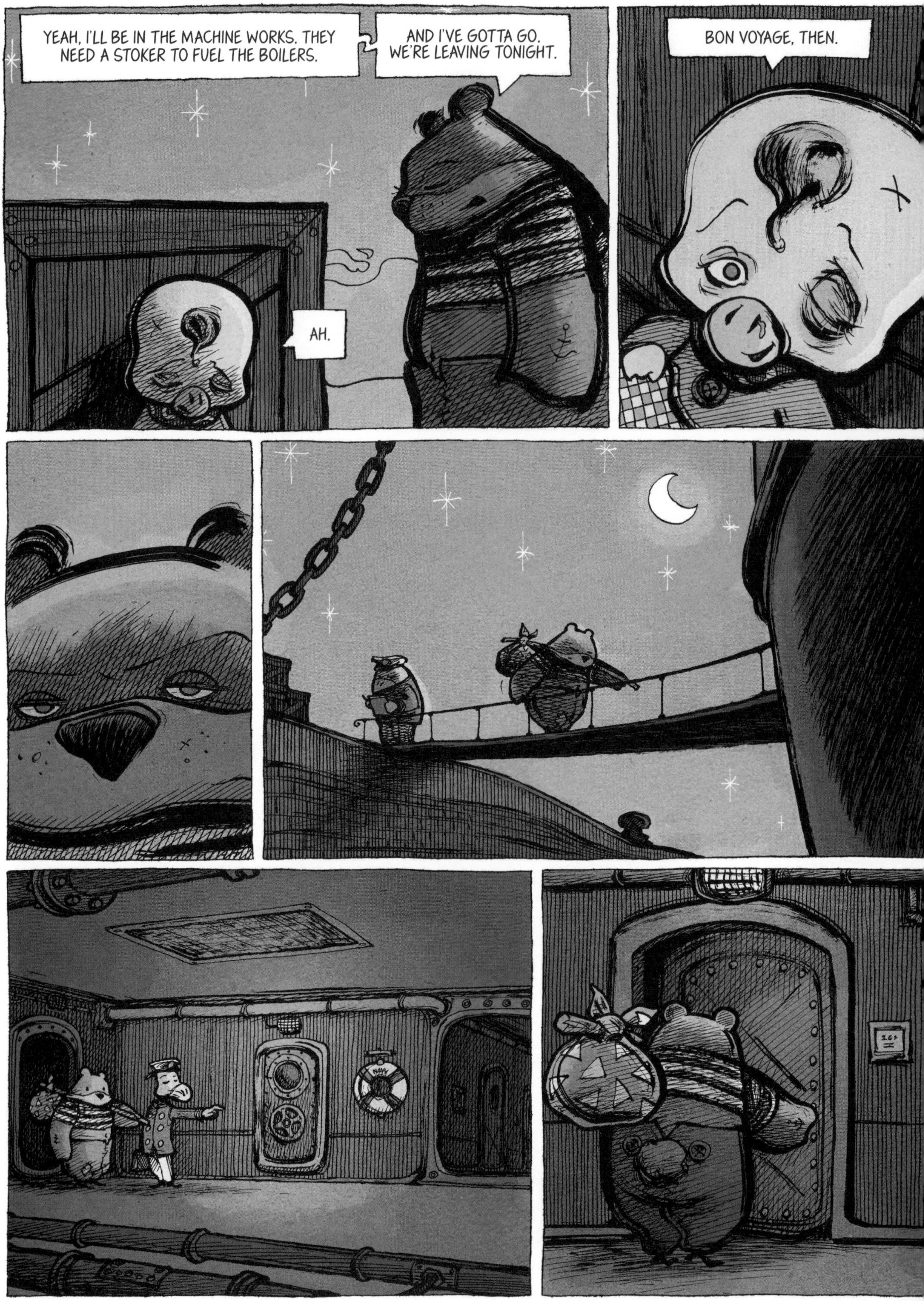
YEAH, I'LL BE IN THE MACHINE WORKS. THEY NEED A STOKER TO FUEL THE BOILERS.
AND I'VE GOTTA GO. WE'RE LEAVING TONIGHT.
AH.
BON VOYAGE, THEN.
NAVY

IT'S OKAY. NOBODY'S HERE.

YOU CAN STAY AND REST HERE. THE MACHINE OPERATOR I'M SHARING THE CABIN WITH IS ALREADY ON HIS SHIFT. YOU'LL LEAVE WHEN I GO RELIEVE HIM.

AFTERWARDS, YOU CAN GO WALK AROUND THE STEERAGE, BUT KEEP FROM GETTING NOTICED.

SAY, GASTON,

HOW DID YOU MEET EPPILY?

EPPILY...

YOU KNOW, HER NAME WAS SUPPOSED TO BE EMILY, IN FACT.

REALLY?

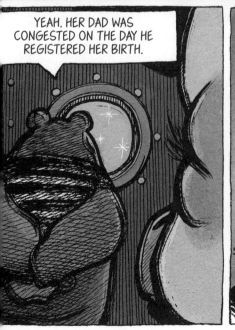
YEAH. HER DAD WAS CONGESTED ON THE DAY HE REGISTERED HER BIRTH.

WHEN WE WERE KIDS, WE LIVED ON THE SAME STREET. WE SPENT OUR TIME FISHING AND PLAYING NEAR THE RIVER.

EVEN THOUGH SHE WAS A GIRL, SHE WAS MY BEST FRIEND.

AND THEN, WHILE GROWING UP, SHE CHANGED.

SHE PLAYED LESS. SHE STARTED PAYING ATTENTION TO HER HAIR AND THE WAY SHE DRESSED. SHE'D IMITATE THE OTHER GIRLS.

IT DIDN'T BOTHER ME NECESSARILY.

I HAVE TO SAY I WAS CHANGING, TOO.

DESPITE ALL THOSE CHANGES, WE REMAINED FRIENDS. BUT IT WASN'T QUITE LIKE BEFORE. WE DIDN'T LOOK AT EACH OTHER THE SAME WAY.

WE GREW APART.

WELL...

HER ESPECIALLY.

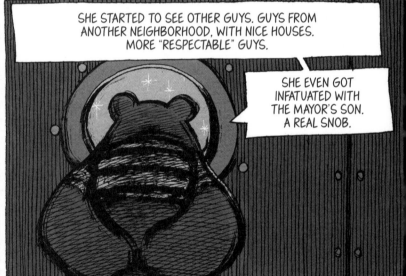

SHE STARTED TO SEE OTHER GUYS. GUYS FROM ANOTHER NEIGHBORHOOD, WITH NICE HOUSES. MORE "RESPECTABLE" GUYS.

SHE EVEN GOT INFATUATED WITH THE MAYOR'S SON. A REAL SNOB.

DAMN CREEP.

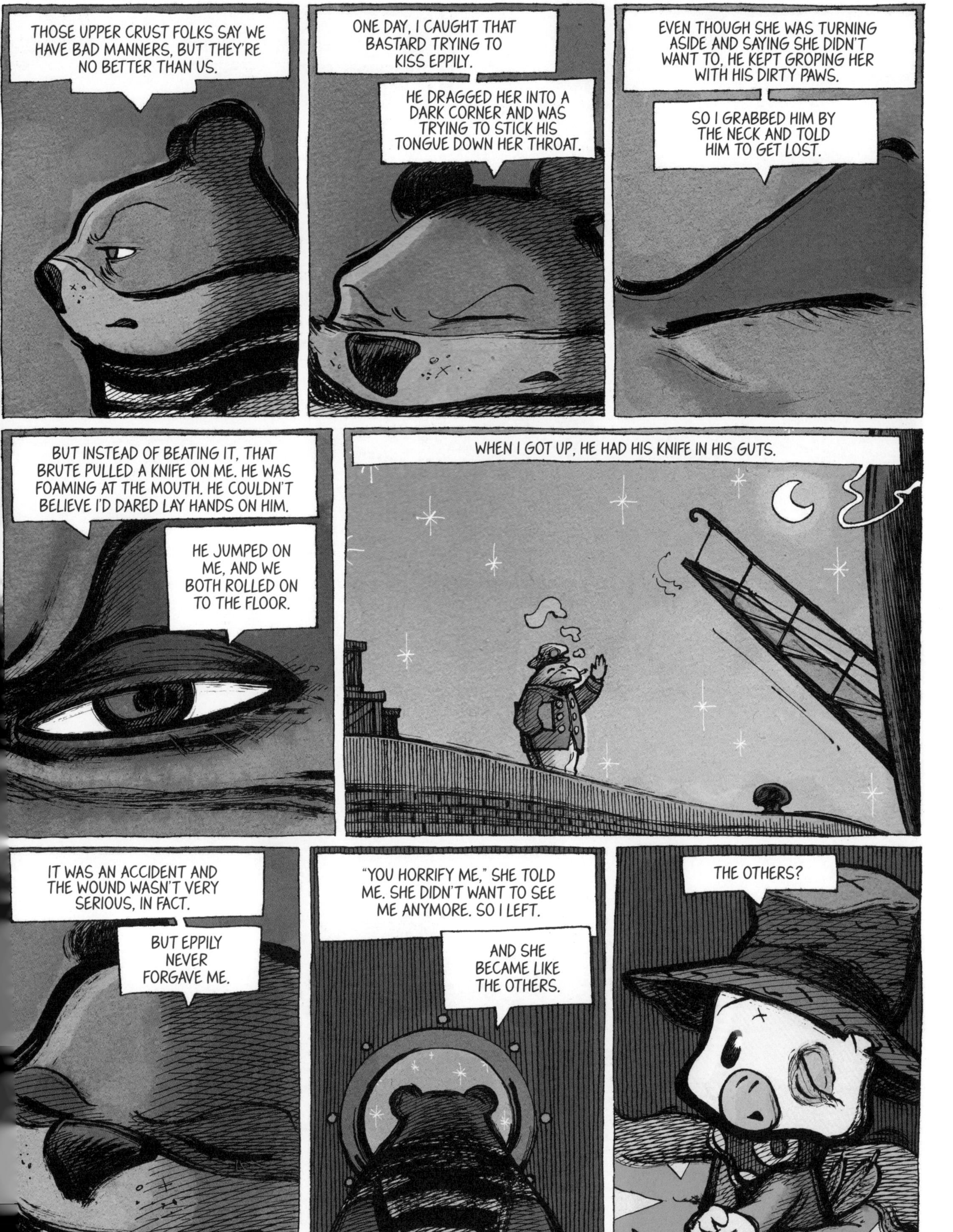
THOSE UPPER CRUST FOLKS SAY WE HAVE BAD MANNERS, BUT THEY'RE NO BETTER THAN US.
ONE DAY, I CAUGHT THAT BASTARD TRYING TO KISS EPPILY.
HE DRAGGED HER INTO A DARK CORNER AND WAS TRYING TO STICK HIS TONGUE DOWN HER THROAT.
EVEN THOUGH SHE WAS TURNING ASIDE AND SAYING SHE DIDN'T WANT TO, HE KEPT GROPING HER WITH HIS DIRTY PAWS.
SO I GRABBED HIM BY THE NECK AND TOLD HIM TO GET LOST.
BUT INSTEAD OF BEATING IT, THAT BRUTE PULLED A KNIFE ON ME. HE WAS FOAMING AT THE MOUTH. HE COULDN'T BELIEVE I'D DARED LAY HANDS ON HIM.
HE JUMPED ON ME, AND WE BOTH ROLLED ON TO THE FLOOR.
WHEN I GOT UP, HE HAD HIS KNIFE IN HIS GUTS.
IT WAS AN ACCIDENT AND THE WOUND WASN'T VERY SERIOUS, IN FACT.
BUT EPPILY NEVER FORGAVE ME.
"YOU HORRIFY ME," SHE TOLD ME. SHE DIDN'T WANT TO SEE ME ANYMORE. SO I LEFT.
AND SHE BECAME LIKE THE OTHERS.
THE OTHERS?

GIRLS FOR WHOM ONLY THE MONEY IS IMPORTANT.

THE KIND WHO PREFER THE PAWING OF THE WELL-HEELED RATHER THAN THE MARKS OF AFFECTION FROM GUYS LIKE US.

YOU'RE WRONG, GASTON. EPPILY ISN'T LIKE THAT.

BELIEVE WHAT YOU WANT.

I'M TELLING YOU, THE EPPILY IN YOUR HEAD IS NOWHERE ELSE. THERE ARE NO PERFECT GIRLS IN EXISTENCE.

AND IT'S NOT JUST GIRLS. IT'S TRUE FOR EVERYTHING. AND EVERYBODY.

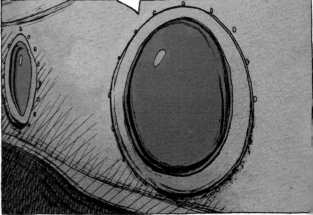

WE ALL HAVE FAULTS AND THINGS WE KEEP HIDDEN INSIDE US. YEAH... WE ALL HAVE A DARK SIDE.

ONLY THE SUN HAS NO SHADOW.

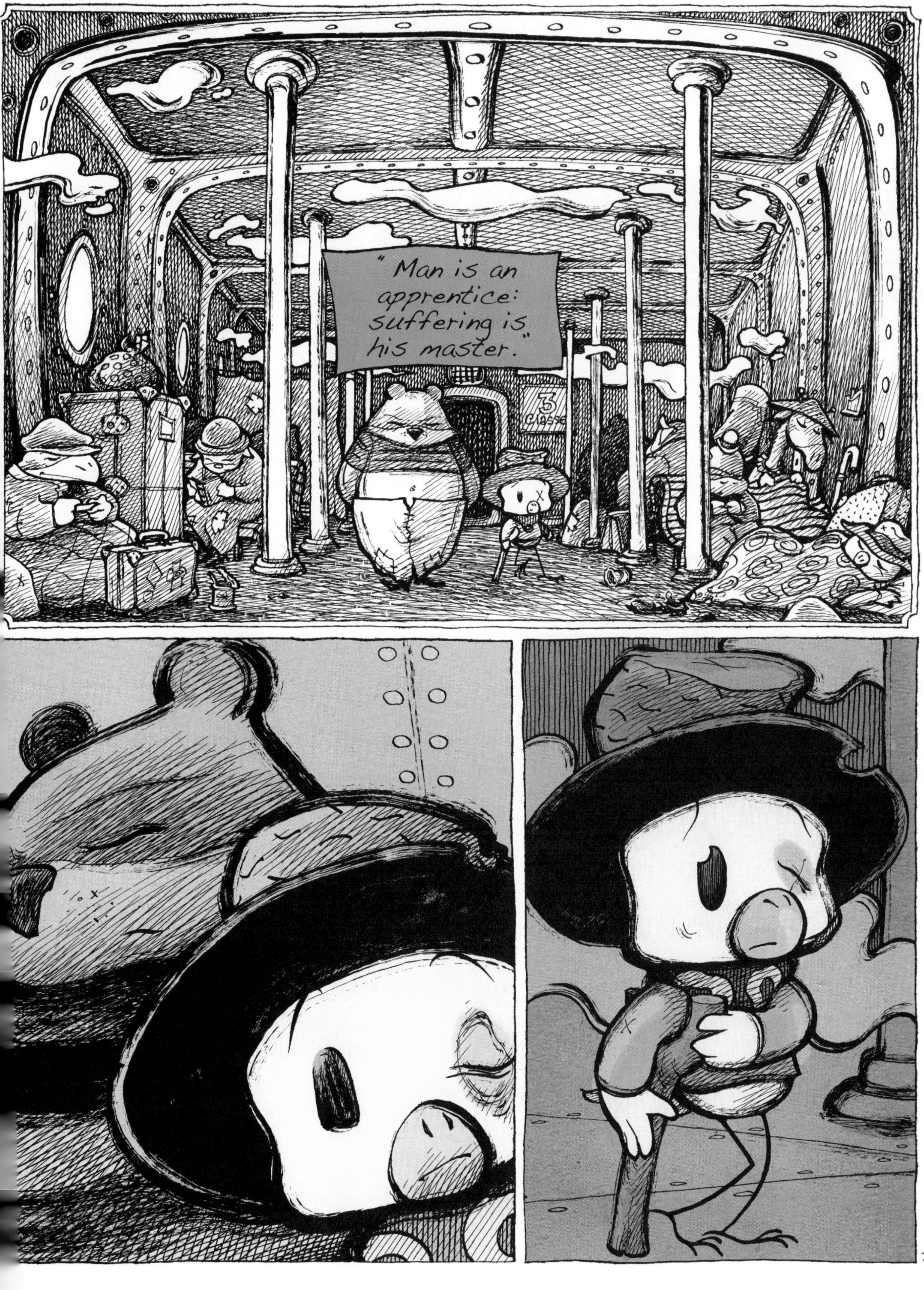
"Man is an apprentice: suffering is his master."
3 Classe

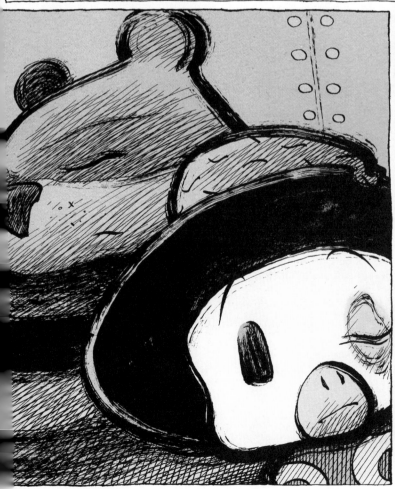

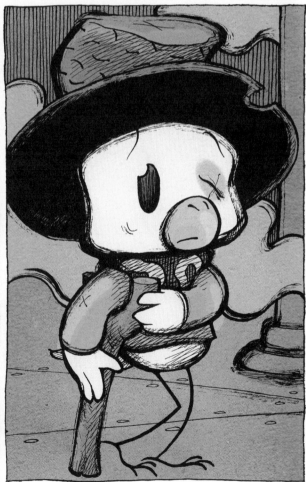

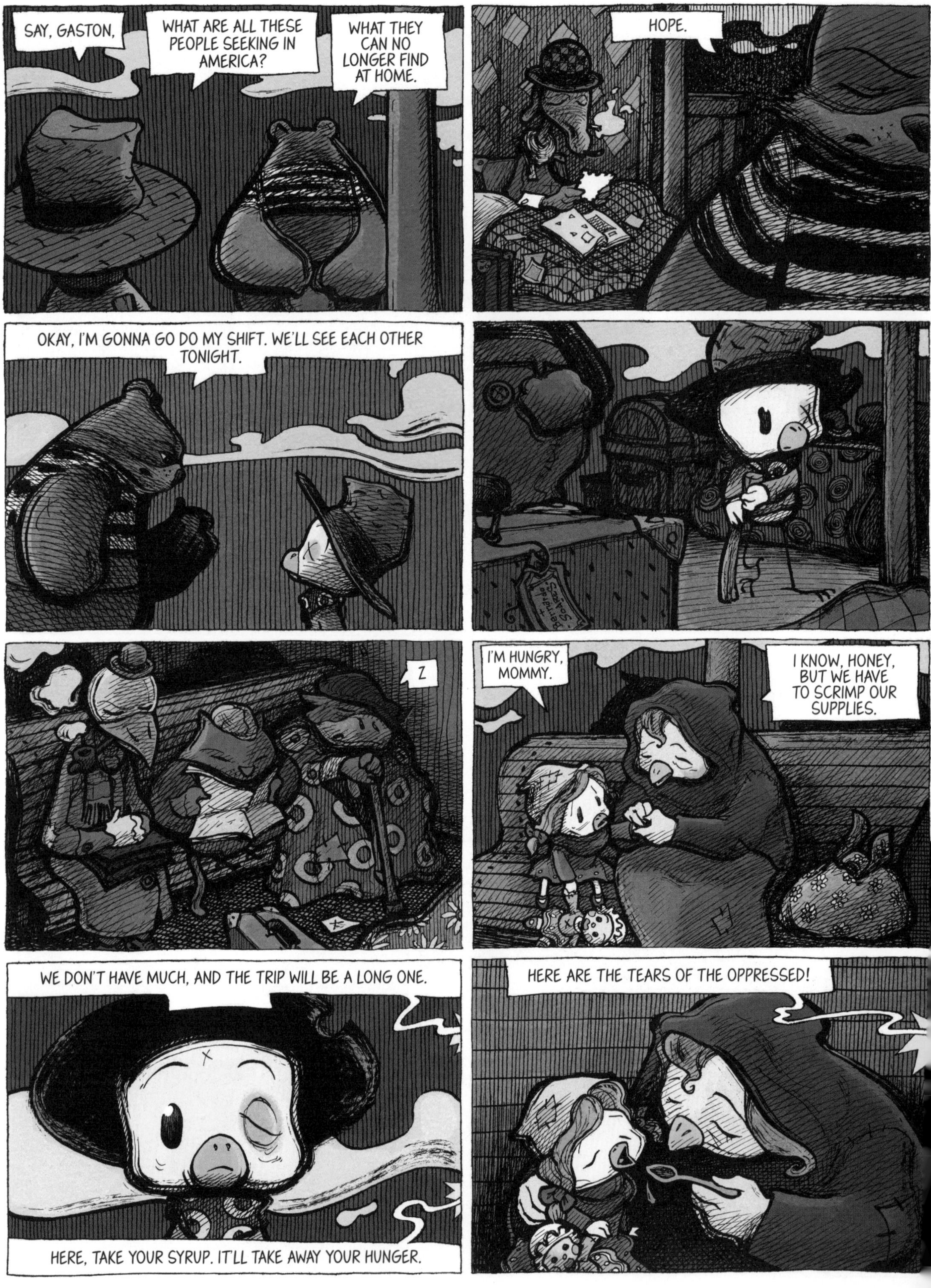
SAY, GASTON,
WHAT ARE ALL THESE PEOPLE SEEKING IN AMERICA?
WHAT THEY CAN NO LONGER FIND AT HOME.
HOPE.
OKAY, I'M GONNA GO DO MY SHIFT. WE'LL SEE EACH OTHER TONIGHT.
Z
I'M HUNGRY, MOMMY.
I KNOW, HONEY, BUT WE HAVE TO SCRIMP OUR SUPPLIES.
WE DON'T HAVE MUCH, AND THE TRIP WILL BE A LONG ONE.
HERE, TAKE YOUR SYRUP. IT'LL TAKE AWAY YOUR HUNGER.
HERE ARE THE TEARS OF THE OPPRESSED!

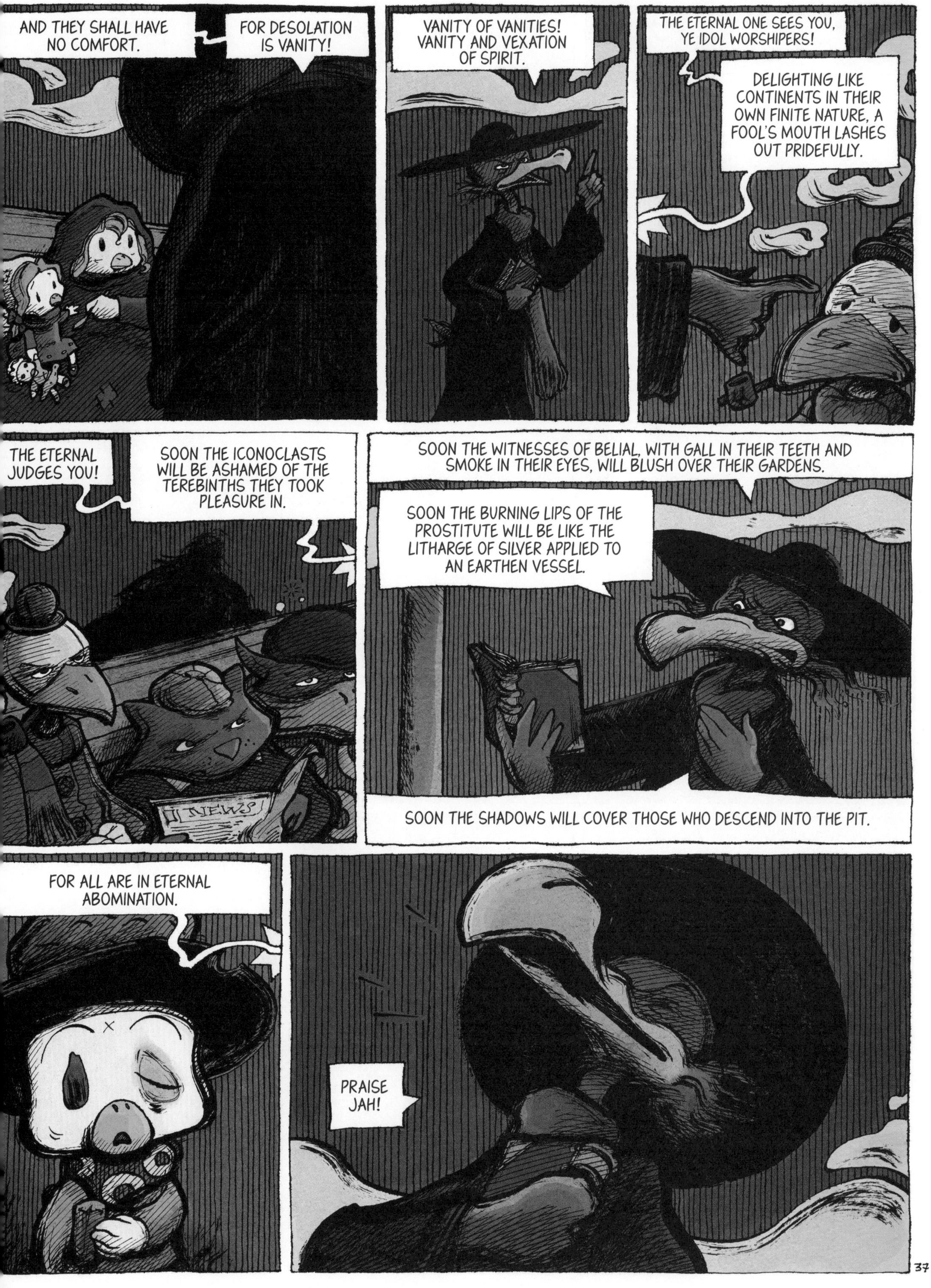

AND THEY SHALL HAVE NO COMFORT.
FOR DESOLATION IS VANITY!
VANITY OF VANITIES! VANITY AND VEXATION OF SPIRIT.
THE ETERNAL ONE SEES YOU, YE IDOL WORSHIPERS!
DELIGHTING LIKE CONTINENTS IN THEIR OWN FINITE NATURE, A FOOL'S MOUTH LASHES OUT PRIDEFULLY.
THE ETERNAL JUDGES YOU!
SOON THE ICONOCLASTS WILL BE ASHAMED OF THE TEREBINTHS THEY TOOK PLEASURE IN.
NEWS
SOON THE WITNESSES OF BELIAL, WITH GALL IN THEIR TEETH AND SMOKE IN THEIR EYES, WILL BLUSH OVER THEIR GARDENS.
SOON THE BURNING LIPS OF THE PROSTITUTE WILL BE LIKE THE LITHARGE OF SILVER APPLIED TO AN EARTHEN VESSEL.
SOON THE SHADOWS WILL COVER THOSE WHO DESCEND INTO THE PIT.
FOR ALL ARE IN ETERNAL ABOMINATION.
PRAISE JAH!
37

BEWARE THE PERNICIOUS TONGUE AND THE LIPS OF INIQUITY! THEY ARE THE ROT OF OVERLY FAT BONES.

AND ENTER NOT INTO THE FIELD OF ORPHANS! FOR THE DEAD FLIES CAUSE THE PERFUMER'S OIL TO FERMENT.

FAITH ALONE SAVES! IT IS THE PATH OF THE MAYBE, WHICH DEATH DOES NOT EXPLOIT.

SO PRAISE JAH AND REPENT, IMPIOUS FAUNA!

THIS VOYAGE IS YOUR FINAL VOYAGE! IT LEADS TO SHEOL AND TO THE ABYSS.

TOMORROW, HERETIC MULTITUDE, YOU WILL RETURN TO THE MIRE. FOR WHAT HAPPENS TO THE BEASTS, HAPPENS TO THE CHILDREN OF MEN. DUST TO DUST.

ASHES TO ASHES.

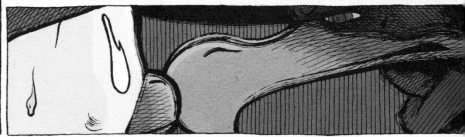

WHOEVER INCREASES HIS KNOWLEDGE INCREASES HIS SUFFERING.

TSSS, CRAZY, OLD FOOL.

COUGH! COUGH!

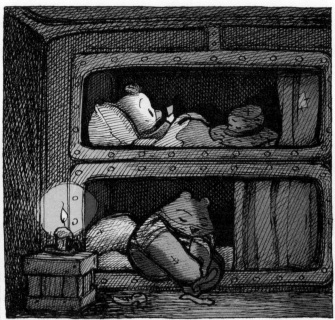

"Anguish is the fundamental disposition that makes us face the void."

SAY, GASTON,

WHERE DO PEOPLE GO WHEN THEY DIE?

TO THE CEMETERY, WHERE DO YOU SUPPOSE?

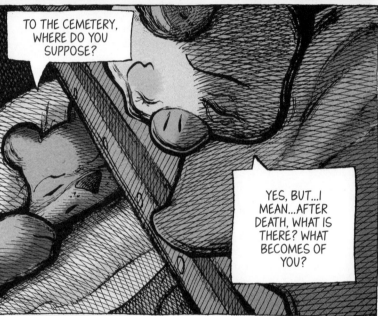

YES, BUT...I MEAN...AFTER DEATH, WHAT IS THERE? WHAT BECOMES OF YOU?

AFTER? NOTHING. YOU BECOME NOTHING. IT'S ALL OVER.

YOU ROT. YOU ROT AND YOU DISAPPEAR TO MAKE ROOM FOR OTHER PEOPLE.

ALL RIGHT. GOODNIGHT.

GOOD-NIGHT.

39

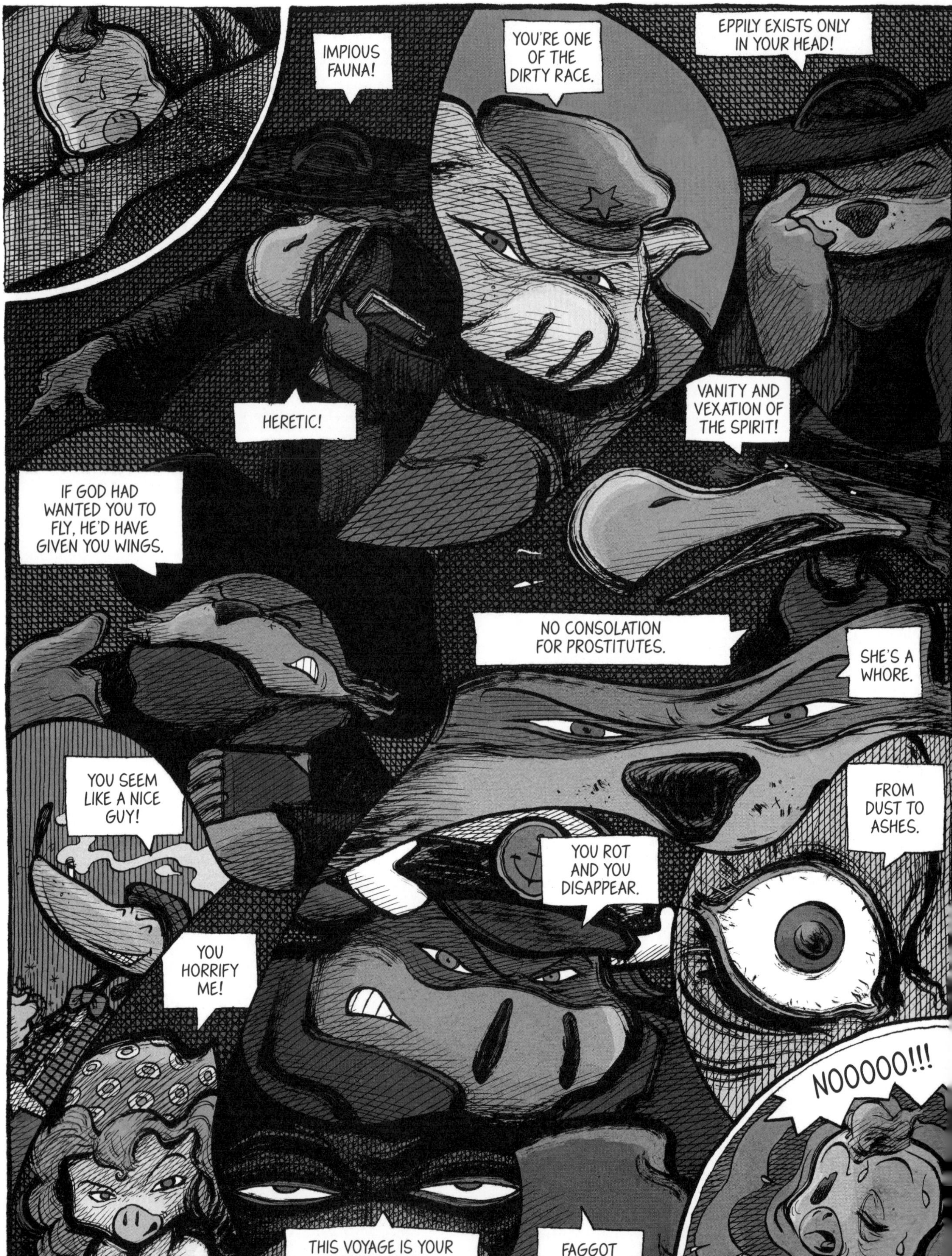
IMPIOUS FAUNA!
YOU'RE ONE OF THE DIRTY RACE.
EPPILY EXISTS ONLY IN YOUR HEAD!
HERETIC!
VANITY AND VEXATION OF THE SPIRIT!
IF GOD HAD WANTED YOU TO FLY, HE'D HAVE GIVEN YOU WINGS.
NO CONSOLATION FOR PROSTITUTES.
SHE'S A WHORE.
YOU SEEM LIKE A NICE GUY!
FROM DUST TO ASHES.
YOU ROT AND YOU DISAPPEAR.
YOU HORRIFY ME!
NOOOOO!!!
THIS VOYAGE IS YOUR LAST VOYAGE!
FAGGOT UNBELIEVER!

HEY, CHECK OUT THAT ONE.

AMPLE CLEAVAGE AND A PRETTY LITTLE ASS WRAPPED IN TAFFETA. JUST WHAT I LIKE.

YES, NICE.

YOU GOTTA ADMIT WE'RE LUCKY

WE WORK OUTDOORS, SURROUNDED BY PRETTY WOMEN.

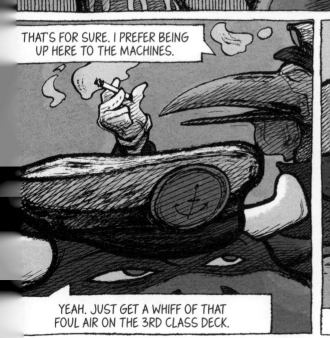

THAT'S FOR SURE. I PREFER BEING UP HERE TO THE MACHINES.

YEAH. JUST GET A WHIFF OF THAT FOUL AIR ON THE 3RD CLASS DECK.

WE'VE BEEN GONE TWO WEEKS. YOU CAN IMAGINE HOW IT STINKS DOWN THERE.

IT REEKS OF ROT, HUMIDITY, VERMIN, AND SWEAT.

THE STENCH'D MAKE YOU PUKE.

THE STENCH'D MAKE YOU COME DOWN WITH A SICKNESS.

41

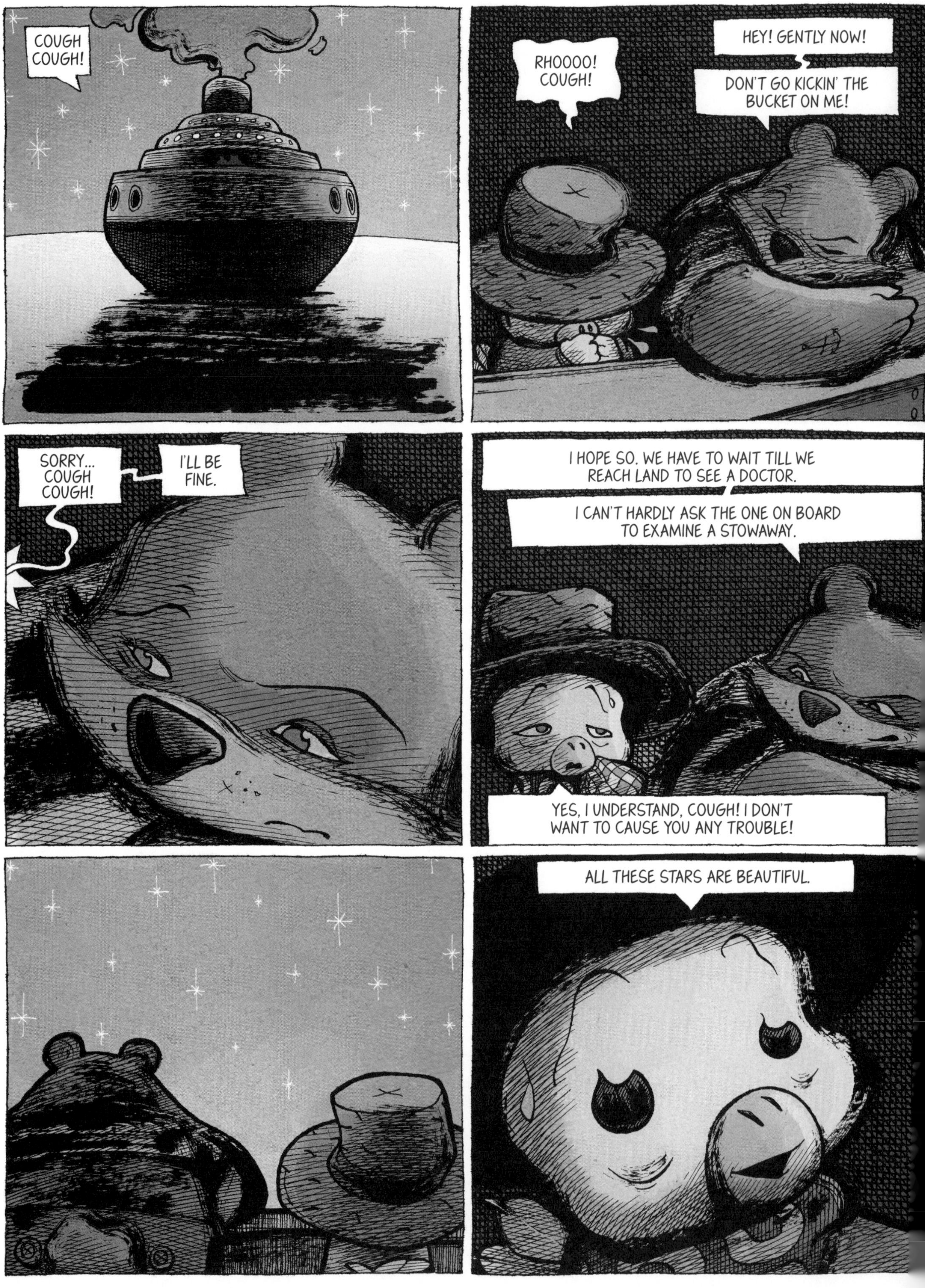
COUGH COUGH!
RHOOOO! COUGH!
HEY! GENTLY NOW!
DON'T GO KICKIN' THE BUCKET ON ME!
SORRY... COUGH COUGH!
I'LL BE FINE.
I HOPE SO. WE HAVE TO WAIT TILL WE REACH LAND TO SEE A DOCTOR.
I CAN'T HARDLY ASK THE ONE ON BOARD TO EXAMINE A STOWAWAY.
YES, I UNDERSTAND, COUGH! I DON'T WANT TO CAUSE YOU ANY TROUBLE!
ALL THESE STARS ARE BEAUTIFUL.

YEAH, THE NIGHTS WOULD BE SAD IF EVER THERE WEREN'T ANY MORE OF THEM.

THEN IT'S ALL THE BETTER IF I DON'T MANAGE TO GATHER ANY.

BAH, ONE OR TWO WON'T MAKE A DIFFERENCE.

THERE ARE MORE STARS THAN FISH IN THE SEA. YOU COULD FILL BOATS FULL OF THEM, AND THERE'D STILL BE BILLIONS LEFT.

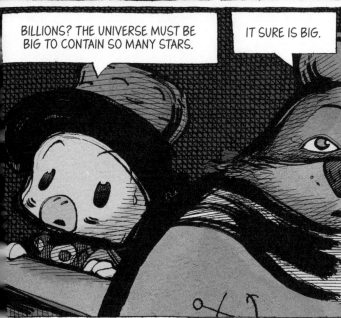

BILLIONS? THE UNIVERSE MUST BE BIG TO CONTAIN SO MANY STARS.

IT SURE IS BIG.

AS BIG AS THE SEA?

BIGGER EVEN. INFINITE!

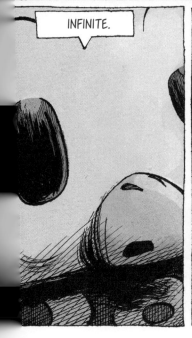

INFINITE.

YEAH, LIKE A HOLE THAT HAS NEITHER AN EDGE NOR A BOTTOM.

A HOLE DARK AND COLD LIKE THE OCEAN.

43

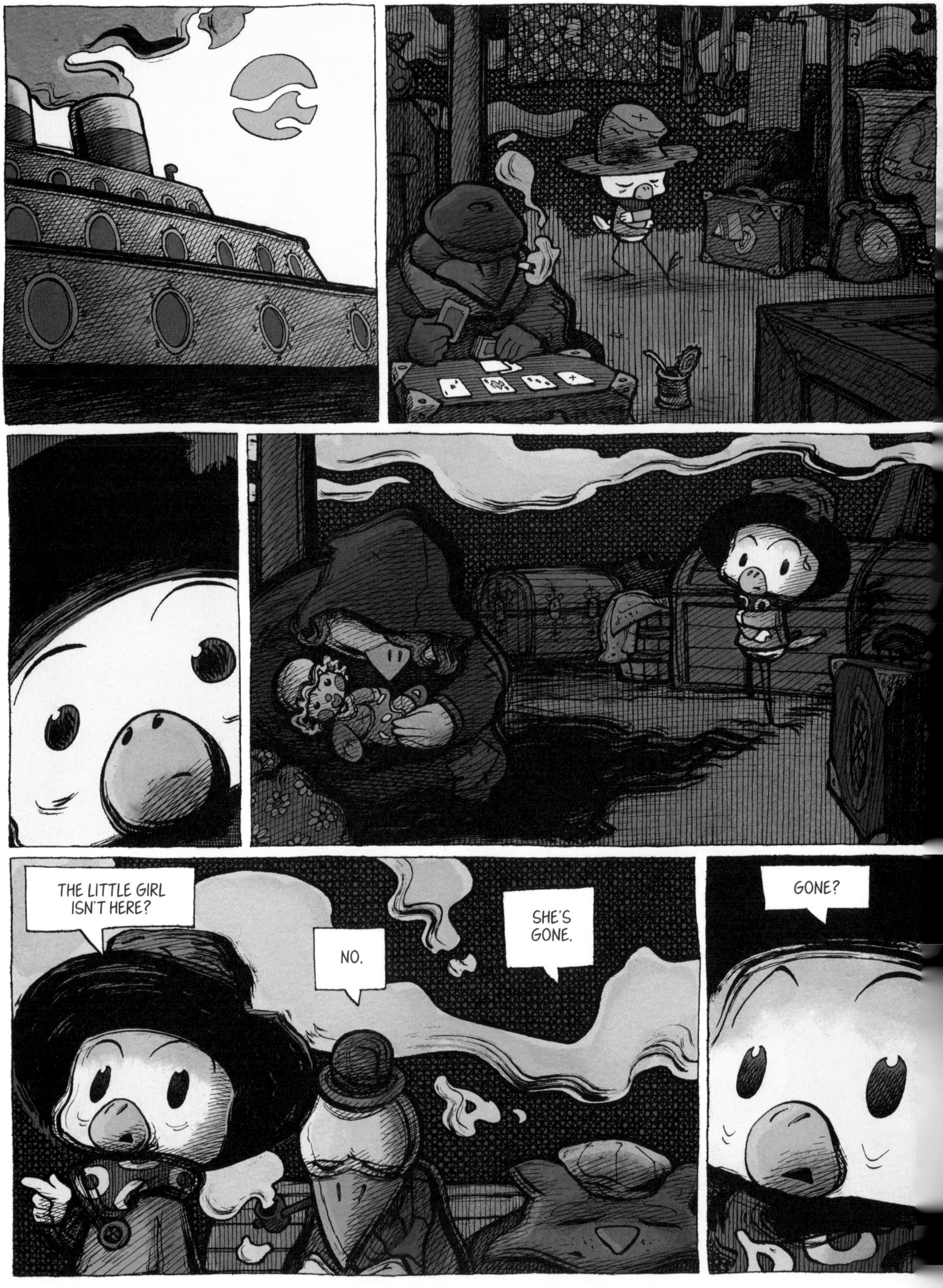
THE LITTLE GIRL ISN'T HERE?
NO.
SHE'S GONE.
GONE?

THISH MORNING.

A FEVER GOT HER.

THE DOCTOR COULDN'T DO ANYTHING FOR HER. DEATH WAS ALREADY THERE. YOU COULD SMELL IT ON THE GIRL'S BREATH.

POOR KID, SHE WAS TOO WEAK TO REZHISHT. SHE DIDN'T EAT ENOUGH.

SHE DIED QUIETLY, JUST LIKE A CANDLE GOING OUT.

TWO CREWMEN CARRIED HER AWAY.

THEY CASHT HER INTO THE DEPTHSH OF THE SHEA! WITH ALL HER CLOTHESZH!

BECAUSE SHE DIED FROM A SICKNESS.

THE CAPTAIN WAS AFRAID OF CONTAGION.

AND YOU GOTTA UNDERSTAND: FOLKS DON'T LIKE CORPSES ON BOARD.

AND SAILORS DO EVEN LESS.

IT BRINGS BAD LUCK! THEY SHAY. PUH! I'LL SHOW YOU BAD LUCK!

ANYHOW, THEY WOULDN'T HAVE LET HER DISEMBARK IN AMERICA.

NEITHER SHICK NOR DEAD! THEY SHAY. THEY ONLY WANT PEOPLE IN GOOD HEALTH.

ALL OF IT'S SAD. REALLY SAD. SHE WAS SO CUTE.

WELL, AT LEAST SHE'S NO LONGER SUFFERING.

YEAH, HER MOTHER, ON THE OTHER HAND...

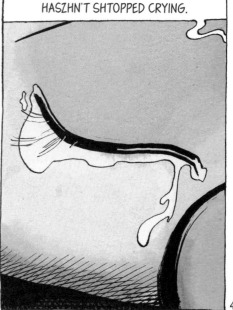

HASZHN'T SHTOPPED CRYING.

45

111

IT'S BETTER IF SHE CRIES. IT'LL DO HER GOOD. IT'S THE BEST WAY TO DROWN HER GRIEF.

YEAH, I'M MORE OF THE IMPRESSION SHE'S GONNA DROWN HERSHELF IN HER DESHPAIR.

WHAT IS "DESHPAIR."

I DIDN'T SHAY "DESHPAIR," I SHAID "DESHPAIR." LIKE IN THE ESHPRESSION: "ASZH LONG ASZH THERE'SZH LIFE, THERE'SZH DESHPAIR."

DESPAIR'S WHEN NOTHING'S IMPORTANT ANYMORE.

IT'S WHEN YOU FIGURE OUT THAT EVERY FINE AND BEAUTIFUL THING YOU EXPECTED IN YOUR EXISTENCE WILL NEVER COME TO PASS.

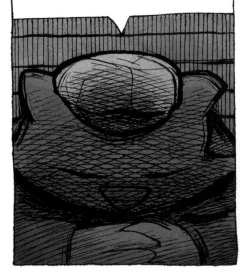

DESPAIR'S WHEN THE BRIGHT PROMISES OF THE FUTURE BECOME THE ILLUSIONS OF THE PAST.

DESHPAIR ISH WHEN YOU TELL YOURSHELF THAT THE FUTURE...

...AIN'T WHAT IT USHED TO BE.

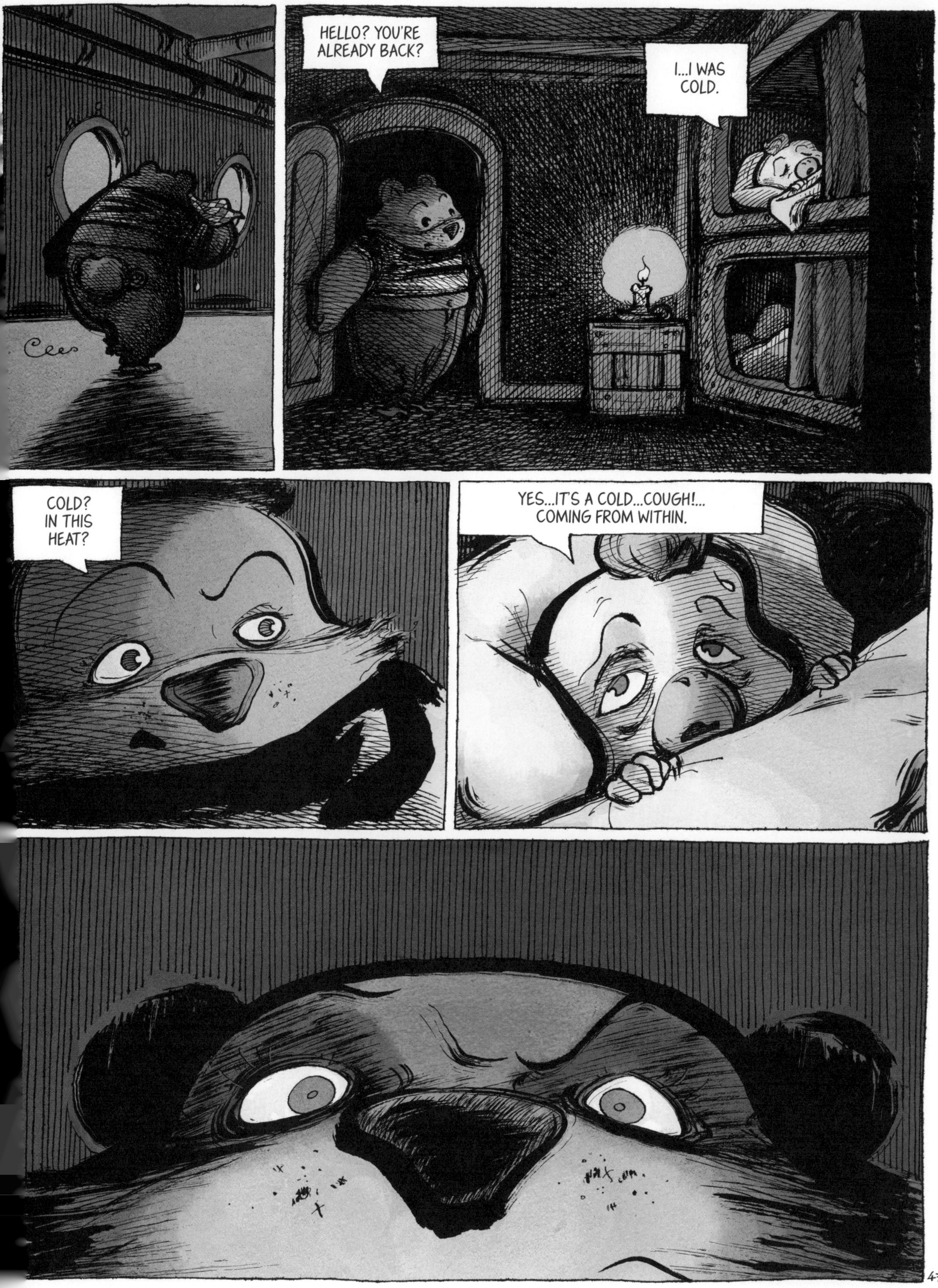

HELLO? YOU'RE ALREADY BACK?
I...I WAS COLD.
COLD? IN THIS HEAT?
YES...IT'S A COLD...COUGH!... COMING FROM WITHIN.

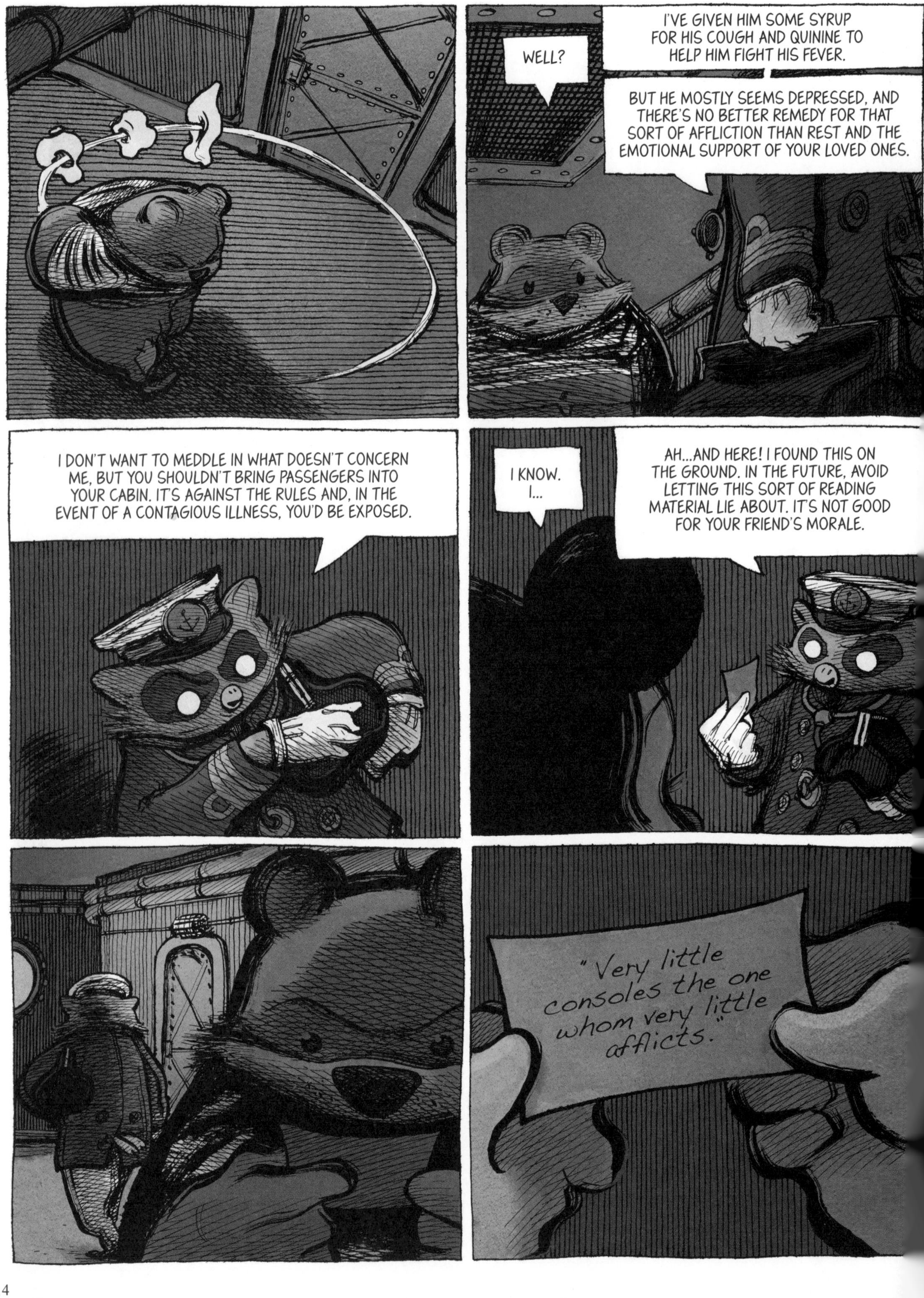
WELL?
I'VE GIVEN HIM SOME SYRUP FOR HIS COUGH AND QUININE TO HELP HIM FIGHT HIS FEVER.
BUT HE MOSTLY SEEMS DEPRESSED, AND THERE'S NO BETTER REMEDY FOR THAT SORT OF AFFLICTION THAN REST AND THE EMOTIONAL SUPPORT OF YOUR LOVED ONES.
I DON'T WANT TO MEDDLE IN WHAT DOESN'T CONCERN ME, BUT YOU SHOULDN'T BRING PASSENGERS INTO YOUR CABIN. IT'S AGAINST THE RULES AND, IN THE EVENT OF A CONTAGIOUS ILLNESS, YOU'D BE EXPOSED.
I KNOW. I...
AH...AND HERE! I FOUND THIS ON THE GROUND. IN THE FUTURE, AVOID LETTING THIS SORT OF READING MATERIAL LIE ABOUT. IT'S NOT GOOD FOR YOUR FRIEND'S MORALE.
"Very little consoles the one whom very little afflicts."

ABELARD.

YES?

I THOUGHT MORE ABOUT THE QUESTION YOU ASKED ME ABOUT DEATH, WHAT THERE IS AFTERWARDS, AND ALL.

AH?

YEAH. WELL, AFTER MY DEATH, I THINK THAT...NO...I'M SURE... THERE'S STILL LIFE.

REALLY? BUT YOU SAID...

I WAS TALKING B.S.! I SPOKE WITHOUT KNOWING.

SO, I THOUGHT ABOUT IT, I'M TELLING YOU.

SO LISTEN, SEE?

IN LIFE, THERE'S LIVING. DO YOU AGREE WITH THAT?

UH, WELL, YES.

AND IN DEATH, THERE'S DYING.

OF COURSE.

BUT IN LIFE, THERE'S ALSO DYING. OTHERWISE PEOPLE WOULDN'T DIE.

THAT'S TRUE.

IT'S INEVITABLE, THEN: THERE IS ALSO LIFE IN DEATH.

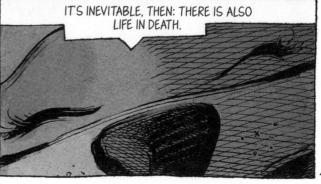

49

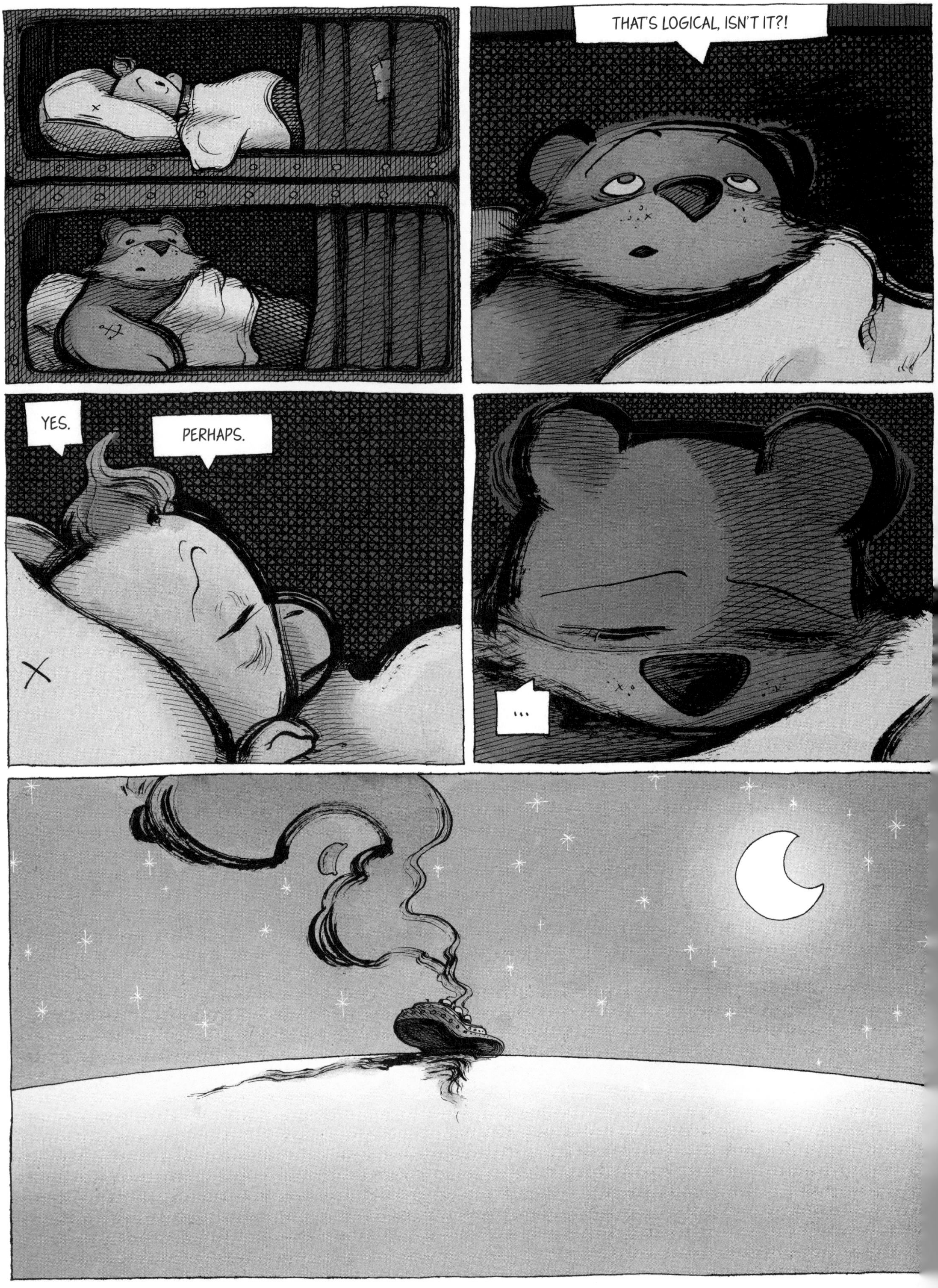
THAT'S LOGICAL, ISN'T IT?!
YES.
PERHAPS.
...

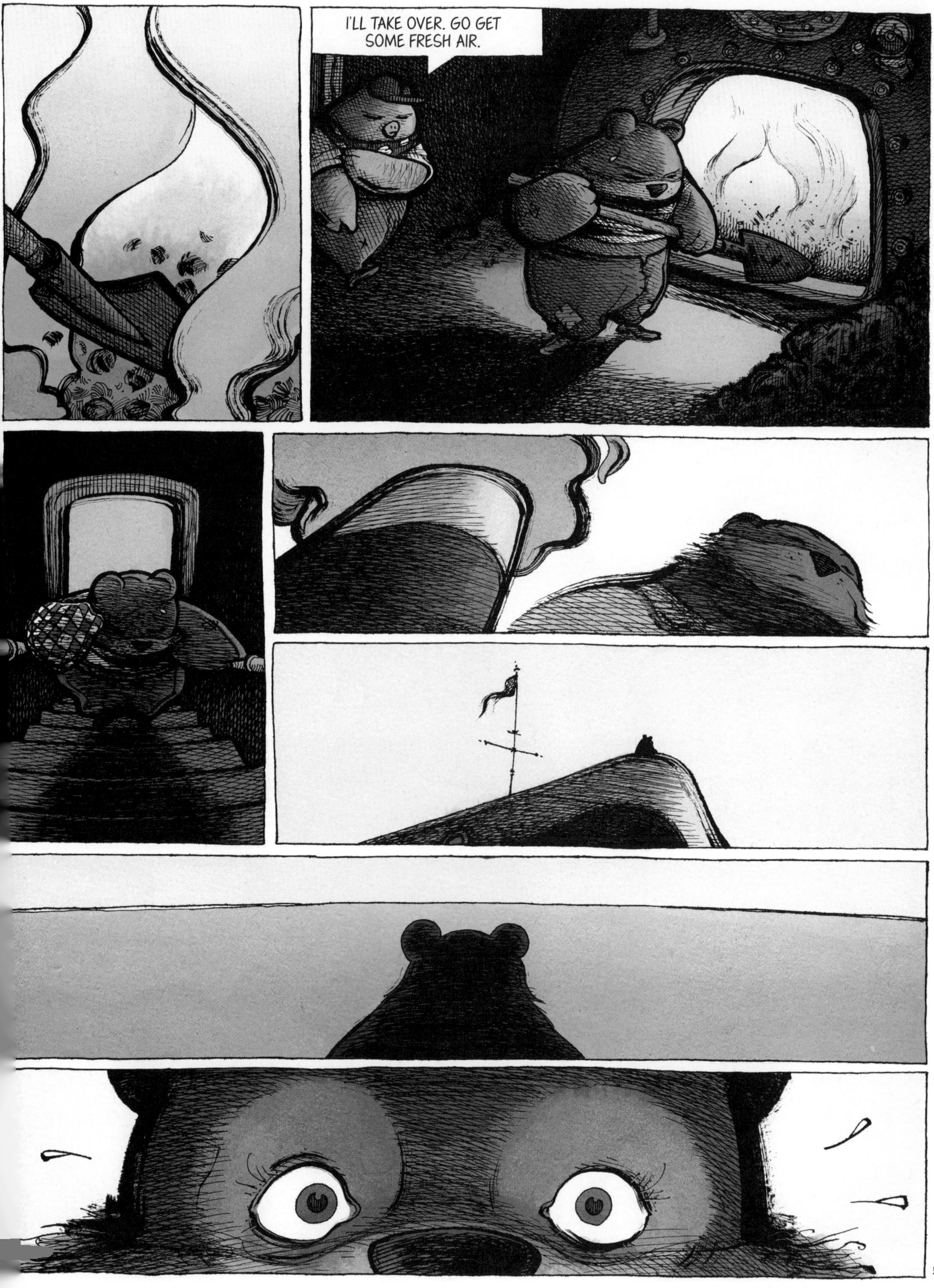
I'LL TAKE OVER. GO GET SOME FRESH AIR.

51

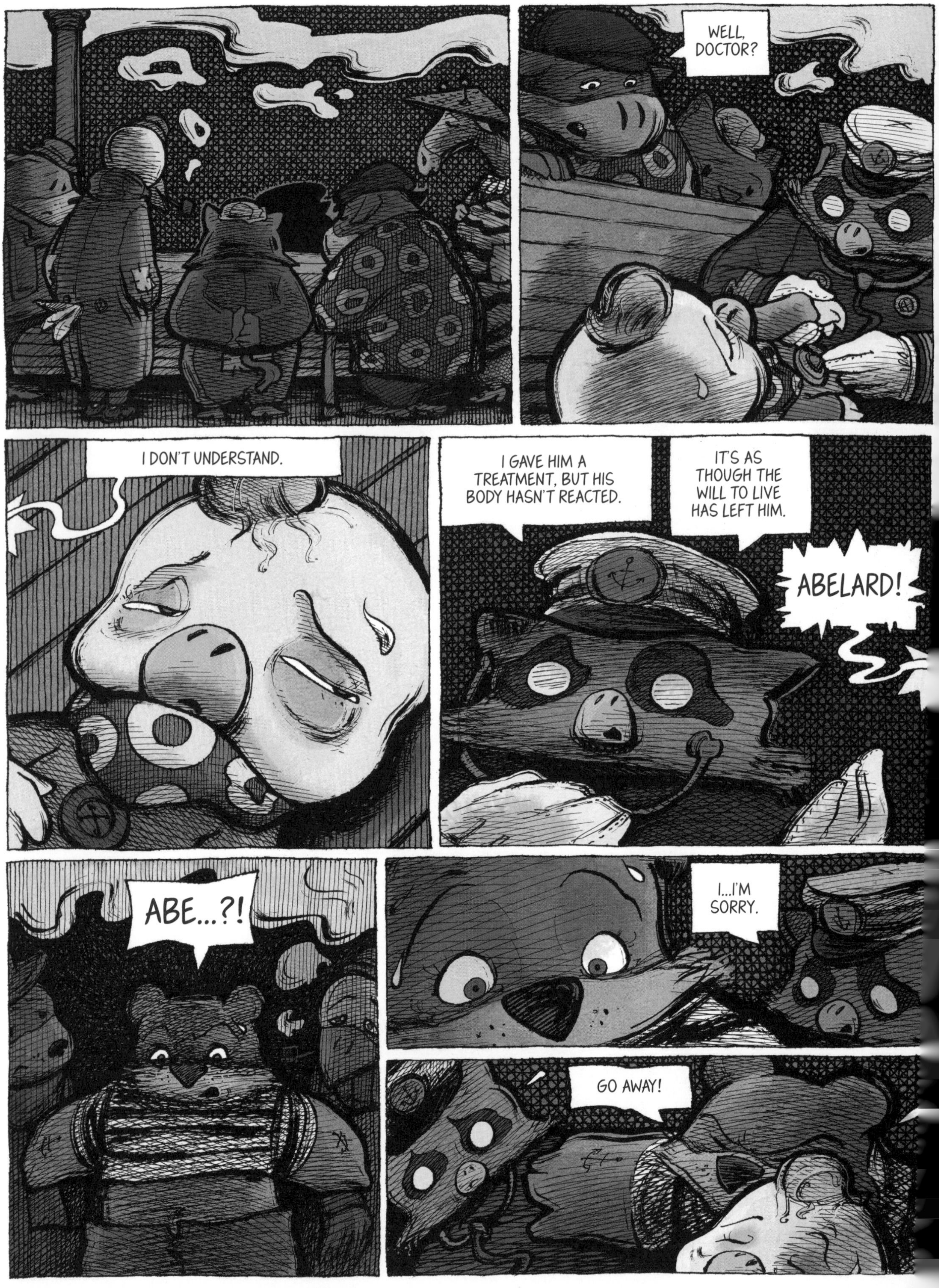
WELL, DOCTOR?
I DON'T UNDERSTAND.
I GAVE HIM A TREATMENT, BUT HIS BODY HASN'T REACTED.
IT'S AS THOUGH THE WILL TO LIVE HAS LEFT HIM.
ABELARD!
ABE...?!
I...I'M SORRY.
GO AWAY!

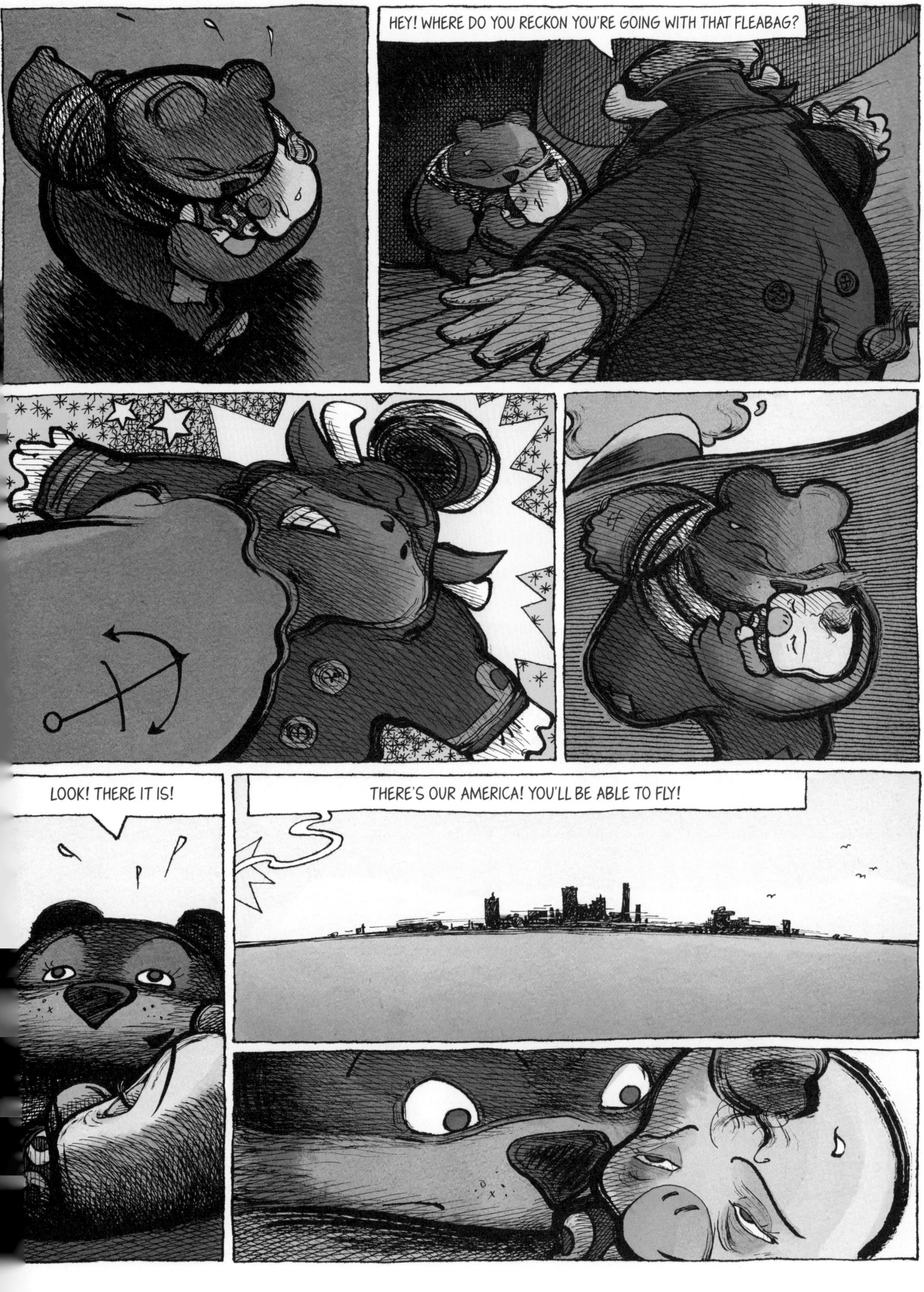
HEY! WHERE DO YOU RECKON YOU'RE GOING WITH THAT FLEABAG?
LOOK! THERE IT IS!
THERE'S OUR AMERICA! YOU'LL BE ABLE TO FLY!
53

COME ON! SAY SOMETHING!

WE MADE IT! WE'RE THERE!

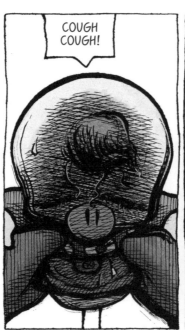

COUGH COUGH!

DON'T LET THEM...THROW ME IN THE SEA.

WHAT?! BUT NO...NO!

YOU'RE NOT GONNA DIE, YA HEAR!!! YOU JUST CAN'T!

NOT LIKE THIS! NOT NOW! NOT WITHOUT SETTING YOUR DAMNED SPARROW FEET ON THIS BLASTED CONTINENT!

NOT IN THE SEA, GASTON.

I'M SO AFRAID OF BEING COLD.

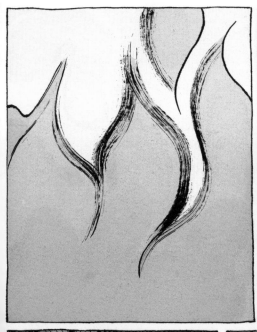
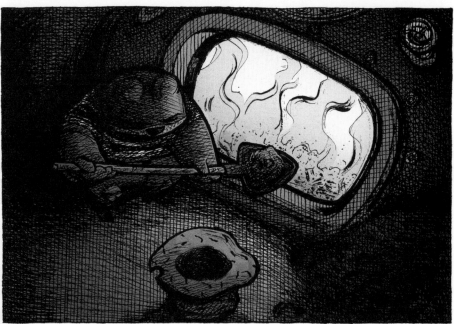

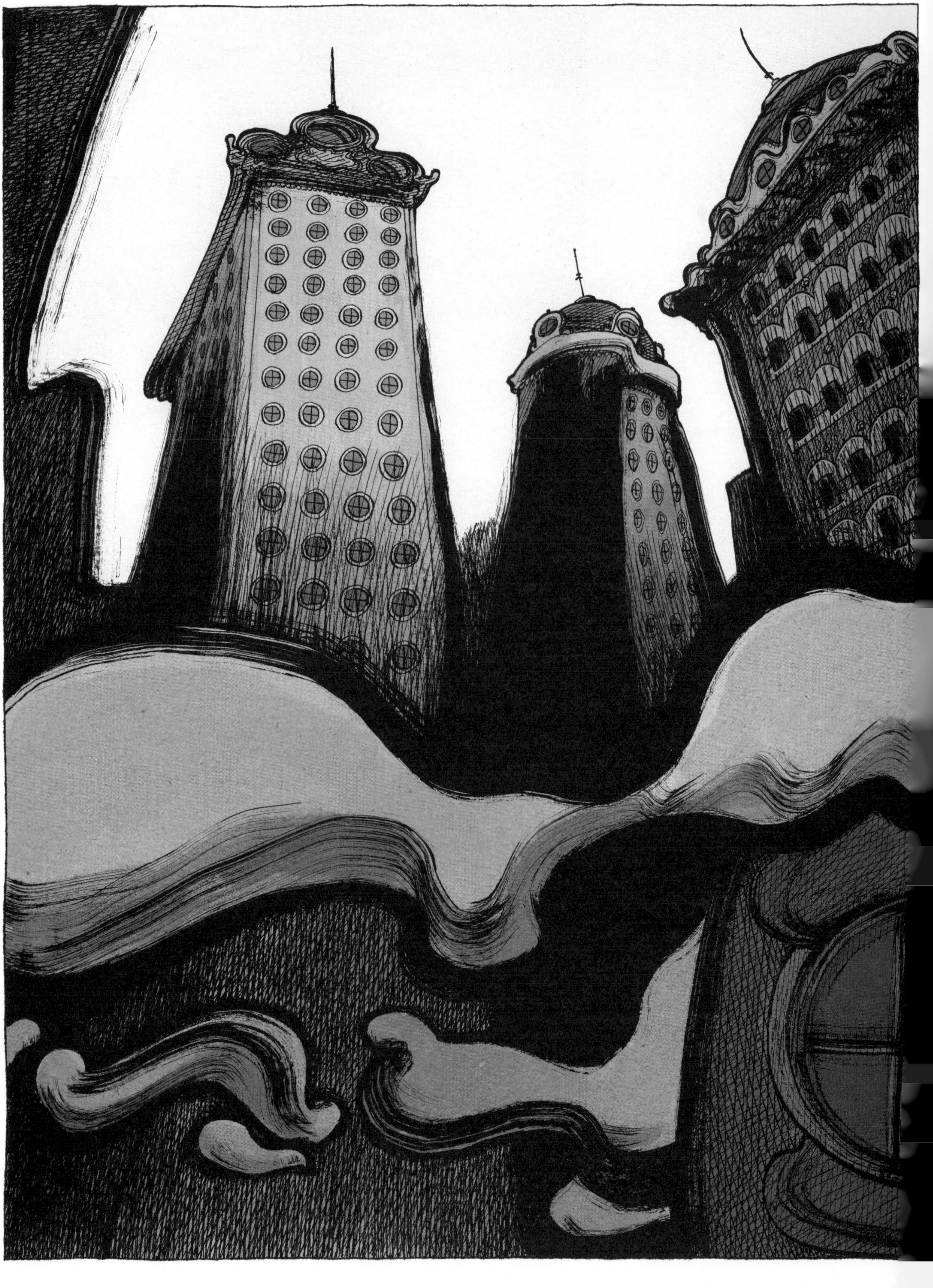

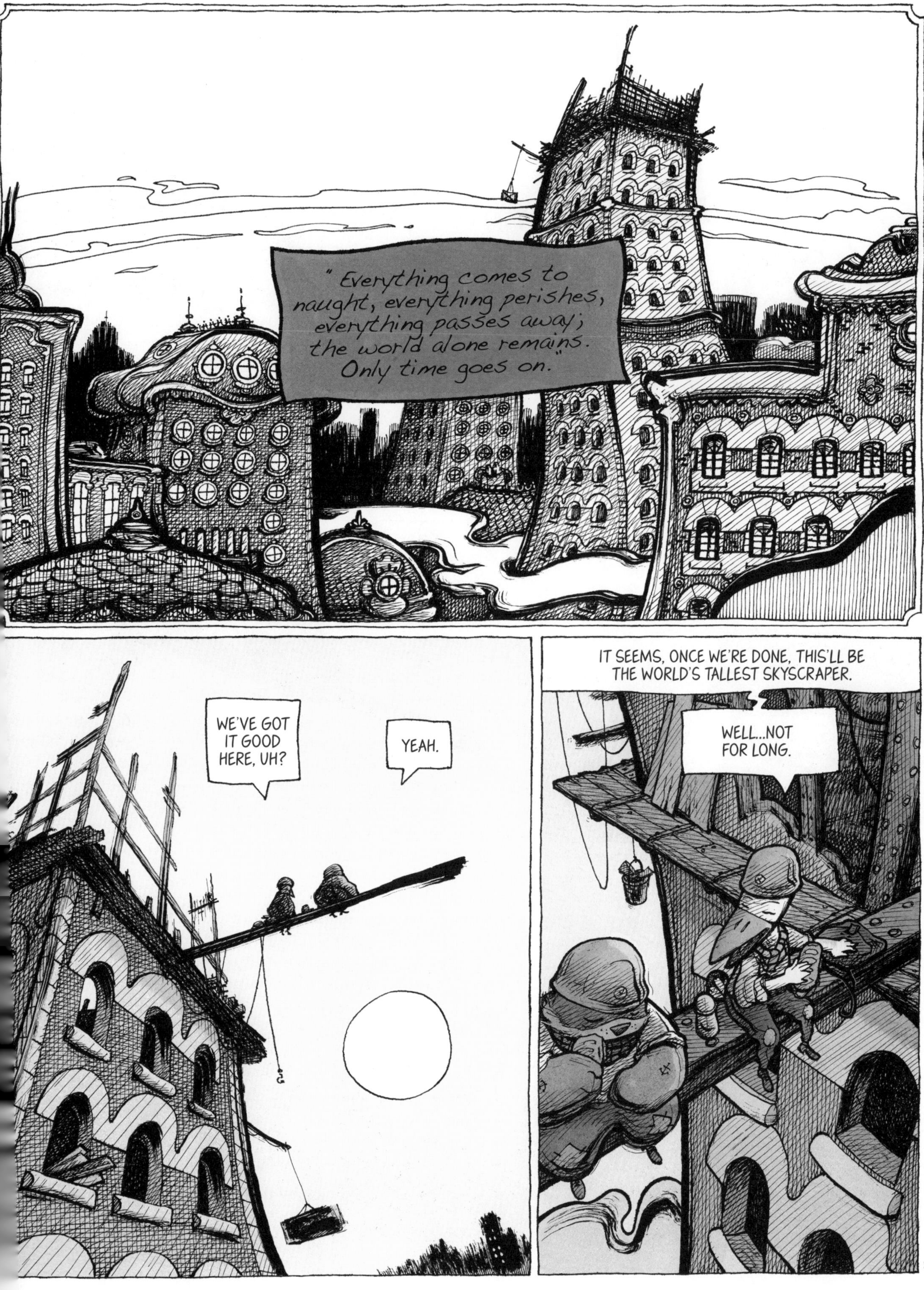
"Everything comes to naught, everything perishes, everything passes away; the world alone remains. Only time goes on."
WE'VE GOT IT GOOD HERE, UH?
YEAH.
IT SEEMS, ONCE WE'RE DONE, THIS'LL BE THE WORLD'S TALLEST SKYSCRAPER.
WELL...NOT FOR LONG.
57

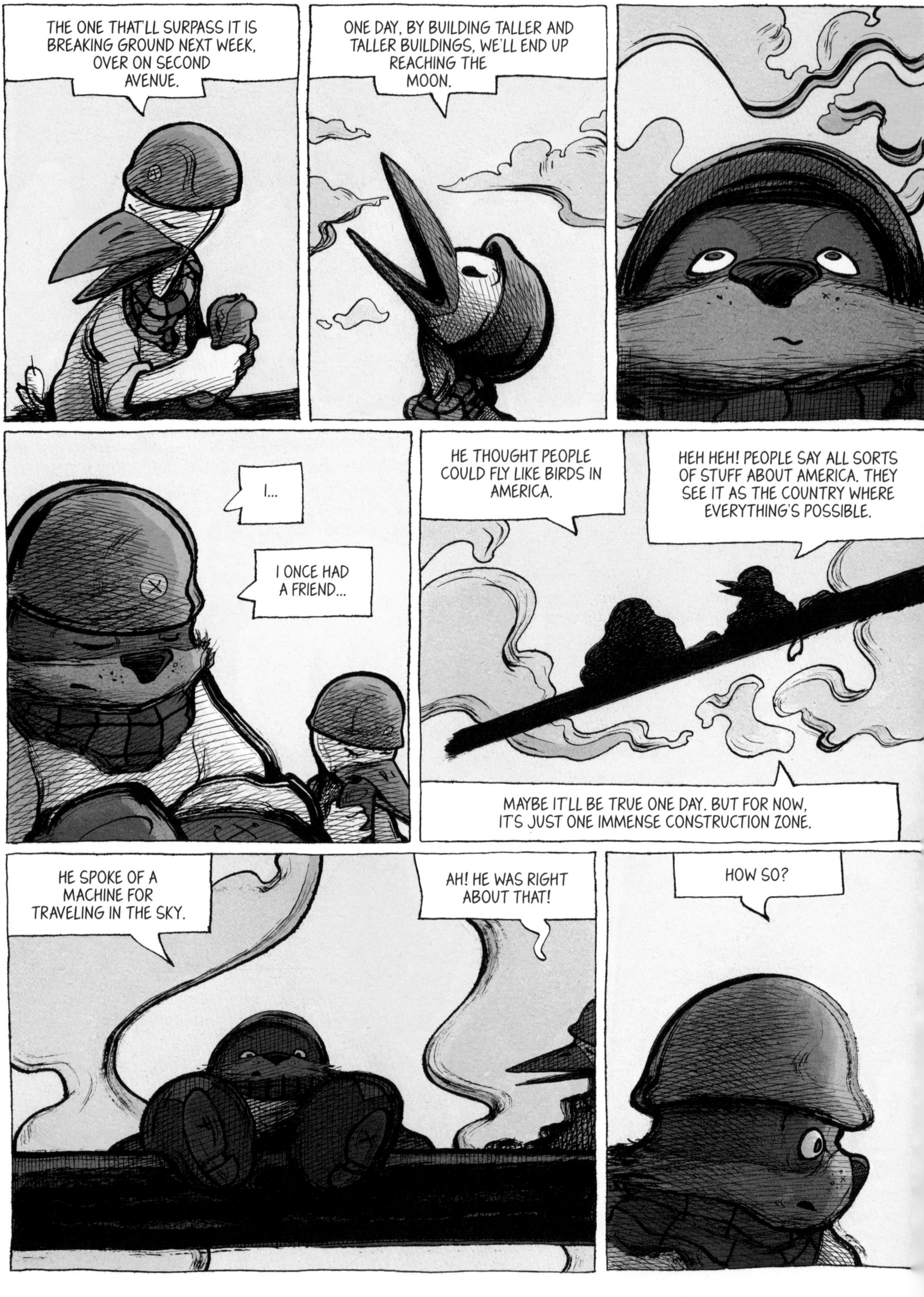
THE ONE THAT'LL SURPASS IT IS BREAKING GROUND NEXT WEEK, OVER ON SECOND AVENUE.
ONE DAY, BY BUILDING TALLER AND TALLER BUILDINGS, WE'LL END UP REACHING THE MOON.
I...
I ONCE HAD A FRIEND...
HE THOUGHT PEOPLE COULD FLY LIKE BIRDS IN AMERICA.
HEH HEH! PEOPLE SAY ALL SORTS OF STUFF ABOUT AMERICA. THEY SEE IT AS THE COUNTRY WHERE EVERYTHING'S POSSIBLE.
MAYBE IT'LL BE TRUE ONE DAY. BUT FOR NOW, IT'S JUST ONE IMMENSE CONSTRUCTION ZONE.
HE SPOKE OF A MACHINE FOR TRAVELING IN THE SKY.
AH! HE WAS RIGHT ABOUT THAT!
HOW SO?

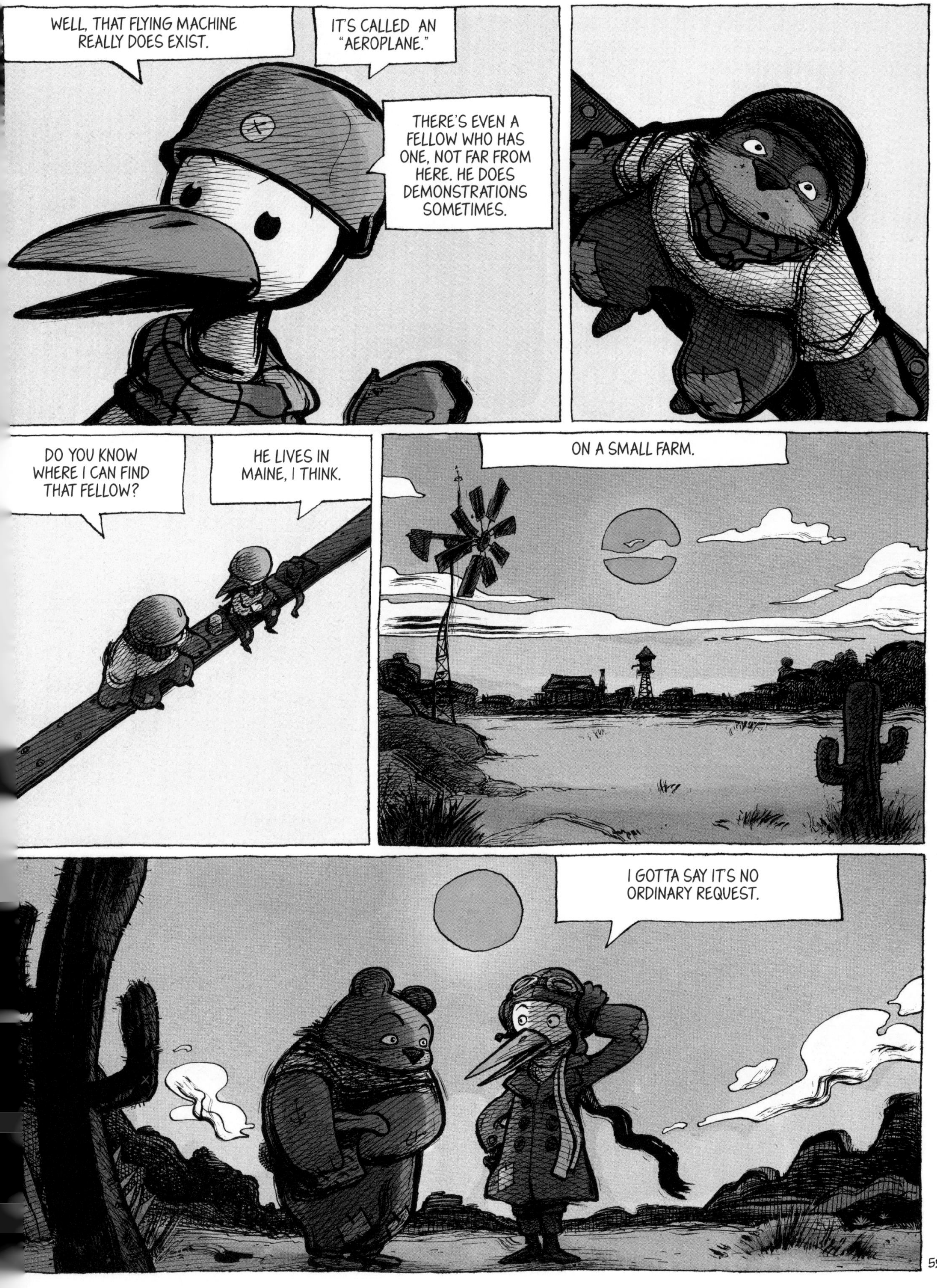
WELL, THAT FLYING MACHINE REALLY DOES EXIST.
IT'S CALLED AN "AEROPLANE."
THERE'S EVEN A FELLOW WHO HAS ONE, NOT FAR FROM HERE. HE DOES DEMONSTRATIONS SOMETIMES.
DO YOU KNOW WHERE I CAN FIND THAT FELLOW?
HE LIVES IN MAINE, I THINK.
ON A SMALL FARM.
I GOTTA SAY IT'S NO ORDINARY REQUEST.
59

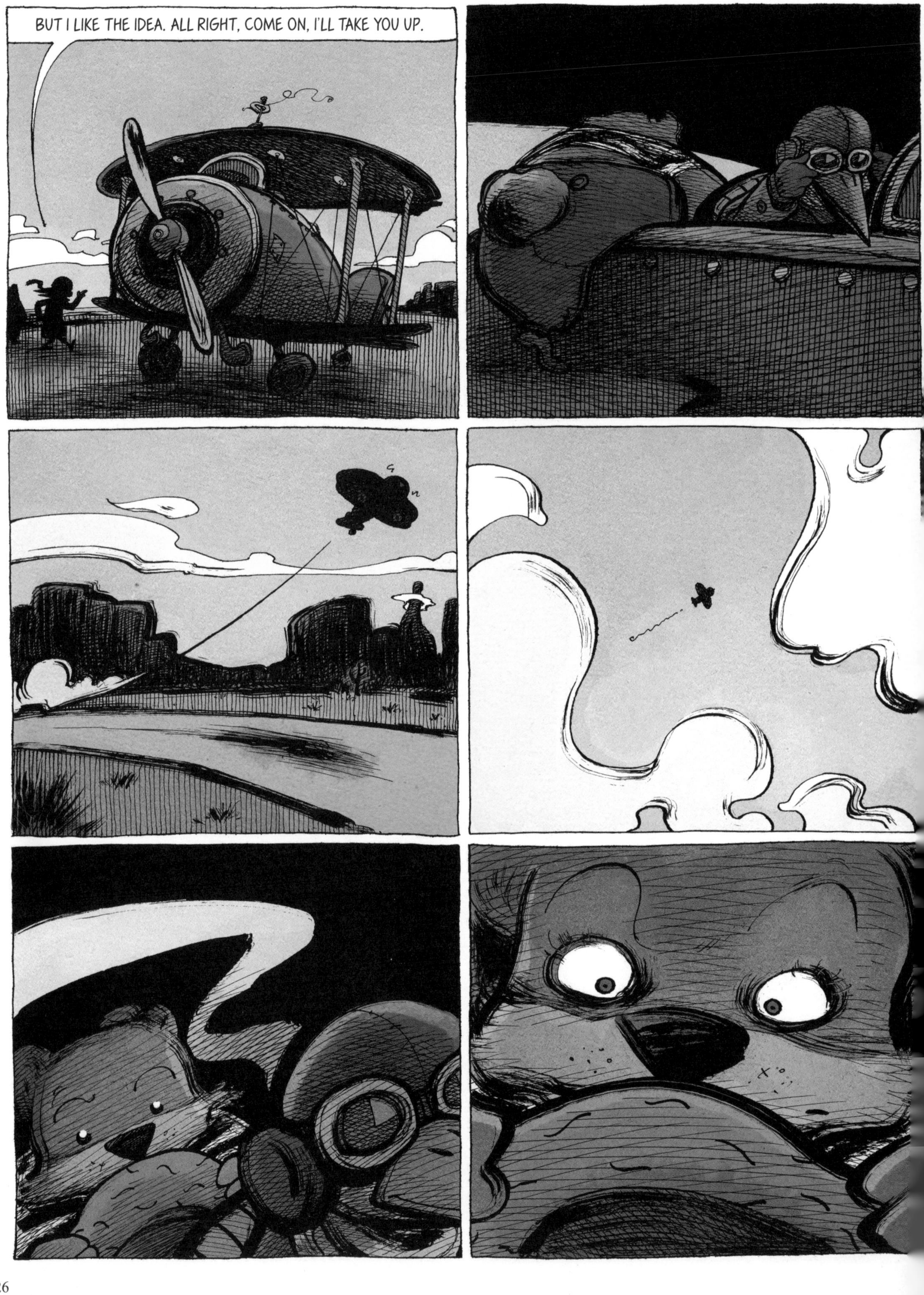
BUT I LIKE THE IDEA. ALL RIGHT, COME ON, I'LL TAKE YOU UP.

A TREASURY OF
American Prints

*A Selection of One Hundred Etchings and
Lithographs by the Foremost Living American Artists*

Edited by
THOMAS CRAVEN

SIMON AND SCHUSTER · NEW YORK

Published by Simon and Schuster, Inc.
386 Fourth Avenue, New York, N. Y.
Manufactured in the United States of America

*OPTAK *from the presses of* Edward Stern & Co., Inc., Philadelphia

*Reg. U. S. Pat. Off.

Introduction

by

THOMAS CRAVEN

One of the most conspicuous occurrences—and at the same time, one of the most important—in the whole field of contemporary expression is the rise of American art to a position of world-wide ascendancy. As historian and active participant in the development of this phenomenon, I can view the present situation with particular satisfaction. A battle has been waged and won, a decisive victory over provincial ignorance, anemic imitation, cheap internationalism, and the postwar hang-over of esthetic snobbery. Only the other day, it seems, our artists, or the dominating group of metropolitan painters, were ashamed of the American label, and opposed, with more vindictiveness than sense, to all efforts directed toward the formation of a native school. Today, save for a few feeble Marxians, and a handful of defeated purists who believe with Picasso that art is a species of vacuous dabbling removed from the pressures of time and place, there is not a self-respecting artist in this country who is not eager to contribute to a movement which has gained the sympathies and the support of the American public.

Never before has French pictorial stock stood so low: the succession of fancy cults emanating from the studios of Paris is dead and, for the most part, forgotten; and the abortions of surrealism—the culminating rot of European gadget makers—have found their proper level as eccentric window dressing for department stores. Never before has anything remotely approximating a popular art movement been seen in America. Schools and museums have multiplied at an amazing rate; universities vie with one another in the size, magnificence, and staffs of their art plants; every city and town has a band of exhibitors; magazines, good and bad, are filled with reproductions of pictures; every child is an artist and, I am sorry to say,

made conscious of the fact; and the number of printmakers is beyond calculation. Some of this is faddish and political; some is transitory and ill-considered; but at bottom, the movement testifies to an organic interest in the production and appreciation of art that cannot be suppressed.

The reasons for this astonishing efflorescence may be briefly enumerated. First, the natural reaction against the hollowness and over-refinement of the modern art of France, which, whatever its validity as an "old and urbane civilization," has no access to American psychology. Second, the organization, by the Federal government, of the art business into a national industry, a bureaucratic maneuver which, by subventions, competitions, and the disbursement of millions of dollars for the purposes of relief, has stimulated professional activity and enormously increased production by bringing into art, for the first time, the measures of pump-priming.

The administration of the Federal art industry has been attended by many evils. Amateurs, hopeless or immature, have been elevated into the ranks of the professionals; acres of walls have been smeared by would-be mural painters; and worst of all, politicians and scheming failures in art have worked hand and glove with the bureaucrats in order to legislate themselves into jobs. Let us take, for example, the amateur Communists and superannuated esthetes who have suddenly found it expedient to love their adopted country. These renegades, notorious in their contempt for everything native, are now whooping it up for American art, and endorsing, for personal gain, every move made by the officials at Washington. Some of them have painted, at Federal expense, large mural eyesores in which the prescribed subject matter has compelled them to reveal their ignorance of American life, and their incapacity in all forms of art not concerned with the sorting of cubes and triangles. When they try to depict an American cow, they contrive an abstraction, or a bloodless, shapeless, milkless beast patterned on Picasso's plunderings of archaic wall decorations.

But the Federal government has rendered inestimable service to the cause of American art: it has recognized the existence of a native movement, and by co-operating with regional boards, it has not only publicized the importance of local themes and subjects but has also helped to restore the artist to his former position as practitioner, or workman. The government, let us bear in mind, did not create the new tendency—it seized upon and promoted a changing order of things. The honor of putting the new tendency in motion—which amounts to the founding of a distinctly American school—belongs to a small group of original artists who, bravely and steadfastly for many years, and in defiance of great opposition, have produced a body of work leading to our cultural declaration of independence. The most prominent of these men—Benton, Burchfield, Curry, Marsh, and Wood— by temperament and training, by intimate knowledge of and sympathy with specific American environments, by character and conviction, have become the leaders of the new school. They are known everywhere, and their followers are legion. Our young artists no longer turn to Europe for inspiration; unhesitatingly they equip themselves to understand and express the significance of the American way of life.

It cannot be denied that an American style in art has definitely emerged; that our most original artists have produced pictures obviously distinct from those made in other countries. The distinction, I believe, is more sharply revealed in our black-and-white art, and it is not a patriotic exaggeration to say that our printmakers are the best in the world. In looking at our finest prints, those characteristically American, we are confronted with the old and perhaps insoluble question of style. What constitutes the American style? What is any style? What does the word mean? In one sense, style may be defined as the outcome of a certain course of

action—but that is not very helpful. When we refer to Italian and French art, we know that the styles employed, technically speaking, are purely Italian or French. Techniques, or procedures, and forms themselves, in the abstract, or geometrical sense, have been traded about from country to country and must be considered as universal developments. Taine got at the root of the question when he treated style as environment affecting form; that is to say, when he stressed, as the most important element in the formation of style, the artist's response to the substance and color of his environment. In this connection, the term localism rather than nationalism is the more fitting designation for geographical differences in art; for these differences existed long before the rise of nationalism as it is understood today.

A new style is born when an artist's acquired technical habits, or methods, are put to work in new surroundings; when his inherited processes are transformed in the crucible of experience; when environmental pressure and interests residing in life, not in art, rouse him to a personal utterance capable of imparting the force and flavor of direct experiences. The subject matter afforded by the American background cannot be enclosed in imported forms; nor can it be convincingly presented in foreign styles. The selection of subject matter, of course, is conditioned by the artist's individual attitude toward life, which, in turn, is conditioned by the prevailing social tendencies of his time. I should say that the American people, in their group attitudes, are essentially pragmatic, or "thing-minded," to use a clumsy word.

Americans are much more interested in things— the objective machinery of life—than in ideas. They have never been strong on the theoretical; and their enormous distrust of long-range planning, at the moment a political fetish with the economic prophets, is a good example of their skeptical attitude toward all that is not plainly at hand and practicable. They have no patience with merely logical conceptions, with absolute systems of philosophy and puzzling abstractions; they are essentially a trial-and-error people. Any native artist who would truthfully represent his people, who would select from the field of experience *that which is characteristically American, must share to a certain extent the group feelings and attributes of his countrymen, their pragmatic absorption in the facts and concrete instruments of living.*

The artists numbered in this collection, with a few exceptions and in spite of individual variations, are preponderantly concerned with materials directly experienced. Like their eminent forebears, Thomas Eakins and Winslow Homer, they are not doctrinaire artists bent on reducing life to a universal symbol or a tidy abstraction; they are preoccupied with things and with people because they like them, because they find these subjects engrossing. Thus it follows that their basic styles are realistic: they do not select their subjects in order to adorn an idea—anything that has come within their observation is their meat. The simple existence of an object or a scene justifies its representation, as it justified the work of Winslow Homer, and, later, the graphic art of George Bellows and John Sloan.

With what extraordinary zeal and vitality these artists—leaders and youngsters alike—dig and delve in the American environment! One might think they had been slaves to a fatal dogma and had suddenly been emancipated into the health-giving atmosphere of personal freedom. Nothing is too venerable or too revolting in its physical aspects for them to tackle. They depict mountains and wildernesses, the clashes of industrialism, the corn belt and the cotton plantation, played-out capitalists and played-out share-croppers, Negroes, tornadoes, night clubs, politicians, slums, parks, factories, and old houses—the vast panorama of American life, uncensored and unrestrained. And what a high level of craftsmanship they display! Clean surfaces, neatness and precision, boldness of execution and a tonal range from the highest light to the deepest dark that makes the engravings of Hogarth, by comparison, look almost gray. Truly, American prints have come a long way since Whistler squinted in the dusk at the London wharves and scratched faintly on smudged copper.

I do not wish to imply that our artists are merely recording appearances with a skillful technique or photographing the various aspects of their country.

Some, in their first enthusiasm and touched, no doubt, by the popularity of the camera, are inclined in that direction, but our major workmen and their more serious followers are concentrated on accomplishments peculiar to a creative medium. With these, draftsmanship is of prime importance; they are more concerned with the anatomy of the human figure and the topography of the landscape than with the appearances of nature at a given moment. Their aim is to get at meanings, to know America, and to design compact structures communicating the poetry and magnificence, the irony, the humor, the shabbiness, the tragedy and, not least, the social significance of their chosen materials.

Artists today are obsessed by the notion of social meanings, an obsession which has unbalanced a number of the young and thrown them under the dominance of those current patterns in social thinking affiliated with Marxist Communism. I am not greatly disturbed over the situation; it is nothing to worry about; the young will grow up, let us hope, and forgetting Communism, develop into artists; if not, they will have to subsist as disgruntled agitators. A few years ago, aggressive young artists were Freudians, and before that, Nietzscheans or aristocratic hedonists. Nor am I disturbed by the wails of those alarmists who detect the bogey of Fascism lurking behind every concerted enterprise. "This nationalism in art," they cry, "leads to regimentation! The next step will be Fascism, state control, and the extinction of individual liberty." If it will make these apprehensive souls feel a little better, I will discard the word nationalism and supply an unimpeachable substitute— localism.

Art is not a philosophical system embracing the whole world; it is an intensely local affair, and the outstanding characteristic of any original style is the local signature, the impress of a specific environment which, by modifying traditional techniques, makes possible a new mode of expression. At present, we are breeding a veritable army of artists in America; and what we shall do with them is not my worry; naturally, only a small number are original in the strictest sense, but the great majority are on the right track—the only course that makes art worth while, that makes it a healthy human activity, springing from and affecting the lives of people. American artists are now delineating what they know and love and understand; they are carrying forward, in a different medium, the spirit of Mark Twain, Dreiser, Sinclair Lewis, and O'Neill—literary artists whose unashamed localism has done honor to America, and lifted American letters to the highest rank. Happily, they are now welcomed and encouraged; for once they have a public. In selecting the prints, I have placed the emphasis where it properly belongs, giving extended space to artists with indisputable interests in the American civilization; but in order to make the record complete and the list fully representative, I have included examples of practically every style and tendency.

The popularity of the print, the black-and-white, is quite in keeping with the general acceptance of the new art movement. Heretofore, the print has been an exclusive and snobbish item, a collector's rarity: it has been the practice of the artist to limit an edition of etchings and lithographs to a few issues, so that scarcity values might be maintained and the vanity of a rich collector delicately flattered. Times have changed, and today, the best prints are within reach of the humblest purse. Furthermore, the artist had discovered that it is better business to release as many prints as the plate, or stone, will bear—better business in dollars and cents, and a wider audience for subsequent works. This, I know, is a bitter pill for the collectors to swallow, but I am not interested in the wounded vanity of monopolists.

No comment on American prints can afford to ignore the services of George Miller, of New York. Artists take him for granted, acknowledge him to be the master lithographer of the day; but to the public, not to mention the specialists, his name means little or nothing. Miller is the man who actually does the printing. Not one artist in a hundred has the experience, the skill, or the apparatus to make his own prints; he draws his picture on a stone slab with a grease pencil, delivers the stone to a little workshop in a dilapidated building in East Fourteenth Street, and Miller does the rest. To the untrained eye, the processes of lithography hold no secrets, but the best printing demands a combination of artist, craftsman, and mechanic, and Miller is exactly that. He printed the first work of George Bellows, and most of the drawings of the contemporary American school are inked and pressed in his shop. Young students who have supposedly learned the craft in art schools come to him to learn all over again—free of charge; and famous practitioners heed him implicitly when he specifies alterations in their drawings—they know the print will be improved. Whenever you see a superlatively fine lithograph, an original print or a reproduction, you may be reasonably certain that George Miller had a hand in the making of it. And that, I conclude, is a service to American art that cannot be ignored.

List of Plates

LIST OF PLATES

LIST OF PLATES

Acknowledgments

Among those who have co-operated generously in making this book what it is, the Editor wishes to thank, first and foremost, Associated American Artists, which from the very inception of *A Treasury of American Prints* has given freely of its staff's time and energy. In addition to placing at the Editor's disposal its own rich files, Associated American Artists worked with other galleries in getting together, for the Editor's perusal, one of the largest collections of prints ever assembled.

Among those who worked tirelessly with the Editor are Margaret Sullivan, of Associated American Artists; Carl Zigrosser, of the Weyhe Galleries, and Leon Shimkin, of Simon and Schuster.

The biographical and descriptive notes accompanying each plate were compiled by the editorial staff of the publishers, in many cases from notes supplied by the artists themselves. They often owe their fullness to information contained in the invaluable *Index of American Artists*. The Editor wishes to thank the College Arts Association for generously lending a complete file of that *Index* while the work was in progress.

Publisher's Note

The prints in this volume have been made detachable, so that those who may wish to remove one or more favorites, for framing, may do so without impairing the appearance of the book as a whole. Because of this, each print bears its own descriptive matter on the back.

A TREASURY OF
AMERICAN PRINTS

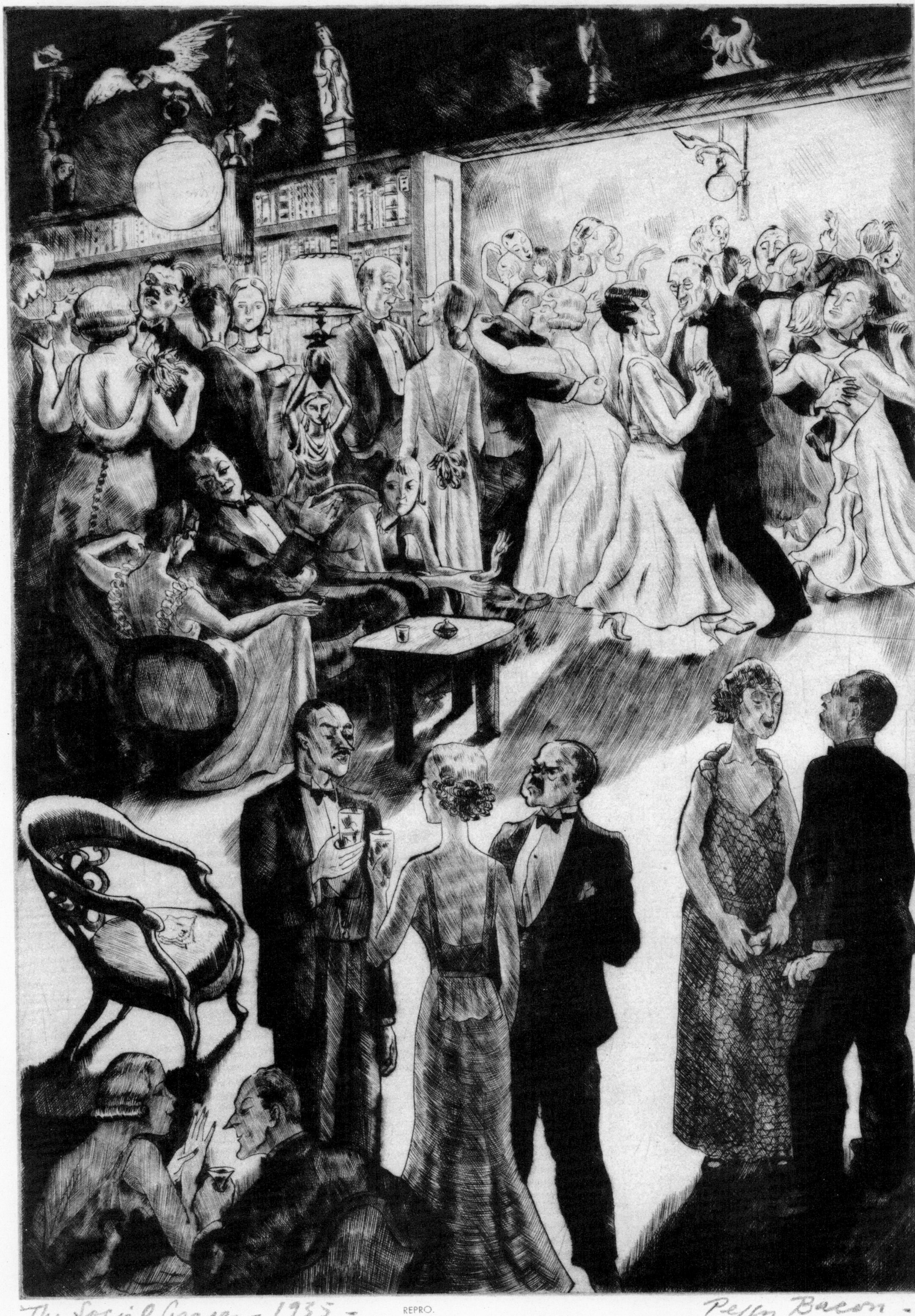

The Social Graces - 1935 - Peggy Bacon -

The Social Graces

BY PEGGY BACON

(See reverse side for plate)

IN HER FORTY-FOUR YEARS, Peggy Bacon has led an extraordinarily full life. She is an etcher, drawer, illustrator, lithographer, teacher, and—not least of all—a writer. She is even a thwarted mural painter, and will probably remain so. Far from trying to hide this appalling fact, she is inclined to brag about it. Besides this, she is married to Alexander Brook, the painter, and has two children. She collects the work of other artists, notably Marsh and Kuniyoshi. She does her share of traveling, goes to her share of parties.

The Social Graces is, like most of Peggy Bacon's work, assembled from sketches made in various places. Possibly no single room contains quite so many terrible statuettes and fixtures, quite so many ridiculous people, as this one, but there are plenty that are as crowded in just the same way. After looking at *The Social Graces,* it may come as a shock to the innocent that Peggy Bacon is still asked to quite a lot of parties.

Pity the Blind · 1933 ·　　　Peggy Bacon ·

Pity the Blind

BY PEGGY BACON

(See reverse side for plate)

PEGGY BACON is a tireless eye. She never takes a vacation from art. She sketches eternally, whether on a transatlantic liner or the subway, doing the galleries or shopping. This passion is easily understandable. Both of her parents were artists, and she subjected her eclectic, individual talent to the enthusiasms of such fine teachers as Jonas Lie, John Sloan, Kenneth Hayes Miller, George Bellows, and Max Weber.

Peggy Bacon's "merciless and mirthful" line has full play in *Pity the Blind*, in which all the dramatis personae, except the blind boy, come off very badly indeed. The mother, who is leading him, is tragic, but there is something of the entrepreneur about her. And the spectators are definitely not nice. Their expressions are dulled, stony, supercilious, gawky. The feet are the more eloquent features: literally, no artist alive understands the expressiveness of shoes better than Peggy Bacon. And there is no better laboratory for studying shoes and their idiosyncrasies than a New York subway train.

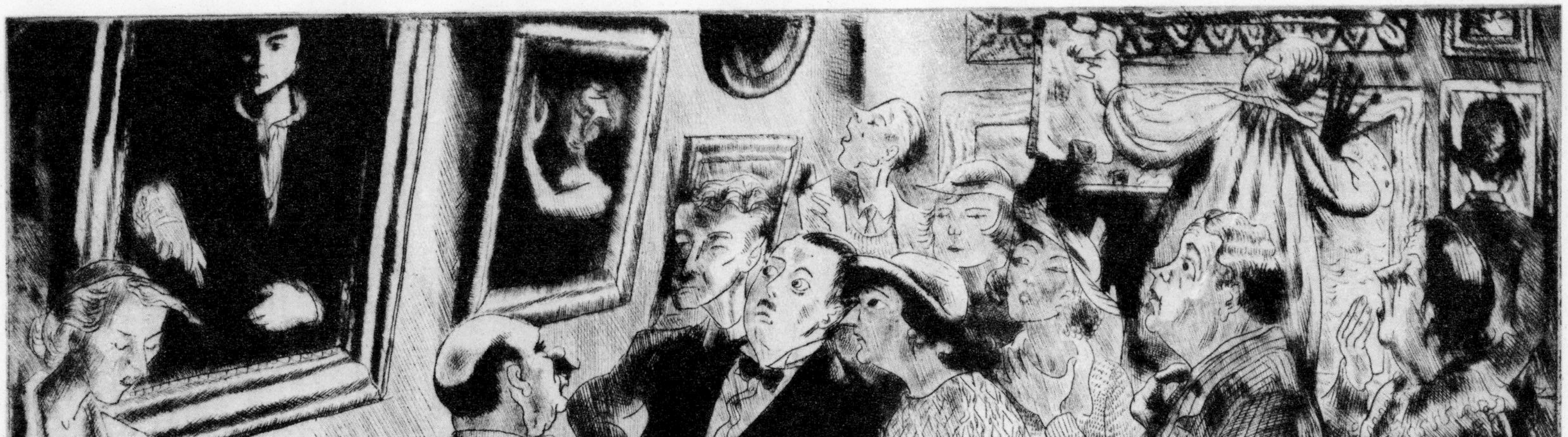

Aesthetic Pleasures - REPRO Peggy Bacon -

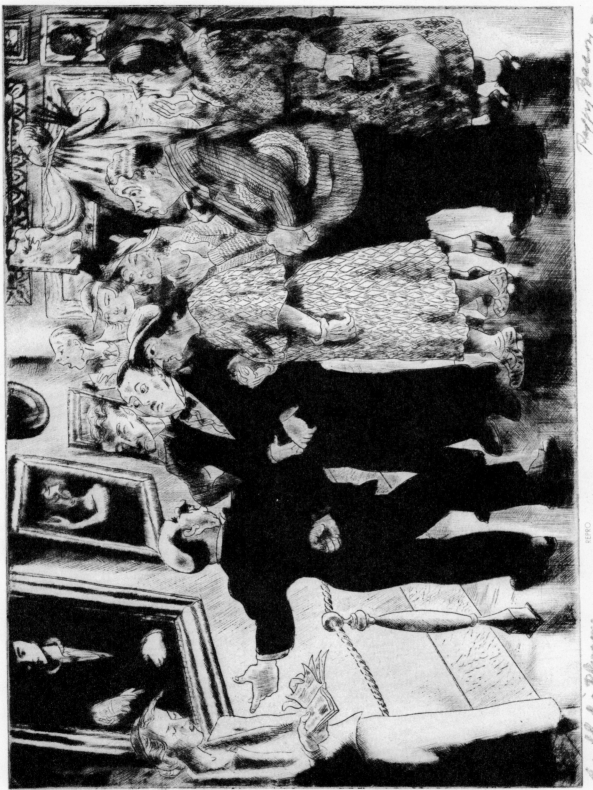

Esthetic Pleasure

BY PEGGY BACON

(See reverse side for plate)

ANY EUROPEAN gallery any free day. As we see, the crowd has halted before a world-famous Titian, and the lecturer is doing his stuff. He is not the kind to inspire confidence, but that does not matter. He has managed to overawe some of his audience, one of whom frankly gapes. Some, however, are neither credulous nor impressed. A woman checks the lecturer's facts with her Baedeker, and a very superior, emaciated man looks sneeringly aloof. It seems, too, as if the married couple (who are very bored with each other) are even more bored with the lecturer. What is that line? Art is long, and time is fleeting. Art is very, very long. . . .

Esthetic Pleasure is one of those rare documents that make one feel, if only for a fleeting moment, that J. P. Morgan was right when he surrounded his gallery with a wall of red tape and official permissions. These yahoos have not earned the right to look at Titian or even at the second-rate Leonardo next door to it. But exactly the right doom has been found for them. They must keep on listening to the mustached lecturer, who looks like a race-horse tout, for the rest of their lives as figures in one of Peggy Bacon's most savage etchings.

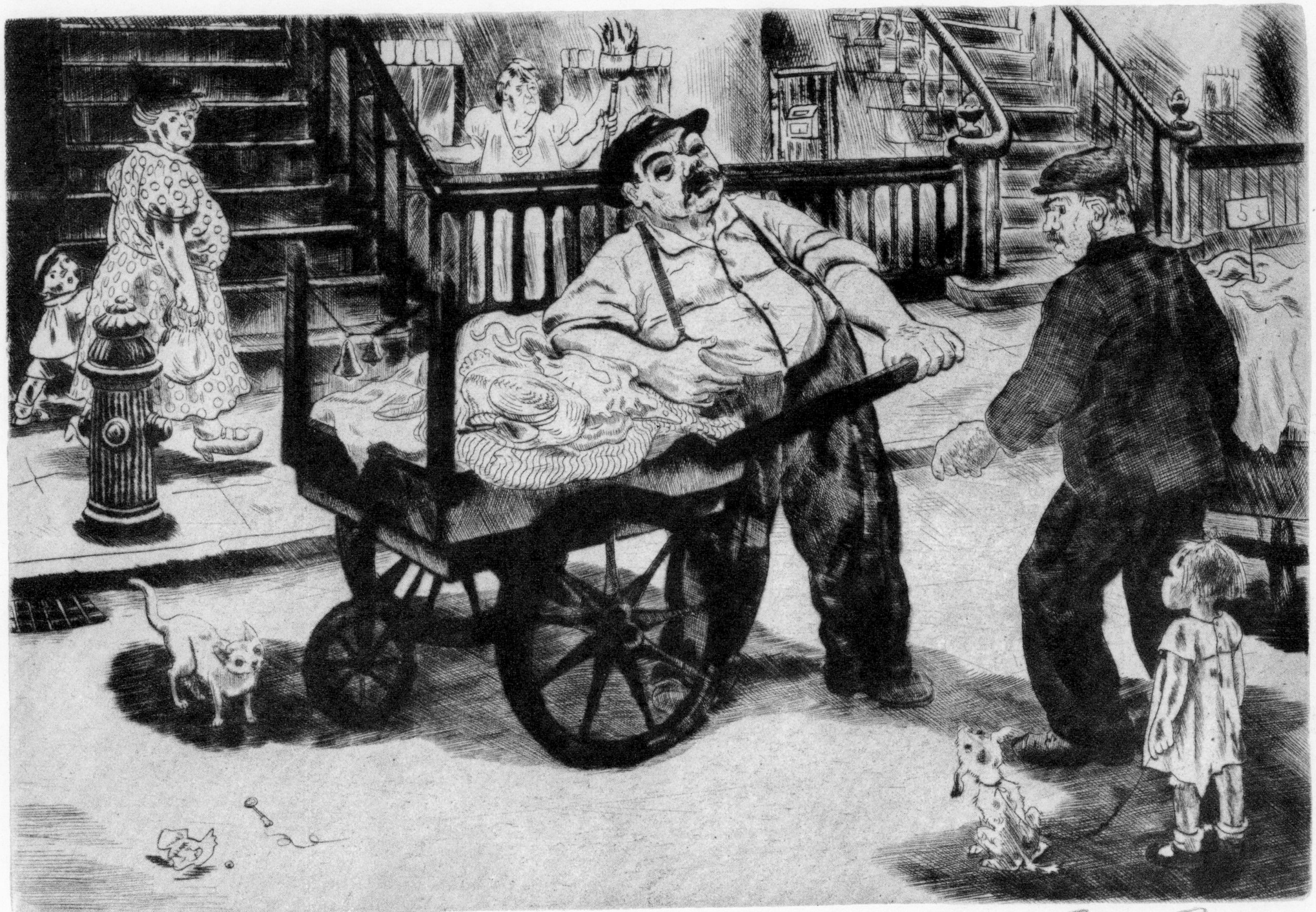

The Rival Ragmen. REPRO. Peggy Bacon.

The Rival Ragmen

BY PEGGY BACON

(See reverse side for plate)

ALEXANDER BROOK was probably being too severe on his gifted wife when he said that her work completely lacked "any ingratiating traits." *The Rival Ragmen* is most certainly a delightful composition, and it does have a spark of love which, however, is kept under strict control. It remains a veritable Bacon. The minuscule cat (definitely not man's friend) is drawn with an archly sympathetic pen that becomes somewhat derisive, even if just, when engaged on the dog (man's friend).

The theme of *The Rival Ragmen* is self-evident, even if the specific cause of their quarrel be forever a thing of mystery. (About the year 2039, it will be a fine subject for a learned monograph from the Berenson of that age.) The etching is hearty in tone, and there is a fruity humor mingled with its still acrid wit. While this scene could have taken place almost anywhere in a large American town, the artist assures us that the actual locale was Twelfth Street, New York, between Second and Third Avenues. The human elements, however, were assembled from sketches made in various places.

Antique Beauty - 1933 -   REPRO   Peggy Bacon -

Antique Beauty

BY PEGGY BACON

(See reverse side for plate)

IT IS A LITTLE difficult to tell whether Peggy Bacon is meaner to the dowager than to the statues. In an unguarded moment, the artist once confessed that she thinks statuary rather silly, and looking at *Antique Beauty* you get just what she means. It is pretty obvious that she does not feel as warm about these marbles as she does about the gallery pictures in *Esthetic Pleasure,* for example. Try to find an old friend among them—if you dare. The lolling siren on the right is as absurd as the runner set on his mark but maliciously devitalized of all his energy. The composition is held together by the grim old woman, who is hedged in by this stone mythology. By some subtle trick, she is made to seem a trifle overawed.

Antique Beauty is not a kind picture. The cruelest comment of all comes from the vest-pocket Venus on the lower left. Allowed some exquisiteness of line and modeling, she makes the point clear, once and for all, that fat old women should not be seen in sculpture galleries. Alexander Brook, Miss Bacon's husband, has called attention to his wife's "crowded plates": so they are, and so is life. *Antique Beauty* is one of the most crowded, and the statues are not to blame.

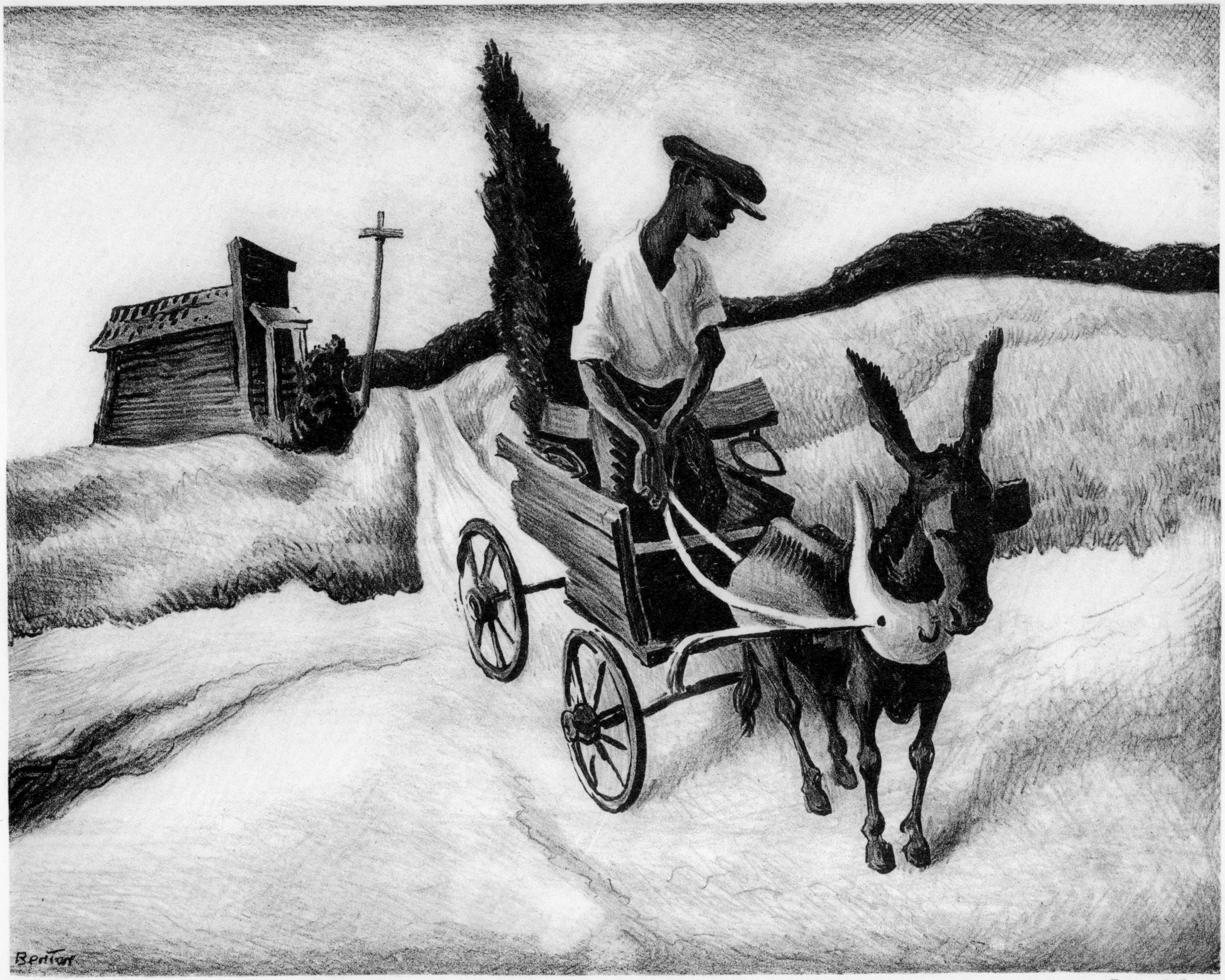
Benton

REPRO

Benton

Lonesome Road

BY THOMAS BENTON

(See reverse side for plate)

SOME OF THE sympathy for the Negro and his woes that eventually led to the downfall of the artist's famous grandfather, the first Senator from Missouri (who, a slaveholder himself, finally came to abhor the whole institution of slavery), can be traced in much of Thomas Hart Benton's work. *Lonesome Road* evokes the conscience-shaking specter of the degrading poverty of whole sections of our country. The utter forlornness of this scene—the dejected Negro, the equally despondent little mule with its absurd haltar, and the poor shack of a general store—is emphasized by the bleak hills that seem to shut out a better world. This is, indeed, one of the lonesomest roads in art.

Thomas Benton was born at Neosho, Missouri, in the heart of the Middle West, fifty years ago, and nothing he has ever been subjected to, including five years of Paris just before the World War, has ever shaken his fidelity to American subject matter. Benton's exhaustive study of the masters of the past, far from injecting academic dead-letter into his work, has swung him into the great tradition. His murals are as rhythmic and strong as those of the Renaissance; his easel paintings, especially his recent ones, suggest that America has a great master of her own. His lithographs, showing a most scrupulous economy of means, are very characteristic works—Benton at his most eloquent, most indignant, and most sad.

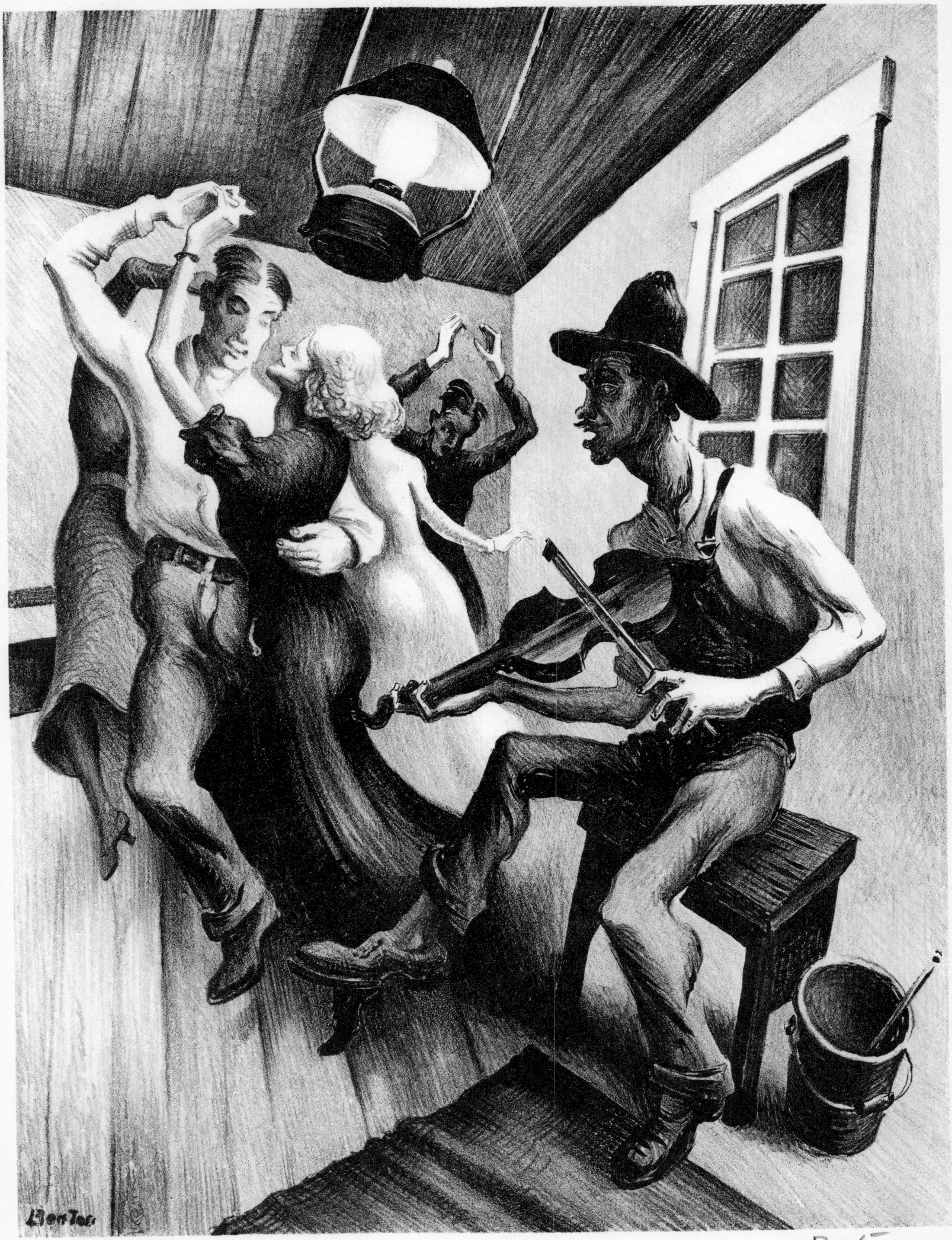

Benton

I Got a Gal on Sourwood Mountain

BY THOMAS BENTON

(See reverse side for plate)

ONE OF THE distinguishing features of Benton's art is the clear evidence, in both his selection of subjects and his treatment of them, of clear and incessantly active intellect. He has not merely reacted: he has thought. He has not merely put his forms down: he has considered their significance as realities. In contradistinction to those far too numerous artists who seem to have started with a desire to paint, or make etchings, or produce lithographs, Benton would seem to have started out with a wealth of observed living, and then to have worked out a brilliant and apposite technique for expressing it. The result —for he is a subtle and sensitive artist—is work that has both pictorial beauty and meaning for the intelligence.

I Got a Gal on Sourwood Mountain is a very striking exemplar of Benton's style. The gaunt, gangling, and humorously seen fiddler, the obviously romantic blond, and the well-brushed farmer out for a gala Saturday night are unmistakable figures out of the southern Middle West. The enigmatic figure in the background, arms raised overhead, supplies the touch of imminent hysteria, the suggestion of cruel repressions about to break out in meaningless and unhealthy ecstasy, that are always likely at such affairs. The bareness of the board floor and ceiling, white window casing, and oil lamp would have produced a dead, unenlivened *décor* in themselves. Benton's very successful way of making them contribute to the somewhat feverish quality of his subject is a perspective distortion that ought to answer once and for all the art vs. photography argument insofar as it applies to pinning down the essential character of scenes.

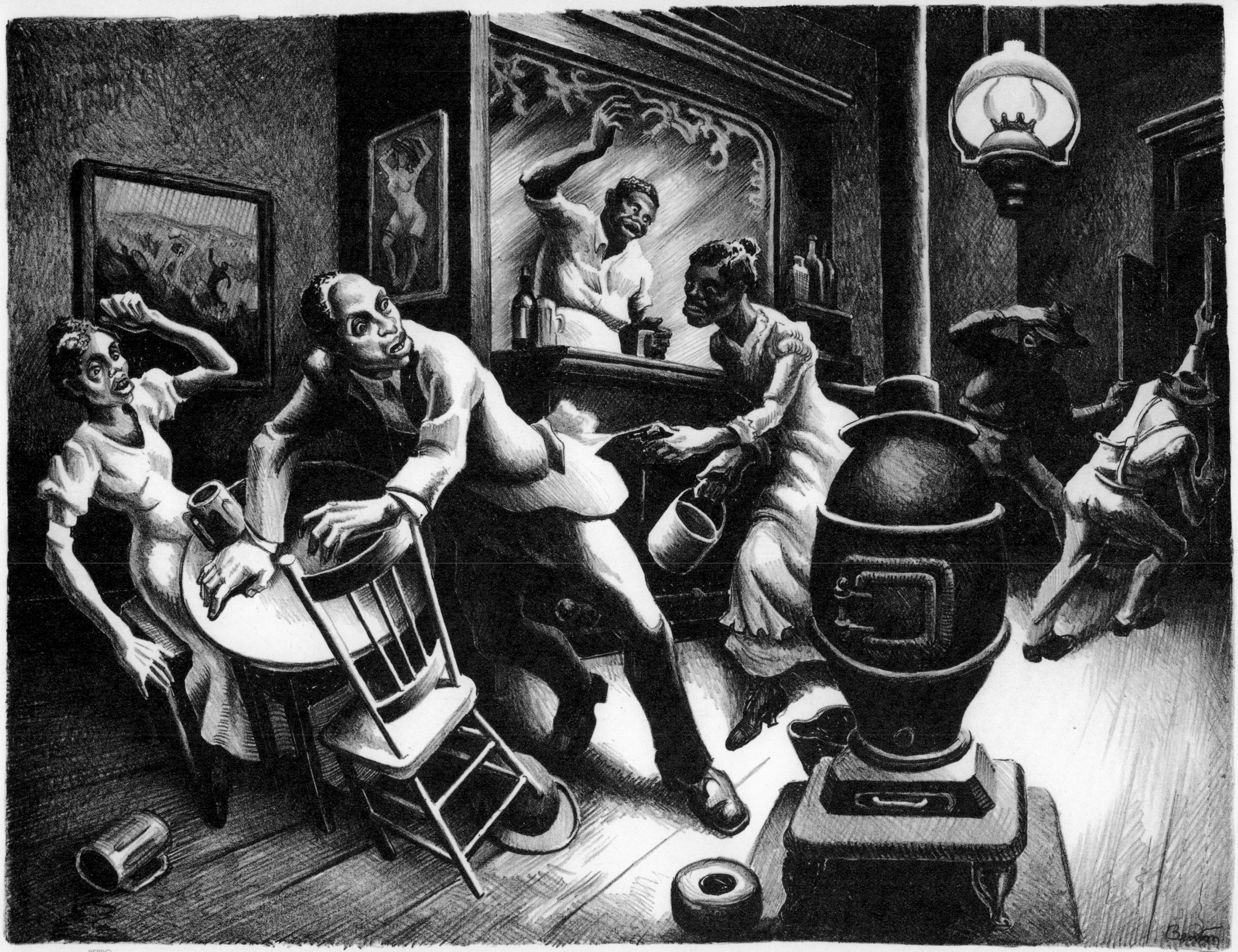

Benton

Frankie and Johnny

BY THOMAS BENTON

(*See reverse side for plate*)

Frankie and Johnny, the ballad that has given so many people with submerged desires to sing a lot of fun on convivial evenings, began to evolve in the mid-nineteenth century, and has been evolving ever since. It has less than a dozen absolutely traditional verses, and scores of extras that vary from locality to locality. For the purposes of Benton's lithograph, it is only necessary to know that "Frankie and Johnny were lovers . . . but he done her wrong." The thrilling drama of revenge runs its inevitable course, rising to a climax in the verses:

> *Frankie went to the Dance Hall, she rang the Dance Hall bell,*
> *She said, "Clear out, you people, I'm going to blow this man to hell:*
> *He was my man—and he done me wrong."*

> *Frankie shot Johnny the first time; Frankie shot Johnny twice;*
> *Frankie shot Johnny the third time, and she took that gambler's life.*
> *He was her man—but he done her wrong.*

Benton has devoted one of his most vigorous lithographs to this catastrophe. It throbs with action and melodrama. Primarily, it is exciting, which it is meant to be.

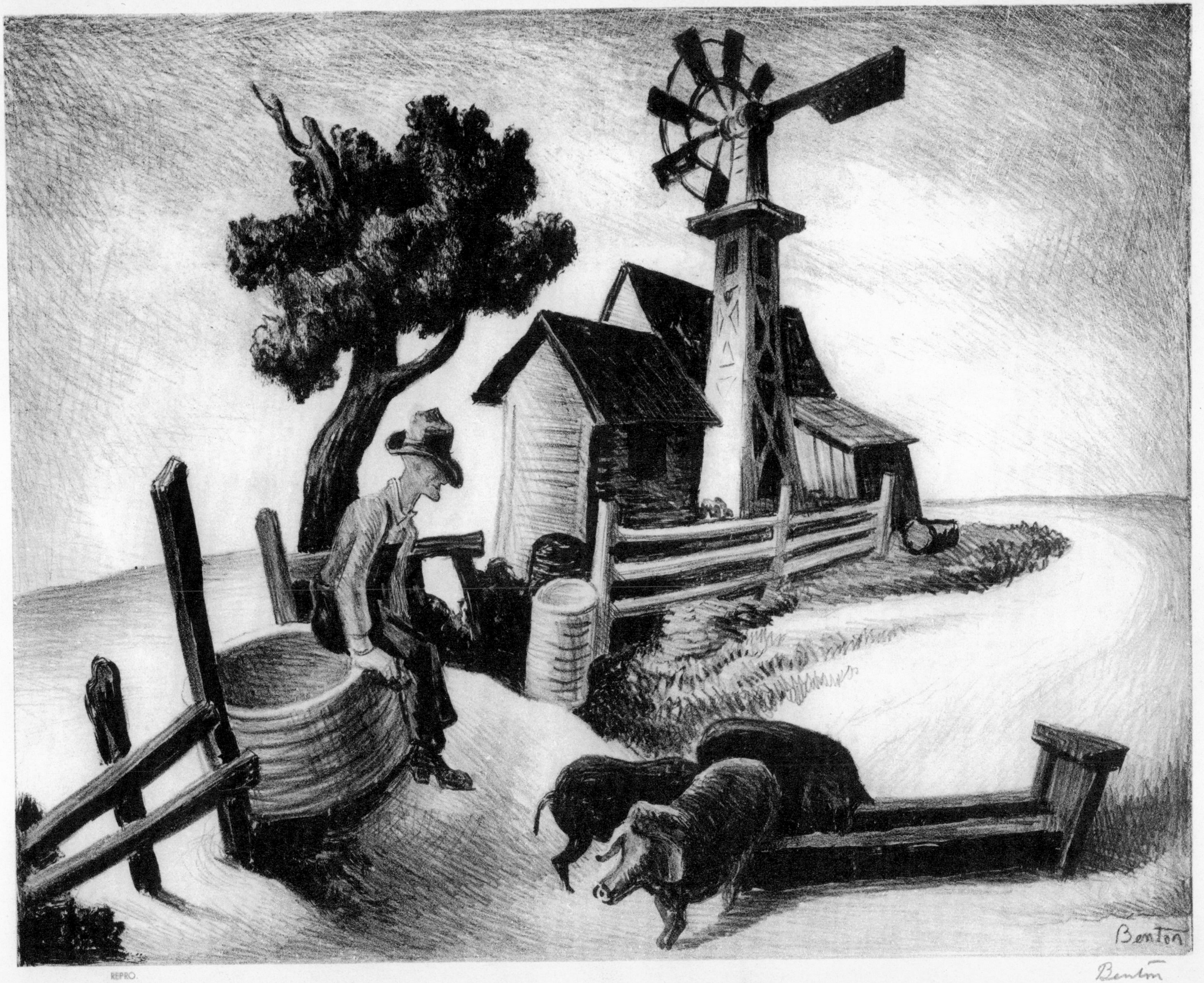
Benton
Benton
REPRO.

In the Ozarks

BY THOMAS BENTON

(See reverse side for plate)

ONE OF THE dreariest parts of Missouri is the Ozark district, which stretches in a southeasterly direction over the lower portion of the state. It is a section that Thomas Benton knows like his own hand—though his tireless curiosity about the folkways of the American people has carried him to practically every part of the United States. But Missouri is his own bailiwick, and on its various aspects Benton has lavished some of his finest lithographs.

In the Ozarks is a powerful piece of work, instinct with humor and pathos, with its elements cunningly selected and arranged. The triangular composition is highly satisfactory to the conventional eye, yet it is no mere academic pattern, but is demanded by subtle considerations of depth and distance. Here are the Ozarks in a nutshell, with their rail fences, point-nosed porkers, windmills, and philosophical, stoical farmers. The scene exudes loneliness: the farm buildings seem like a not too green oasis in a desert.

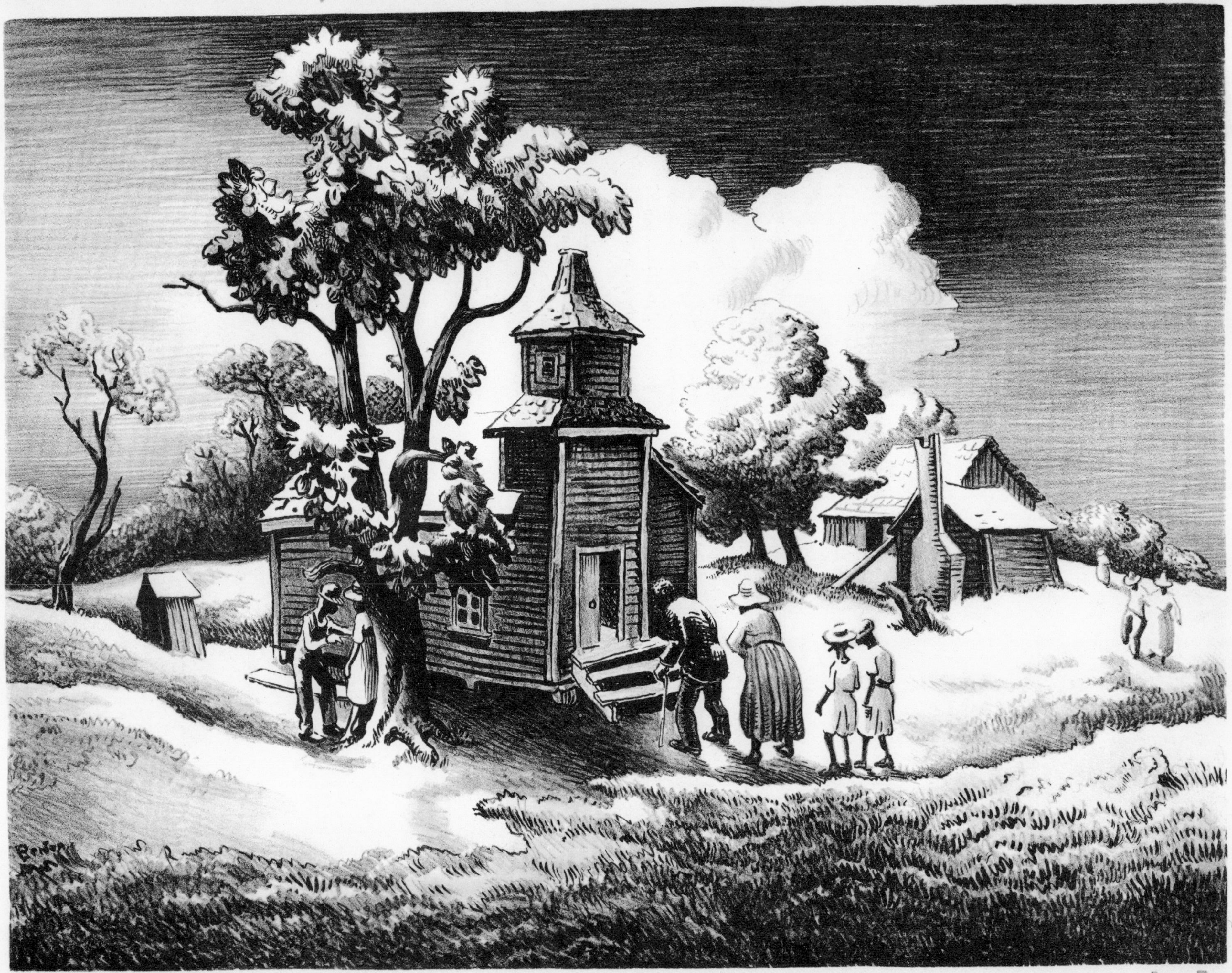
Benton

REPRO.

Benton

Sunday Morning

BY THOMAS BENTON

(See reverse side for plate)

BENTON HAS OFTEN been accused of lack of feeling. It is true that in his great murals sympathy is sometimes submerged by compositional brilliancy and a reporter's instinct, but his lithographs testify to his greatheartedness and his understanding of the underprivileged. *Edge of Town* and *Lonesome Road* reflect the hopelessness of barren lives: *Sunday Morning* strikes a different note, for at least one day a week a thin wedge of hope enters into these lives. The Southern Negro, though naturally optimistic and gay, gets bogged down in the oppressive conditions of daily existence. The little rural church is the answer for the old folk and for some of the younger ones.

Sunday Morning is less bleak, less unrelieved than most of Benton's lithographs. Light and shade are distributed with less dramatic contrast than usual, and the blacks are not so emphatic. For the first time, the artist has modified the slashing conciseness of his effects by recourse to detail, but without sacrificing power and impressiveness.

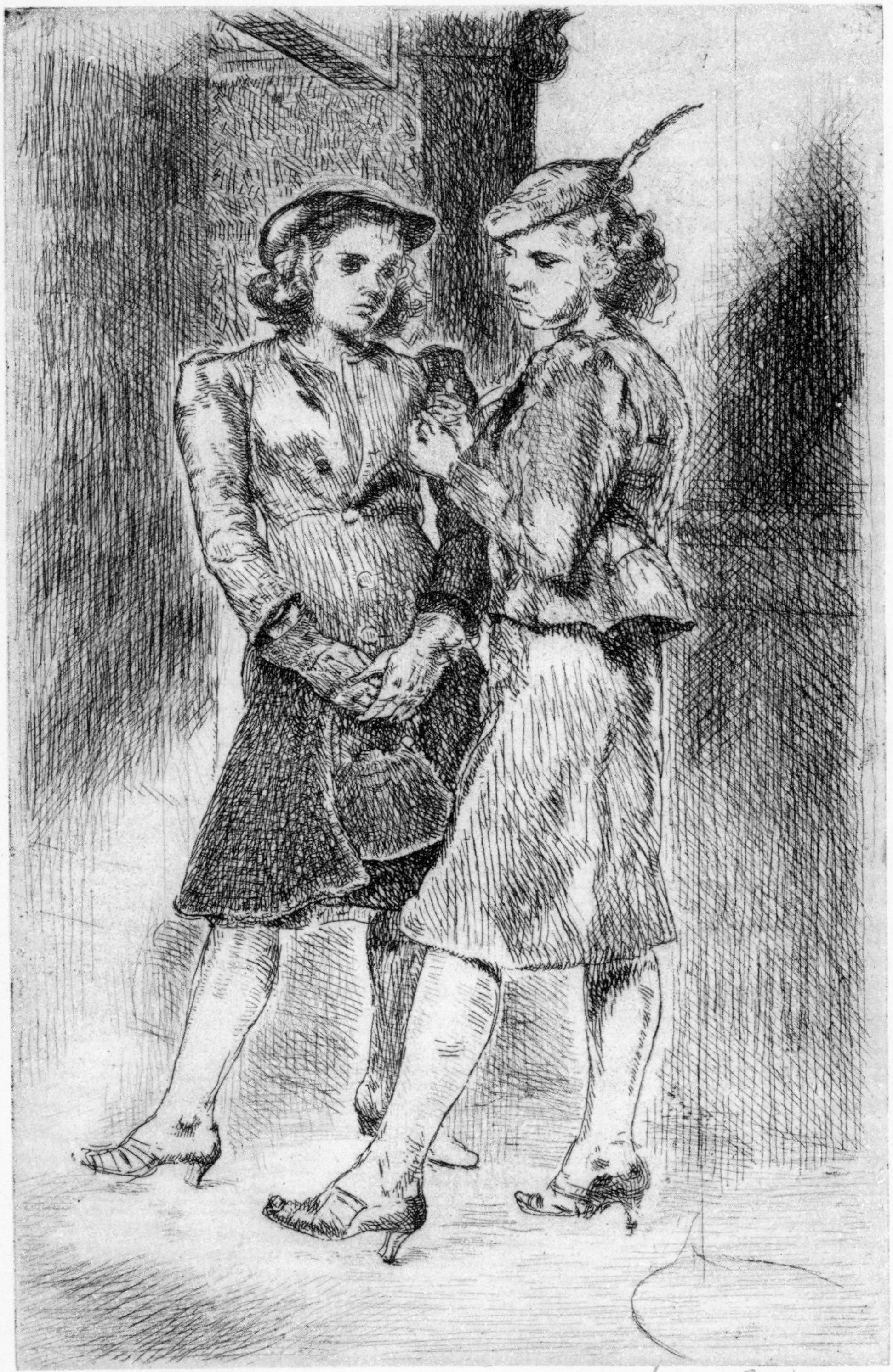

REPRO.

Isabel Bishop

Office Girls

BY ISABEL BISHOP

(*See reverse side for plate*)

ISABEL BISHOP drifted into art more or less accidentally, but she is very glad that she did so. She was born in Cincinnati in 1902, but her family moved to Detroit several years later, and she went to school there. Here people noticed that she had a marked aptitude for drawing—"my only aptitude," she says modestly—and suggested she become an illustrator. So, after a few Saturday classes while she was going to high school, Isabel Bishop went to New York, and entered the New York School of Applied Art for Women. She was sixteen years old, and perhaps a bit flurried by the skyline. At any rate, instead of entering the commercial-art classes, she enrolled in the life class. Since then, the thing has just got into her blood, and she has had no time for, or interest in, commercial art. She has taught composition and life at the Art Students' League, and has made four gallery tours of Europe. She says that the thing that makes her happiest is that she saw the Prado pictures before they got carted off to God knows where.

Office Girls is a picture without a story. It is frankly a study of two girls who work near Isabel Bishop's studio.

REPRO.   Isabel Bishop

Schoolgirls

BY ISABEL BISHOP

(See reverse side for plate)

THIS IS ONE OF ISABEL BISHOP'S most characteristic etchings, showing her abiding interest in the complexities of design raised by one or two figures. In this case, she has found her subjects in two high-school girls exchanging confidences.

The scene is a simple but wholly attractive one: it is a pleasant moment caught by an accurate and sympathetic eye. The Union Square fountain, on which the two schoolgirls are perched, stands at the edge of the Square, against a background of hedges and shrubs, and faces a busy street. Almost any time of the day—or night, for that matter—it is a favorite resting place of the Square's milling, varied life. "The casual way in which people in the public squares sit all over the steps and monuments, as well as on the benches," Miss Bishop says, "sometimes seems to have an informal charm that one finds is usually reserved for rural surroundings."

The artist's problem in this etching is, though subtly solved, relatively simple: "beveling" the form from the center. The modeling is turned back from the spectator, beginning with the head and shoulders of the nearer figure.

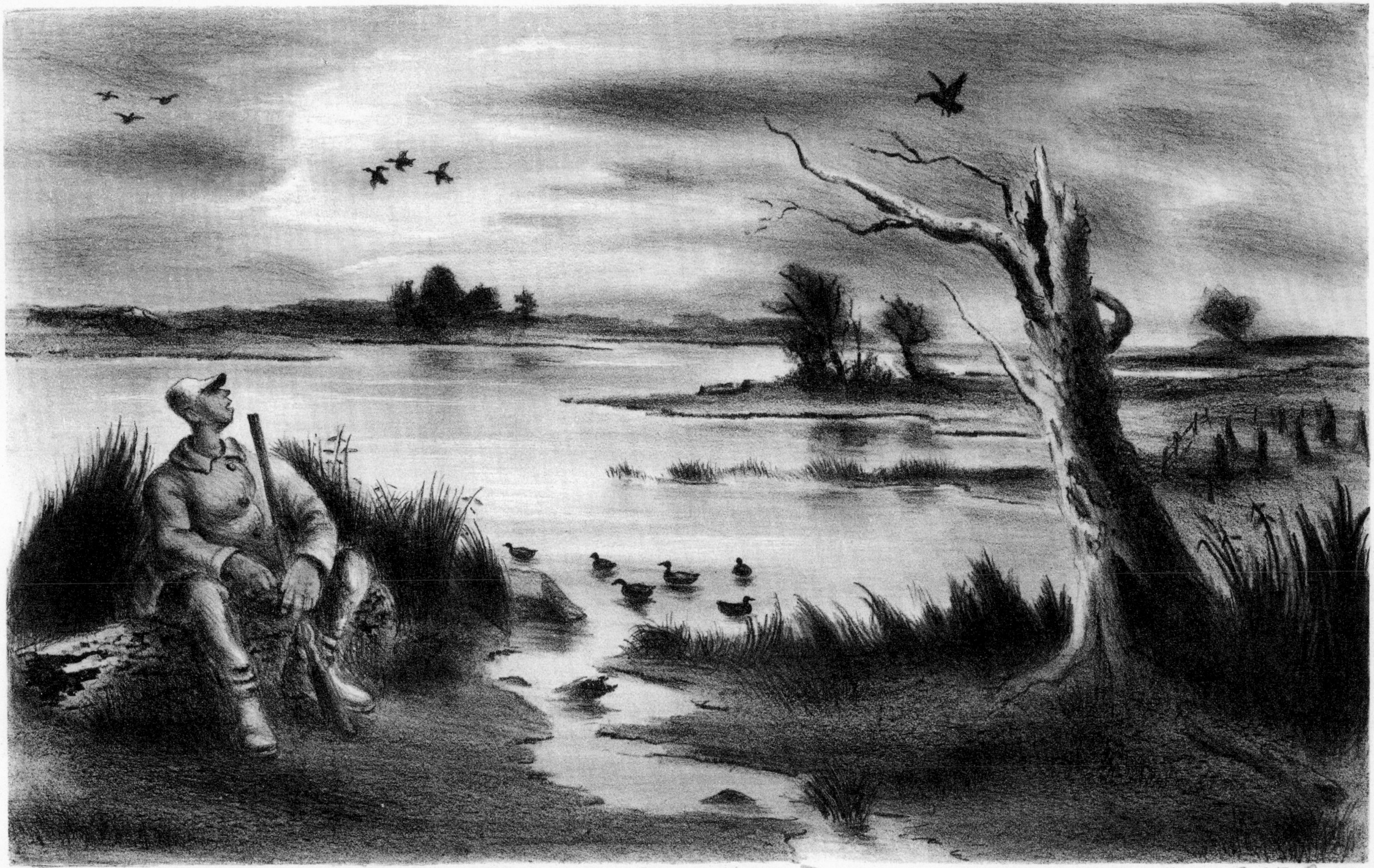

REPRO

Duck Hunter

Arnold Blanch

Duck Hunter

BY ARNOLD BLANCH

(See reverse side for plate)

ARNOLD BLANCH was born at Mantorville, Minnesota, on June 4, 1896. After some work at the Minneapolis School of Fine Arts, he came to New York, and studied with Kenneth Hayes Miller at the Art Students' League. He also went to Sloan, Henri, and F. Luis Mora for instruction. He looked around Europe, and haunted the great galleries, but without it affecting his style invidiously. In 1933 he received a Guggenheim fellowship for creative work in painting. He teaches painting and drawing at the Art Students' League.

Duck Hunter is somewhat autobiographical, for the artist loves the sport. Even the cold, murky mornings that figure so largely in the annals of duck-hunting are doubtless dear to his heart. There is a kind of desolation, possibly laid on thick with half-humorous intent (though there is usually little comedy in his work) that gives this lithograph an attractive excess of atmosphere. The hunter himself has been caught in a lethargic moment. Possibly he is even asleep. At any rate, the ducks are having it all their own way.

Along The Hudson

annapel Branch

Along the Hudson

BY ARNOLD BLANCH

(See reverse side for plate)

ARNOLD BLANCH AND LUCILE, his equally famed painter wife, have their home at Woodstock, midway between New York and Albany. The river, woodlands, and farms of the surrounding countryside are old friends, though Mrs. Blanch is not as interested in landscape as her husband.

Along the Hudson is a remarkably attractive lithograph, with its long views way to the other side of the Hudson, the river islands, and the opulent farmlands in the middle distance and foreground. The reaper is at its work, depositing little heaps of grain, and there is a fine, primly disposed apple orchard on the left. A more conventional artist would have disclaimed, and deleted, the feather-duster tree in the foreground rather than cut his composition into two parts. Here the result excuses the bold device: the otherwise rather blonde and empty foreground gets needed weight and interest. The richness and variety of this scene is in sharp contrast to the artist's well-known New England landscapes.

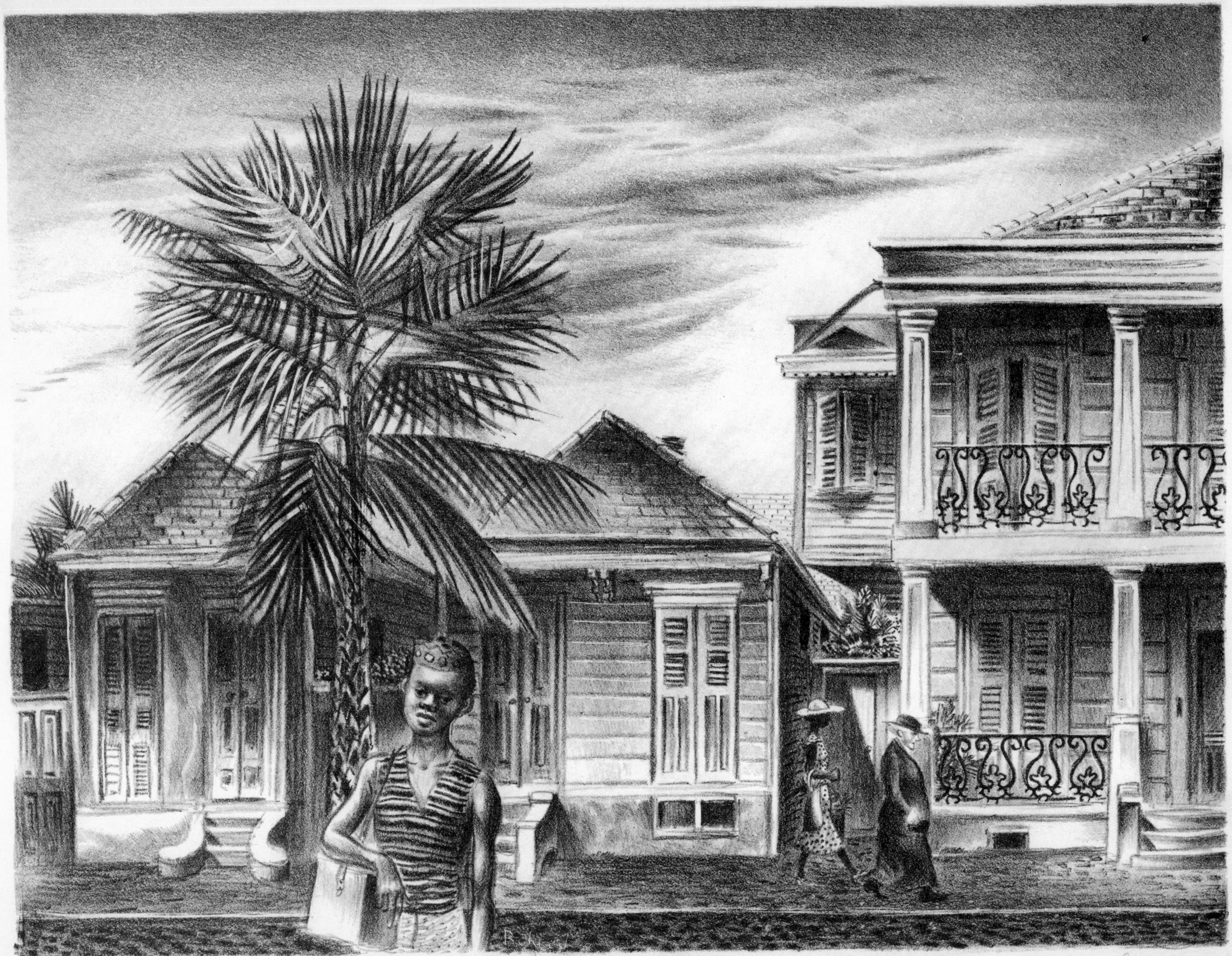

Aaron Bohrod

New Orleans Street

BY AARON BOHROD

(See reverse side for plate)

AARON BOHROD has generally concentrated on scraps of the Middle West in which—at Chicago, in 1907—he was born. But like many of his contemporary confreres, he has traveled widely, having studied in New York as well as Chicago, and having twice had a Guggenheim fellowship. Returning from New Orleans with pictures that look, at first sight, like some scene from Jamaica or Trinidad, he has shown such proofs as *New Orleans Street* that the United States is not all metropolitan skyscrapers, vast plains, and mountains. "New Orleans, to me," he says, "has a distinct 'different world' flavor." It is exactly that flavor that he has perfectly caught in this lithograph.

The elements of the most attractive, least modernized sections of our most flavorsome city are all present in *New Orleans Street*. Here is the old mansion on which decay now lays its toll. Here the clapboard shack which is not quite content to be drab entirely, but must let down small, flaring steps to the sidewalk. Here the Southern Negro, not yet entirely robbed of his taste for exuberant color. Here, most characteristic and—to a Northerner—most exotic of all, the palm outside a conservatory. These details Mr. Bohrod has presented faithfully, by means of a shrewd selection of telling minutiae, but without comment. The result is a very true and satisfactory picture.

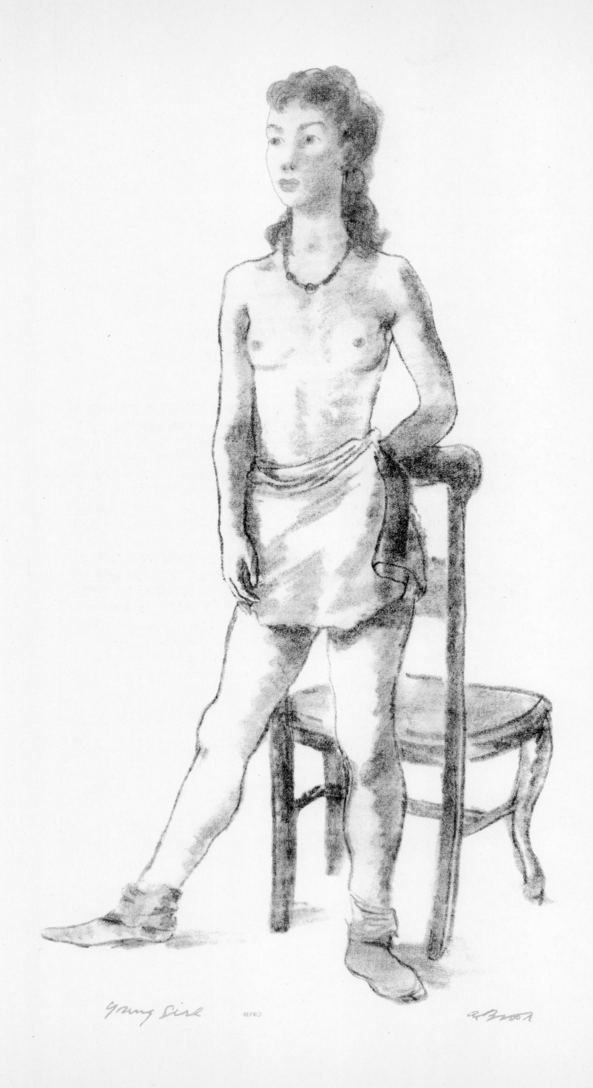

Young Girl   REPRO

Young Girl

BY ALEXANDER BROOK

(See reverse side for plate)

THE CAREER OF THIS distinguished artist has been brilliant in a variety of ways. First, he is a fine painter and lithographer. Second, he is a former Guggenheim fellow. Third, he is a thinker of real distinction, whose views on all phases of art are always interesting and deeply individual. Finally, he is married to Peggy Bacon. Brook is forty-one years old, a New Yorker by birth. He has received several important awards, and is widely represented in museums throughout the country. He has taught at the Art Students' League, and some years ago organized a school of painting at Cross River, New York, where he has a summer home.

Young Girl is simple and gracious in its appeal, artistically notable for fine draftsmanship and economy of means. This succinctness is characteristic of Brook. There is nothing overdone in his work, nothing fussy, no striving after effect. Young Girl is a memorable study, fresh and modern in its appeal, but with its roots deep in the living soil of a great tradition.

PLATE NUMBER SEVENTEEN

Sleep

BY ALEXANDER BROOK

(*See reverse side for plate*)

THIS BEAUTIFULLY considered study of a young woman may be contrasted with *Young Girl*. Here are the same economy of means, the same linear sensitiveness, the same native appreciation of essential structure. Here they are made to subserve the exposition of mature female amplitudes, yet the whole quality of *Sleep* is detached and passionless.

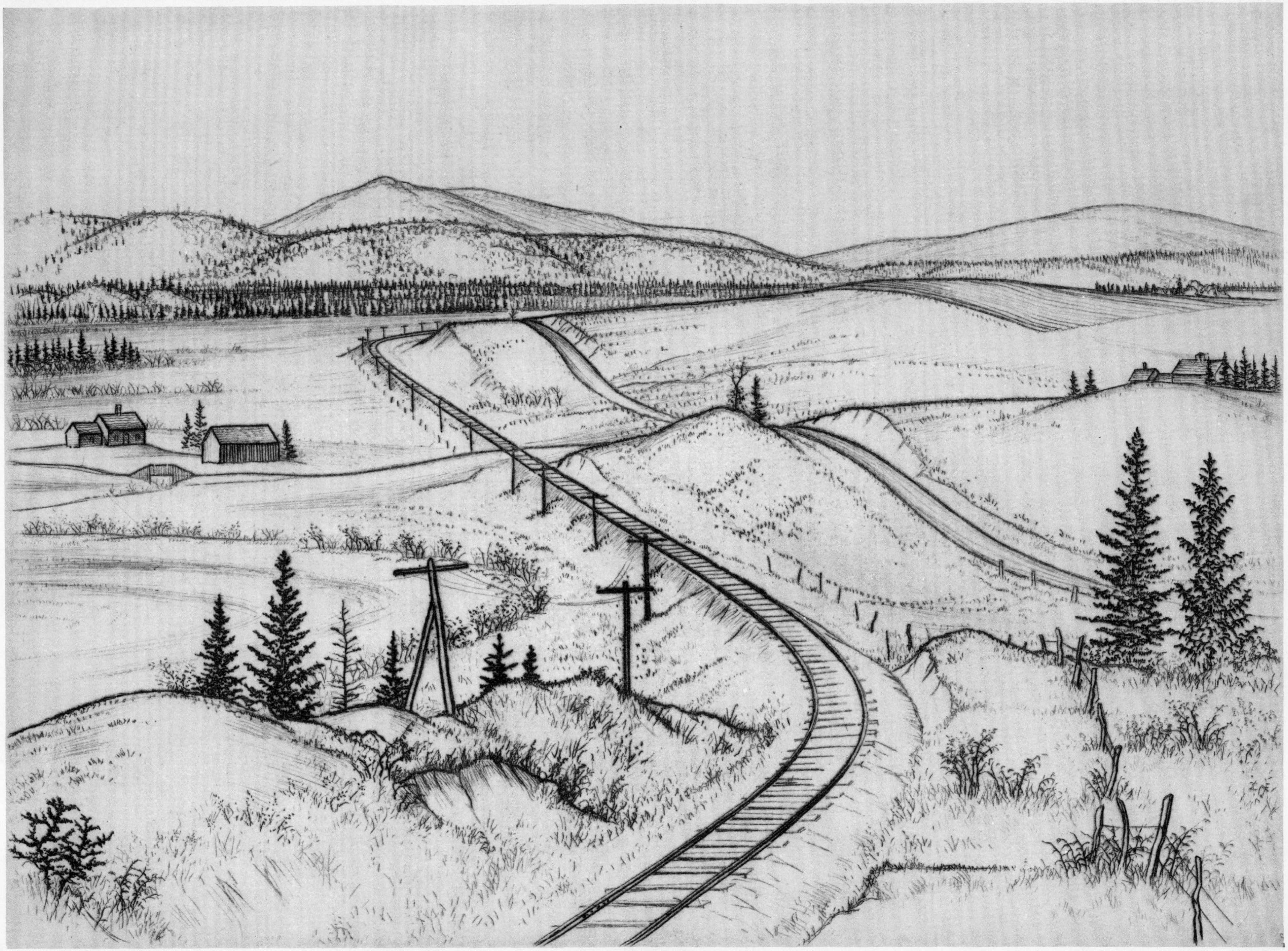

REPRO.

Andrew Butler '33

Mount Holly

BY ANDREW BUTLER

(*See reverse side for plate*)

ANDREW BUTLER paints and etches the countryside he loves. A native of Yonkers, and now a resident of Manhattan, he has farmed in the Southwest and in Virginia. The land got into his blood, and for some time he rashly thought that he might be able to combine farming and painting, but "found that either one would be entirely consuming." Anyone who has seen his eloquent rural scenes will agree that the artist has lovingly sublimated his yearning actually to till the soil.

Mr. Butler was born in 1896. He was educated at the National Academy of Design and the Art Students' League, where his teachers were Frank Du Mond, Eugene Speicher, and Luis Mora. He later returned to the League to study etching with Joseph Pennell.

The village of Mount Holly lies about fifteen miles southeast of Rutland, and this etching is a typical scene of high, bleak Vermont—of that part of the state lying against the backbone of the Green Mountains. It is quite open, and is very northern in its quality.

The artist, in his own words, set himself the problem of "a three-dimensional design, with a moving rhythm around the static element supplied by the near-by bank and the hill to the right. It was my intention to make the track, the stream, and the road move through these masses into the flatland and the forest in the background."

REPRO.

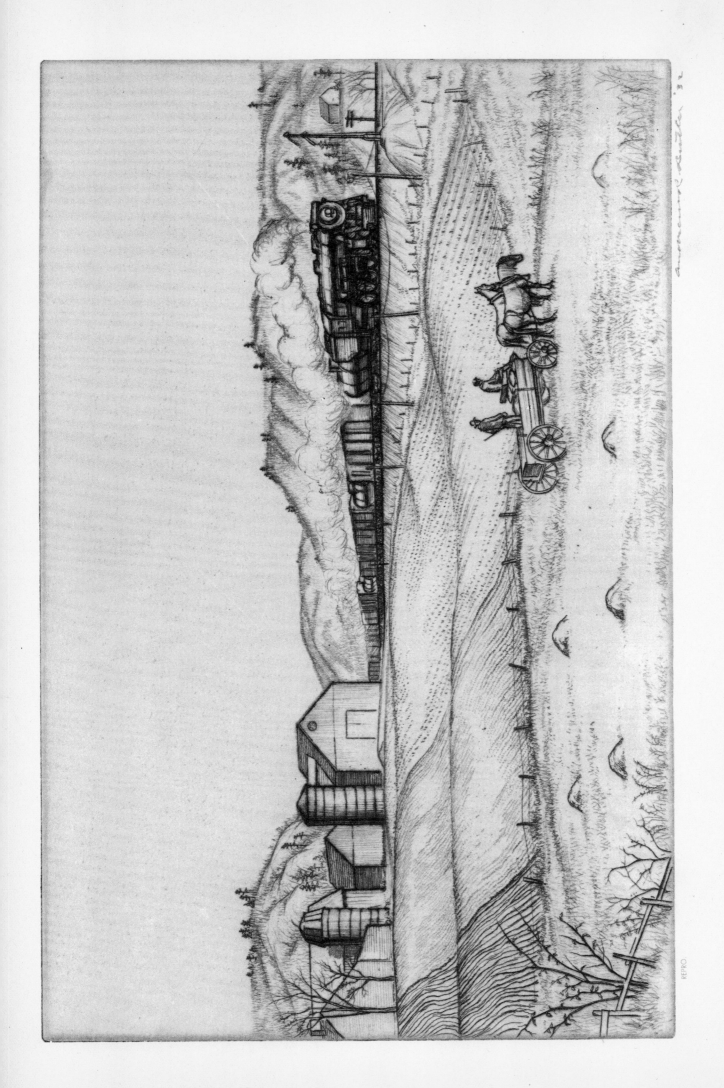

New England Scene

BY ANDREW BUTLER

(See reverse side for plate)

THE ELEGANCE and precision of Butler's line are strange instruments with which to subdue the sobriety and bleakness of New England. Yet, they prove to be oddly effective, even if the result is somewhat more gentle than the reality. Butler has an almost Japanese reverence for formal linear values that is inclined to sacrifice everything to the working out of the artistic problem at hand. So, in this *New England Scene* we must not take as realistic the neat railroad train, the precise tracks, the toy horse-and-buggy, the ideal far view: they are the elements of a composition fraught with rhythmic and dimensional complexities. This is, perhaps, not a profound art, but one that is perfect as far as it goes. Decoratively, at least, it is satisfying.

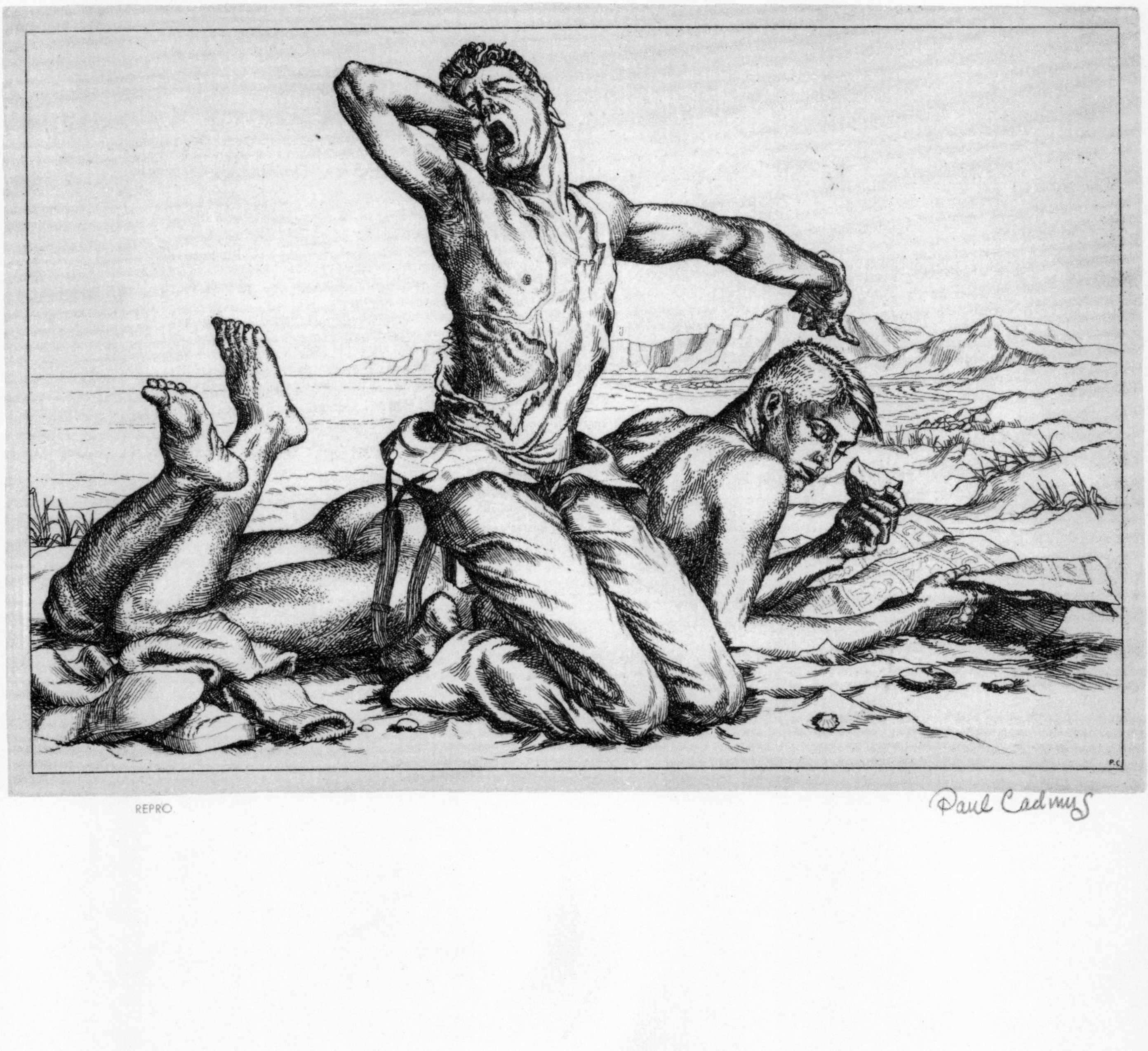
P.C.

REPRO.

Paul Cadmus

Two Boys on a Beach

BY PAUL CADMUS

(See reverse side for plate)

SOME YEARS AGO, a young man by the name of Paul Cadmus leapt into fame overnight by the print of a painting that he had called *The Fleet's In*. The print was so frank, and its implications were so obvious, that the Navy Department filed an official objection. The original painting now hangs in the Walters Gallery in Baltimore. When the author of this outrage was ferreted out he was found to be a shy, retiring youngster, rather scholarly and bookish in his tastes, with all his sensationalism in his paintings and prints. Paul Cadmus is less than thirty-five years old, and the way he has clung to a sure-fire but unvarying technique may give some of his well-wishers an uneasy feeling that he was not quite ready for the fame so unceremoniously thrust upon him when *The Fleet's In* burst upon the world. However, there is no question that Cadmus has a fine and distinctive talent. It remains to see what he will do with it. He needs to forget his market for a while, sit back and take stock of himself, and see precisely where immaturity persists in his work.

In practically all of Cadmus' work there is a hint of violence—actually taking place, imminent, or latent. *Two Boys on a Beach* sounds drowsy enough, but the suppressed power of the yawning boy is eloquent of Cadmus' preoccupation. It is an interesting motif, but it finally becomes monotonous. Here, however, the contrast has a telling effect: the relaxed youth lying on his stomach, and the other boy flung back on his knees in a paroxysm of weariness.

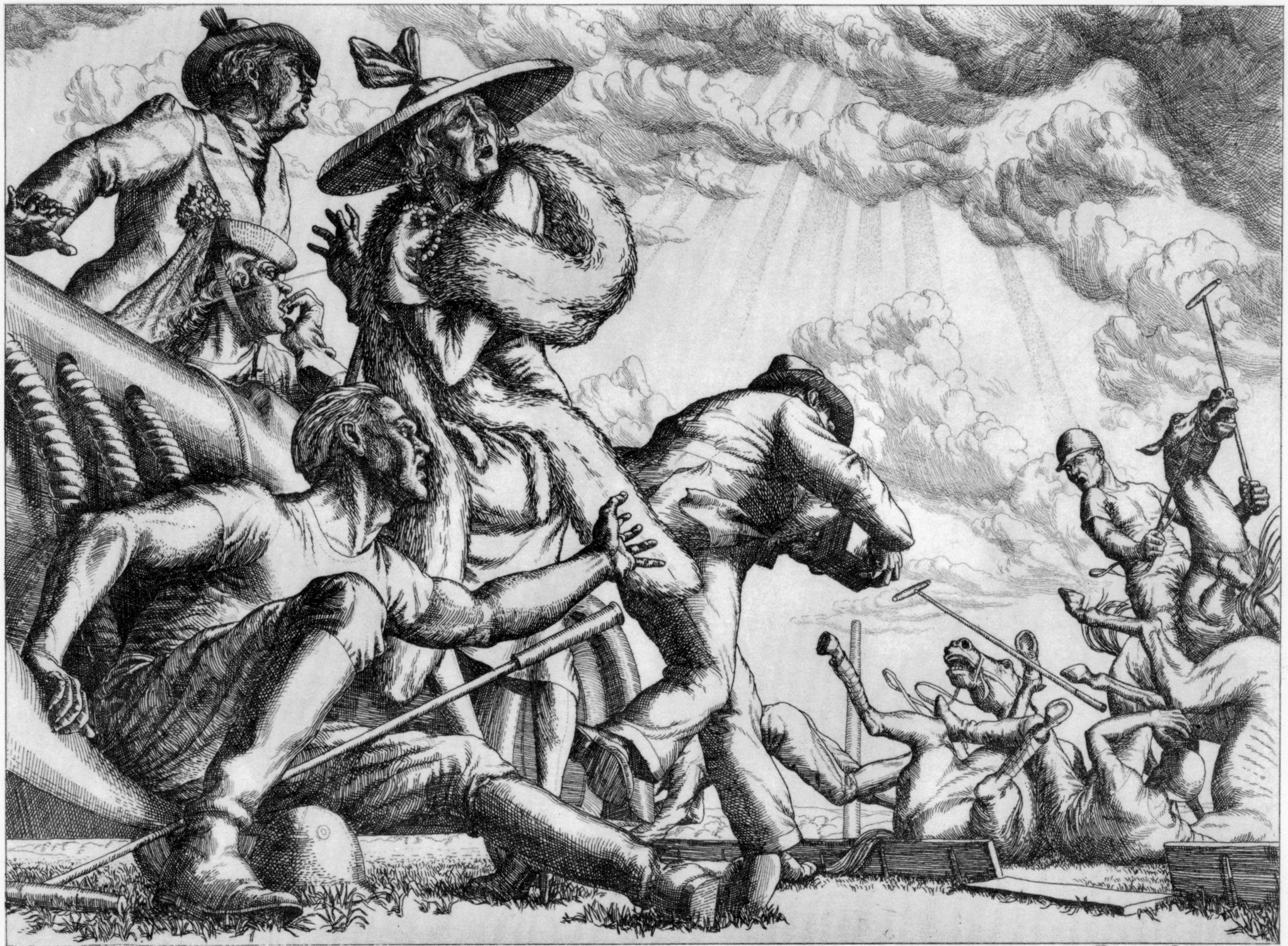

REPRO.

Paul Cadmus

PLATE NUMBER TWENTY-ONE

Aspects of Suburban Life—Polo Spill

BY PAUL CADMUS

(*See reverse side for plate*)

CADMUS WAS WELL TAUGHT. He is a pupil of Joseph Pennell, Auerbach-Levy, Charles Locke, and Jared French. His work throbs with native genius controlled by carefully learned lessons. Yet, Cadmus' style is his own, or at least he has chosen his own shrines at which to worship. *Polo Spill*, a print made after the original mural in the American legation building at Ottawa, Canada, is medieval in style and flavor. The caricature, the violence of the attitudes, the stylized glory from the heavens—all derive from Dürer and Schongauer. But there is something here, much indeed, that is not merely derived. There is an innate appreciation for the dramatic moment, a sense of the tragicomic, and a flair for effective extravaganza. All these are, of course, allied to his preoccupation with violence, and tend to hallmark his work, which is in danger of becoming stereotyped because of the excessive narrowness of his traditional sources.

No one can deny, however, that *Polo Spill* has the power of keeping the spectator's eye riveted on the catastrophe. It is composed with climactic intention, and comes off. There is no doubt that the lavishness of the stage business is humorously piled on to make something of a burlesque out of the entire situation.

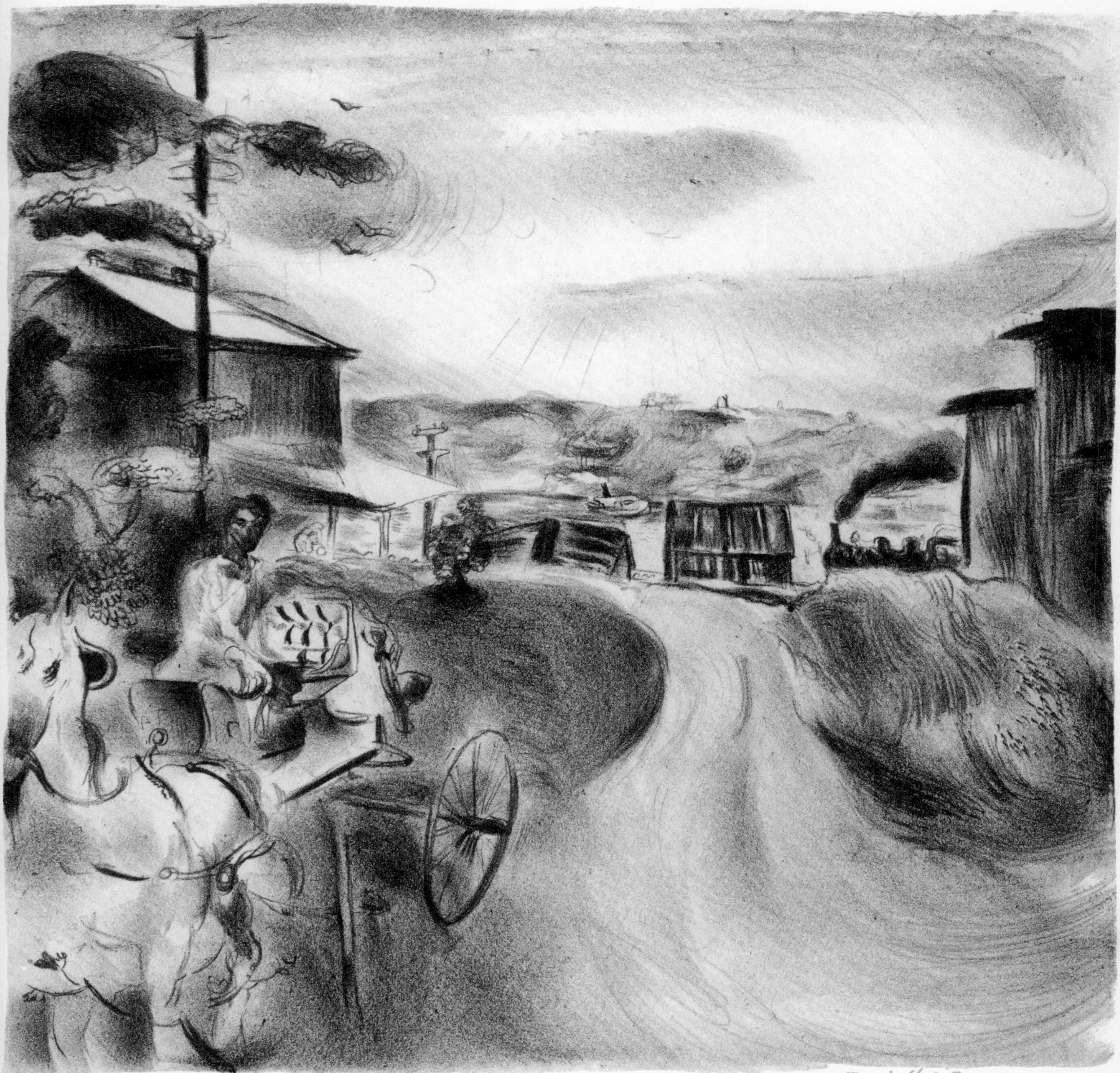

REPRO. *Morning Train* *Francis Chapin*

PLATE NUMBER TWENTY-TWO

Morning Train

BY FRANCIS CHAPIN

(*See reverse side for plate*)

FRANCIS CHAPIN is a Chicago artist whose facility in water-color painting is making a name for him throughout the country. The brilliancy of his water-color technique has been carried over into many of his lithographs, of which *Morning Train* is an especially fine example. The black-and-white contrasts are managed with an ease and sureness that give a great sense of brio to the entire handling of the scene. The delicate tone arrangements show a sensitive feeling for minute color gradation. Finally, a dazzling technique has achieved a satisfactory composition, notable for nice balance and rhythmic emphasis.

Mr. Chapin, who was born in Bristolville, Ohio, forty years ago, makes his summer home in Saugatuck, Michigan. He teaches painting and lithography in the Art Institute of Chicago school. Speaking of *Morning Train,* he says that he made the lithograph to provide a setting for the train—"which itself was not present in the Saugatuck landscape, the nearest tracks being the Pere Marquette, five miles away at New Richmond."

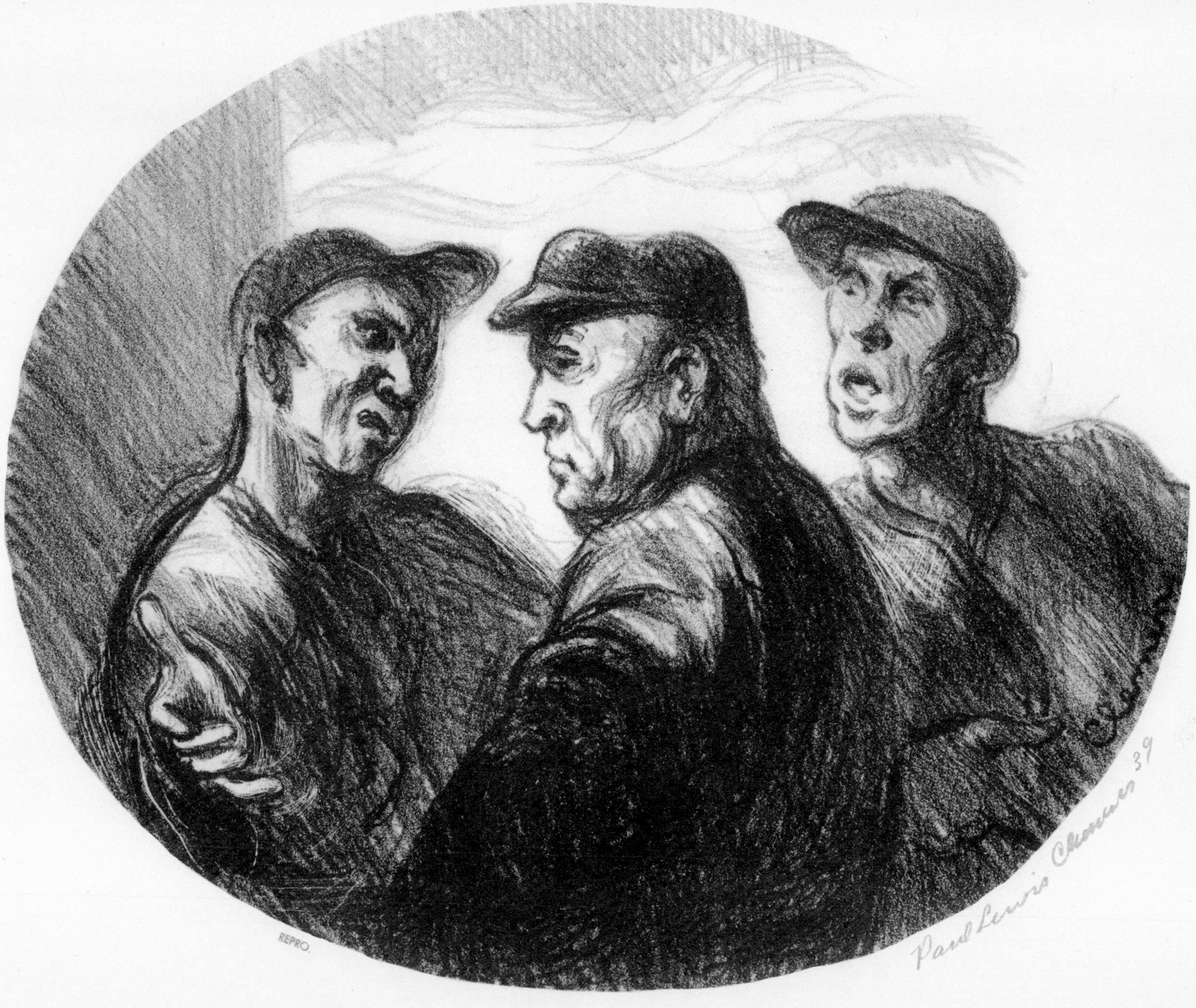
REPRO.

PLATE NUMBER TWENTY-THREE

Baseball Argument

BY PAUL LOUIS CLEMENS

(See reverse side for plate)

YOUNG PAUL LOUIS CLEMENS is probably the only serious American artist devoting most of his creative energy to the world of sports. A native of Superior, Wisconsin, and a student of Oskar Hagen at the art school of the University of Wisconsin, the twenty-eight-year-old artist has remained true to the enthusiasms of the old vacant lot whence come the future Sultans of Swat. In *Baseball Argument,* a couple of the Sultans are putting it up to the Old Man, and obviously getting no place with him at all.

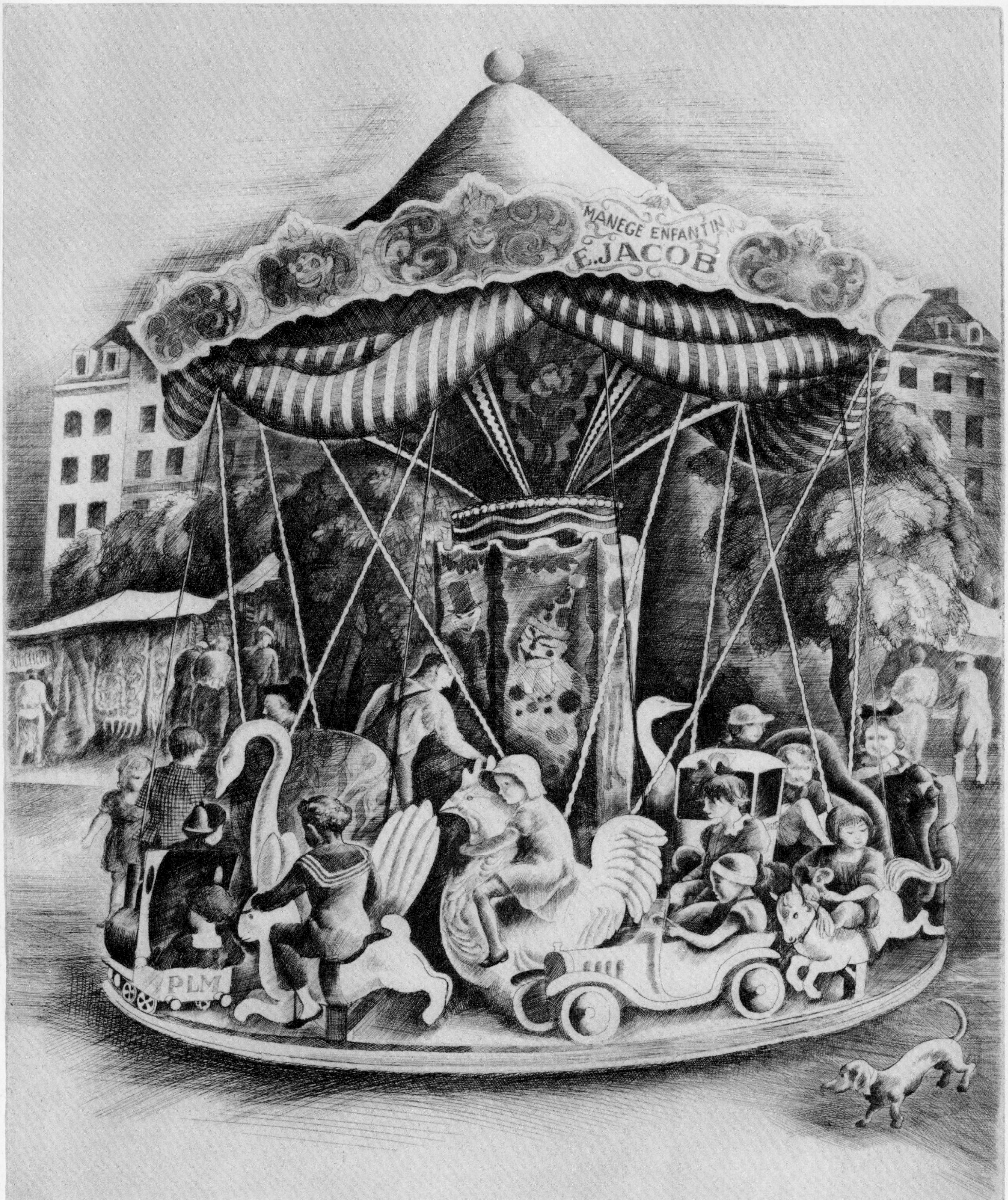
MANEGE ENFANTIN
E.JACOB
PLM

REPRO.

Howard Cook 1931 exp.

PLATE NUMBER TWENTY-FOUR

Merry-Go-Round

BY HOWARD COOK

(*See reverse side for plate*)

THIS DELIGHTFUL ETCHING comes from the pen of a man whose subject matter, if often, or even usually, exotic, is rarely as light and charming as this. Howard Norton Cook is a widely traveled and highly sophisticated artist whose vagabonding and varied interests have much influenced his choice of subjects. He came to the graphic arts after some years devoted to tobacco farming and advertising, and this fact, too, is not without significance in uncovering the sources of his interests. A native of Massachusetts—he was born at Springfield in 1901—Cook received his training at the Art Students' League. In 1934, he was granted a Guggenheim for creative work in print making. His work has appeared in *Fifty Prints of the Year* for five consecutive years, and he is widely represented both here and abroad.

Merry-Go-Round is a delicate capturing of a typical Parisian scene. Everything is touched with a poetic imagination, and a droll eye for detail is allowed its way with just the right measure of restraint. The treatment is adroit without being slick, showing a strong feeling for design nicely balanced against the realities of the situation.

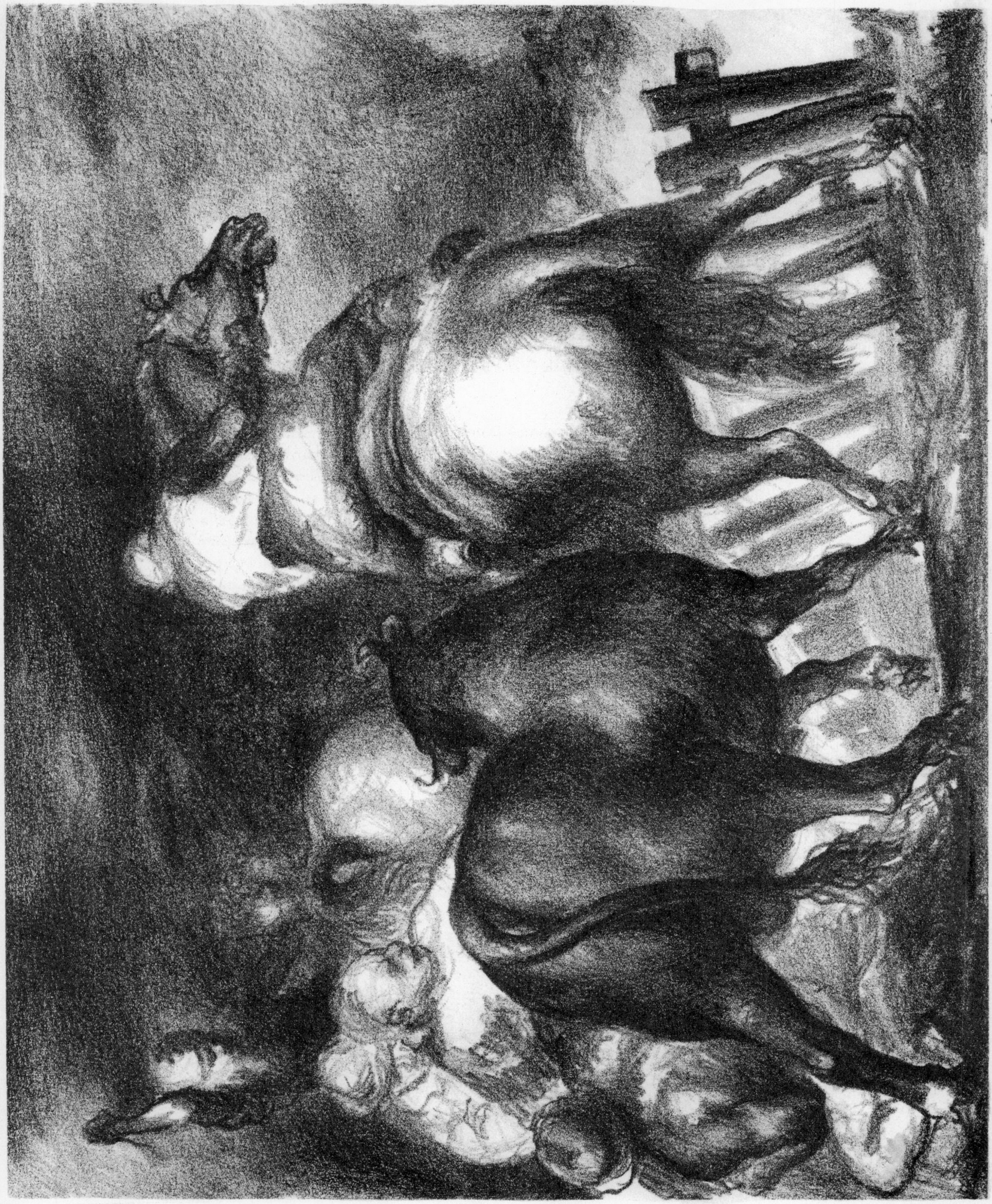

PLATE NUMBER TWENTY-FIVE

Escaped Bull

BY JON CORBINO

(*See reverse side for plate*)

ALTHOUGH JON CORBINO is of Italian ancestry—he was born in Vittoria, Italy, in 1905—his highly individual work has an American vigor. He has twice been the recipient of a Guggenheim fellowship. When his artistic sources become less obvious, he may well emerge as an artist of ponderable distinction. It may be true that his debts to Delacroix and Goya are large. To the Frenchman he seems to owe the almost physical strength of his crowded designs, to the Spaniard his unsparing treatment of human meanness and ugliness. But the raw power of the animal subjects he delights in has a distinct New World tension.

Escaped Bull owes much of its dramatic potency to Corbino's intensely selective eye and habit of drawing from memory rather than from life. The subject at first hand would probably have been more suitable to the camera than to the lithographer's stone, but as arranged by Corbino it is perfectly adapted black-and-white material. Lending the whole excited scene a quality of alarm by placing the legs of the bull and the frightened horse in awkward, strained positions, intensifying the importance of brute muscle by relegating the human beings to carefully selected secondary positions, and weighting the entire quadrangle of gray, white, and black down with a threatening and unsympathetic sky, Corbino has produced a lithograph which seems to live by virtue of some vigor native to itself.

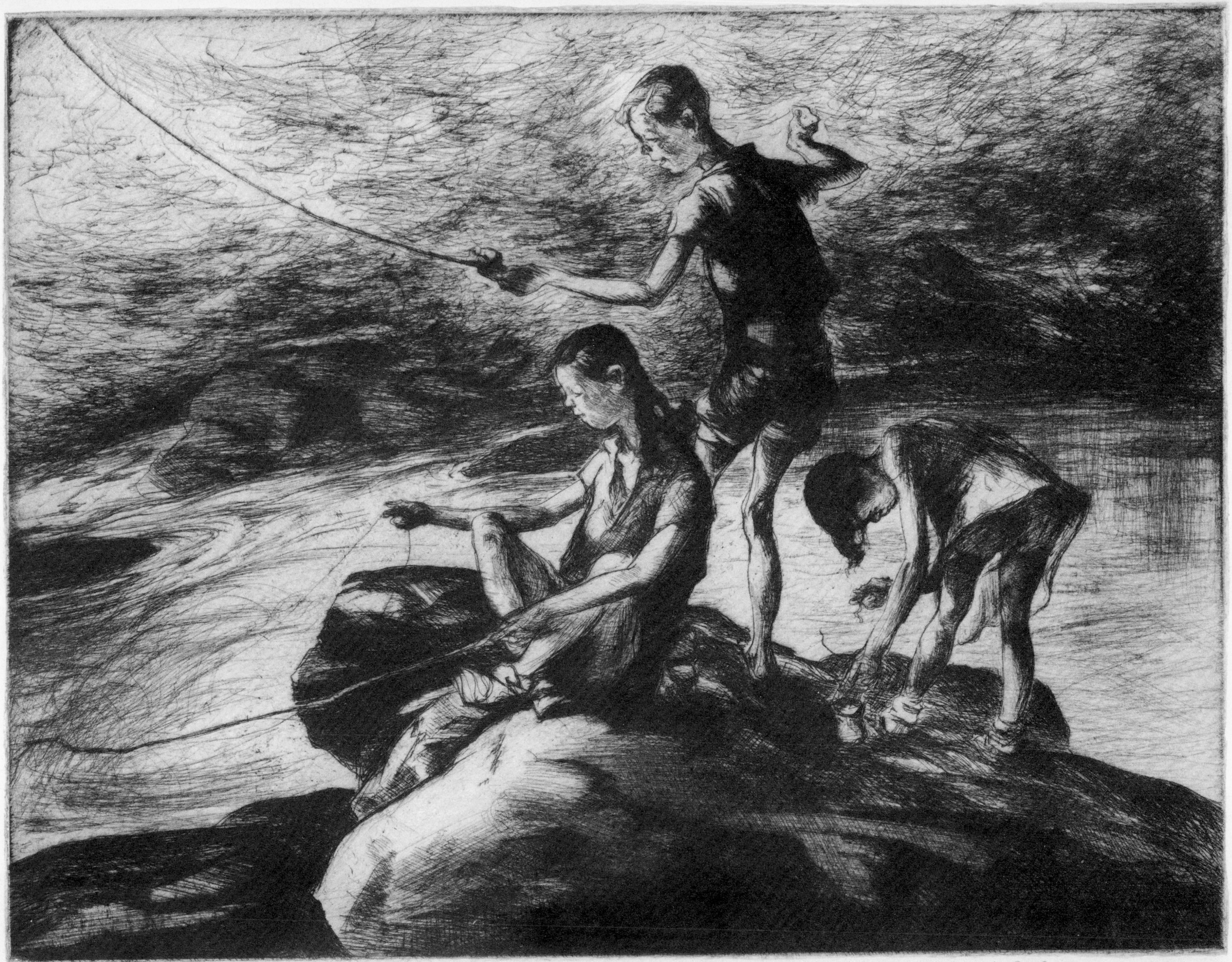

REPRO.

J. E. Costigan N.A.

PLATE NUMBER TWENTY-SIX

Fishermen Three

BY JOHN E. COSTIGAN

(*See reverse side for plate*)

JOHN E. COSTIGAN is an unusual phenomenon among American artists: he is self-taught. Born in Providence fifty-one years ago, he went to New York at the age of eighteen, and for ten years did posters for theaters. In the early 1900's, there was still a lot of leisure around (even in New York), and Mr. Costigan tried experimenting in oils. His development was interrupted by the World War, during which he saw service overseas. After returning to America, he went to live in the country. His home is a farm near Orangeburg, New York, and here he raises livestock and lives a typical farmer's life—when he is not painting or etching, of course. He is deeply attached to the soil, and conceives of the city only as a market place for the products of the country.

Mr. Costigan has come far from that day in 1904 when he got his first job doing posters. Now an esteemed artist, his works are in no less than sixty-two museums both here and abroad. *Fishermen Three* is an adaptation of a watercolor sketch of Mr. Costigan's three children fishing in a stream that wanders through the farm at Orangeburg. With a fine sense of etching quality, he has, in transferring the original to the plate, simplified the background. The result is an attractive picture of peace, of youthful awkwardness and spontaneous childish concentration on the pastime at hand.

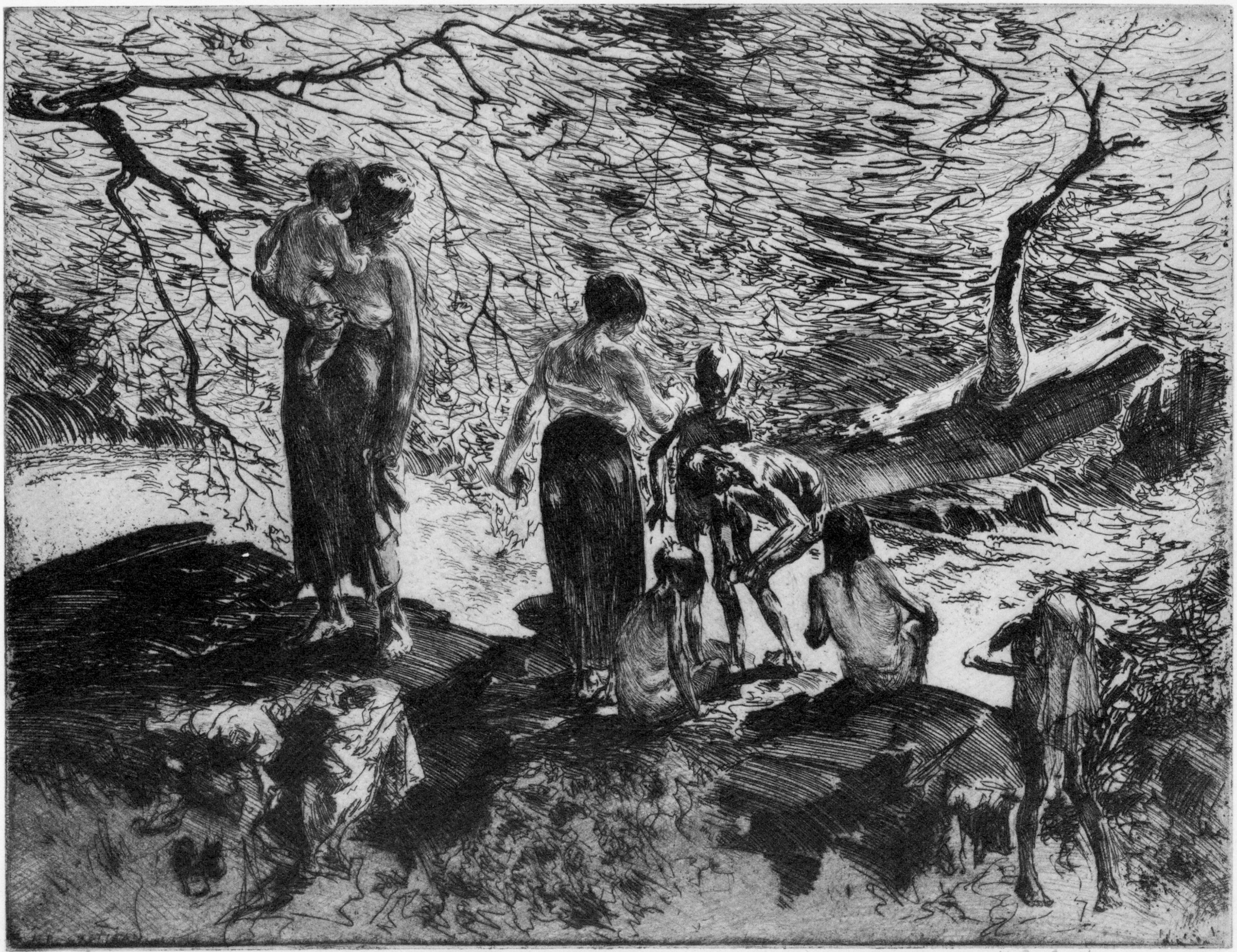

Bathers REPRO. J. E. Costigan N.A.

PLATE NUMBER TWENTY-SEVEN

Bathers

BY JOHN E. COSTIGAN

(*See reverse side for plate*)

Bathers is a study in repose. Although not one of the eight figures in the scene is lying down, and only two of them—and they almost the least important—are sitting down, the whole scene is full of relaxation, of time enjoyed slowly. The very quality of light filtered through branches, of reflected radiance coming from the water below rather than from a direct sky overhead, contributes immeasurably to this sensation of peaceful enjoyment.

By looking long and thoughtfully at the commonplace events taking place about him, on his own farm at Orangeburg, and by refusing to be distracted by whatever more dramatic events he has witnessed, Costigan has been able to draw off the essence of everyday American life on a residential farm. His work is not likely to appeal to those who like violent movement, exposures of events in crisis, or social interpretation. But such a print as *Bathers* is the very essence of that much discussed, but seldom realizable quality—the poetry of everyday life.

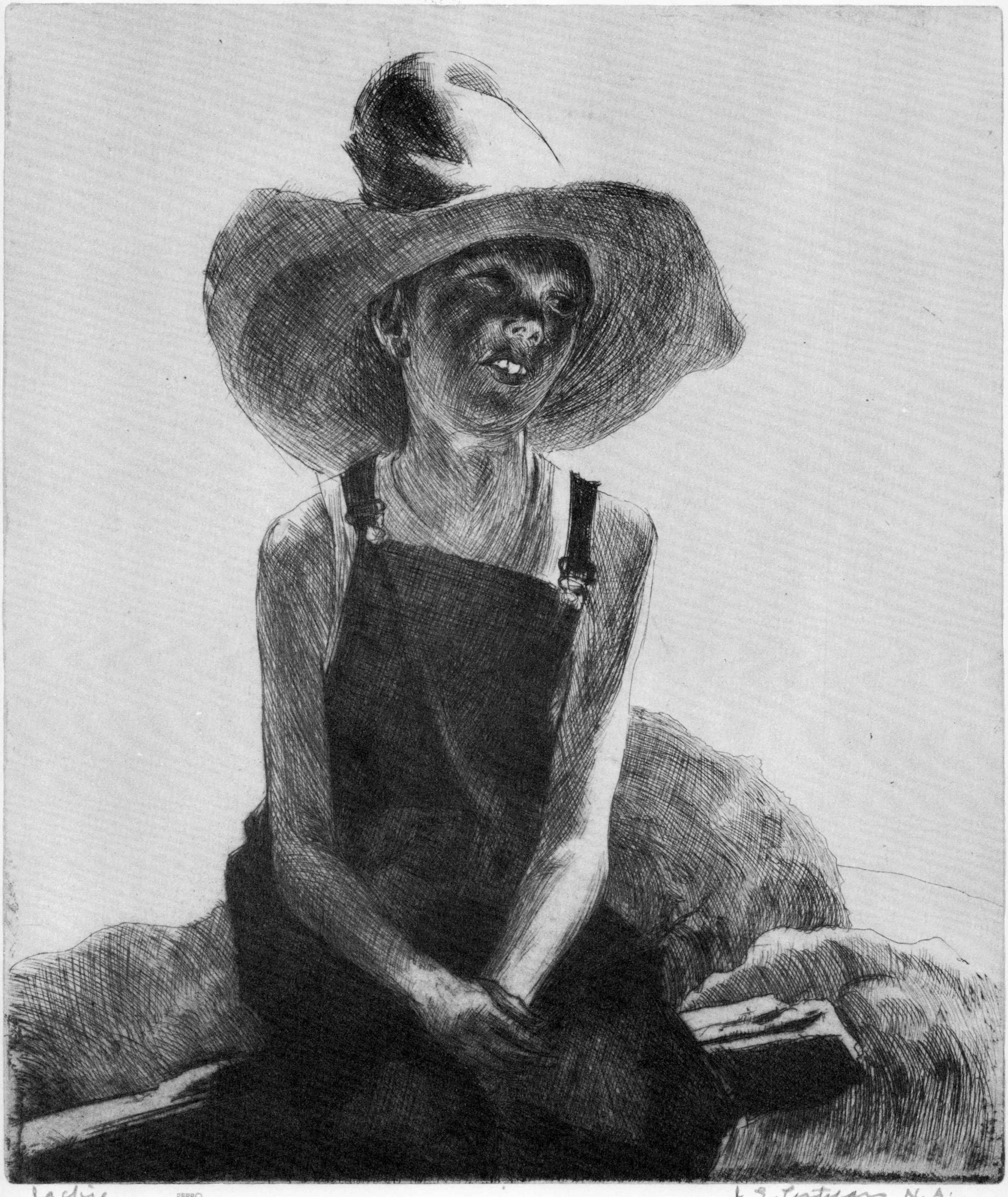

Jackie

REPRO.

J. E. Costigan N.A.

PLATE NUMBER TWENTY-EIGHT

Jackie

BY JOHN E. COSTIGAN

(*See reverse side for plate*)

COSTIGAN, with his intensely sincere approach to home subject matter, is the ideal man to deal with the "barefoot boy, with cheek of tan." *Jackie* is a study of the artist's small son. The subject wears an immense straw hat, reminding us that the Costigans are practical farmers, and that Jackie probably sat for his father after helping out with a good day's haying.

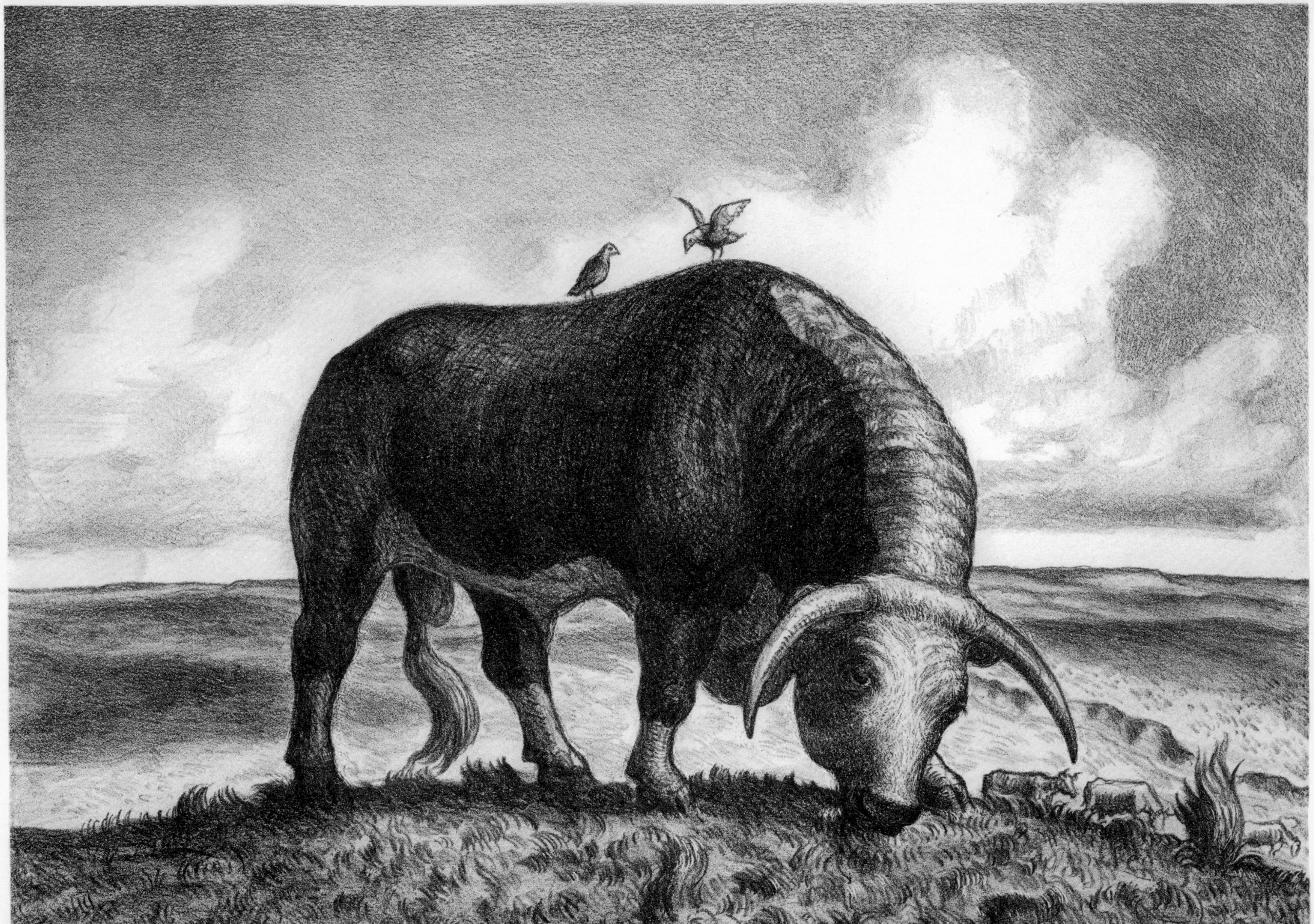
J. CURRY

"Ajax" REPRO. John Stewart Curry 1932

PLATE NUMBER TWENTY-NINE

Ajax

BY JOHN STEUART CURRY

(See reverse side for plate)

JOHN STEUART CURRY is a man whom no transient ambitions and no will-o'-the-wisp of fame could ever lure away from an essential devotion to rural America, specifically the Kansas of his birth. He was born in that state forty-two years ago, and until 1916, when he had his first taste of art school, first in Kansas City and then in Chicago, he spent most of his time on the farm, with his eyes always wide open. He came East in 1919, and tried illustrating. Though his work appeared in *The Saturday Evening Post* and *The Country Gentleman*, after several years he retired of his own volition, saying that he was not clever enough for magazine work. He married, went to Paris, and came back unimpressed. Meanwhile he kept on painting, and in 1928 exhibited *Baptism in Kansas*, which can fairly be called one of the landmarks of American painting. Since then, always gaining in knowledge and stature, Curry has proceeded in a straight line. As his goals are hard by the sources of his fertility, he is assured of a really creative life as long as he can wield a brush.

Ajax is the result of Curry's observations of Hereford bulls roaming the Heart Ranch in Barber County, Kansas. He saw an old range bull in 1933 that looked, he says, "like a prehistoric animal compared to the modern streamlined edition." This is *Ajax*, a more strenuous retired emperor than any Paul Potter ever painted.

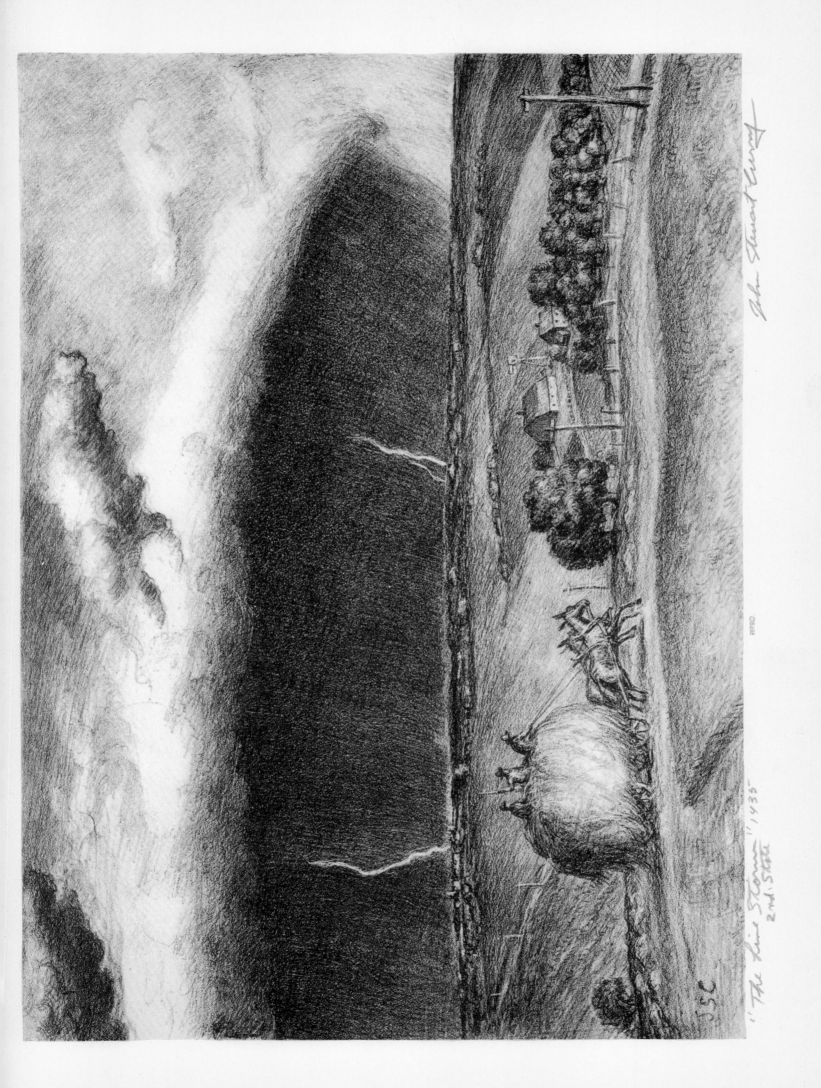

"The Lime Storm" 1935   John Stewart Curry
2nd State

The Line Storm

BY JOHN STEUART CURRY

(See reverse side for plate)

CURRY BEGAN TO MAKE lithographs in the winter of 1927 at the Art Students' League, under the tutelage of Charles Locke, "and has worked at stones off and on ever since." He often makes lithographs of his paintings, and such is *The Line Storm*, after the famous painting of the same name (considered by many to be Curry's masterpiece), in the collection of Sidney Howard, the playwright.

Curry himself has said significantly that *The Line Storm* was done "from memory of many such storms before which we fled." No one, almost in the whole range of painting, manages to communicate the terror caused by the convulsions of nature as Curry does. Thomas Craven has said of this picture (and the same things apply to the lithograph made from it) that it is "a masterpiece in which the elements and earth and sky and the whole landscape together with the frightened animals are transformed into an enormous personality alive with dramatic terror. Timid New Yorkers have called such pictures theatrical; they would say the same of *King Lear*. . . ."

The title of the lithograph may baffle some who are not used to Midwestern colloquialisms (Webster localizes the term in New England, where, indeed, it may have originated). A line storm is merely an equinoctial storm of first-rate dimensions.

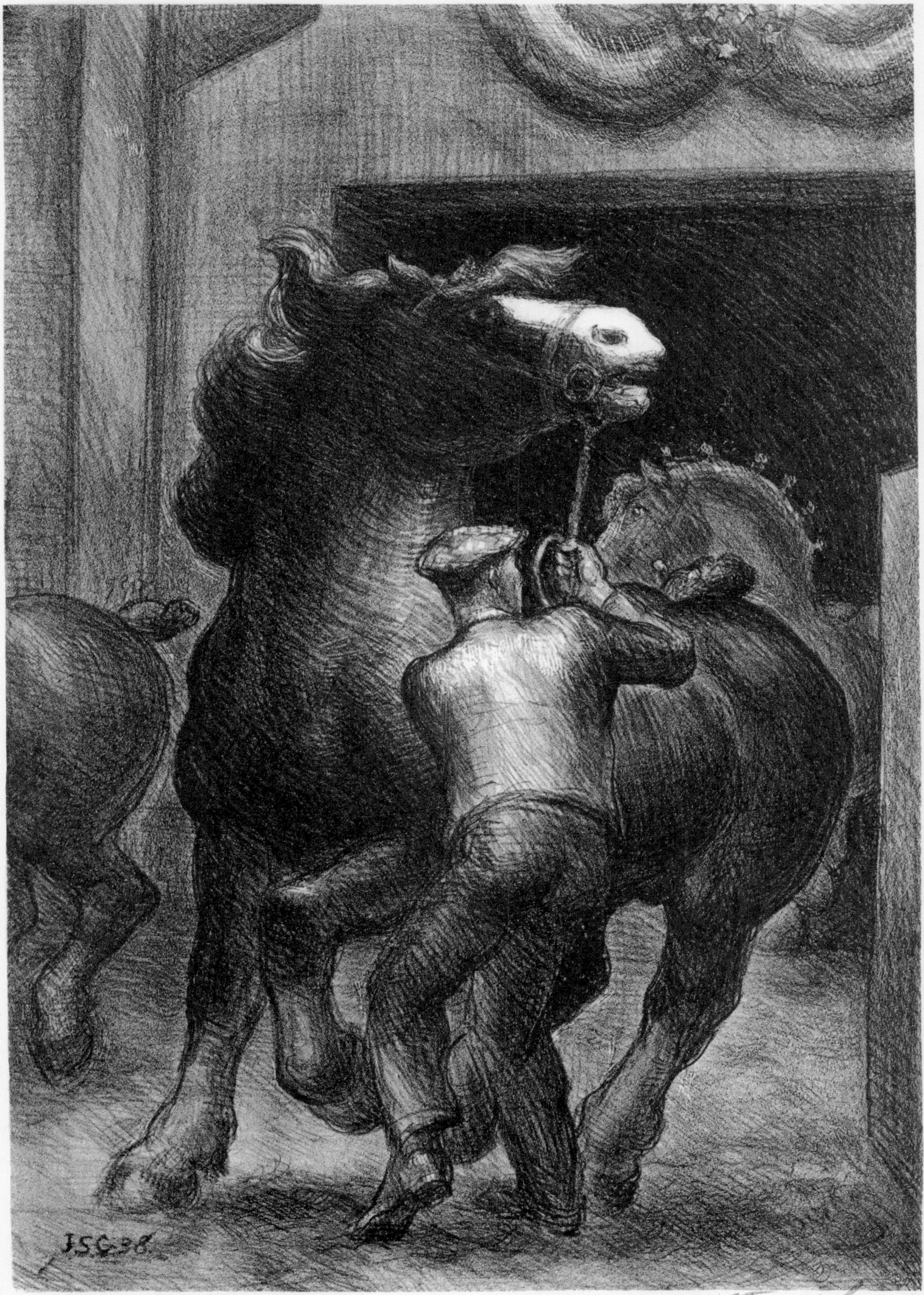
J.S.C. 38

"Prize Stallions"

REPRO

John Steuart Curry

PLATE NUMBER THIRTY-ONE

Prize Stallions

BY JOHN STEUART CURRY

(*See reverse side for plate*)

THE TAUT VIGOR of horses in action has, since the earliest beginnings of art, been a favorite subject, concentrating the attention of everyone from the first scratchers on cave walls to Rosa Bonheur, from El Greco to Giorgio di Chirico. The huge, beautifully balanced anatomy of a prize stallion being led from its stall has given John Steuart Curry a fine point of departure in this handsome lithograph. An interesting insight into the difference of two artists' conception of relatively similar subjects can be gained by comparing the huge animal in this lithograph with that in Jon Corbino's *Escaped Bull* (Plate 25). Mr. Curry has, so to speak, searched out the individual, nervous character of a particular prize stallion, while Mr. Corbino has been more interested in the dynamic physical voltage of a frightened horse.

Prize Stallions is a picture that radiates out from its center, where the light on the man's back and the stallion's chest seems to flow downward to the ground on which his hooves are momentarily planted, and upward—past the high-point of light on his head—to the less sharply drawn building and looped bunting. The result is an instant concentration on the center of physical energy, a depth and plasticity of perspective that make the stallion seem almost to be moving forward off the print.

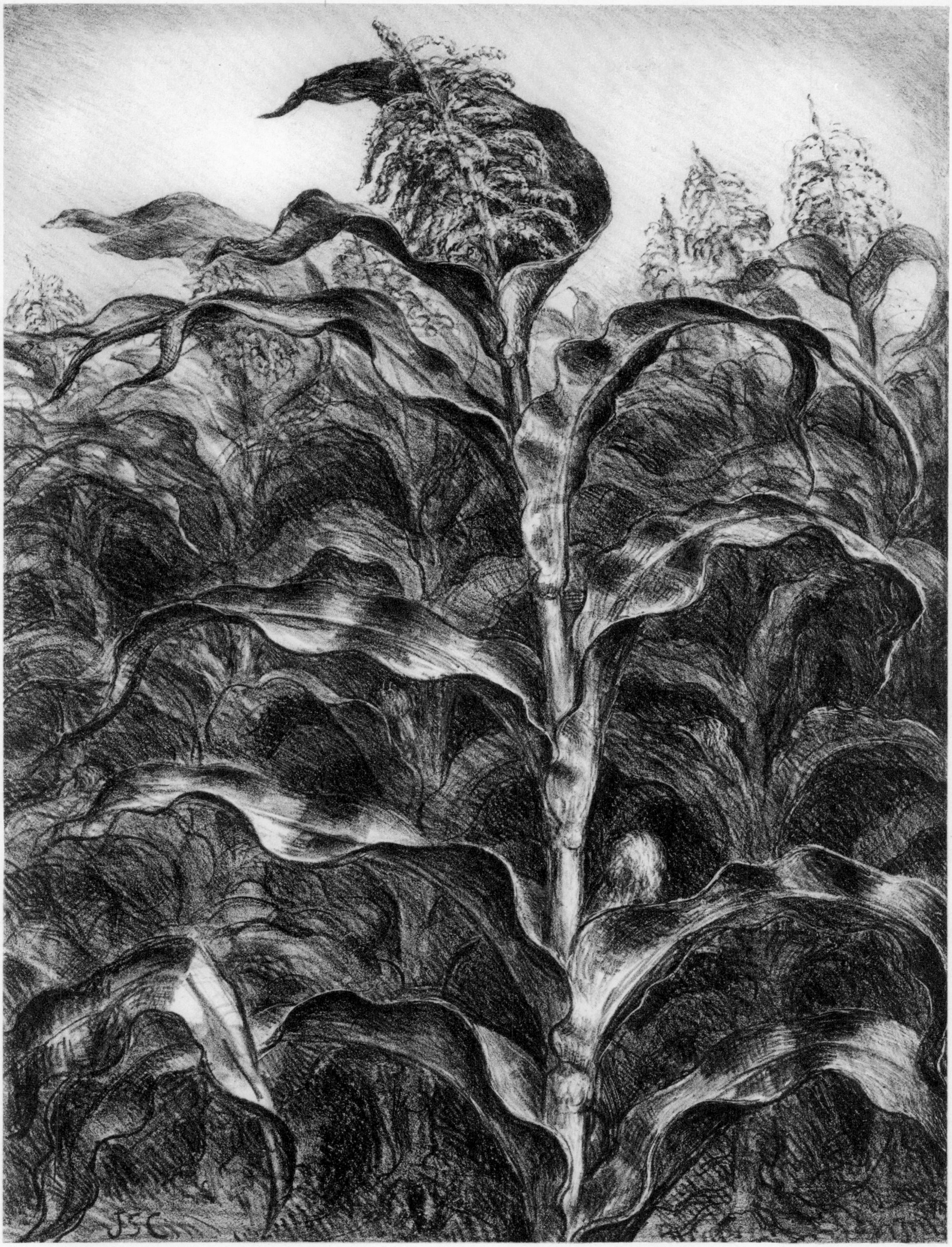
JSC

John Steuart Curry 1935

PLATE NUMBER THIRTY-TWO

Corn

BY JOHN STEUART CURRY

(*See reverse side for plate*)

ONLY THOSE WHO have watched the cycle of growing corn, and have helped in its planting, reaping, and threshing, can have a true sense of the majesty of the grain. Curry, who has worked with corn at every stage of its career, and who likes nothing better than a good roasting ear, has devoted this lithograph to an intimate study of ripe corn. Rarely does an artist take us into the field for a close-up of this sort. The result is magical, for the rows of stalks can be as impressive as the aisles of a great church.

The original oil painting, from which this lithograph was made, now hangs in the Wichita Art Association.

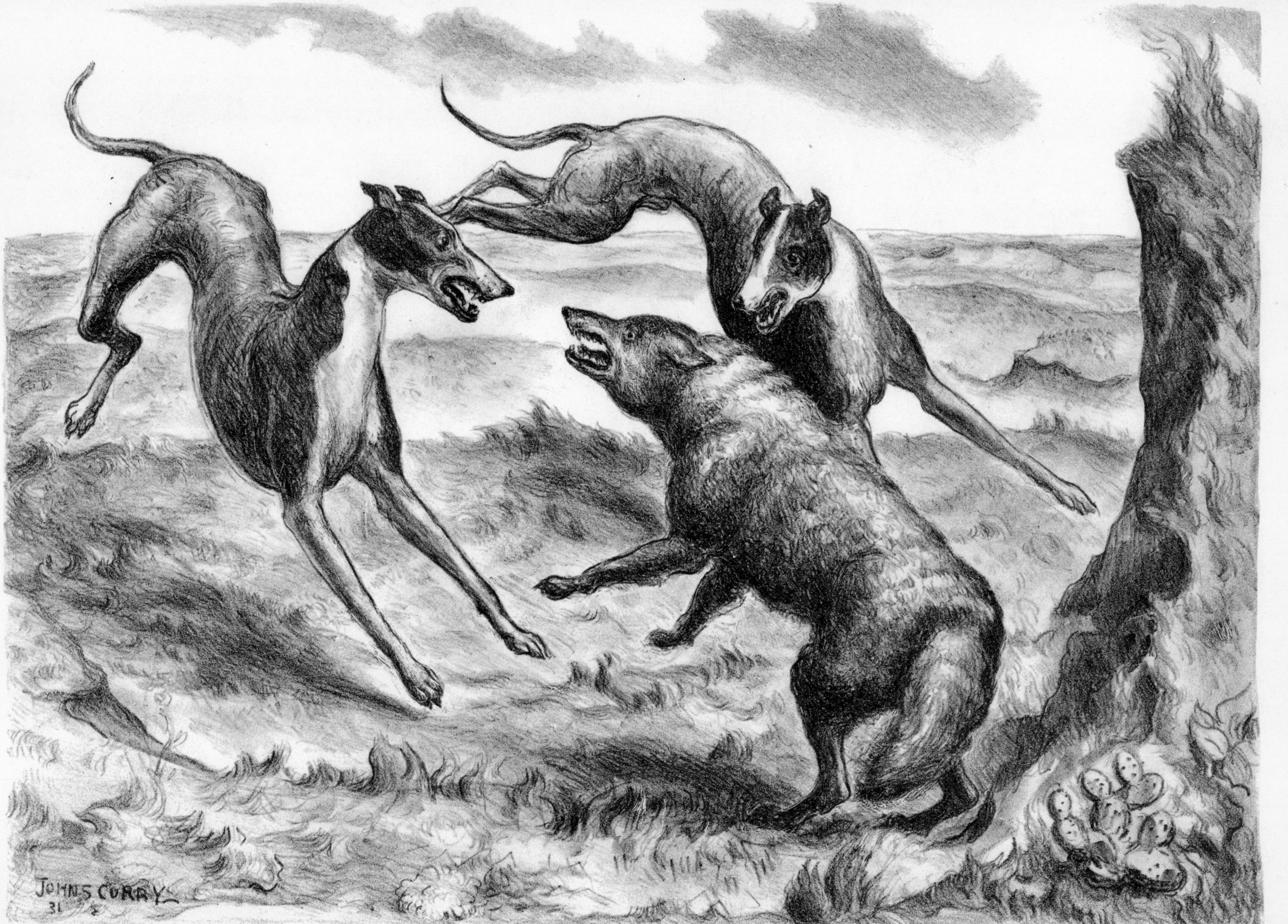
JOHNS CURRY
31

"Hounds and Coyote"

REPRO.

John Steuart Curry 1931

PLATE NUMBER THIRTY-THREE

Hounds and Coyote

BY JOHN STEUART CURRY

(*See reverse side for plate*)

CURRY IS FASCINATED by animals, whether tamed or wild. In 1932, he followed "The Greatest Show on Earth," and made several superb circus pictures and lithographs. Curry himself considers *Hounds and Coyote* one of his best lithographs. The three animals are vessels of the most violent action, and there is real untrammeled ferocity in this Kansas night scene. The coyote, an animal of great swiftness and considerable cunning, rarely allows itself to get within such close range of dogs, and undoubtedly the encounter Curry represents is not of the coyote's seeking. But, as we can see, it is a nasty customer when cornered, though it much prefers staying in the rut of its cowardly ways. The long, lean anatomy of the combatants is effective in enhancing the rapid movement of the composition.

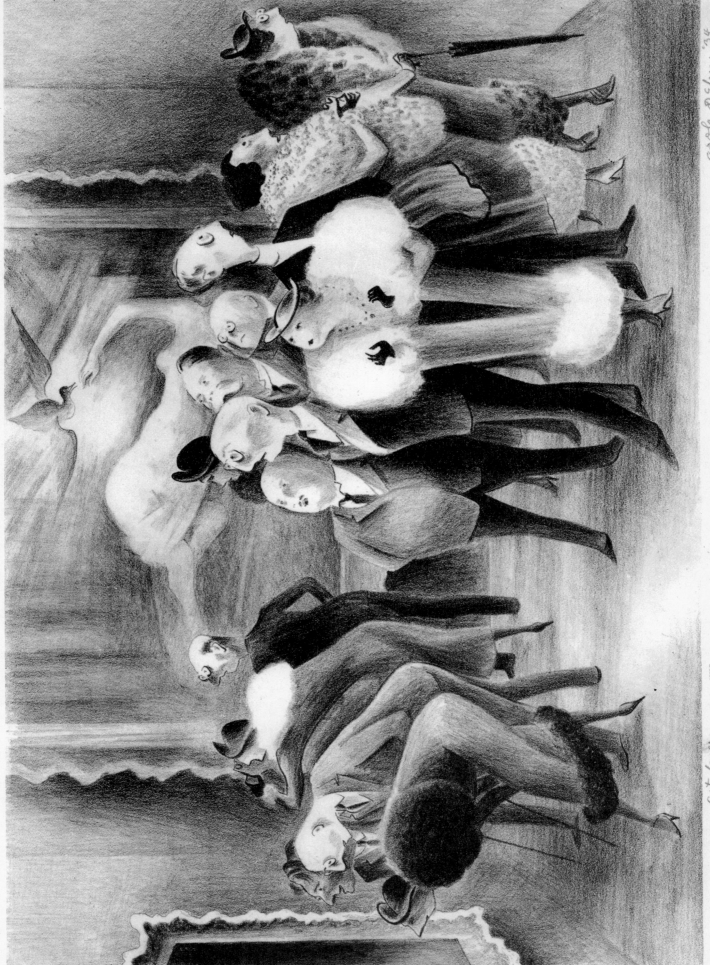

art lovers.

REPRO.

Adolf Dehn '34

PLATE NUMBER THIRTY-FOUR

Art Lovers

BY ADOLF DEHN

(See reverse side for plate)

ADOLF DEHN hates sham, and is amused by it. Here he is spying on a smart *vernissage,* than which, perhaps, there is nothing shammier. With Dehn, the commentator rarely has any work to do, for Dehn has done it all for him. Here, the victims do everything but speak—which is just as well. You do not have to look closely to identify the art-gallery regulars. The goateed man who seems to recoil with an esthetic "wild surmise" is a veteran, and so is the rapt fat lady who holds the center of the stage. It is just like this cynical fellow Dehn to have netted these specimens at a show of his own work, for no place and no time are sacred to his sacrilegious eye.

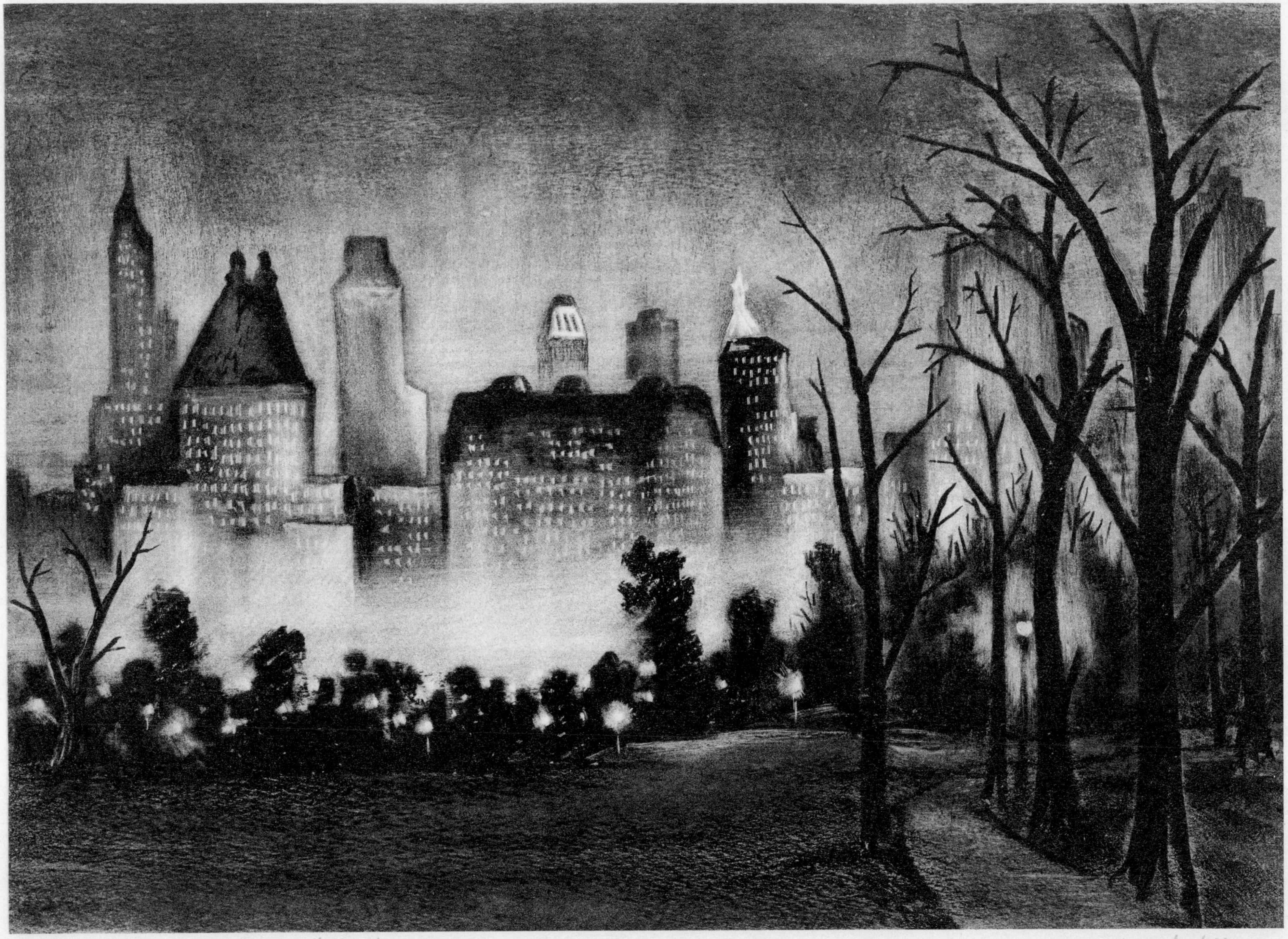

Central Park at Night REPRO Adolf Dehn '34

PLATE NUMBER THIRTY-FIVE

Central Park at Night

BY ADOLF DEHN

(*See reverse side for plate*)

EXPLAINING WHY he made the lithograph *Central Park at Night*, Dehn said, "The towering splendor of New York's skyline rising out of the glow of lights from the streets below, all of which was silhouetted against the black trees at night, was the thing that excited me." He set himself a difficult task: "My lithographic problem was to try to get the velvet blacks of the foreground, the intense glow of light, and the dull glow of the sky with the skyscrapers towering, and yet marching across the format of my paper. This I tried to do by combining pure washes with rubbed tones, scratching and scraping these down to light grays and pure whites, and then drawing strong blacks over the rubbed and washed tones."

The precise locale of the lithograph is the southeast corner of Central Park, looking toward Fifth Avenue, with the Plaza, the Savoy Plaza, and the Sherry Netherlands prominent on the sky line.

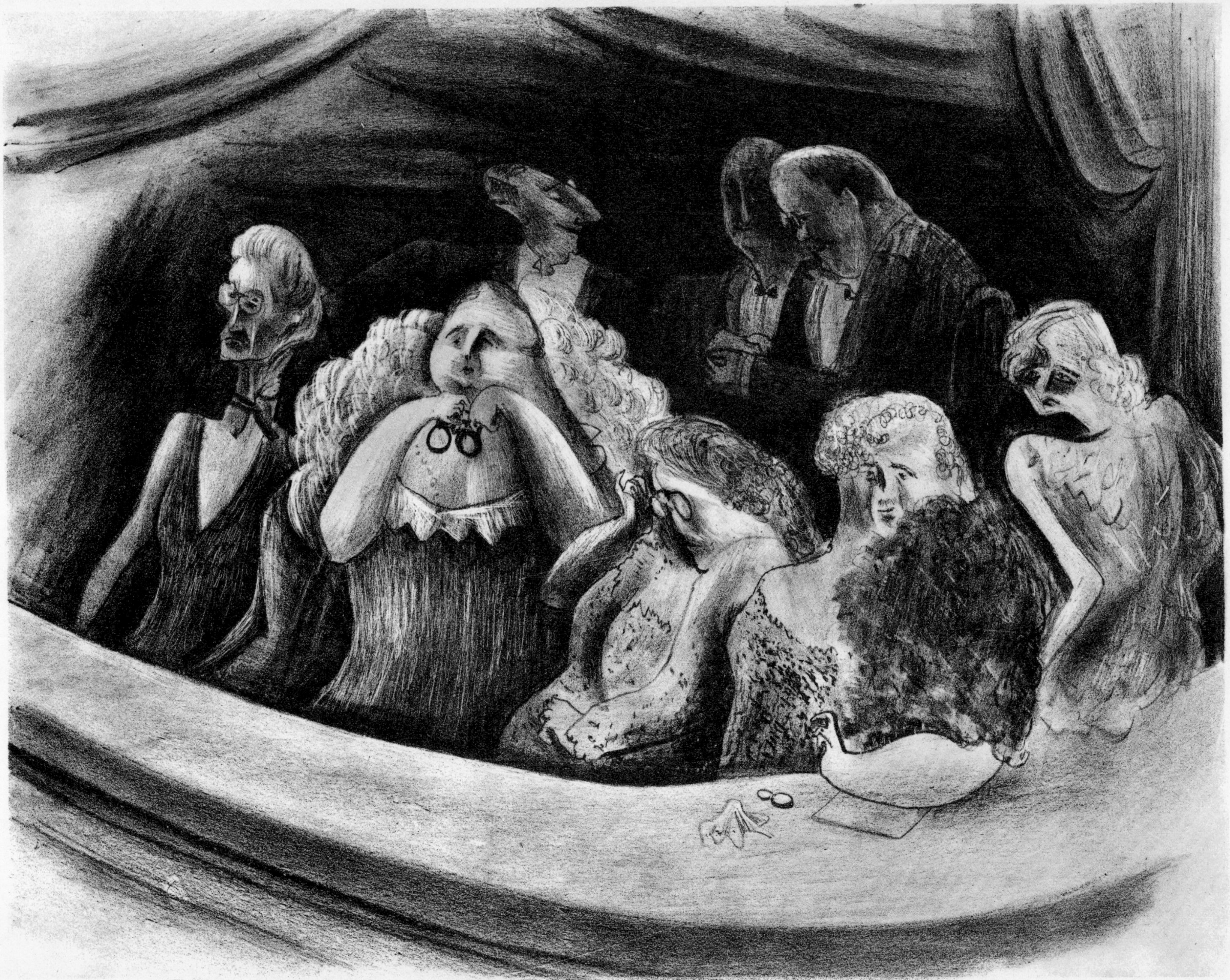

REPRO.

Adolf Dehn 1927

PLATE NUMBER THIRTY-SIX

Beethoven's Ninth Symphony

BY ADOLF DEHN

(See reverse side for plate)

HERE DEHN INVADES the holy of holies—Carnegie Hall on the day the Ninth Symphony of Ludwig van Beethoven (who loathed society) is being performed. Naturally, society is out in battle gear for this event.

It is plain that the symphony has already been on for some time. The men in the rear of the box (who probably loathe Beethoven as much as he would loathe them) are deep in the latest crop of stories. Or they are discussing the market—anything but Beethoven, in fact. The women are more formidable than the men, except for the deb on the right. The battle-ax on the left has not lost an argument in fifty years. The vague, large creature who practically obliterates the deb gets that way because she is trying to do her artistic and social duties simultaneously, that is, watch Toscanini and her friends in the other boxes with only one pair of eyes to turn the trick.

Beethoven's Ninth Symphony is one of Dehn's most savage satires. It has practically none of that amiability that takes the sting out of many of his social scenes.

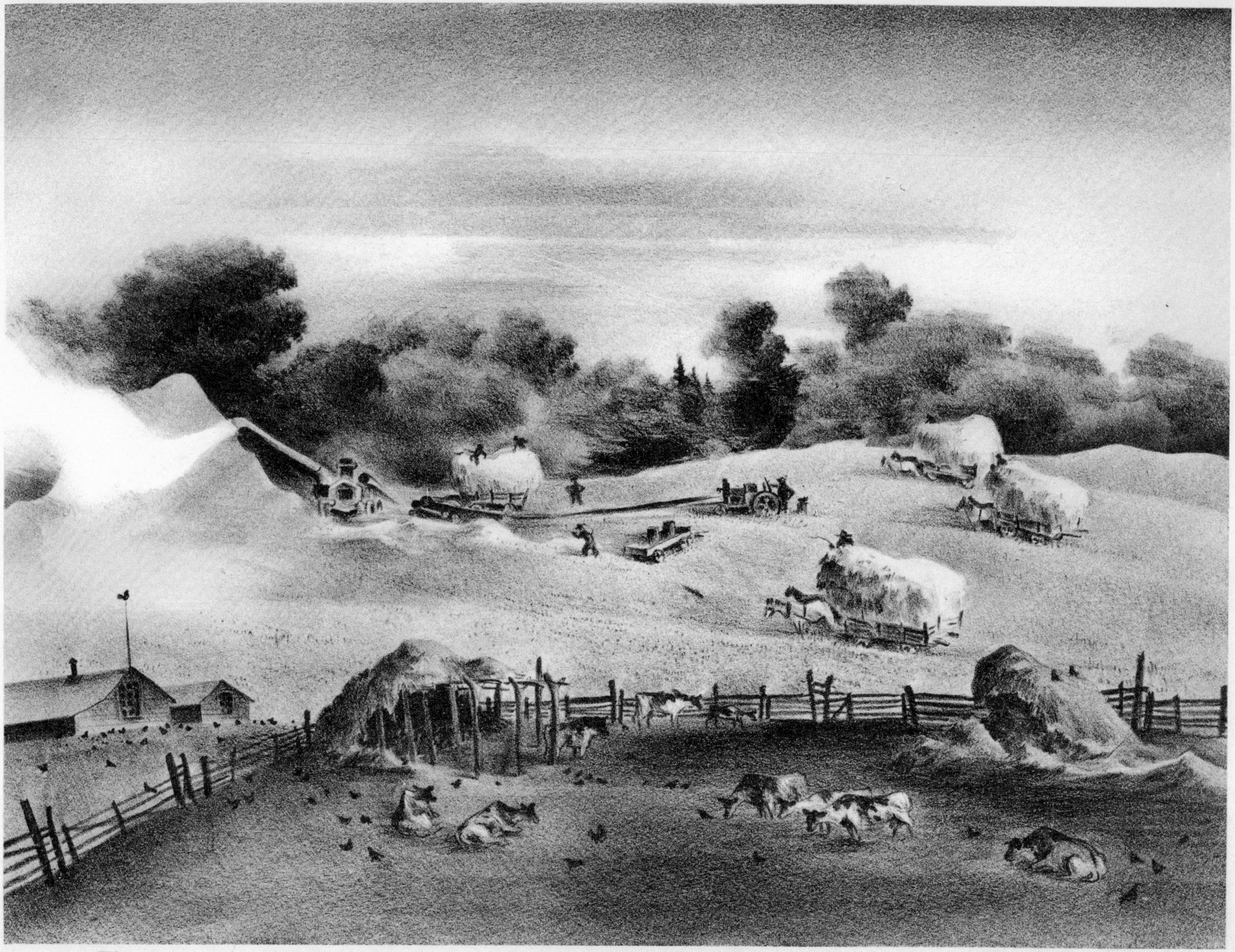

REPRO.

Adolf Dehn

PLATE NUMBER THIRTY-SEVEN

Threshing

BY ADOLF DEHN

(*See reverse side for plate*)

THE ROUGH TECHNIQUE of Dehn's satiric studies is in sharp contrast to the loving care the artist lavishes on his landscapes. There is a fascinating psychological problem here. Dehn has great love for the country in which he was reared, and still takes long vacations in Minnesota. He feels tender toward landscape, not toward the people who inhabit the cruel areas of his social sketches.

Threshing conveys the almost voluptuous plenty of that Minnesota farmland. Everything, except the peaceful enclosure in the foreground, seems deluged by the golden grain, which billows up with the exuberance of a snowdrift. In this fabulous agricultural Golconda Dehn was born forty-four years ago, and thence he came to New York with a scholarship at the Art Students' League, where he studied with Boardman Robinson. He spent eight years in Europe, looking at pictures, acquiring the feel of great civilizations, and earning a livelihood by selling drawings to magazines. Already a great caricaturist, he had done his best work in drawing, mainly line. In 1927 he found his own expressive idiom in lithography, and has since become one of the world's most distinguished lithographers.

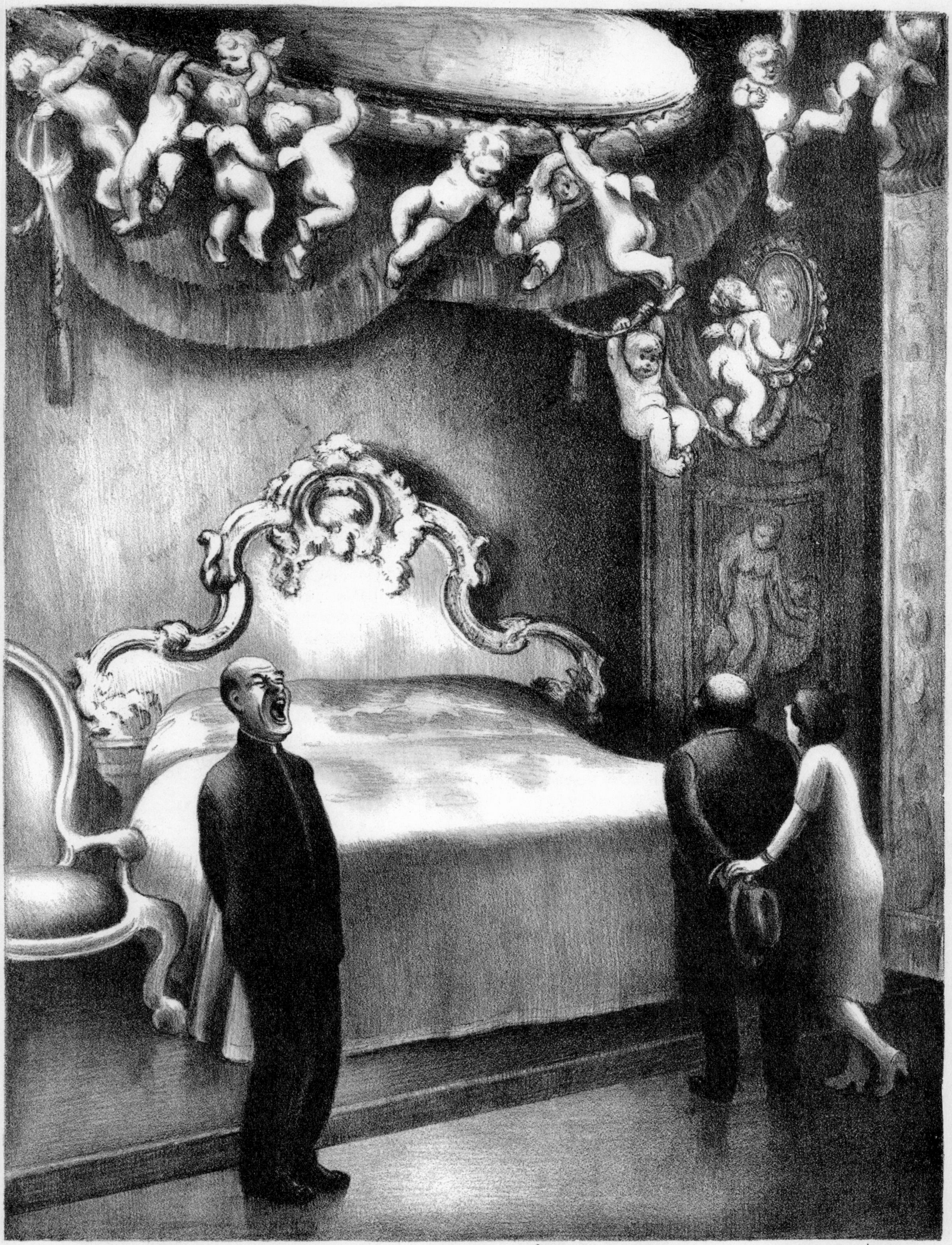

REPRO.

Museum Guard

Mabel Dwight

PLATE NUMBER THIRTY-EIGHT

Museum Guard

BY MABEL DWIGHT

(*See reverse side for plate*)

MABEL DWIGHT, who was born at Cincinnati, Ohio, in 1876, studied art in San Francisco when she was young, but did not work at it seriously until she was middle-aged. In 1927 she made her first lithograph. Since then she has exhibited regularly and with great success. Her work is widely represented both here and abroad. She confines her efforts to water-color painting and lithography.

Mabel Dwight's story of *Museum Guard* is so interesting that it must be quoted *in toto:* "While working in the Metropolitan Museum, I used to talk with the guards. They told me how tired they became from the long hours of standing. No stools are provided for them as in European galleries. The authorities say the guards would go to sleep if they could sit down. The job seems to have a paralyzing effect on the men, and some of them crack under it.

"A woman copyist in one of the period-furniture rooms once scolded a guard for his indifference to the rare opportunities for studying the history of furniture. 'Do you know the difference in the legs of a Louis XV chair and a Louis XVI chair?' she asked. 'Well, mam,' he replied, 'I'm more interested in the trouble in my own legs—I don't care about Louis' legs.' I made the sketch for this lithograph in the Venetian Room. The vast, ornate bed with its silly legs and the great yawning armchairs back of a man nearly dead with weariness and exhaustion struck me as ironical and absurd. I wanted to portray this idea."

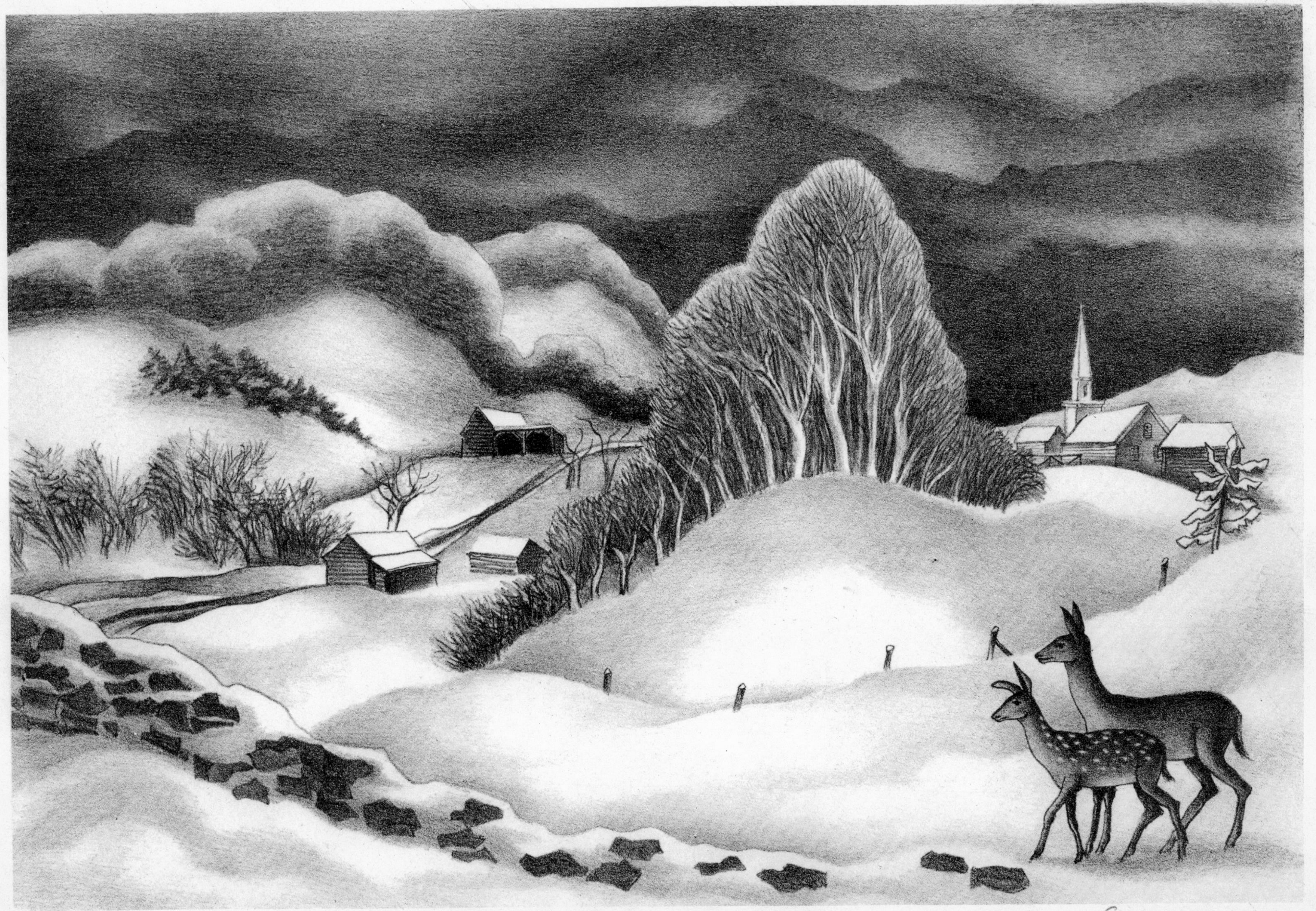

Ernest Fiene 36

PLATE NUMBER THIRTY-NINE

Winter Evening

BY ERNEST FIENE

(*See reverse side for plate*)

ALTHOUGH BORN in the Rhineland in 1894, Ernest Fiene has spent most of his years in the United States. He received his art instruction at the National Academy of Design and the Art Students' League. He works in oil, water color, *gouache*, lithography, and etching, and is an expert technician in each. Not only does he know technics, but he can also communicate them to others, for he is an excellent teacher. In 1932 he received a Guggenheim fellowship.

The lithograph *Winter Evening* was made from drawings the artist made from his window when he was snowed in for four days during the blizzard of 1934. When the storm was over, the deer came out from the woods in search of food. So it is in every way an actual scene. The locale is near Southbury, which lies in southwestern Connecticut, between Danbury and Waterbury. The snowed-under, steepled church hints at the geography. The scene has great decorative charm, mirroring Fiene's interest in design and formal values. Yet, this snowscape is by no means cold: it has a sincerity and truthfulness that lift it above purely pattern interest.

REPRO.   Lauren Ford

Early Rising

BY LAUREN FORD

(See reverse side for plate)

LAUREN FORD is the daughter of Simeon Ford, who for years was considered Chauncey Depew's only rival as America's ace after-dinner speaker, and Julia Ellsworth Ford, author and philanthropist, who in 1934 established an annual contest for encouraging literature for the young. Lauren Ford shares her mother's interest in children, but much of her work is marked by a deeply religious quality, too.

Early Rising is, however, just a little genre scene—a view into an old-fashioned room with two girls of the primmest sort the center of attention. The larger girl is tying her little sister's hair bow. The atmosphere of the picture is partly Kate Greenaway, partly Louisa May Alcott—and all homespun. The scene has a dozen quaint, tenderly observant touches. The little dog, the disorderly bureau, the miniature on the wall—all testify to the artist's feeling for a charming past.

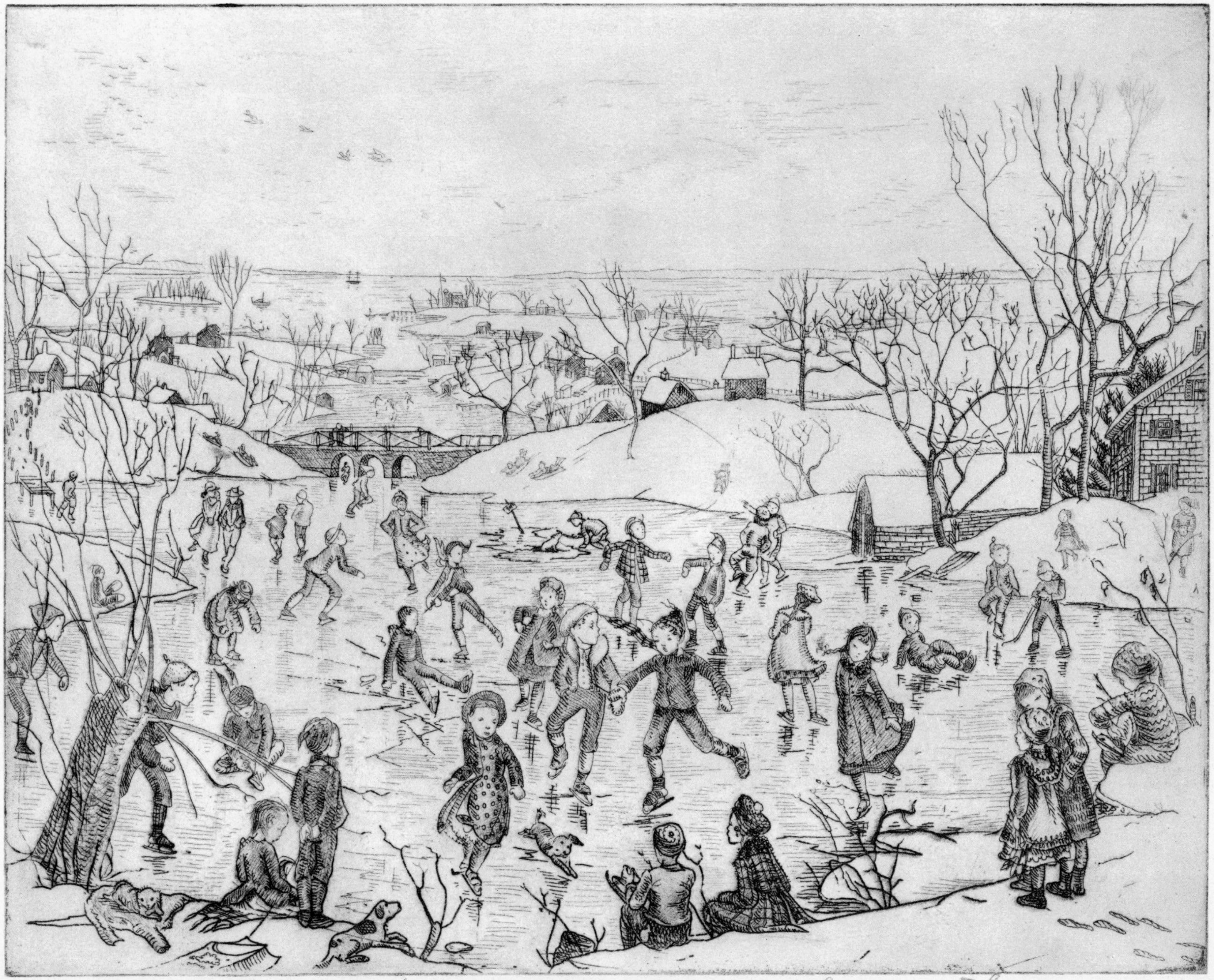

REPRO.

Lauren Ford

Milton Pond, Thanksgiving Day

BY LAUREN FORD

(See reverse side for plate)

Milton Pond, Thanksgiving Day is a work of exquisite fancy and finical detail. The scene is, to establish the realism of the setting beyond question, the Great Pond at Milton, Massachusetts, where the Indian sachem Chicataubot wept over his lost lands that the palefaces had stolen from him. Miss Ford has not depicted this unhappy moment, but has peopled the pond with some of the most delightful children in modern art. The etching deserves the closest attention, for a dozen tiny incidents and minute catastrophes are used within the confines of this nicely devised composition.

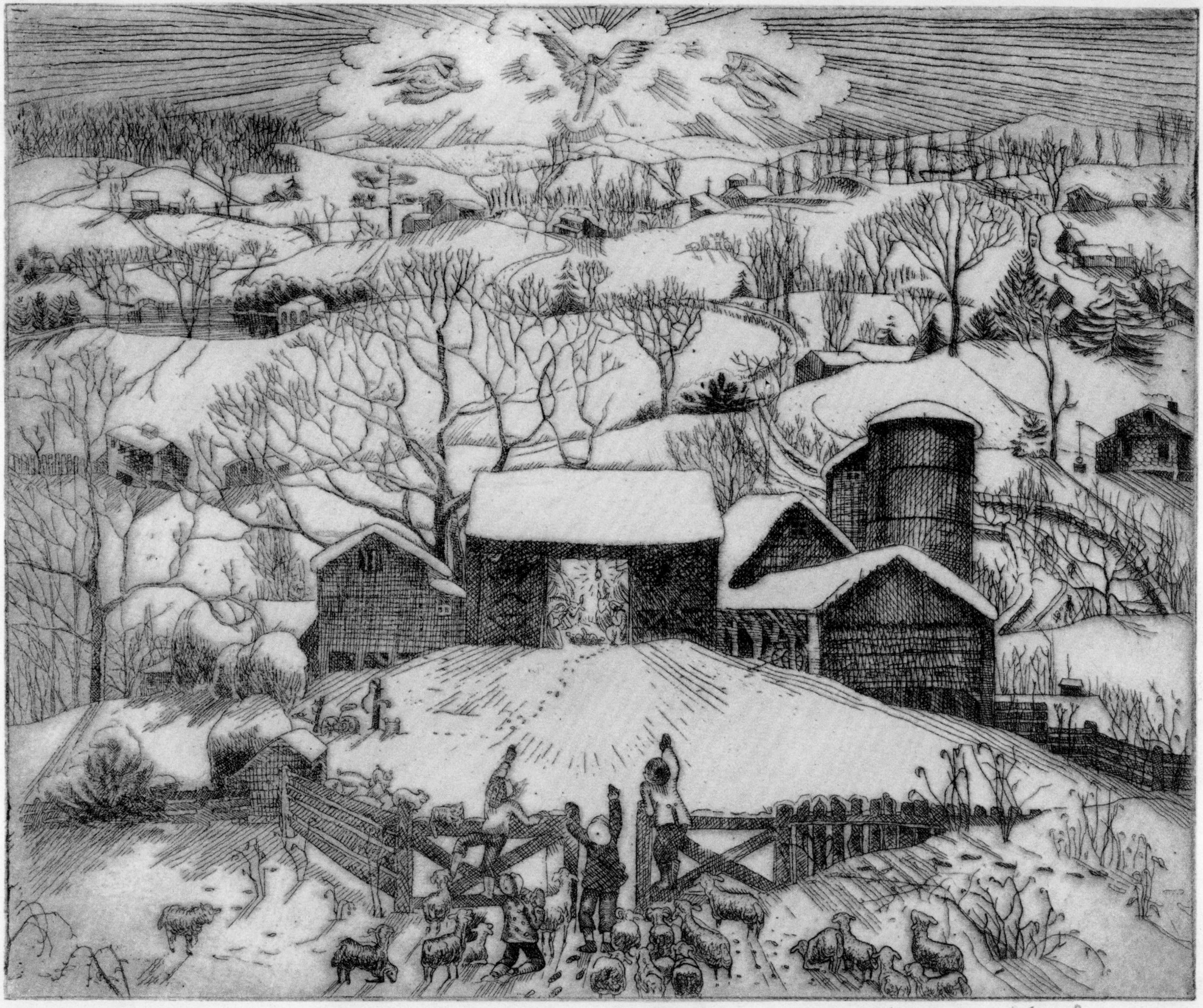

REPRO.

Lauren Ford

The Nativity

BY LAUREN FORD

(See reverse side for plate)

TO LAUREN FORD, Christ and His teaching are so living that she has devoted much of her art to making them live for other people. This *Nativity*, as tenderly devout as any by Fra Angelico, is brought right down to modern times, and shown as if it had taken place on her own farm near Bethlehem, Connecticut. It is something of a miracle that the barns, the towering silo, the typical New England farmhouses, the rail fence, and the pump add to, rather than detract from, the impressiveness of the scene. The children in their snug winter clothing, the sheep, and the cats on the fence are delightfully observed. The Nativity drama itself has the charm of a miniature by one of the Sienese masters.

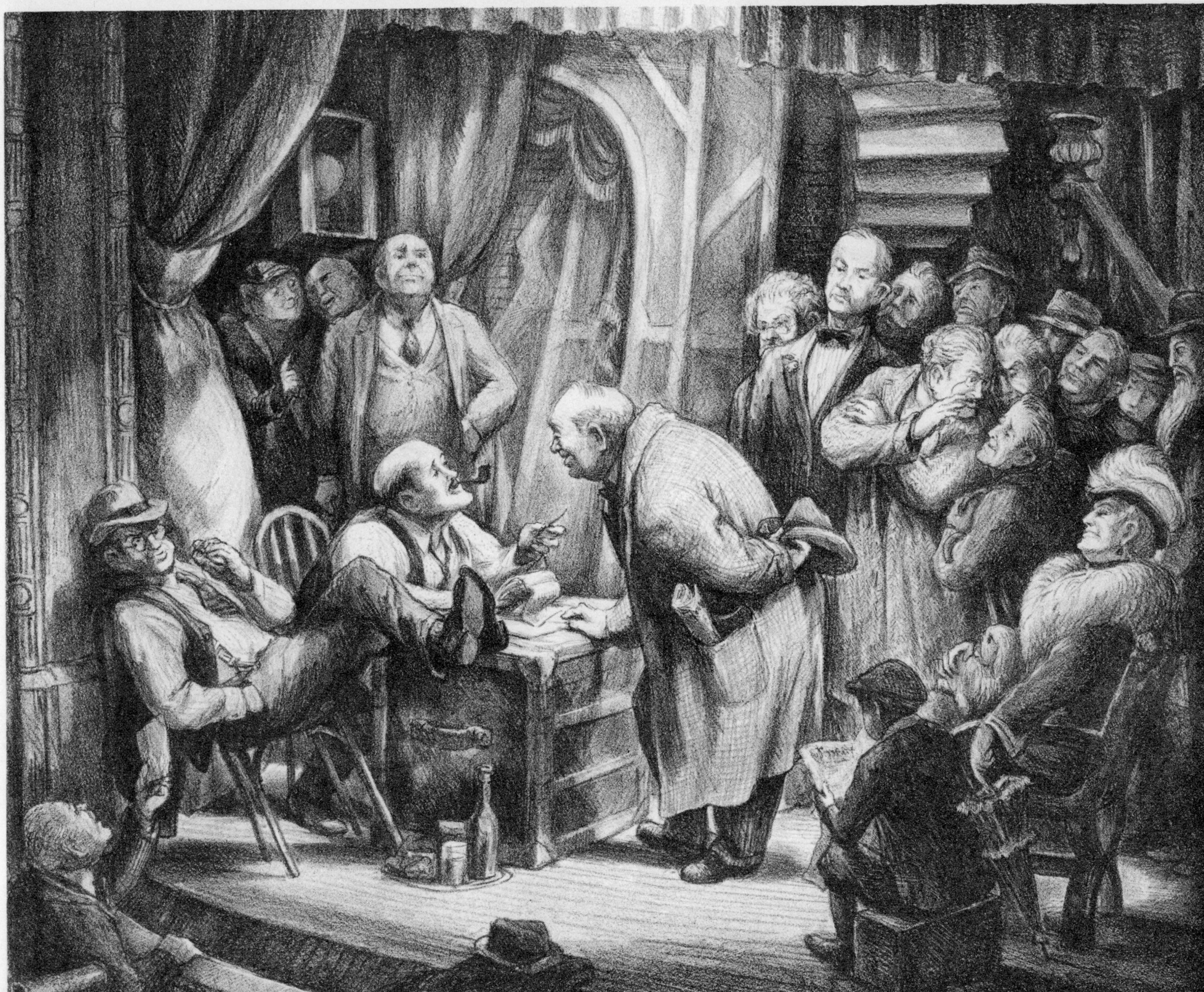

Don Freeman

PLATE NUMBER FORTY-THREE

Casting for Character

BY DON FREEMAN

(*See reverse side for plate*)

LIKE MOST OF THE artists and writers who have dwelt lovingly on the vari-colored life of New York City, Don Freeman comes from somewhere else—in his case, California, where he was born at San Diego in 1908. After attending high school in St. Louis, he became an itinerant trumpet player. Even while practicing his "hot licks" on the trumpet, however, he was drawing as a pastime. With training under (among others) John Sloan and John Steuart Curry, he began a new career as a caricaturist, with special emphasis on theatrical subjects, and is now a free lance, producing posters for shows and work for various newspapers and magazines. He has been a Guggenheim fellow.

Casting for Character is Mr. Freeman's interpretation of an actual scene he came upon accidentally while walking down a side street just off Broadway. In a splash of artificial light the casting director—whom Mr. Freeman describes as "very amiable"—is interviewing applicants for a type part. A clutter of scenery, sluggish supernumeraries, a tray of refreshments, and a lady with dog in a property chair are congealed in a print that gives the required feeling of being crowded, without appearing jumbled. The framing of the chief character in the scene is aptly achieved by the lighting and the placing of the three figures nearest him. The humor of the situation is implicit rather than obvious, and is a tribute to Mr. Freeman's selective eye.

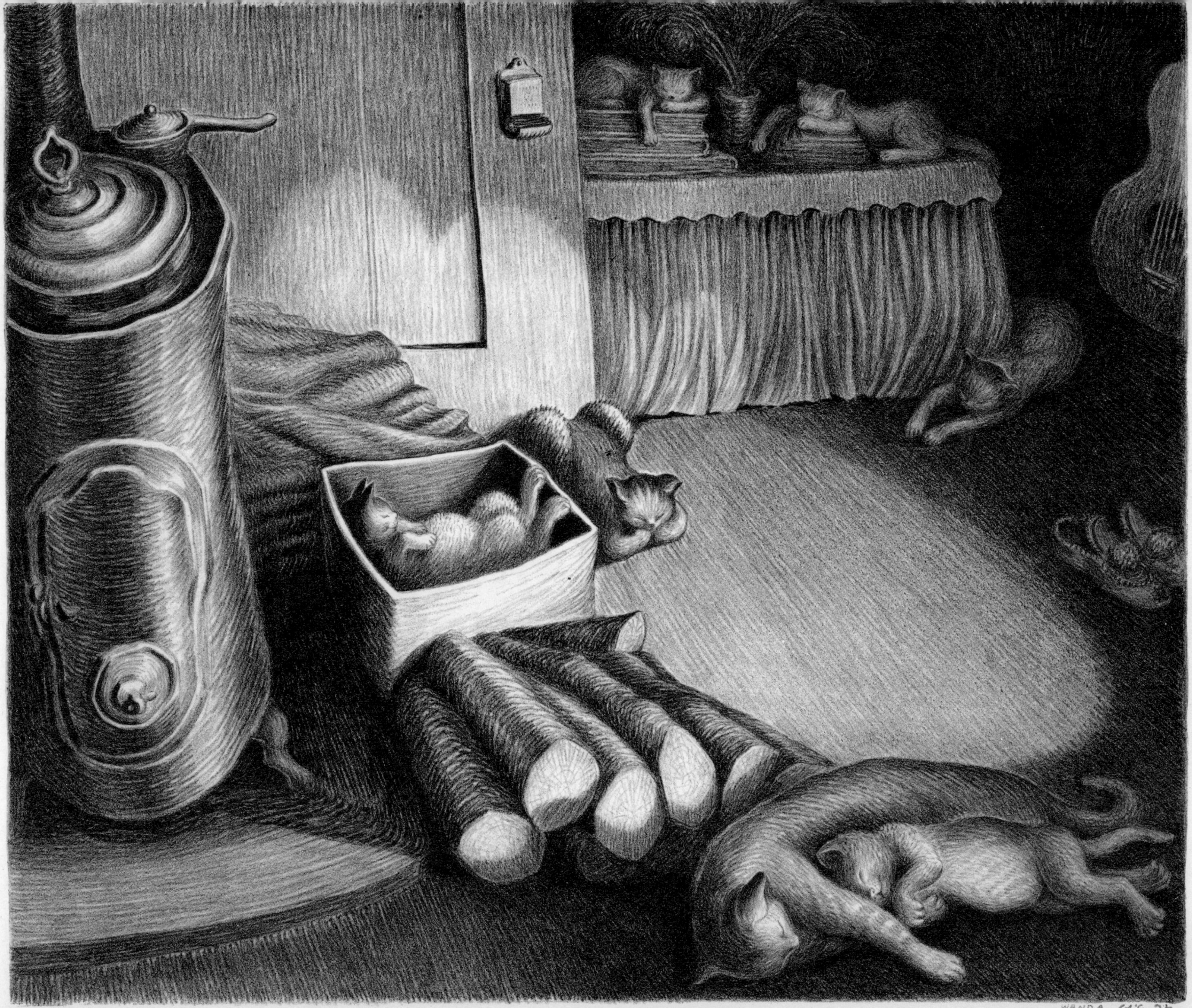

REPRO

WANDA GÁG 33

PLATE NUMBER FORTY-FOUR

Siesta

BY WANDA GÁG

(*See reverse side for plate*)

WANDA GÁG pronounces her name Gaag, to rime with jog. She was born in New Ulm, Minnesota, forty-six years ago, the child of Austro-Bohemian parents. After studying in the art schools of the Twin Cities, Miss Gag enrolled at the Art Students' League. It is a bit difficult to think of this vigorously intelligent artist "painting lamp shades, fashion drawings, making batiks, and so on," but this was practically her lot until 1923, when she went to live in the country—first Connecticut, then New Jersey. There she really found herself, partly through the reading of Thoreau's *Walden.*

Besides being in the van of America's distinguished graphic artists, Miss Gág writes extraordinarily well. It would be supererogatory to add a word to her delicious exposition of *Siesta:*

"*Siesta* shows a family of cats basking in the warmth of an early autumn fire. I am always amused at the natural tendency of cats to fit themselves into and over all sorts of places and spaces—and from an artistic point of view I am interested in the interrelation of forms resulting from this.

"I felt the room as a space in which cylinders (stove, wood), cubes (box, bench), flat surfaces (floors, walls), and the more pliable forms of the cats all had their place. Since I wanted a mood of calm and comfort, I used a simple composition of familiar objects grouped around a nucleus of light and arranged so that the eye could travel easily from one to the other.

"Technically I was interested in bringing out the delicacy rather than the forcefulness of the lithographic medium, so I built up this drawing by the use of many fine lines."

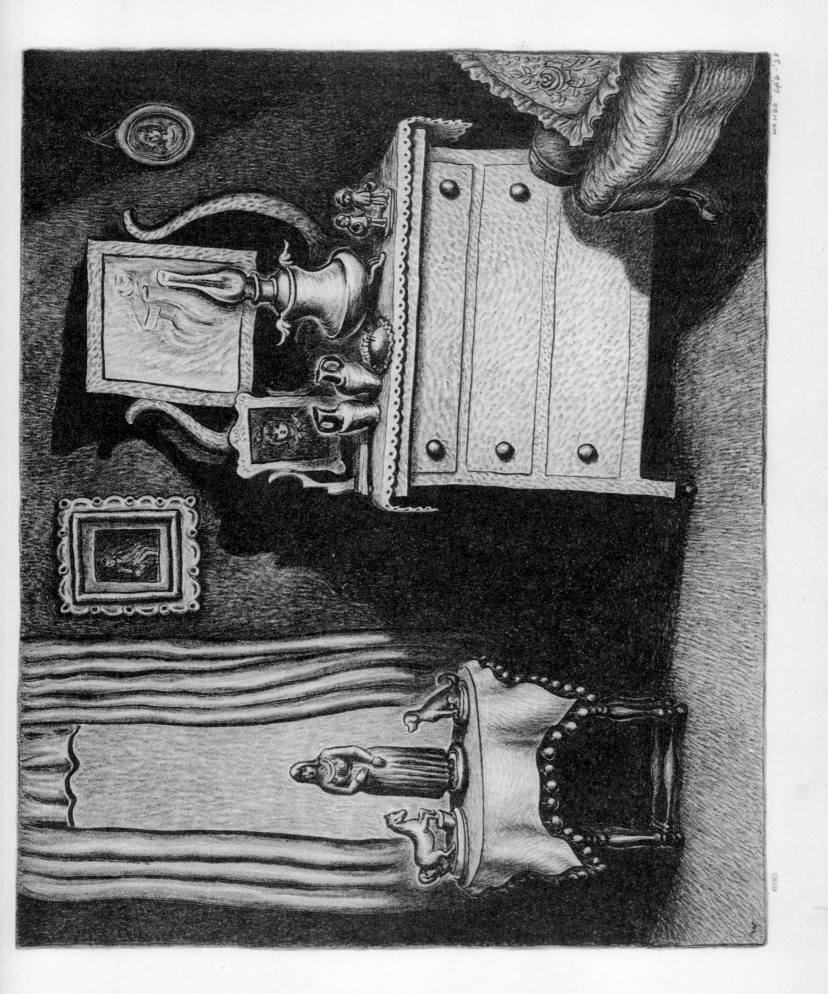

WANDA GÁG '31

PLATE NUMBER FORTY-FIVE

Grandma's Parlor

BY WANDA GÁG

(*See reverse side for plate*)

OF THE LITHOGRAPH *Grandma's Parlor,* Wanda Gág has written:

"When, after many years, I returned to Minnesota and again saw the front room Down At Grandma's, it seemed to me the epitome of Parlor—a staid, rather cold place, the clean, dustless repository of objects too 'artistic' to be sullied by use. That, at least, is how it impressed me objectively. Subjectively a host of childhood associations crowded themselves into the scene, softened its lines, and gave it a life of its own.

"Out in the kitchen sat my solid peasant forbears—here in the parlor was this baroque display, their naïve acceptance of mid-Victorian 'beauty.' It was amusing but touching too, and so when I began to draw, a wave of tender tolerant mirth flowed through me and over my paper. That, I suppose, is why the picture came out as it did: the Grand Rapids dresser atilt with gaiety, the lamp like a clumsy gosling poising its ridiculous wings for flight, and the two little pitchers swaying and saying, 'Let's dance.'

"Technically I tried to get all the richness possible out of the lithographic medium. An old-fashioned parlor, arranged mainly for show rather than use, has something theatrical about it; and to portray this, I used a strong black-and-white design—an almost spotlight effect—to bring out the rococo pattern against the rich black shadows."

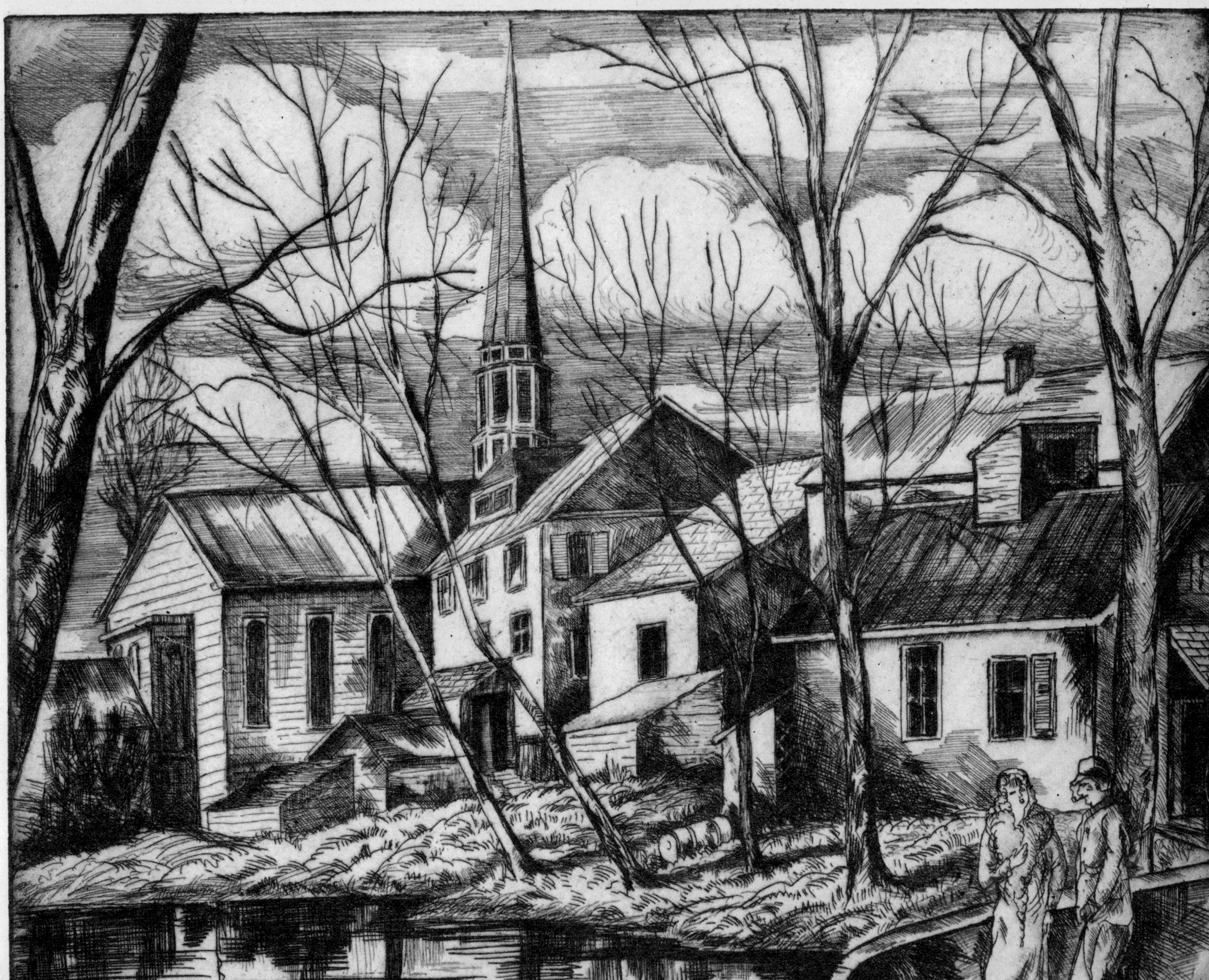

Bearsville

Ganso 31

Bearsville

BY EMIL GANSO

(See reverse side for plate)

EMIL GANSO was born in Halberstadt, Germany, in 1895, but has lived in the United States for many years. He is of mixed German, French, and Spanish ancestry. He had a hard struggle to make ends meet when he first came to America, and except for a few weeks at the night school of the National Academy of Design, he is largely self-taught. Largely on the advice of E. Weyhe, the well-known dealer, Ganso (who was then working in a bakery) decided to devote himself exclusively to art. He works in many media, lithography being among his favorites. In 1933 he received a Guggenheim fellowship for creative work, and accordingly spent the next year studying and painting in Europe.

Ganso's landscapes are not as often seen as his flowers and nudes, but they have a fine, fresh quality. Bearsville is a tiny village near Woodstock, New York. Its spired church completely dominates it, and provides the natural focus for any painting or view of the locality. While Ganso's work is usually distinguished for its cunning balance of lights and darks, *Bearsville* seems saturated with sunshine or glistening with rain.

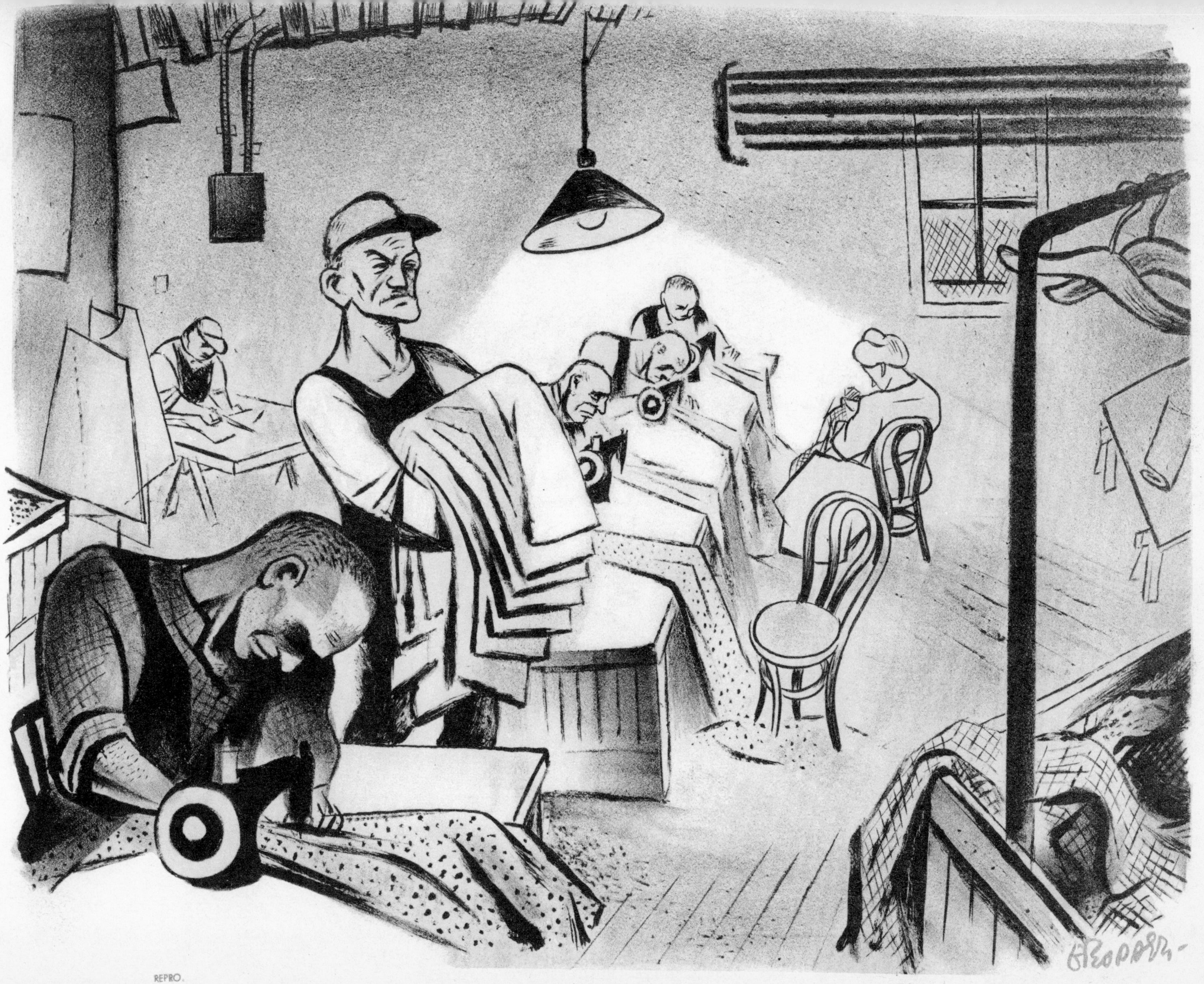

PLATE NUMBER FORTY-SEVEN

Sweatshop

BY WILLIAM GROPPER

(*See reverse side for plate*)

WILLIAM GROPPER, one of America's most powerful illustrators and cartoonists, was born in New York City, on December 3, 1897. "Poor parents," he writes, "so began to work the minute I was born, and have been at it ever since. Resolved, will never become a millionaire even if I live to be 398 years of age." Gropper studied with Bellows and Robert Henri, and received many prizes. In 1937 he received a Guggenheim fellowship. Much of his work has appeared in *Vanity Fair, New Masses*, and *Art Front*. Speaking of his political cartoons, Gropper has said, "I drew them for Red publications because no other newspaper has enough courage to allow an artist his freedom of expression."

Sweatshop is a hard-hitting slam at one of the most noxious institutions in industrial life. It tells its story as directly as a Daumier, and far more eloquently than a Dos Passos tract. There is merit in Gropper's statement that "I draw pictures of this world of ours, and they're not all pretty pictures."

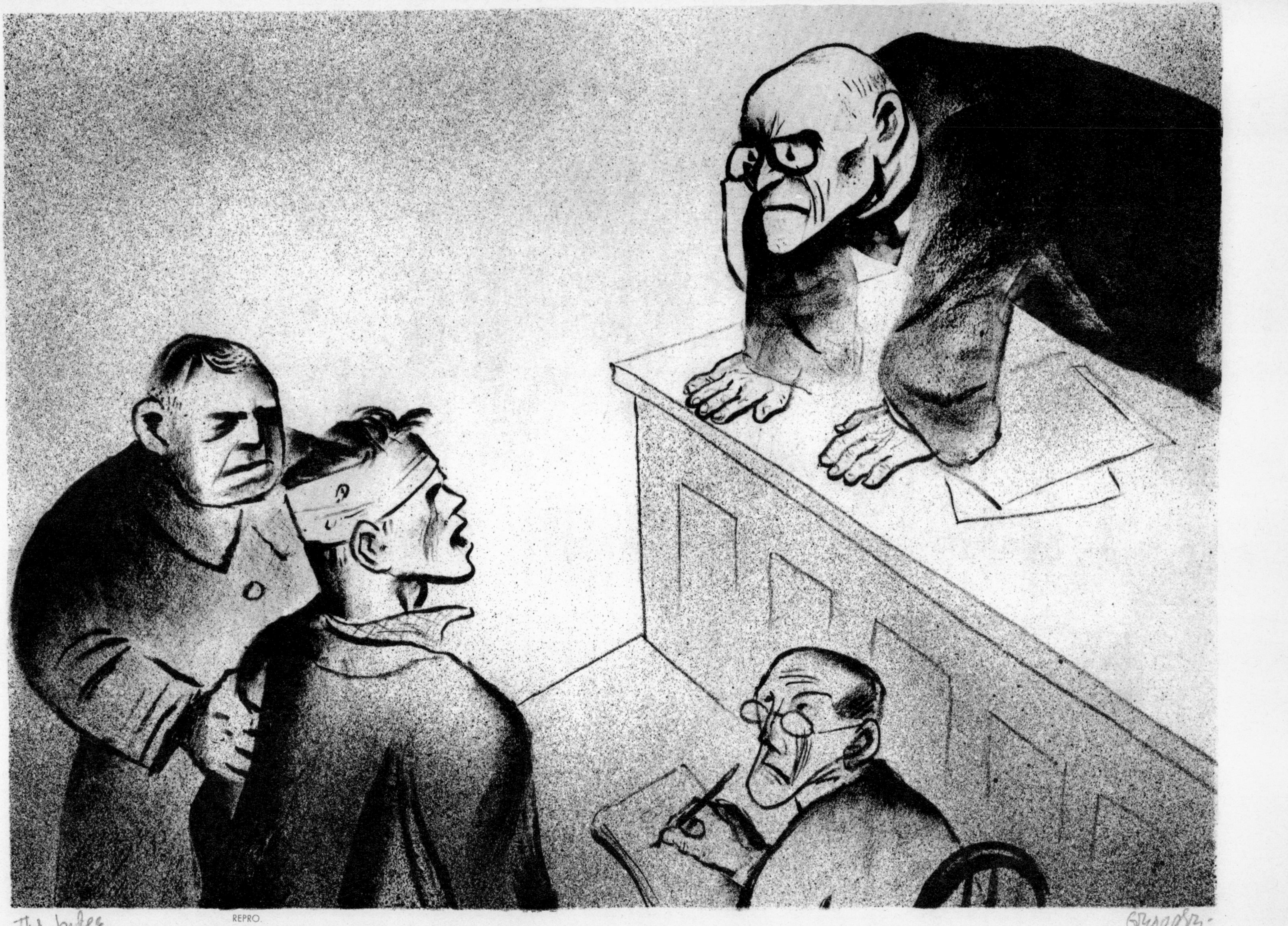

The Judge

PLATE NUMBER FORTY-EIGHT

The Judge

BY WILLIAM GROPPER

(*See reverse side for plate*)

GROPPER HAS MET this savage jurist—he once gave him a parking ticket. "When my case came up," Gropper remembers, "he asked me what business I was in, and how much money I had. I told him I was broke, so he fined me five dollars." After that the artist made a number of visits to the court as a visitor, and sketched the judge several times before doing this lithograph. He began to wonder how this man of all men became a judge, and how he had such power over other people, and what chance an honest lawyer, "who is not a politician," had to become a judge. These questions bothered the artist a lot, but at last he found a judge who answered them for him.

Here, in *The Judge,* is a modern example of the notorious "hanging judges" of the seventeenth and eighteenth centuries. The prisoner at the bar is not less browbeaten than the court stenographer, who must have the judge as a daily diet. Only the policeman preserves his stolidity.

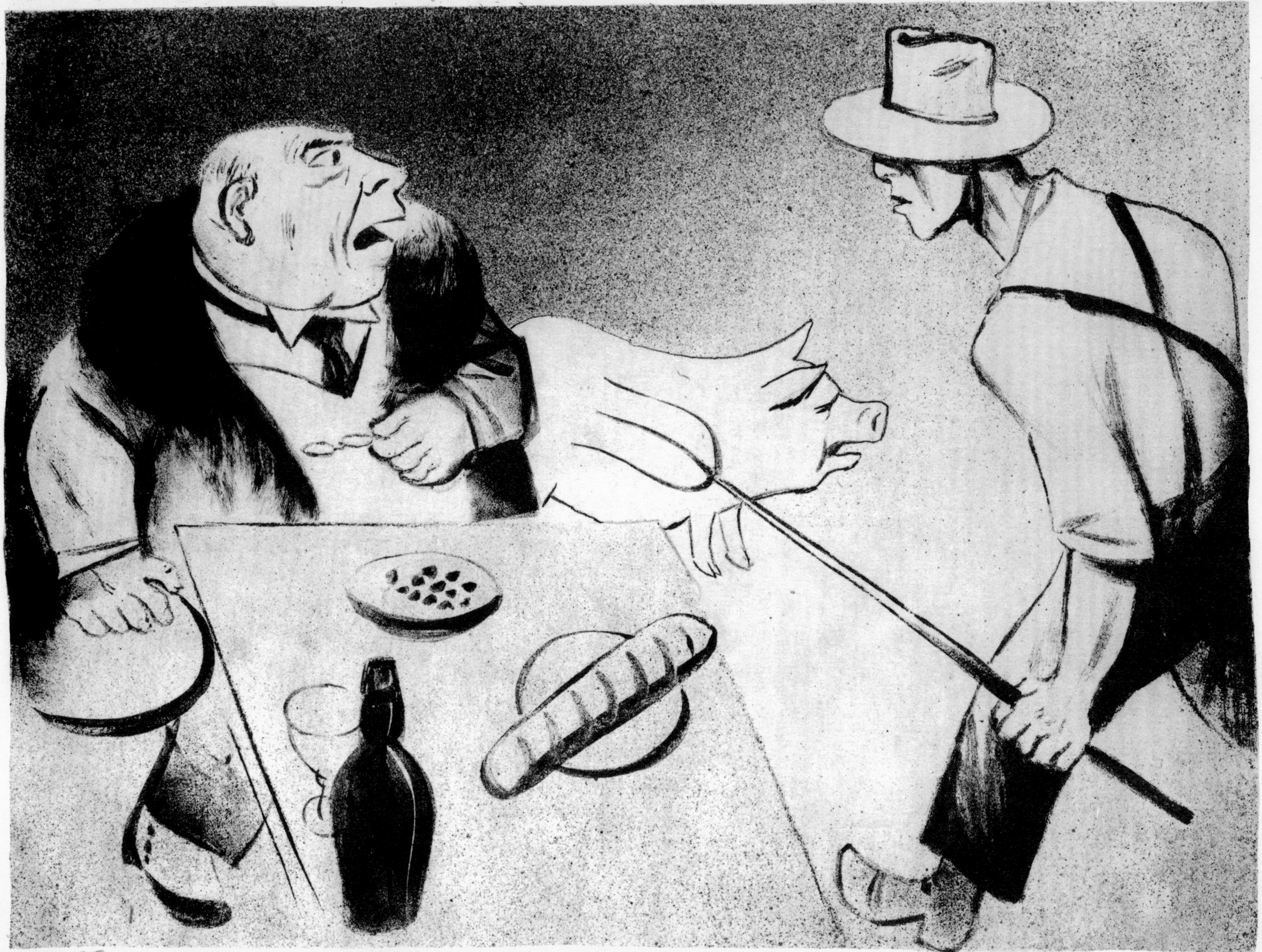

RELIEF

REPRO

GROPPER

PLATE NUMBER FORTY-NINE

Relief

BY WILLIAM GROPPER

(*See reverse side for plate*)

MR. GROPPER, whose work appears regularly in *New Masses*, does not seem to love the human race any more than that lamented bard who admitted flatly—

I do not love the human race.
I do not love its ugly face.

While *Relief* is not as readily understandable as certain others of his cartoons, it is extraordinarily powerful. The wing-collared Neanderthal man at the table impersonates graft, and you may attach any specific label to him you wish. His resemblance to the hog is too vivid to be fortuitous. It should be noted that the table is the "groaning board," the plate of beans, hard roll, and wine bottle and glass being the artist's shorthand for the concept *plenty*. When the "embattled farmer" gets through with Homo Neanderthalensis, there is little doubt that some of the relief money will be diverted into its proper channels.

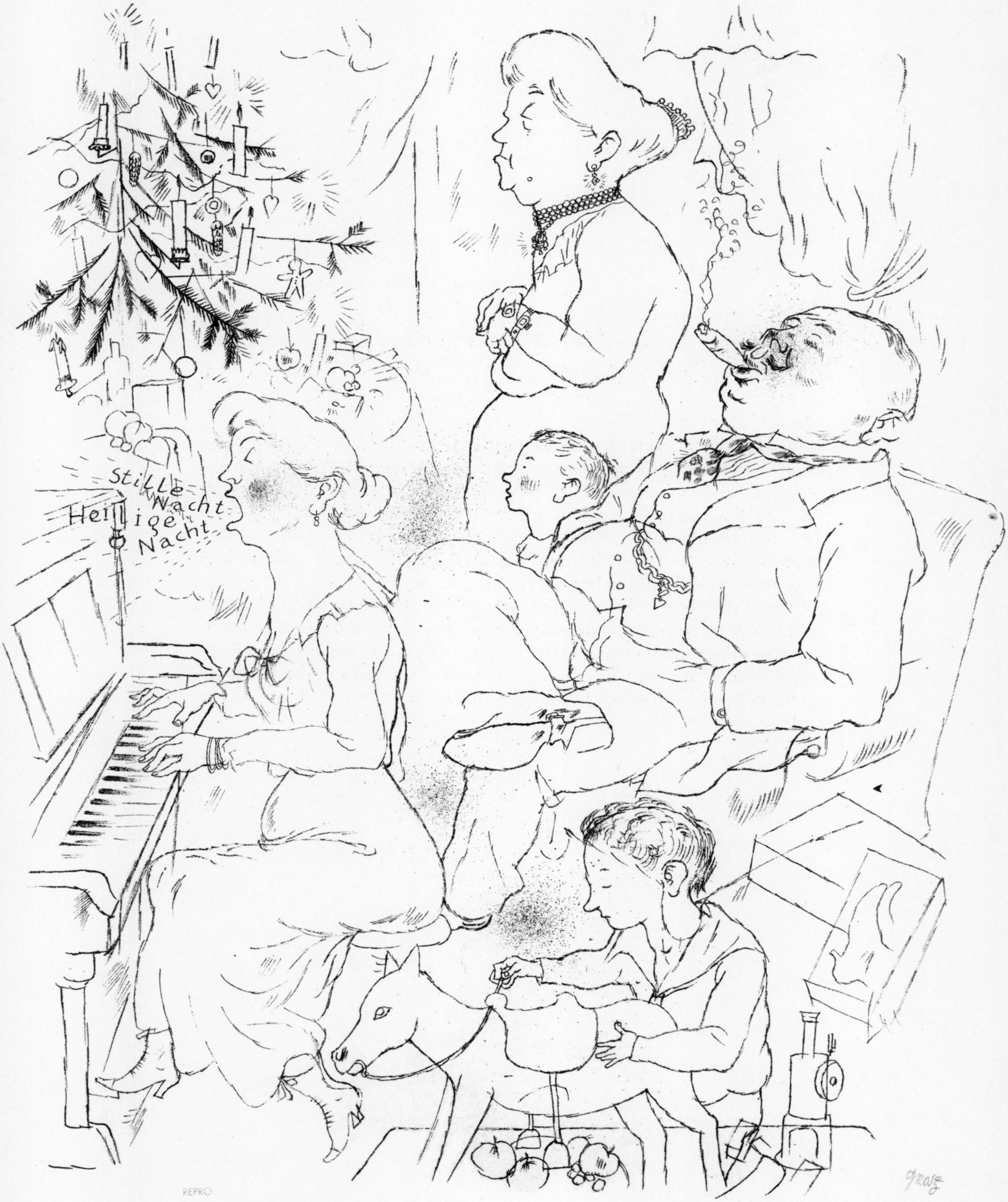
Stille Nacht
Heilige Nacht

Heilige Nacht

BY GEORGE GROSZ

(See reverse side for plate)

GEORGE GROSZ was born in Berlin in 1893, and as his father lost his money shortly afterwards, the artist had an unhappy early childhood, much of which was spent in the sour slums of North Berlin. Finally, after her husband's death in 1900, Frau Grosz got a job as housekeeper in a little town near the Baltic Sea. In this invigorating atmosphere Grosz was introduced to the delights of healthy boyhood. Thereafter, until he mixed with the martinets of the local high school, his life was to be happy.

The smug plenty of *Heilige Nacht* was, in any event, never part of Grosz's childhood. It represents, with sardonic explicitness, that mixture of sentimental benevolence and grossness which typifies many a German family in the expansiveness of a high feast. Amid this tumescence and sluggishness, much of the holiness has been subtracted from the night.

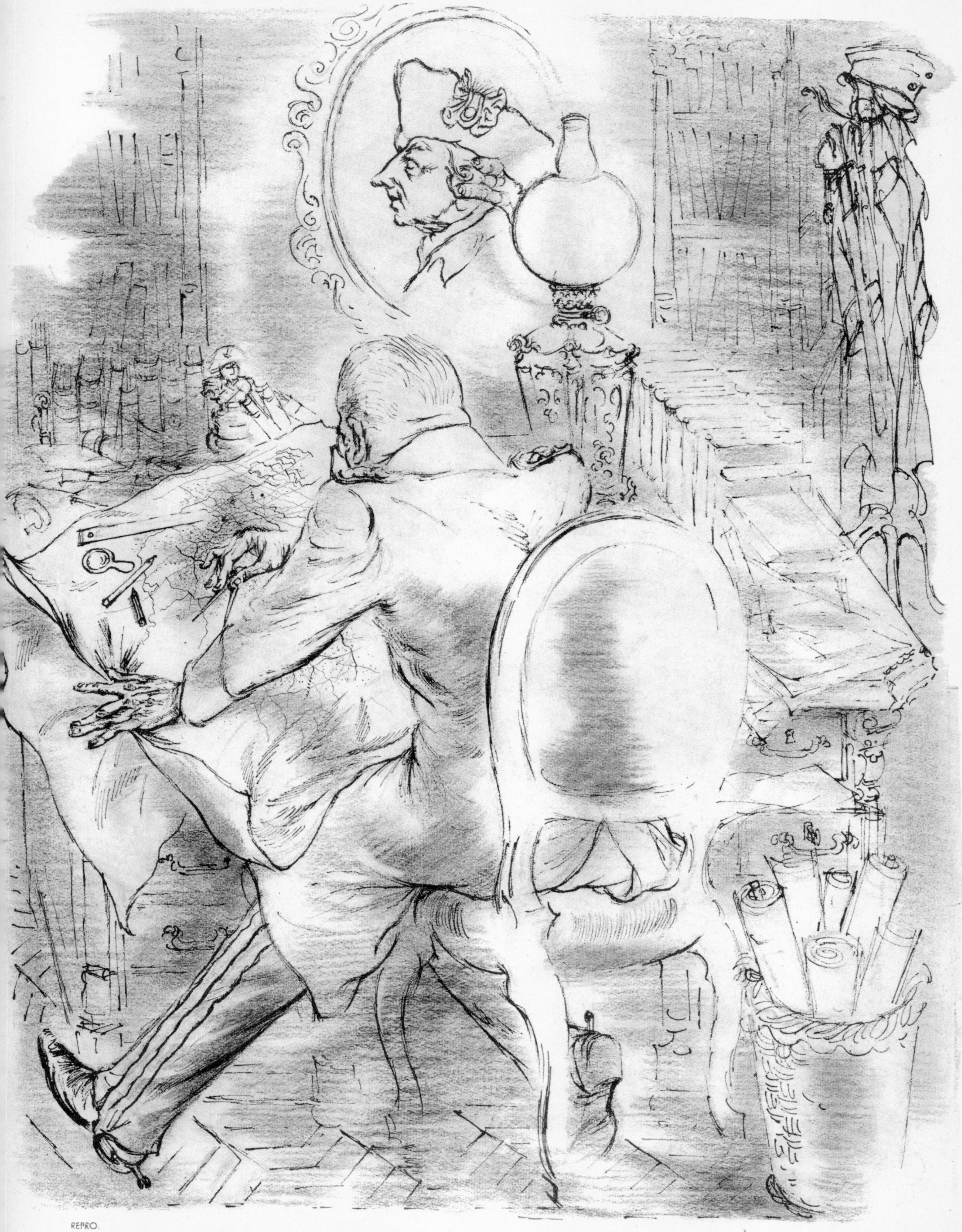

REPRO.

grosz

PLATE NUMBER FIFTY-ONE

The General

BY GEORGE GROSZ

(See reverse side for plate)

THIS COMES FROM the pencil of the Grosz who is the "scourge of *Junker*," from the Grosz whom the militarists sent to the Western Front first-line trenches, and prayed that a French bullet would do the rest. *The General* is a magnificent and repellent figure—the type of Prussian officer who will frown over the strategic puzzles of the next World War. Here are all the stage properties of a General Staff officer, including, on the wall, a profile portrait of Frederick the Great, idol of the Prussian military clique. The only thing lacking from the ensemble are the ten volumes of Von Clausewitz, the Delphic oracle of army strategy, and doubtless these are well assimilated in the regions above that creased, bull neck.

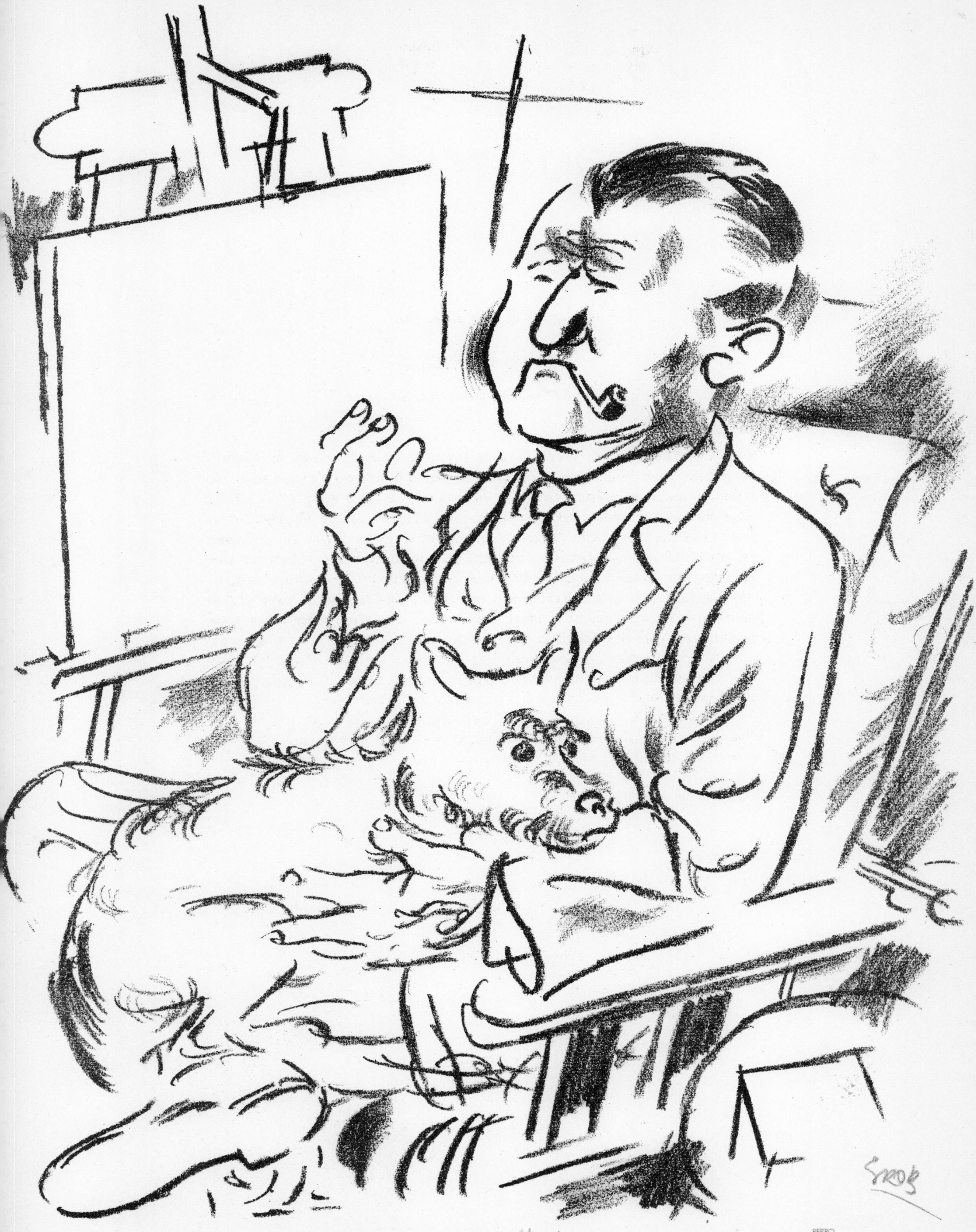
Grosz

Selbstbildnis

PLATE NUMBER FIFTY-TWO

Self-Portrait

BY GEORGE GROSZ

(See reverse side for plate)

SEVERAL YEARS AGO, Thomas Craven began a chapter on George Grosz in *Modern Art* with these words: "He will tell you, in his quiet way, that there are many Groszes; he will say this with scrupulous modesty, with a self-analysis containing no egoism. One Grosz is in the cellar, skeptical and faithless, buried in the litter of a senseless world; one is a romantic traveler, a Gothic visionary in line and verse, treasuring sentimentally in distant lands the memories of a happy boyhood in the Fatherland. There is the terrible Grosz whose fame has gone around the world—the scourge of *Junker*; the most explicit and pitiless satirist of the social habits of man since Swift. There is yet another Grosz: methodical and humorous, domestic, unafraid of bourgeois emotions, incessantly industrious and very kindly—the Grosz you may meet one day among the riffraff of Sixth Avenue, or prowling in Central Park, notebook in hand, observing the aimless vitality of unoccupied Americans."

And here is Grosz's portrait of himself—of Germany's greatest artist of this century. He sits here blandly thinking about life and art, puffing on his pipe and holding his little dog in his lap.

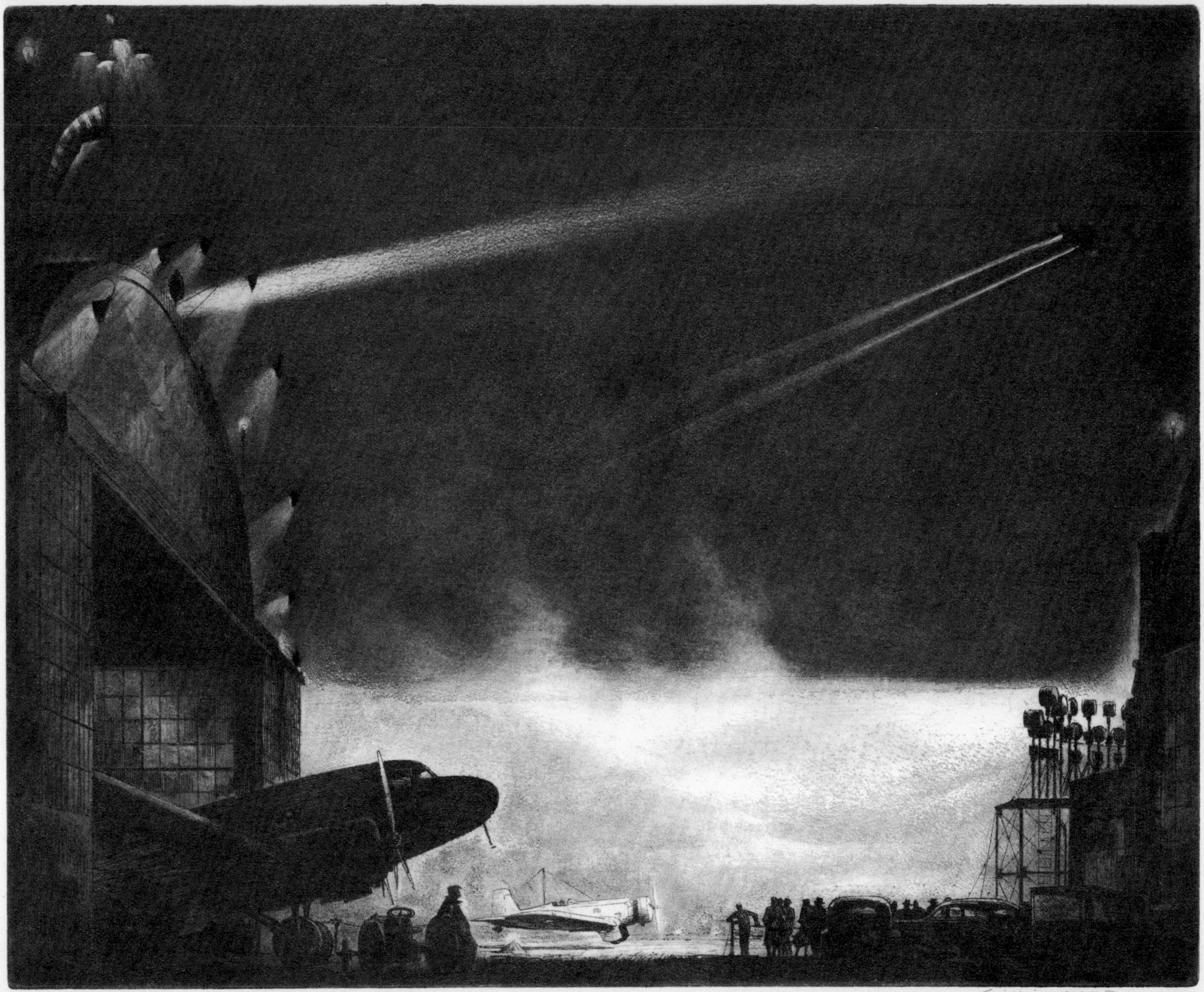

AIRPORT. REPRO.

PLATE NUMBER FIFTY-THREE

Airport

BY WILLIAM HEASLIP

(*See reverse side for plate*)

Airport comes from the pen of a former member of the Royal Flying Corps, in which Heaslip served during the World War, and therefore has none of the self-consciousness of an academic study. The artist, whose interest in flying is unabated, went out to the Newark airport, and made some night flights as the guest of the superintendent, both taking off and landing in the floodlights. He has caught the tense hurry and the mysterious impressiveness of an airport at night in this brilliant impression.

Heaslip, who was born in Toronto, Canada, in 1898, came to New York after his war service was over, and studied at the National Academy of Design and the Art Students' League. As he has pungently expressed it, "I won the Suydam Medal at the former institution, and a point of view at the latter." His prints are in many private collections. He is a deft illustrator whose work has appeared in *The Saturday Evening Post, Collier's,* and other magazines.

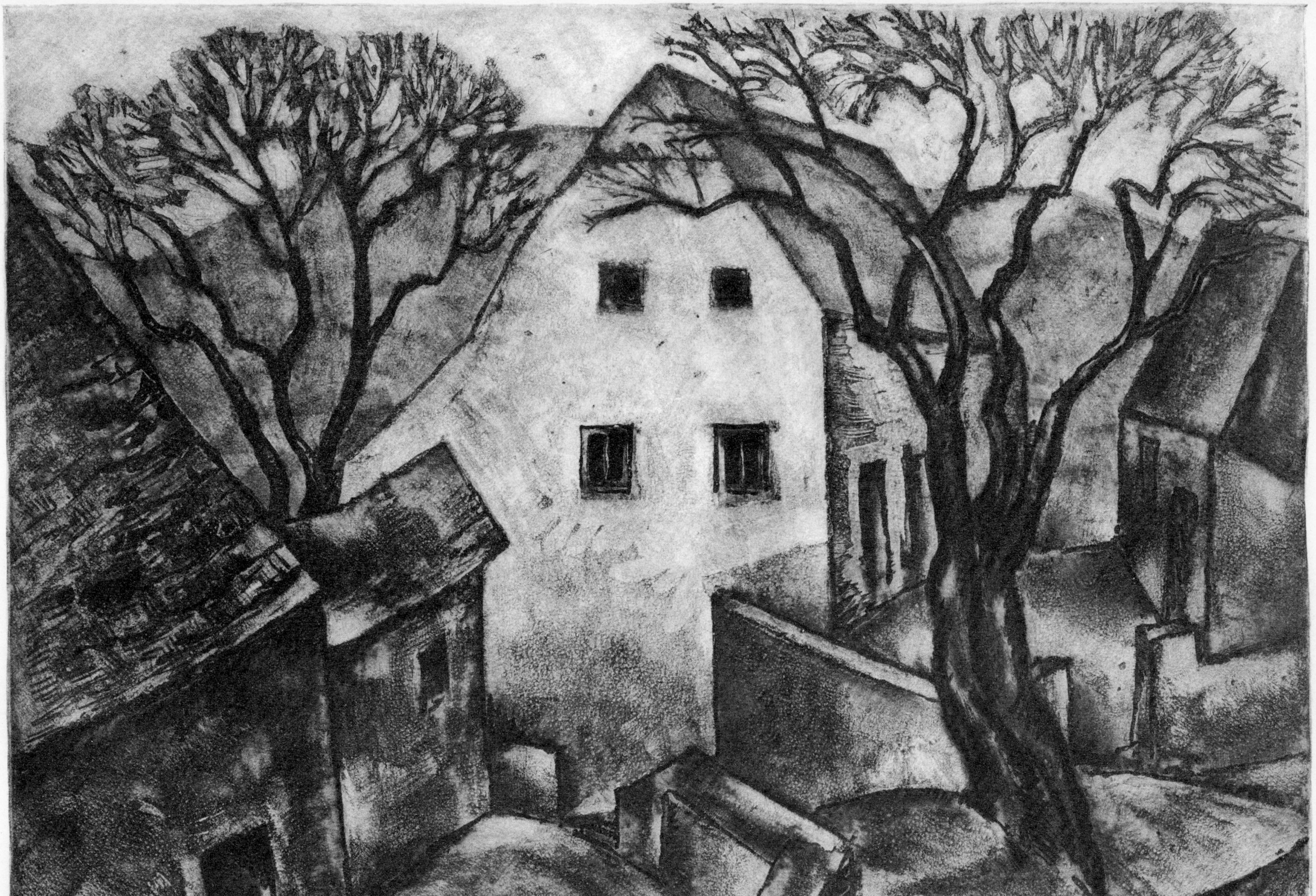

The Side Street

Albert Heckman

PLATE NUMBER FIFTY-FOUR

The Side Street

BY ALBERT HECKMAN

(*See reverse side for plate*)

THE INFLUENCE OF Cézanne weighs rather heavily on this otherwise interesting village scene by the versatile Albert Heckman. While the great Frenchman properly made his and future generations of artists increasingly aware of the formal dynamics of painting, he unfortunately made some positively self-conscious about them. *The Side Street* suffers somewhat from a rather too literal interpretation of the fundamental form of objects, but otherwise it maintains its individuality. The prevailing note is one of sobriety, of bleakness even—the mountain in the background crowds the scene, dehumanizing it further. Altogether a discouraging place for human habitation.

Heckman is forty-six years old. Born in Meadville, Pennsylvania, he finished his art studies at the Leipzig Institute of Graphic Arts. Working in many media, he is also a teacher of note. He is the author of *Paintings of Many Lands and Ages*.

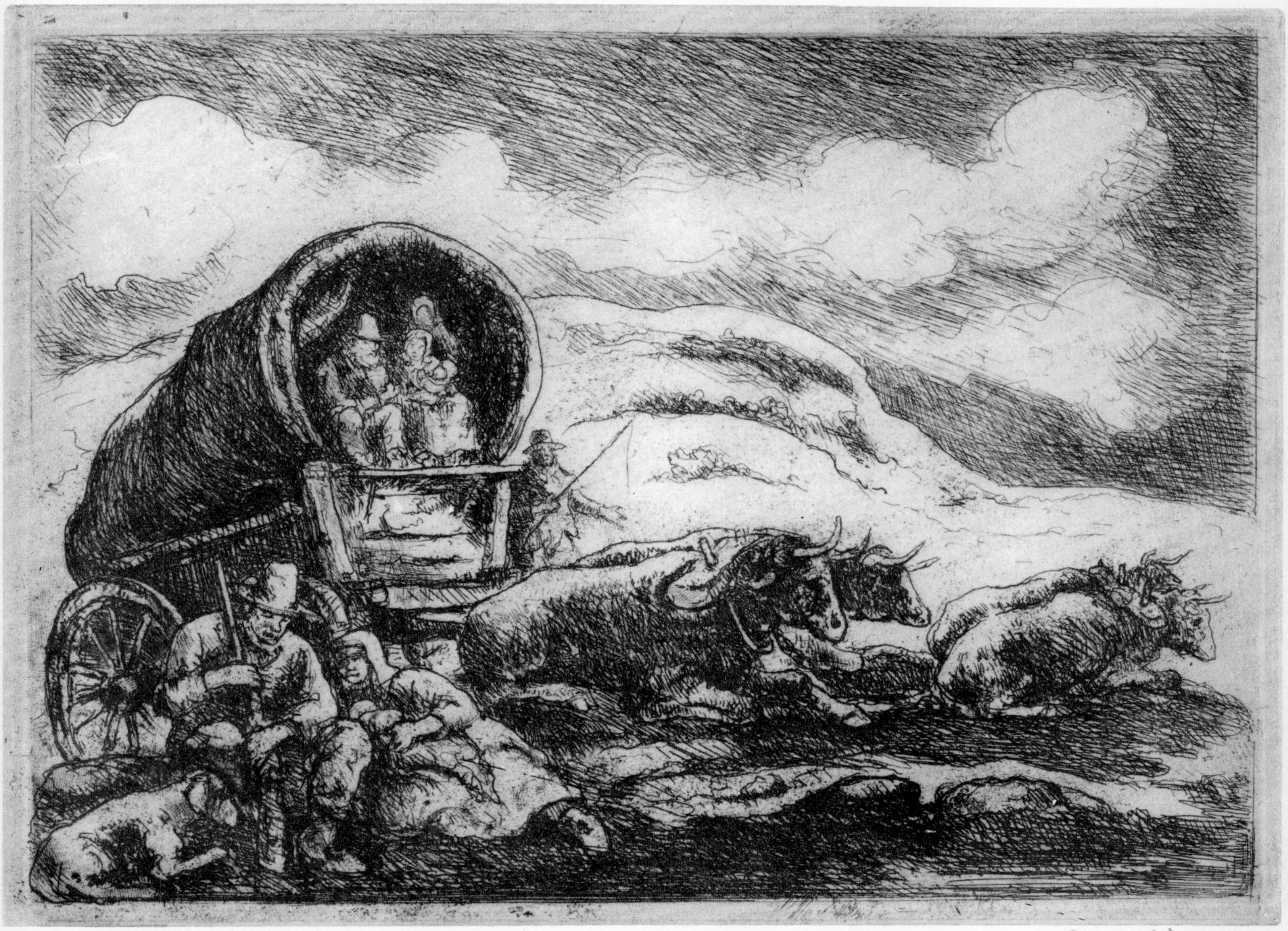

REPRO.

Eugene Higgins

PLATE NUMBER FIFTY-FIVE

Pioneers Resting

BY EUGENE HIGGINS

(*See reverse side for plate*)

EUGENE HIGGINS has been called "America's Millet." In this connection, it is interesting to note that, though born in the United States—at Kansas City, Missouri, in 1874—he studied in France under such men as Jean Paul Laurens, Benjamin Constant, and J. L. Gerôme. His work may be described as the successful adaptation of traditional European techniques to the American scene. It has won him numbers of prizes, and placed his ample, old-masterly pictures in galleries in the United States, England, and France.

In *Pioneers Resting,* Mr. Higgins says, he aimed at "a monumental design." There can be no question of his success. Although he has deviated from what must have been exact reality only in the matter of carefully deployed sections of subject matter, he has invested the covered wagon and the tired pioneers and animals with symbolic grandeur. By choosing to view them from a spot somewhat below them, and by thus placing them against the sky, he has given them a feeling of importance larger than life. "I have been doing this all my life," he remarked about this sort of subject, "hoping to get something really fine." *Pioneers Resting* is sufficient comment on his modesty.

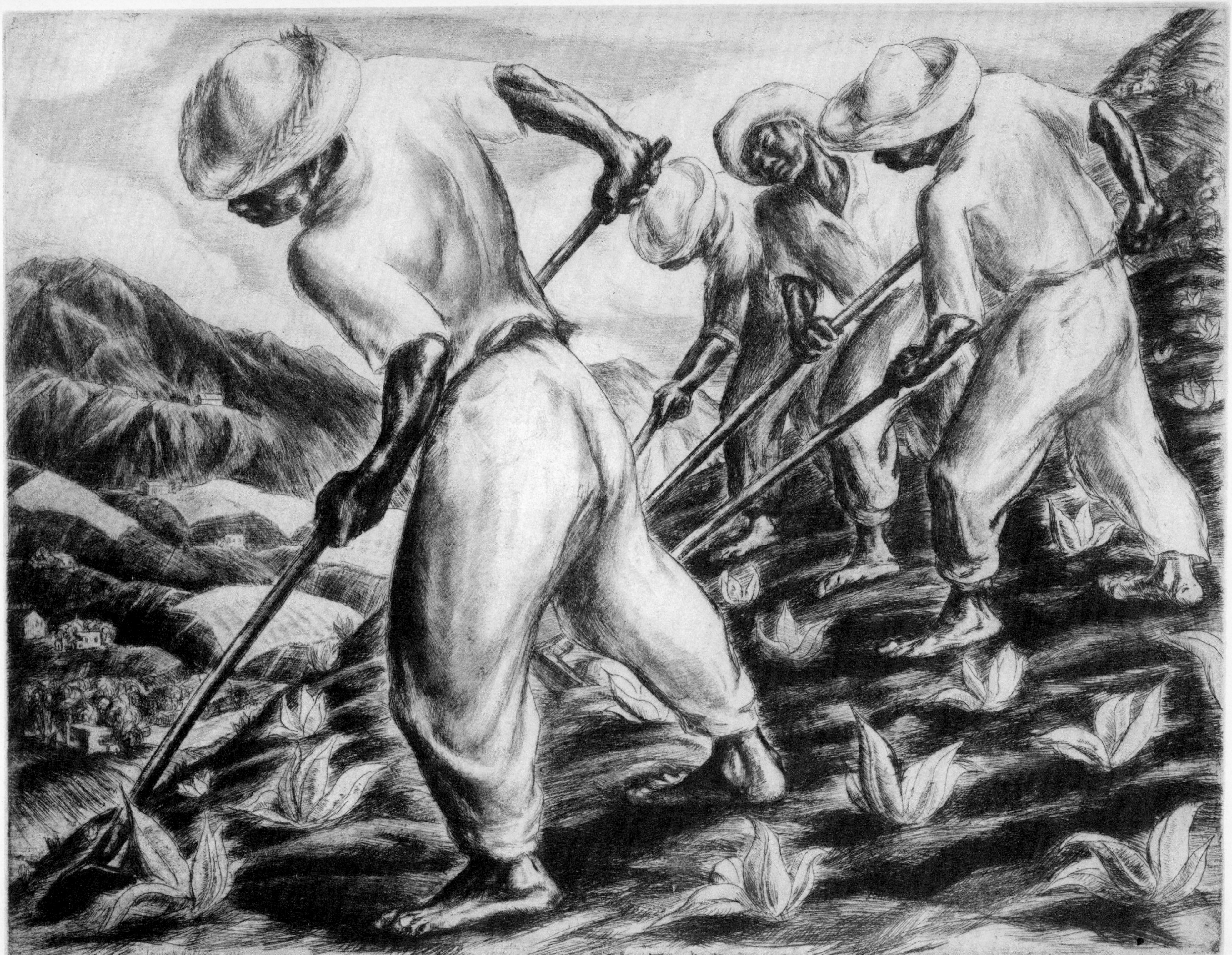

Pastoral, Puerto Rico -

REPRO.

Irwin D. Hoffman

Pastoral, Puerto Rico

BY IRWIN D. HOFFMAN

(*See reverse side for plate*)

BORN IN BOSTON in 1901, Irwin D. Hoffman has, in choosing subjects for his somber paintings and full-bodied etchings, turned his back on the city and New England life close at hand. Instead, he has become a recognized interpreter of mining and boiler-room scenes, and, more latterly, of the peasant and worker of nearer Latin America, particularly Mexico and Puerto Rico. His more recent work shows the invigorating influence (by no means undigested) of Diego Rivera and José Clemente Orozco. It is a tribute to the vigor of his native talent to say that he has learned from these men without losing any of his individuality.

Pastoral, Puerto Rico, is a fine example of the artist's ability to fill the spaces of his picture without crowding them. The diagonal line of the hillside on which the four white-clothed men are at work, the almost parallel lines of the handles of their hoes, are remarkably counterpoised by the antithetical slant of the more distant ridges of hills, and by the placing of the largest and most important figure against the open space. Intentionally or by accident, Hoffman has presented us with men doing backbreaking work for a mere pittance. He has not found it necessary to enlist ugliness in the presentation of an implied social criticism.

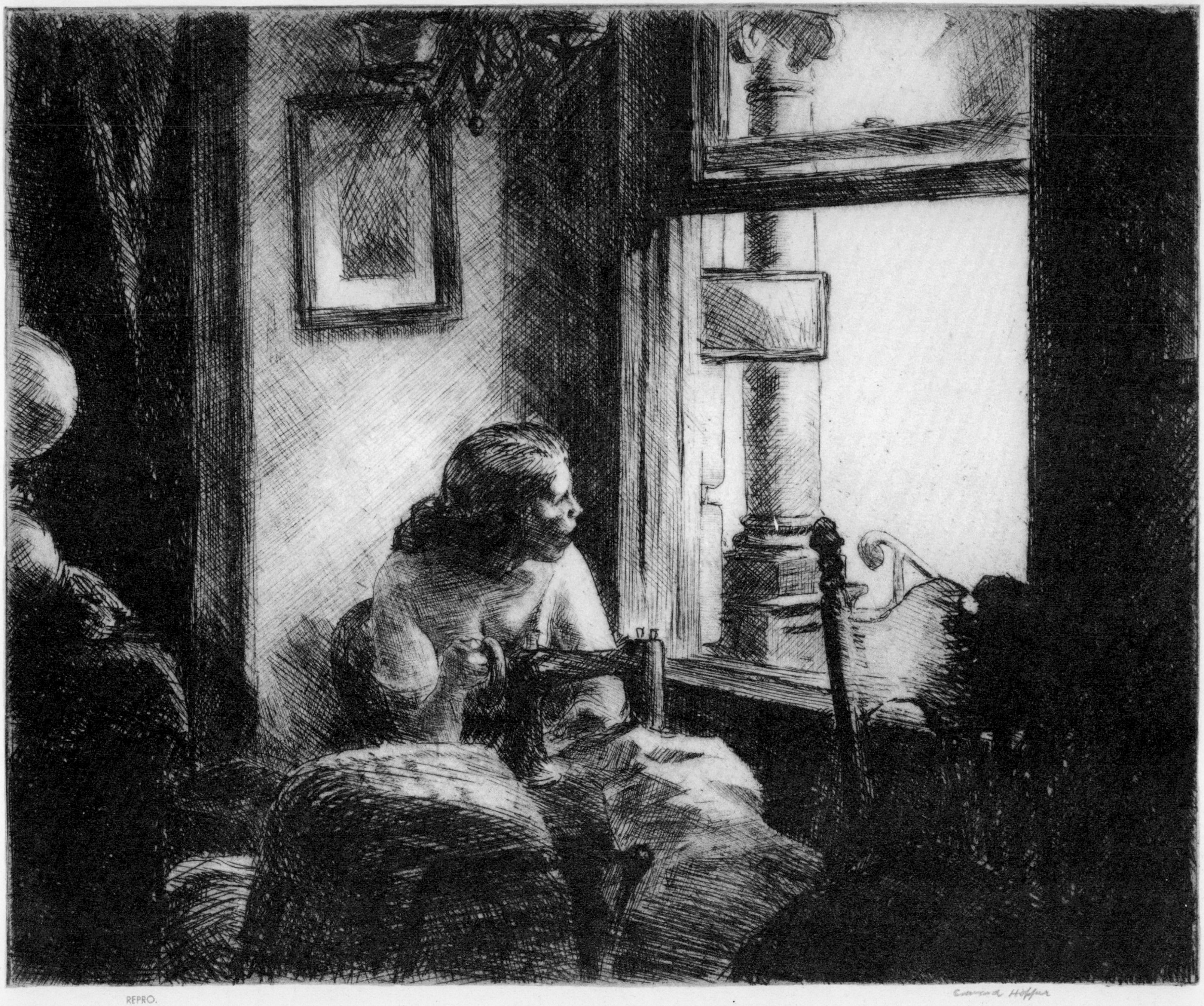

REPRO.

Edward Hopper

PLATE NUMBER FIFTY-SEVEN

East Side Interior

BY EDWARD HOPPER

(*See reverse side for plate*)

EDWARD HOPPER, portrayer par excellence of water, boats, and the sort of squarish wooden house characteristic of towns and villages near the water in the eastern states, was appropriately born at Nyack, New York, famous as the building port for racing yachts. It was 1882, and within a few years the boy was thoroughly familiar with the beautiful landscapes of the near-by Hudson valley, the rigging and form of yachts, and the outline and mass of the water-front buildings. For he has an astonishing sharpness of vision, a pertinacious memory for detail, an uncanny power of revealing the beauty in things and places others might pass by as completely undistinguished. His training in New York, under Robert Henri and Kenneth Hayes Miller, his self-education in Paris and elsewhere, have sharpened his tools, given him the unmistakably personal technique that he uses so persuasively. But his materials, the apparent commonplaces he loves so understandingly, have remained unchanged.

East Side Interior is a fine example not only of Mr. Hopper's way of laying bare the beauties of design and substance to be found in ordinary scenes, but also of his characteristic way of using light. A scene which many an artist might have valued for the indications of sordidness with which it could easily be invested, has here been given the poetic quality of a moment suspended forever in time. It is realism, if you like, but realism illuminated with a love for the surfaces light brings out of darkness, of the forms it rounds out of space, or the quality it lends the drabbest house and room.

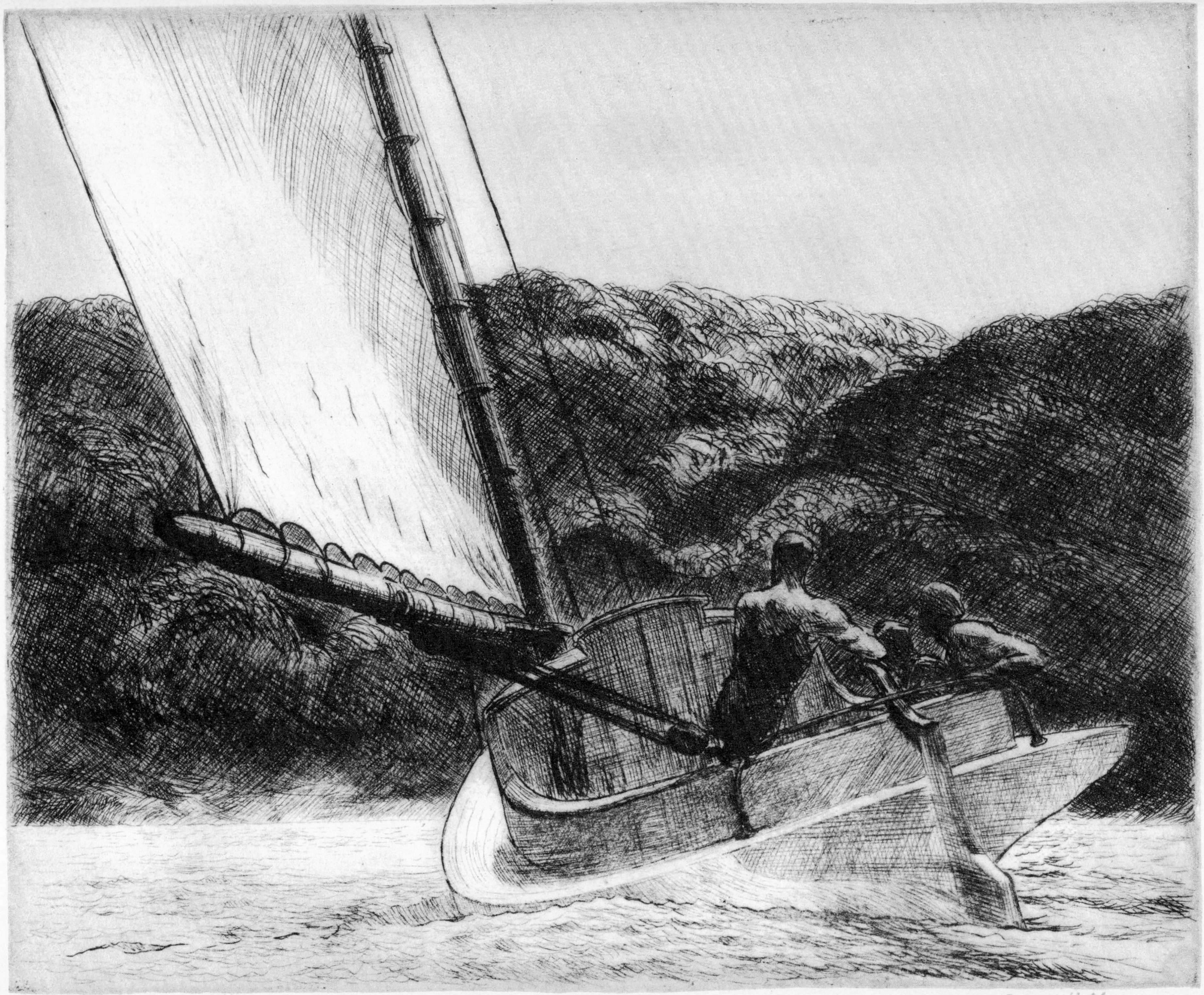

REPRO.

Edward Hopper

PLATE NUMBER FIFTY-EIGHT

The Catboat

BY EDWARD HOPPER

(*See reverse side for plate*)

OF MOST OF EDWARD HOPPER'S paintings and etchings it would be true to say that they are completely static. The lens of his artistic vision has flicked open for a fraction of a second, and caught the material selected in one of the succession of tiny unmoving postures of which motion is made. The houses, boats, and people in his pictures have just moved or changed, may be about to move or change again; at the exact fraction of a second in which they are revealed they are neither changing nor moving. It is indeed an impersonal and motionless and unchanging world. In *The Catboat*, water, boat, and sail are lovingly, convincingly etched. But the entire scene has been silenced, made rigid forever. The men are mere incidents in the design, the hilly background a changeless unpopulated land.

Here is none of the swinging motion Winslow Homer knew how to portray, but rather, the beautifully architectural drawing of a boat and its rigging by a man who loves things for their tactile, palpable surfaces, their suggestions of ponderability and depth, their way of catching and reflecting light. It is the extremely well seen and smoothly set down vision of an intensely objective man.

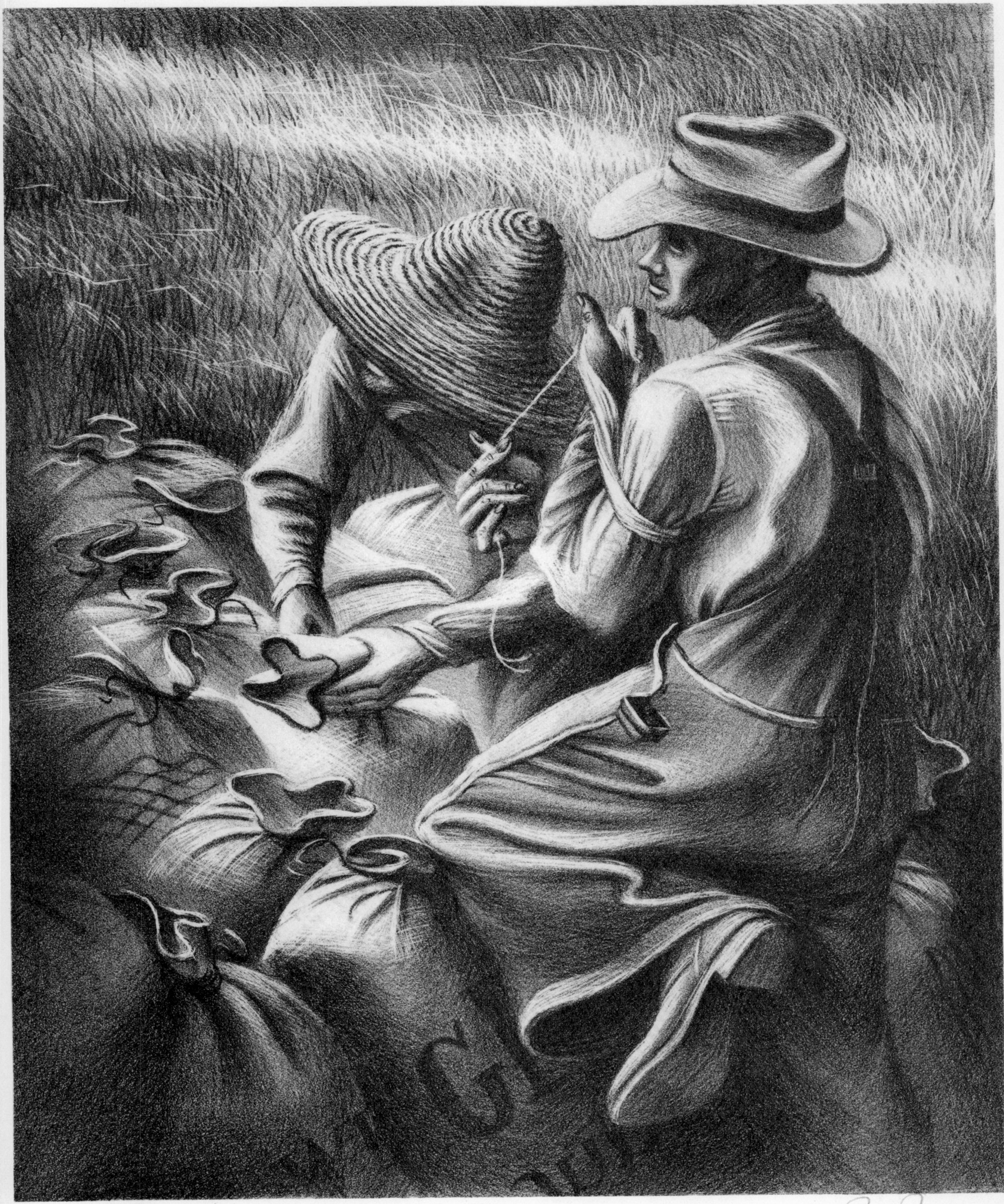

REPRO.

Joe Jones

PLATE NUMBER FIFTY-NINE

Missouri Wheat Farmers

BY JOE JONES

(See reverse side for plate)

JUST THIRTY YEARS OLD—he was born in St. Louis, where he still lives, in 1909—Joe Jones has for some years been one of the most excitedly discussed artists in America. Entirely self-taught, he won prizes at various exhibits in his early twenties, and in 1937 was awarded a Guggenheim fellowship. He has been hailed as a proletarian artist because of his exclusive interest in the lives and work of laborers, and because he is vocally a member of the Communist Party. His principal admirations in painting are, he says, "El Greco, Titian, Daumier, Goya, Rembrandt, Rubens, Picasso, George Grosz, and Orozco." In view of this extraordinary catholicity of taste, it is gratifying to discover in Mr. Jones himself an artist of considerable originality.

Missouri Wheat Farmers makes brilliant use, in building up a very handsome design, of such paraphernalia of trade as a thick-soled shoe, a round straw hat and a crushed felt one, overalls, and wheat bags. Extreme simplification of texture and outline, a brilliant use of light coming from one side and producing almost sculptural shadows on the other, a welcome absence of the underscoring from which so much "proletarian" art suffers—in short, a willingness to let clearly envisioned and adeptly set down reality bring its own persuasions to bear—make Mr. Jones' comment on two men at rather dull work a beautiful picture to see.

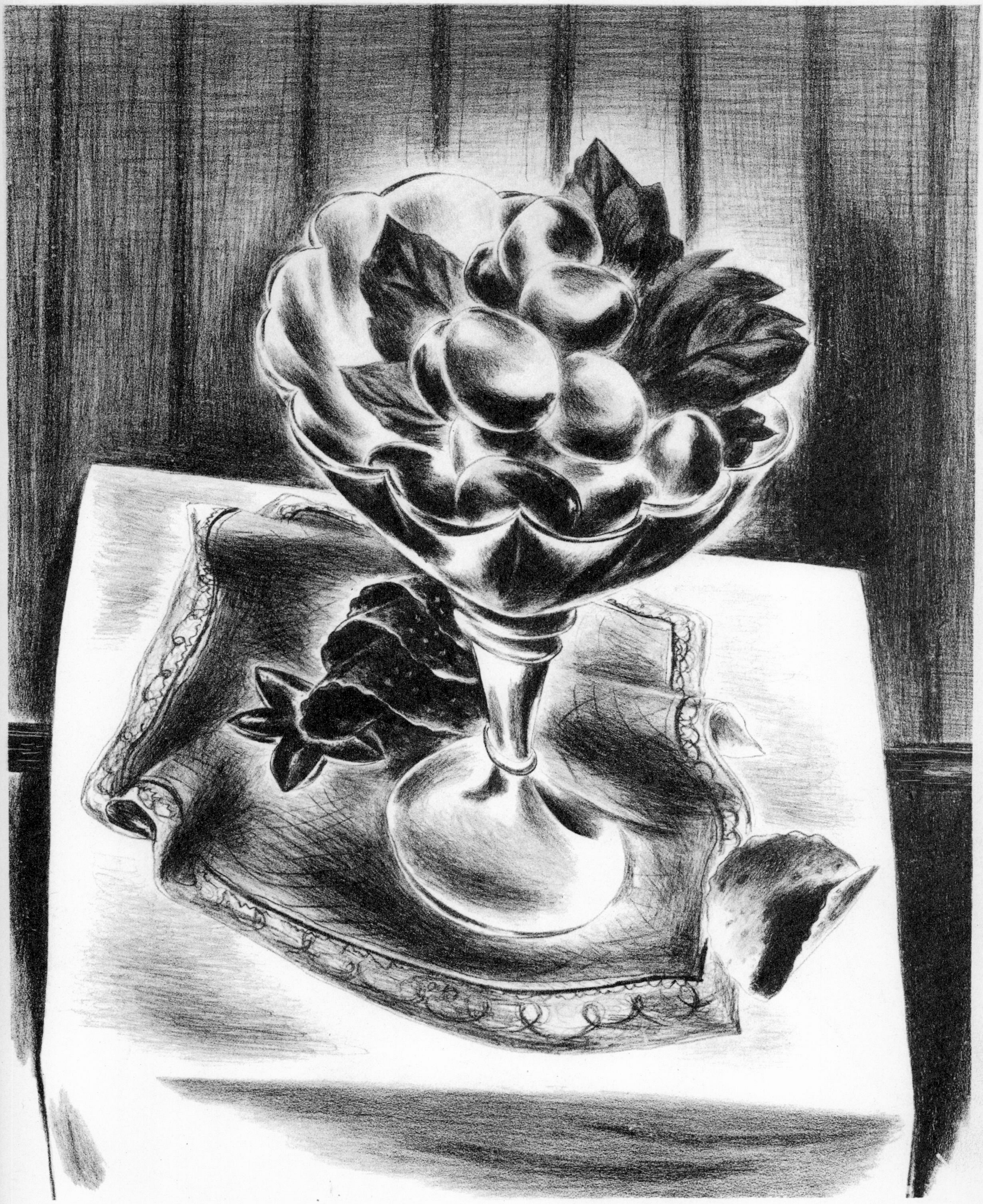

REPRO.

Y. KUNIYOSHI

Grapes in a Bowl

BY YASUO KUNIYOSHI

(See reverse side for plate)

YASUO KUNIYOSHI was born in Okayama, Japan, in 1893, and came to America at the age of eighteen. He studied in various American art schools, but his most vital absorption of Western influence came during trips to Europe in 1925 and 1928, when he looked at all the Daumiers and Delacroixs he could, finding in them the plasticity of form and subjectivity that he needed to give body to his inherited decorative flair. He has not abandoned the exquisite design and refinement of the East, however, and he has managed to combine them with what he has learned from the West without seeming merely an interesting hybrid. He has himself succinctly expressed his aims: "I have wished to express the thoughts of the East, my race, using the tradition of expressing the inner thoughts through the full realization of the matter of my experience. . . ." So perfectly assured is he of which direction his own art is going that he has become a teacher in the art school at Woodstock, New York, where his summer home is located.

Grapes in a Bowl is an unpretentious but charming arrangement, rather conventional but utterly satisfactory as a decorative composition.

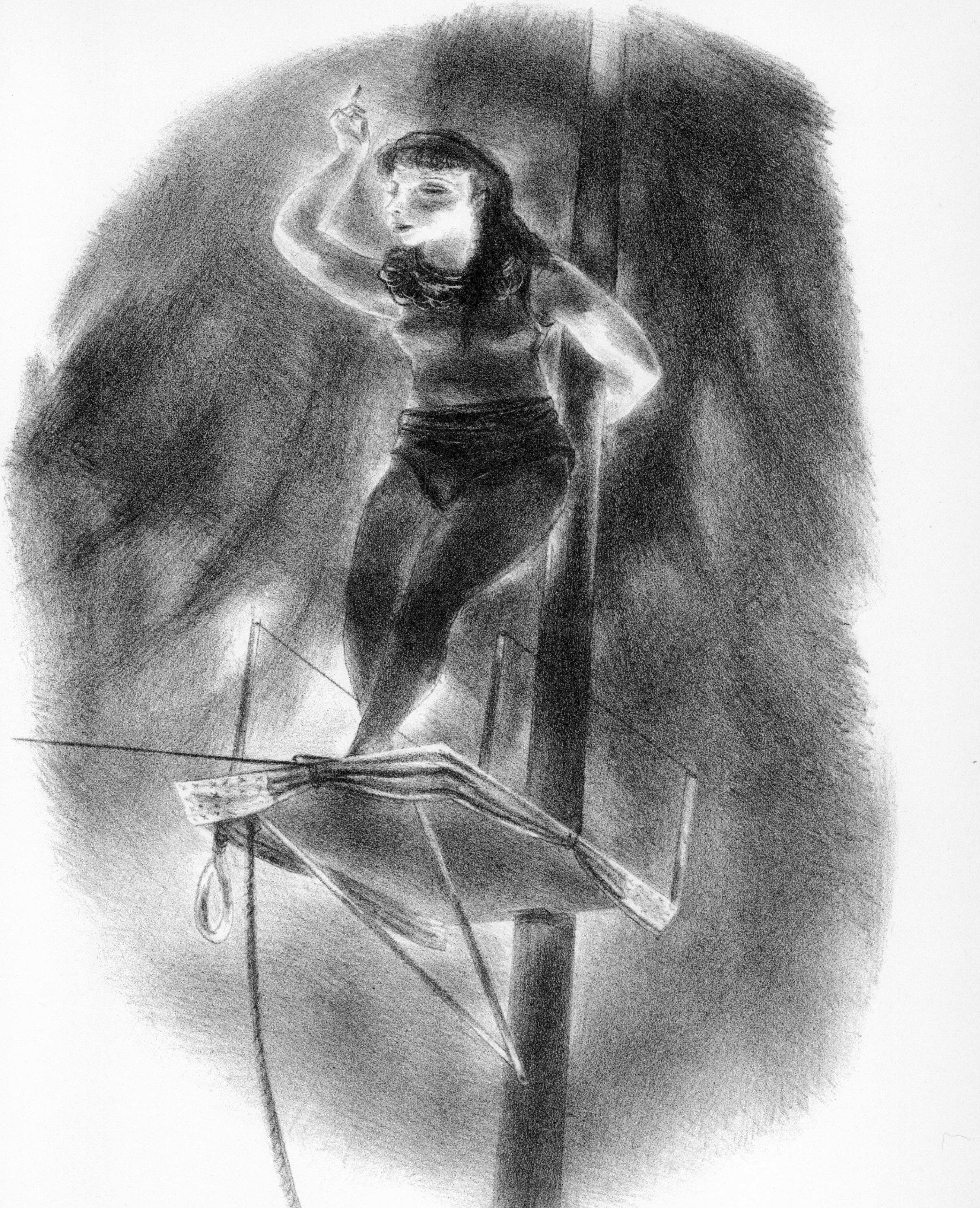

REPRO. Tight rope performer Yasuo Kuniyoshi 36

Tightrope Performer

BY YASUO KUNIYOSHI

(See reverse side for plate)

THIS DELICIOUS COMPOSITION has "zero hour" tension. The acrobat is poised on her aerial platform, ready to take off across space. With one arm around the pole, she steadies herself for the effort; the other arm gives the signal that she is ready. The eyes calculate the chances. The upper vastnesses of the big circus tent lower about her. *Tightrope Performer* is one of Kuniyoshi's most satisfying compositions, neatly, gracefully conceived and executed with delicacy and refinement.

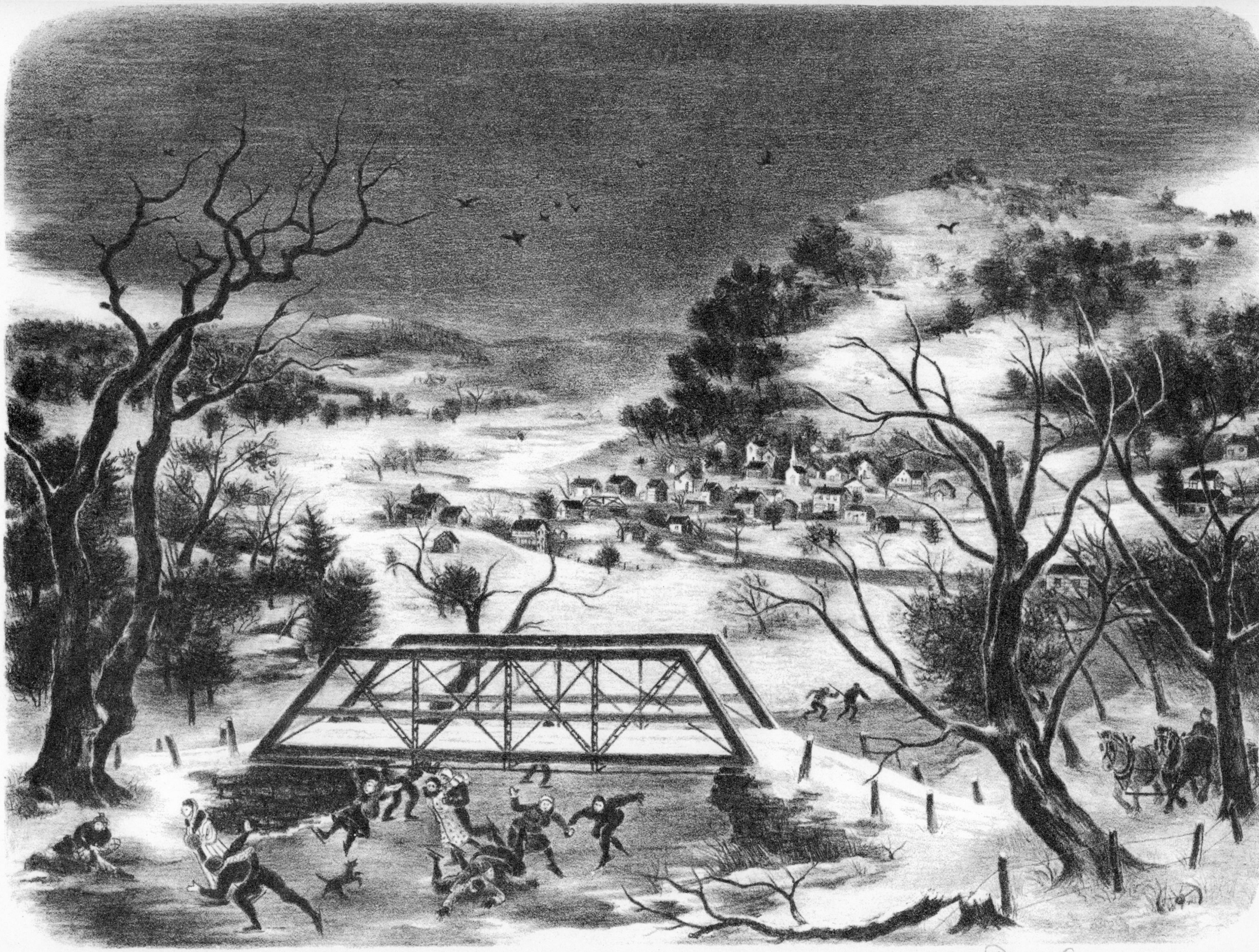

REPRO.

Doris Lee

Winter in the Catskills

BY DORIS LEE

(See reverse side for plate)

OUT OF ILLINOIS, Doris Lee began to attract wide public notice when she won the Logan Medal of the Art Institute of Chicago in 1935. Success after success has rewarded her sometimes controversial work, which finally won her the commission for murals in the new Post Office in Washington, D. C.

Winter in the Catskills suggests that Miss Lee may love the spare and naïve landscapes of early American painters. For there is present in it in large quantity the delicate and precise pictorial charm of many so-called primitives. Except for the modern bridge in the foreground, it could easily be a fine print of some New York or New England painting of the early nineteenth century. It has the idiosyncrasy of vision and forthrightness of conception that make the works of those bygone, untutored masters so appealing to the modern eye. That a very contemporary young woman should be able to achieve this pictorial immediacy without any sense of imitation or condescension is a proof of important talent. Few lithographs so successfully combine interest of small detail with unrolling space. The wintry sky, gaunt trees, sharply defined bridge, white snow, and busy skaters are unified into the single impression that is the aim of every artist's technique of integration.

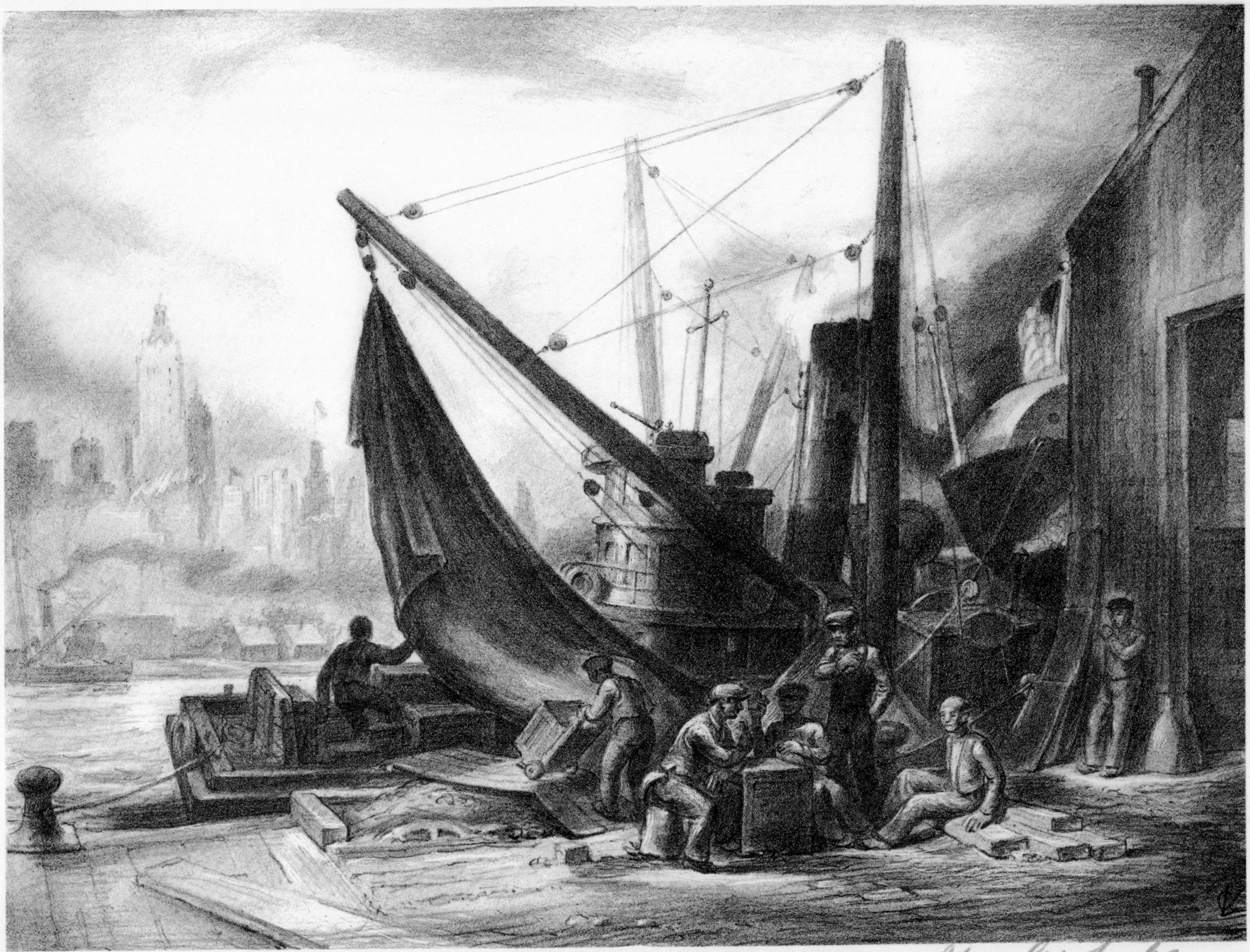

REPRO

Charles Locke

PLATE NUMBER SIXTY-THREE

Water Front

BY CHARLES LOCKE

(*See reverse side for plate*)

CHARLES WHEELER LOCKE was born in Cincinnati in 1899. After studying at the Art Academy there, he became assistant in lithography to Joseph Pennell at the Art Students' League, later becoming Pennell's successor there. He now lives in Brooklyn, New York, not far from the vantage point from which the general outlines of *Water Front* are seen. Just so, by walking down to the east bank of the East River, can he look across the busy stream toward the towers of downtown Manhattan.

There is something not very common in contemporary art, a certain monumental quality reminiscent of other times—a quality that Joseph Pennell often achieved—in *Water Front*. Its smoky vagueness, the very tangible softness of its lithographic technique, the centering of interest on building, barge, and sky—all contribute to the undefinable, if unmistakable "past recaptured" quality of the print. Perhaps it would be better to say that Mr. Locke has seen a Brooklyn water front scene *sub specie aeternitatis*. For he has not falsified or sentimentalized the material chosen: he has merely looked at it from a point of view that has become rare.

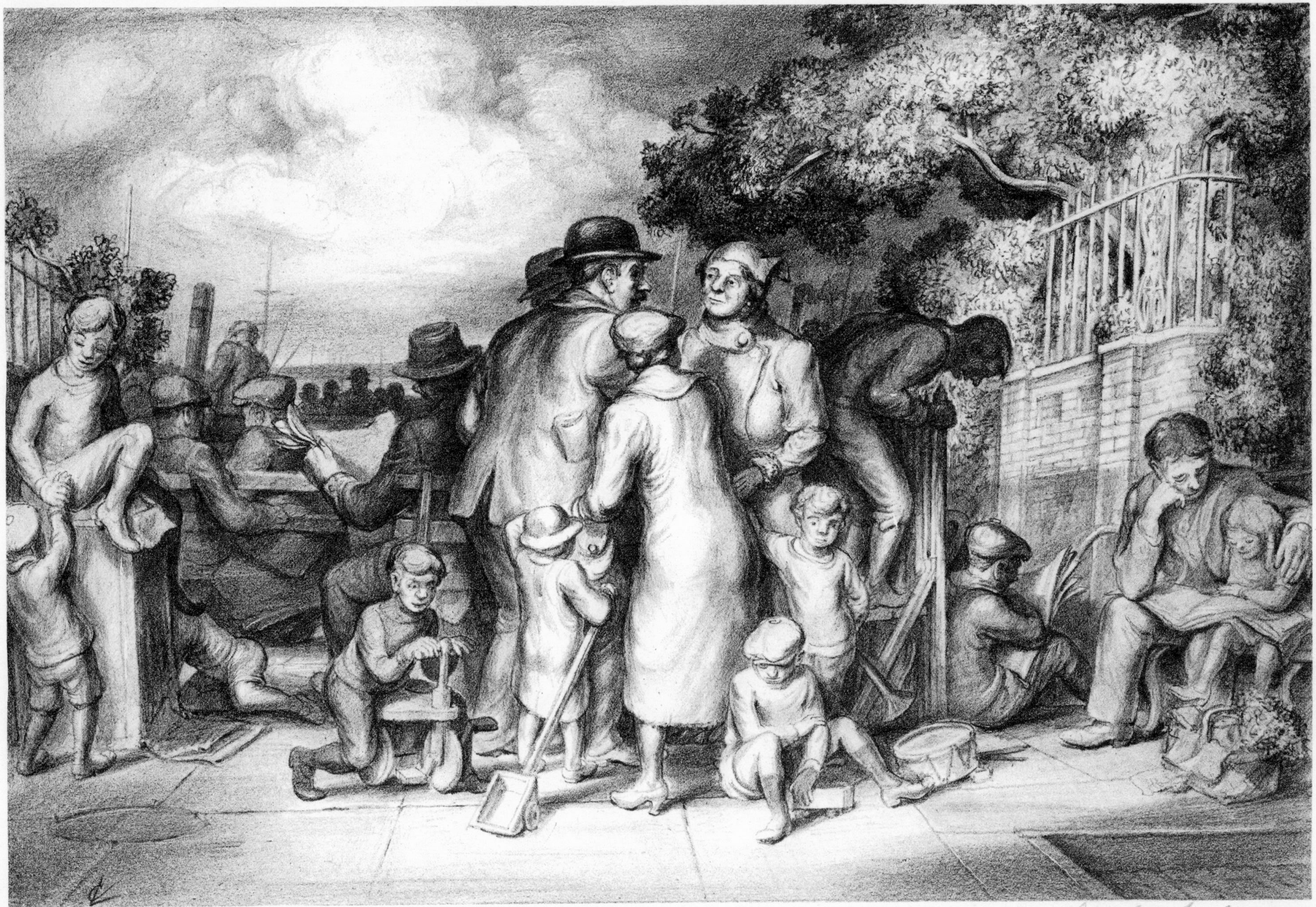

Charles Locke

PLATE NUMBER SIXTY-FOUR

The Terrace

BY CHARLES LOCKE

(*See reverse side for plate*)

THE LOCALE OF *The Terrace* is the foot of Montague Street, in Brooklyn. This open-air conversation piece brings into sharper focus some of the qualities of *Water Front.* The forms, again, are sculptural, and again the human note is an echo of the past. "This print," the artist has said, "is in no sense a portrait." That is correct. Here, rather, is a point of view that brings together, with some nostalgia perhaps, an association of forms in "an attempt," as Locke says, "to translate the atmosphere of such a place into a design suitable to my purposes." And these purposes, whatever their incidental motivations, are overwhelmingly and satisfactorily esthetic. Locke has a largeness of design and an understanding of the business of organizing the elements of a picture that unify and invest with power the rather unsensational materials of his inventions.

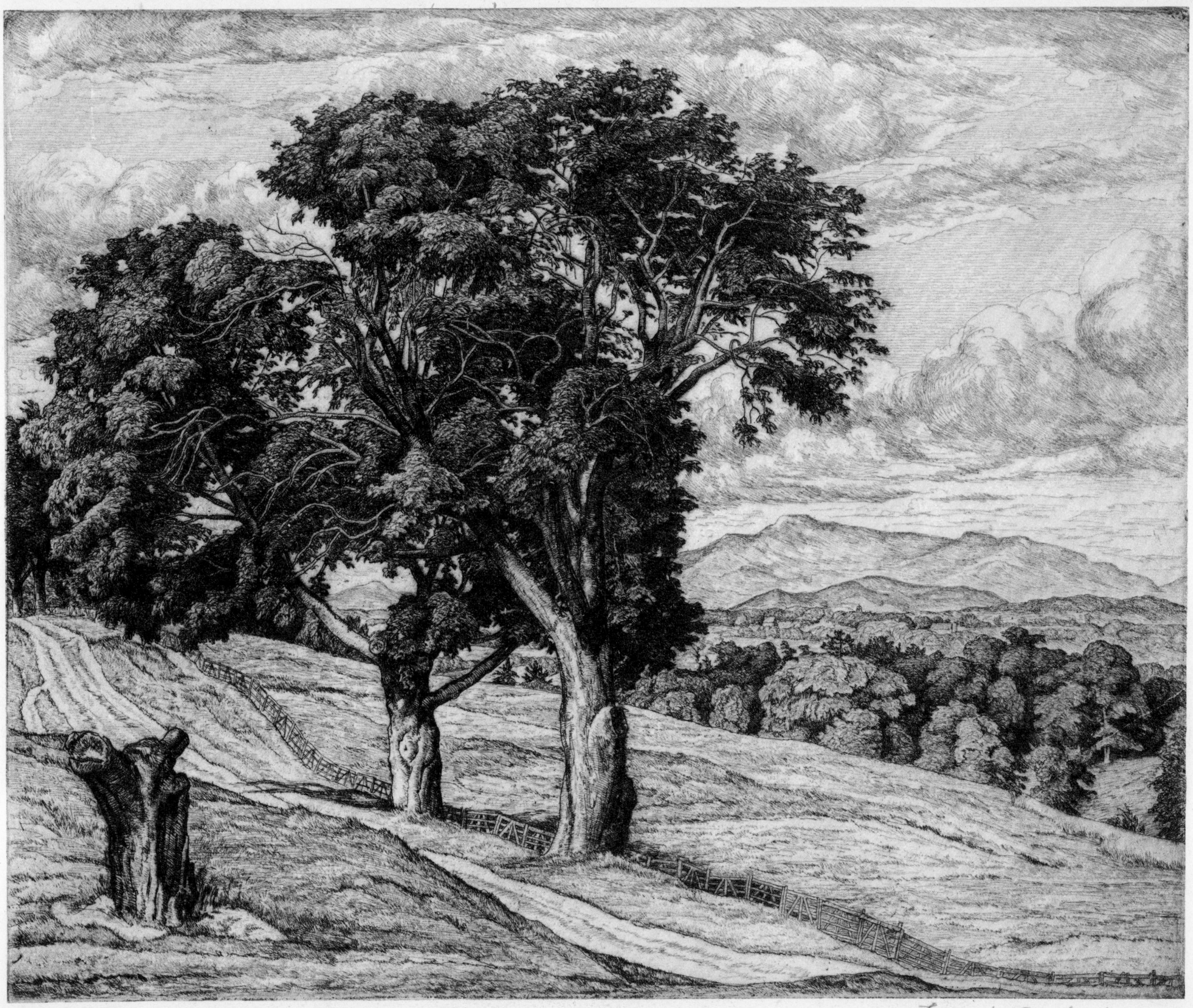

REPRO.

Luigi Lucioni

PLATE NUMBER SIXTY-FIVE

Trees and Mountains

BY LUIGI LUCIONI

(*See reverse side for plate*)

THE BEST INTRODUCTION to an understanding of Lucioni's art is his own statement of his aims: "I admire fantasy in art, but realizing that it is not in my make-up I try more and more to create reality with the simplest means and with all essential detail. But I feel that all this should be part of a design, which I believe every canvas must primarily possess." *Trees and Mountains*, an excellent illustration of this point of view, exemplifies, too, the lengths to which he carries his almost photographic realism. The scene is the Vermont highland area he never tires of painting, with its splendid mountains, noble trees, straggling roads, and hidden farms.

Lucioni was born in Malnate, Italy, on November 4, 1900. After his family came to America, he entered the night art classes at Cooper Union. He remained there four years, and an equal period at the National Academy of Design. His career has been brilliant, and it is difficult to say whether his landscapes are the most prized of his work, for his still lifes and portraits seem equally esteemed. He has received various awards, and is well represented both in public and private collections throughout the country.

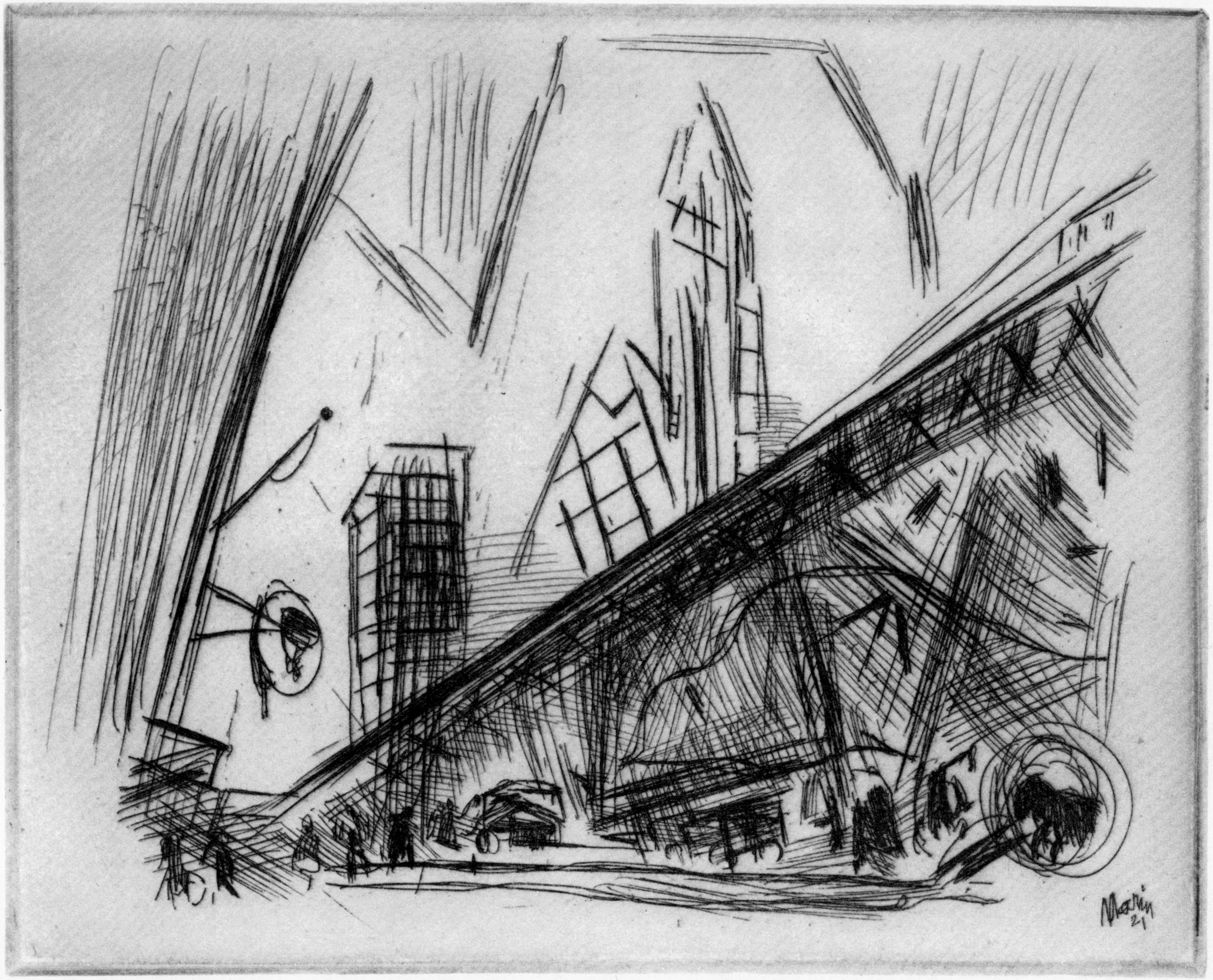
Marin 21

John Marin

Downtown New York

BY JOHN MARIN

(See reverse side for plate)

IT IS A LITTLE DIFFICULT to think of John Marin as an oldster, and yet he is almost seventy years of age. It cannot truly be said that his long career is the history of American art, for from the first he has isolated himself from national tendencies to become an experimenter. *Downtown New York* is typical of his aloof style—a thoroughly mature production of one of America's most accomplished technicians. Realistic truth and perspective have been sacrificed to emphasis and the play of the artist's eclecticism. While Marin has gone far on the road to distortion, grace remains, and this personal impression of a New York scene is easy to look at and, as personal idiosyncrasy, difficult to quarrel with.

Marin, born in Rutherford, New Jersey, in 1870, comes of English-Dutch and French ancestry. After studying in Philadelphia and New York, for some years he devoted himself to his art without notable acclaim. Fame came to him after 1909, when Alfred Stieglitz invited him to join that coterie of expressionists known as the "291" group. By many critics this shy, limelight-avoiding man is considered the greatest water-colorist alive.

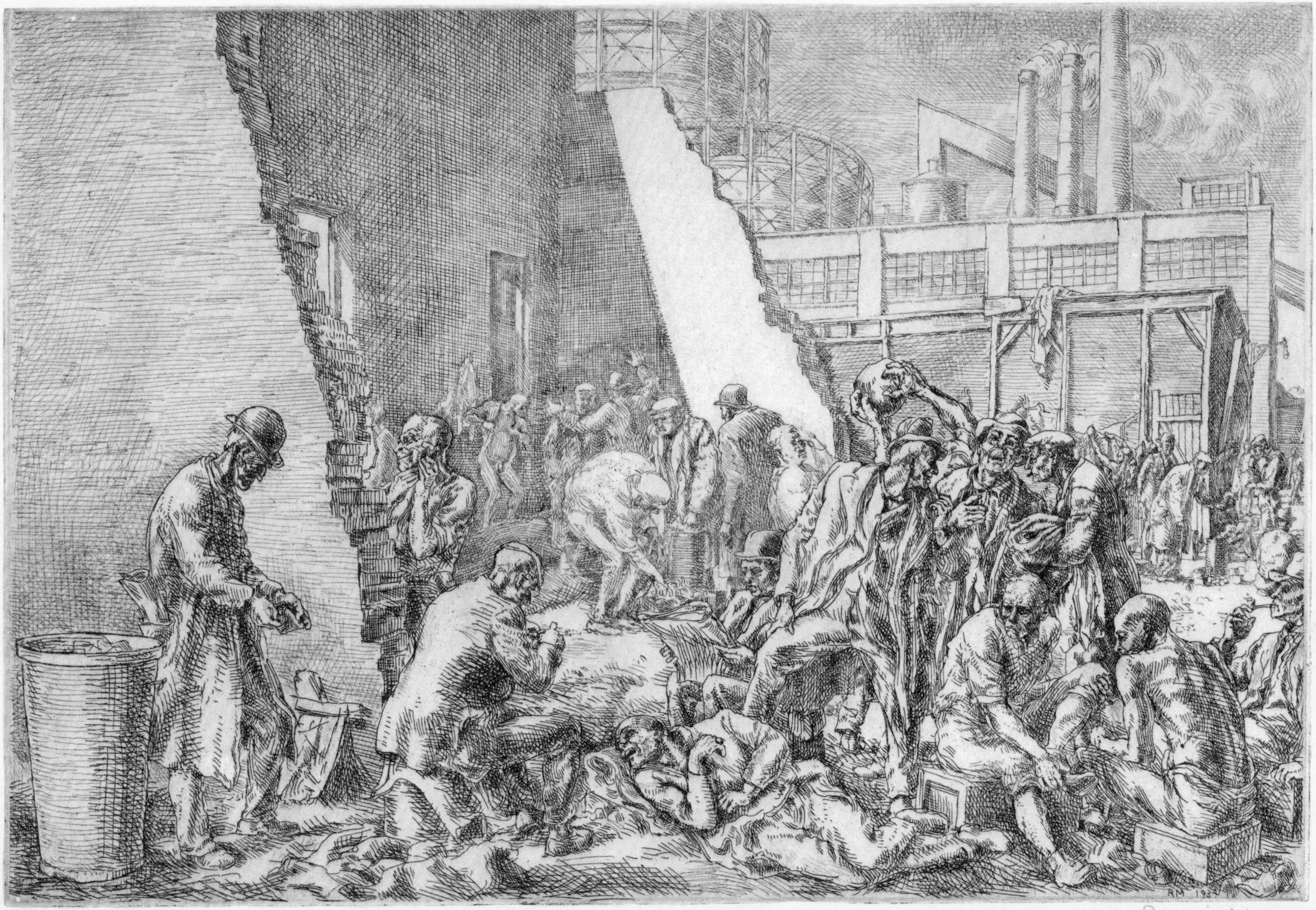
RM

Reginald Marsh

PLATE NUMBER SIXTY-SEVEN

The Jungle

BY REGINALD MARSH

(*See reverse side for plate*)

REGINALD MARSH, one of the best satirists of the American scene, was born in Paris in 1898. Both his parents were artists, and a conventional career at Lawrenceville and Yale did nothing to quench his own interest in the arts. At first a drummer, and then a maker of verse, he finally approached his métier through the art editorship of *The Yale Record*. After graduation, he tried cartoons, caricatures, and stage sets. An uneasy feeling that technically he still had much to learn sent him first to the Art Students' League, and then abroad to study the great traditionalists under Mahonri Young. Since then he has been an untiring chronicler of New York life in all its manifold aspects. In 1930 he held his first one-man show, and since then has shown often. He is well represented in public and private collections, and has done two frescoes for the new Post Office Building in Washington, D. C.

The Jungle penetrates the mildew the average New York never sees—this is part of *The Jungle* Upton Sinclair wrote about near the beginning of the century (though that was, of course, Chicago). Here is a sad congress of down-and-outers, men precariously clinging to life, not even on the fringes of an acceptable existence. The etching is crowded, but the details are fine and shrewdly observed.

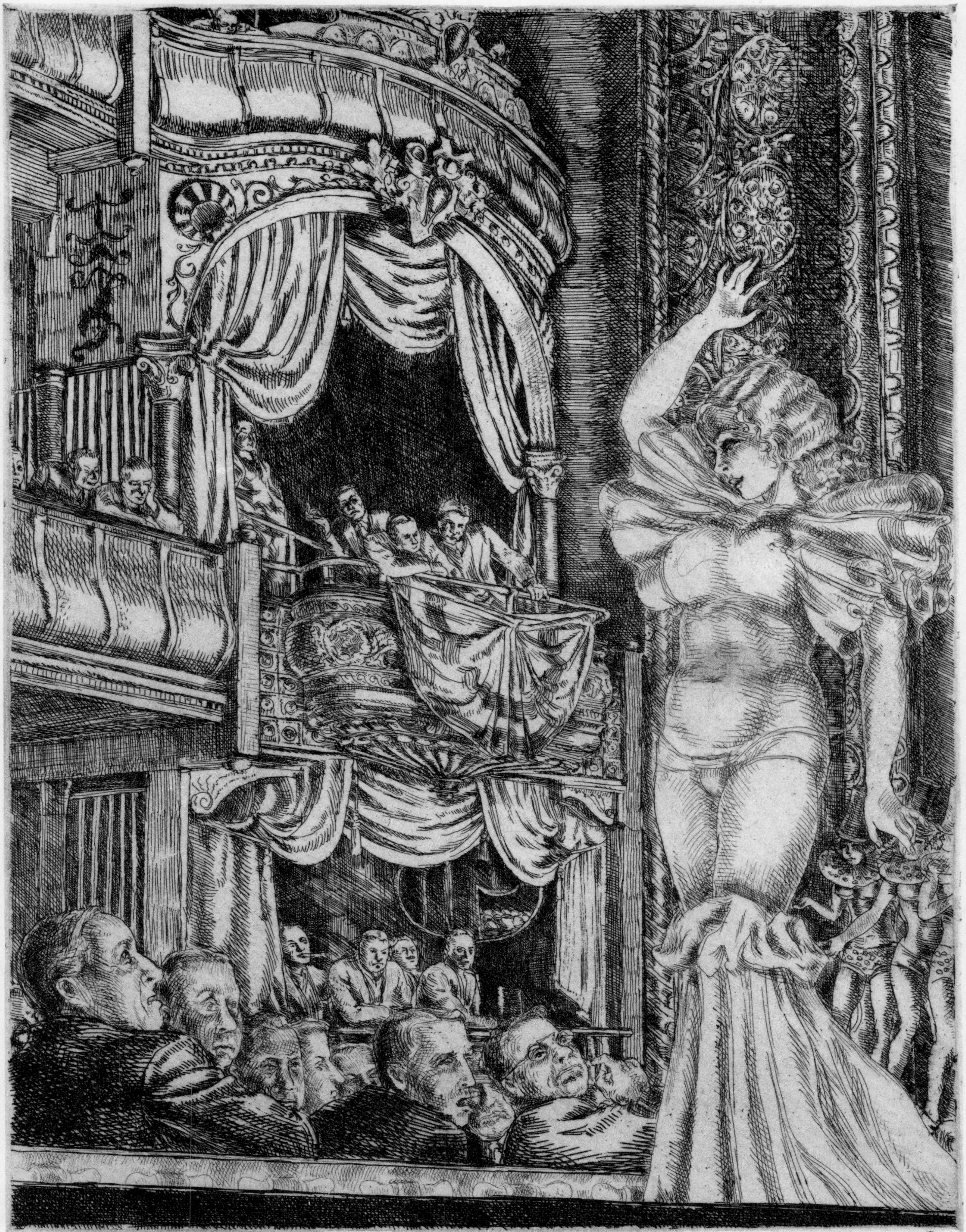

Star Burlesk 1933 REPRO. *Reginald Marsh*

PLATE NUMBER SIXTY-EIGHT

Star Burlesque

BY REGINALD MARSH

(*See reverse side for plate*)

IN THE MIDDLE TWENTIES, Marsh's interest in the theater became marked, and he began to design stage sets. John Murray Anderson gave him a commission to do a curtain for *The Greenwich Village Follies,* composed entirely of cartoons, and this led to Robert Edmond Jones asking him to help design the sets for a Provincetown production. Later he did some work for Paramount Publix and Sandór Gluck's Dance Theater. Since then, Marsh has been fascinated by theatrical material.

Star Burlesque is a subject that is obviously as attractive to Marsh's witty eye as it must be abhorrent to the Arguses of the Watch and Ward Society. There is no tut-tut attitude lurking behind this etching, only a sympathetic and vivid reporting of a significant slice of New Yorkese. There is no cynicism here, either. Yet, Marsh is not invariably gentle. When asked what artistic problem he attempted to solve in *Star Burlesque,* he replied, "Traditional form independent of what current cant tries to make us think what it is."

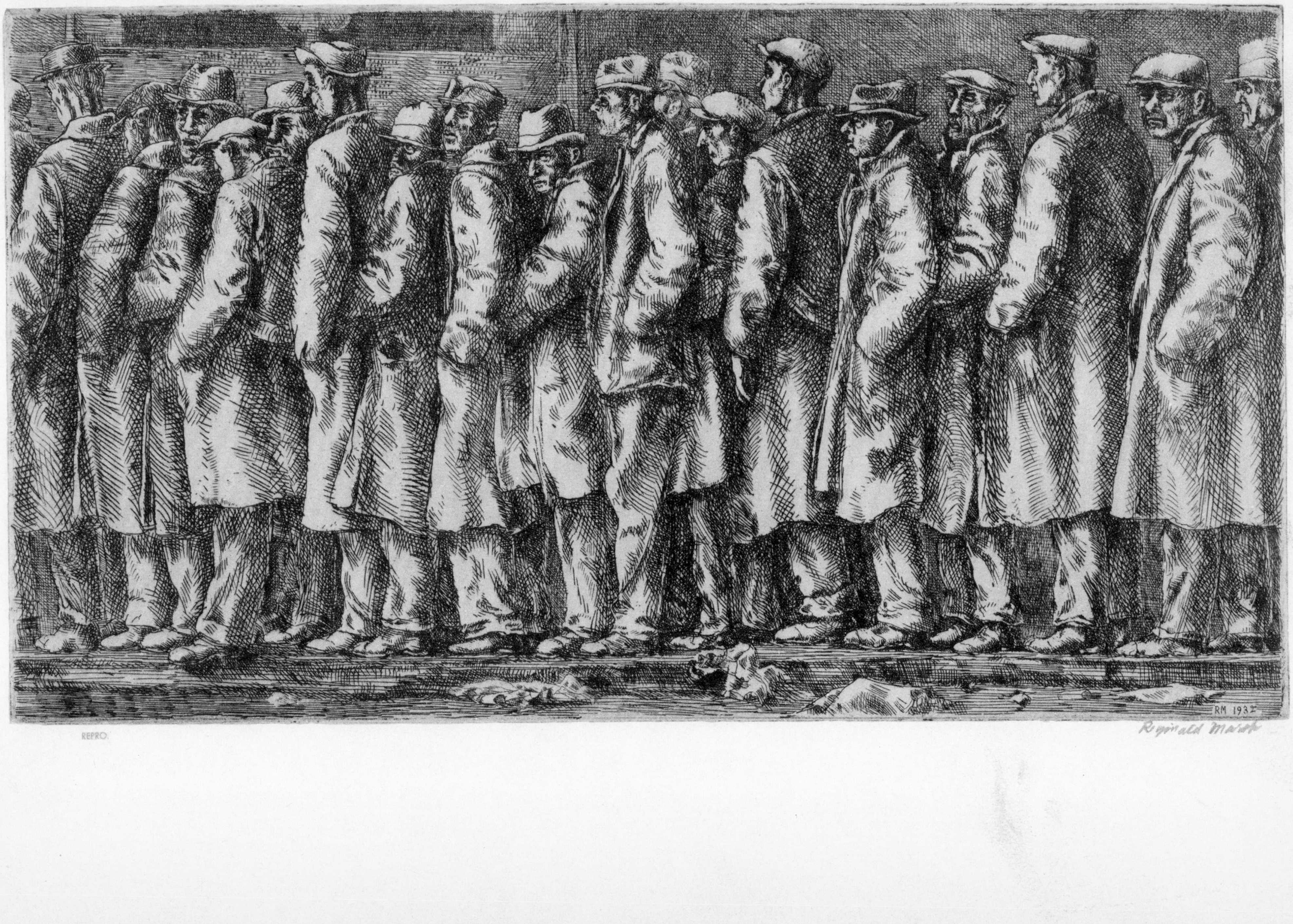
RM 1932

Reginald Marsh

PLATE NUMBER SIXTY-NINE

Bread Line

BY REGINALD MARSH

(*See reverse side for plate*)

MARSH, whose chief deficiency is composition, here reaches a compromise between his natural tendency to put down his facts without eliminating anything and a pull towards establishing a satisfactory relationship between forms. *Bread Line* is a sure-fire way of making the compromise, and if it lacks formal imagination of the highest kind, it has tremendous concentration. *Bread Line* was etched in 1932, which is almost all one need know about it. There is a rare assortment of faces in it, from downright mugs, chronic down-and-outers, and panhandlers to at least one man who has seen better days. While Marsh rejoices in an equable temperament, there is a latent anger in *Bread Line* that gives it more eloquence than many of the artist's more elaborate compositions.

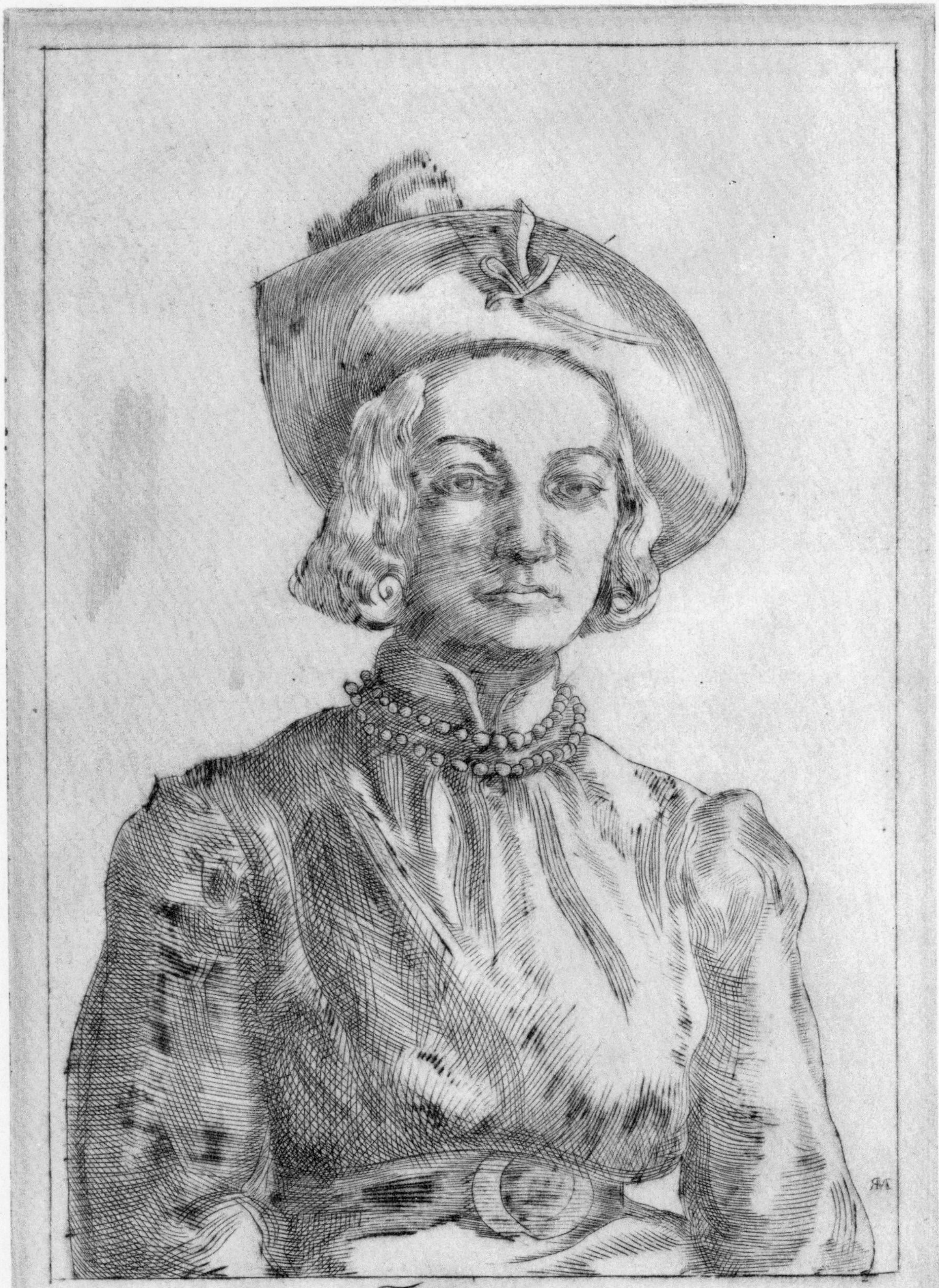
Felicia

REPRO.

Reginald Marsh

Felicia

BY REGINALD MARSH

(*See reverse side for plate*)

Felicia is a copper line engraving of Reginald Marsh's second wife, Felicia Meyers, who is also an artist. While Marsh's is not an overintellectualized art, *Felicia* has a certain naïve hauteur that recalls certain portraits of the Renaissance. It reminds one that Marsh has studied the Old Masters intensively. Here he has caught the secret of the greatest portraits: getting something of the sitter's substance as well as her likeness. The quaint, grave charm of *Felicia* represents a side of Marsh's art that may surprise those who know only his studies of Manhattan low life.

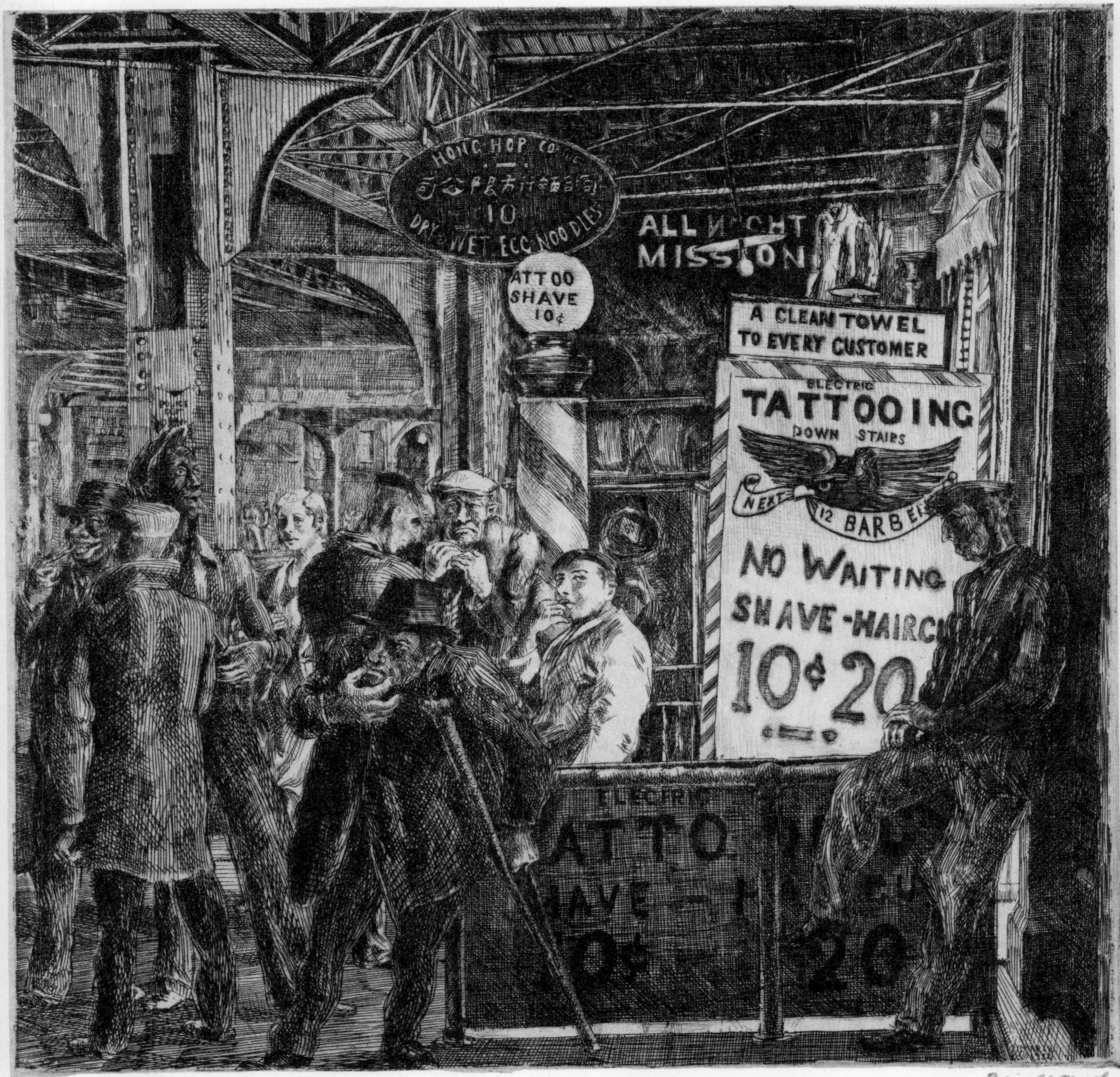
HONG HOP CO.
10
DRY WET EGG NOODLES
ATTOO
SHAVE
10¢
A CLEAN TOWEL
TO EVERY CUSTOMER
ELECTRIC
TATTOOING
DOWN STAIRS
NO WAITING
SHAVE-HAIRC
10¢ 20
ELECTRIC

REPRO.

Reginald Marsh

PLATE NUMBER SEVENTY-ONE

Tattoo—Haircut—Shave

BY REGINALD MARSH

(*See reverse side for plate*)

REGINALD MARSH'S consuming passion is the drama of Manhattan, and he has set it down in so many of its multifarious aspects that he can truly be called the Boswell of its sordid side. His preoccupation with the shady side of New York life is, of course, linked up with the fact that the denizens of Coney Island, the Bowery, the docks, and Fourteenth Street are more picturesque than those of Park Avenue, the east Seventies, and Gramercy Park. While he completely lacks the reforming urge, Marsh produces work instinct with satire and quick wit.

The locale of *Tattoo—Haircut—Shave* is the Bowery, of which this is a fair sample. Marsh has made an etching of tremendous vitality and pace. As is usual in Marsh's scenes of Manhattan low life, he has whelmed down everything within a certain segment of his vision, without troubling himself to select. This does not always work, but here it is effective. It is this sort of scene that will be of incalculable benefit to the historian of a thousand years hence, for it condenses a hundred pages of text into a quick view. The dwarf in the foreground is as evil as any that ever stepped from the pages of Goya, and the other figures can be classed as dangerous characters. The signs are characteristic of the district: A Clean Towel to Every Customer is worth the price of admission alone.

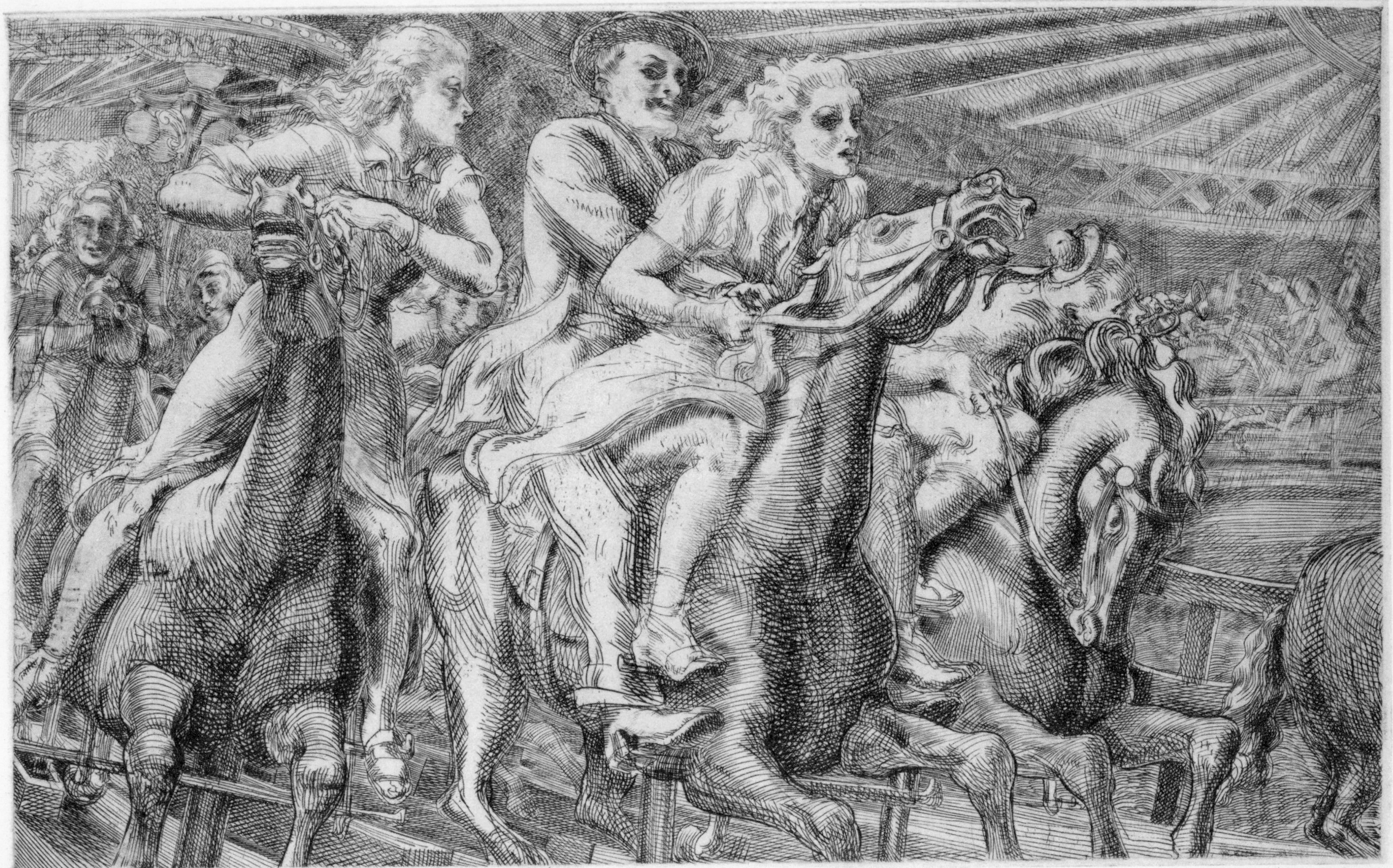

Reginald Marsh

PLATE NUMBER SEVENTY-TWO

Merry-Go-Round

BY REGINALD MARSH

(See reverse side for plate)

RECENTLY, when asked about the size of an edition of one of his etchings, Marsh answered, "Probably a dozen." Then he was asked how many of that edition were still available, and he answered, "Probably a dozen." He went on to elucidate: "Since I do practically all my own printing, I do not limit the edition. The buyer limits the edition—he rarely buys, I rarely print. I usually print fifteen or twenty and sell one or two in the next five years—so why limit the edition?" There is not a little cynical legpulling in this account of the extreme unrarity of Marsh's etching, for many of them are in much demand.

Merry-Go-Round is one of Marsh's many Coney Island subjects, and is very popular. It is feverish in tempo, in marked contrast to Howard Cook's handling of a similar scene (Plate 24). It is not impeccably composed, but it is vivid and candid, with splendid, perfectly done bits.

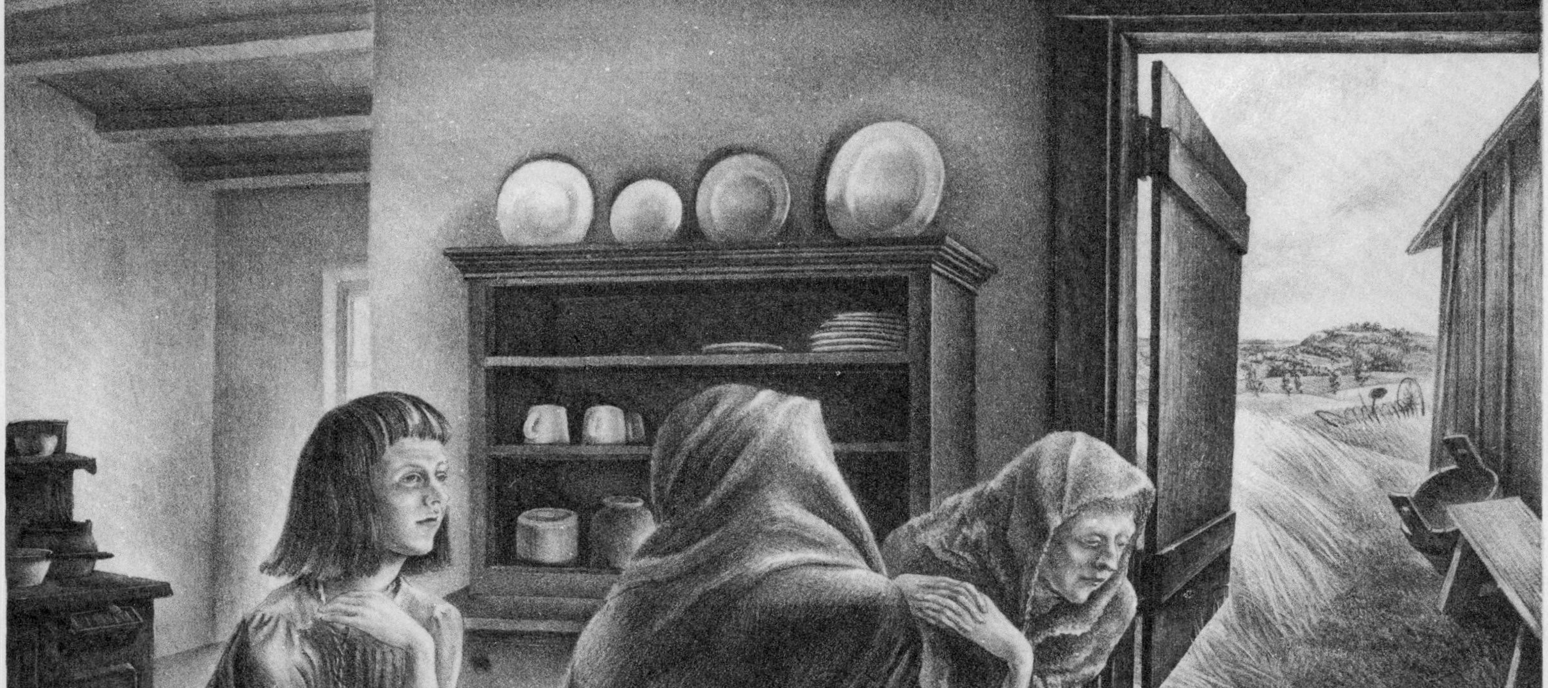

REPRO.

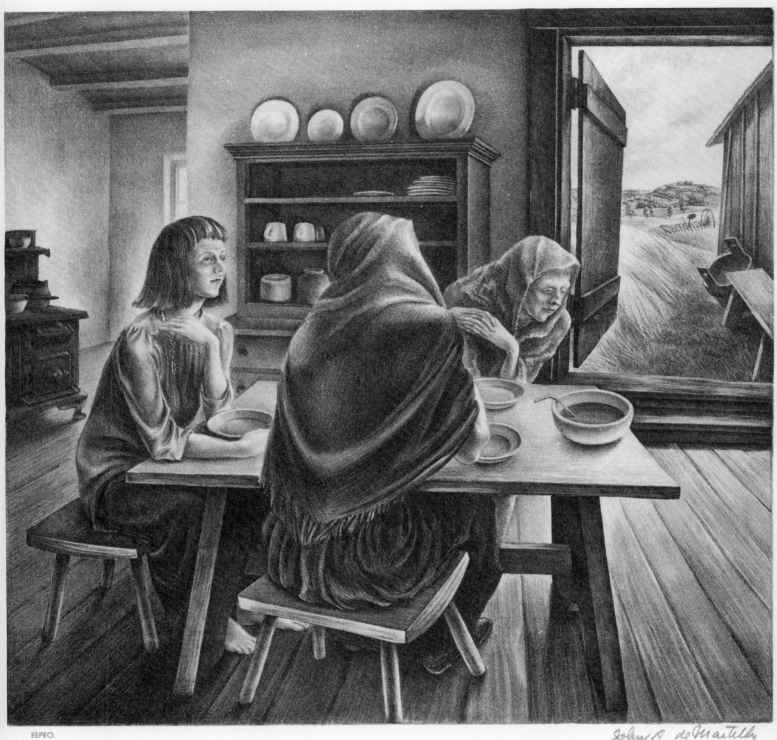

John S. deMartelly

PLATE NUMBER SEVENTY-THREE

Give Us This Day

BY JOHN S. DE MARTELLY

(*See reverse side for plate*)

ALTHOUGH THE LOCALE OF *Give Us This Day* is Missouri, the lithograph has a timeless quality. Yet, as Mr. de Martelly has been at pains to point out, the dry, brilliant warmth of a late summer sun that pervades the picture is a locally observed phenomenon. The effect of that sunlight is something of a technical triumph, but it was not this that chiefly prompted the artist to create *Give Us This Day*. Rather, it was his sympathy with his fellow men in their battle with life. Mr. de Martelly has said with undue modesty: "There is a slight touch of the spiritual that has stolen into *Give Us This Day*."

John S. de Martelly, though born in Philadelphia, has resided in Kansas City, Missouri, for many years, and knows the state and its people thoroughly. Painter, etcher, lithographer, illustrator, and teacher, the thirty-six-year-old artist has achieved a more than local eminence. His best work shows appreciation of, but not subservience to, tradition. In short, he bears watching.

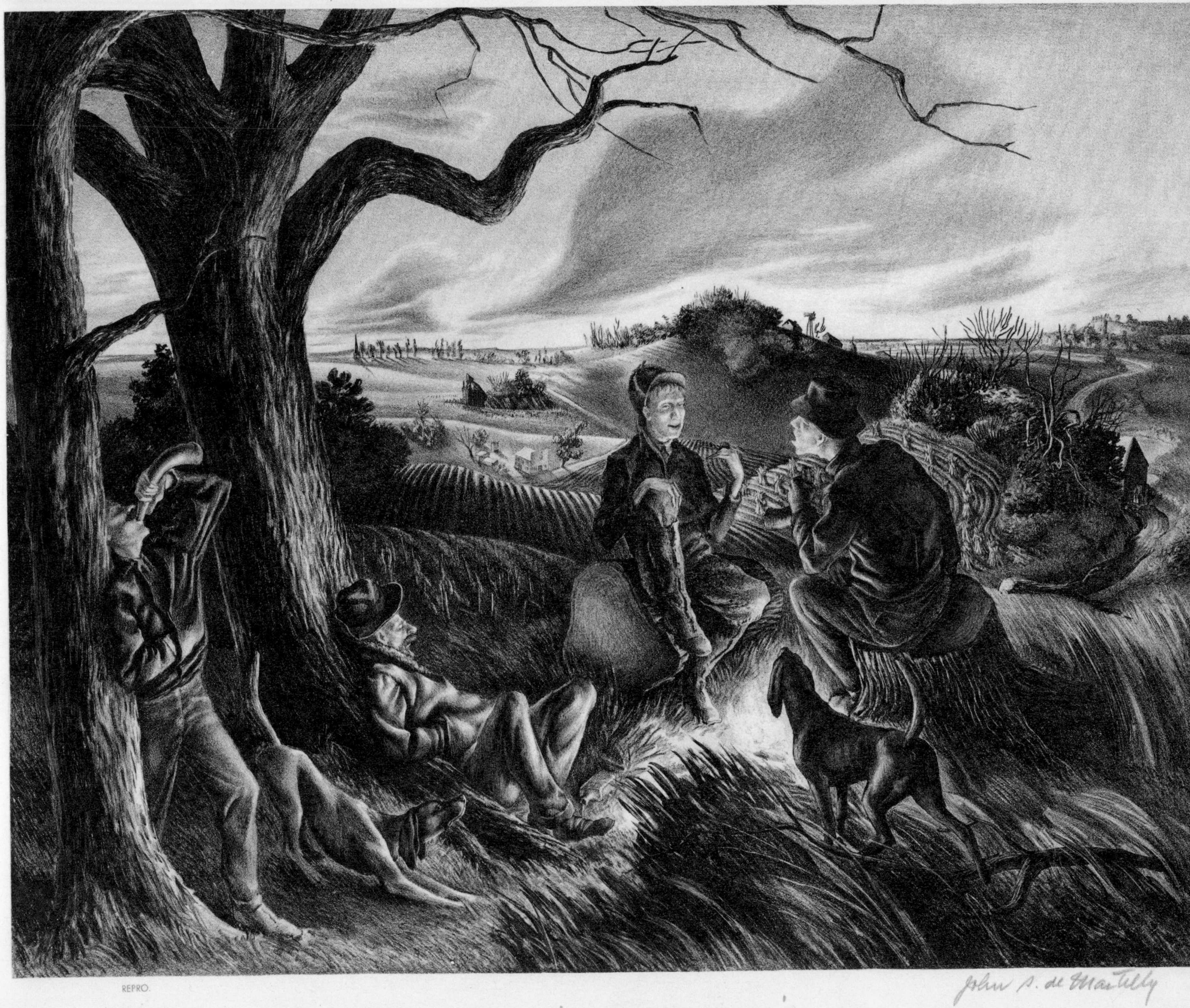

REPRO.

John S. de Martelly

PLATE NUMBER SEVENTY-FOUR

Blue Valley Fox Hunt

BY JOHN S. DE MARTELLY

(*See reverse side for plate*)

THIS LITHOGRAPH IS the end result of many efforts. The artist tells us that its design or composition was achieved only after a dozen drawings were made. To those who find solace in thinking of an artist as a hard-working economic unit, it is pertinent to note that almost one hundred and fifty hours were consumed in bringing *Blue Valley Fox Hunt* to perfection.

It is easy to gather that the English form of hunting the fox does not obtain in the Blue Valley of Missouri. "The sport," as Mr. de Martelly explains it, "is derived from listening to the voices of the baying hounds, and from wagering as to the hound in the lead." This is, then, mainly an esthetic pleasure, which the fox "hunters" can enjoy as they sit at their ease.

The Breughel-like quality of *Blue Valley Fox Hunt,* which is as apparent in the wonderful feeling for distance as in the aspect of the countrymen, makes the lithograph peculiarly attractive to those whose appreciation is stimulated by finding some immediately recognizable traditional thread. The dimensions of the chase are admirably shown by the subtle relationship of the foreground forms to the middle and far distances. The feeling of dawn is conveyed by a pervasive gray that gives the artist ample opportunity to differentiate the texture of forms.

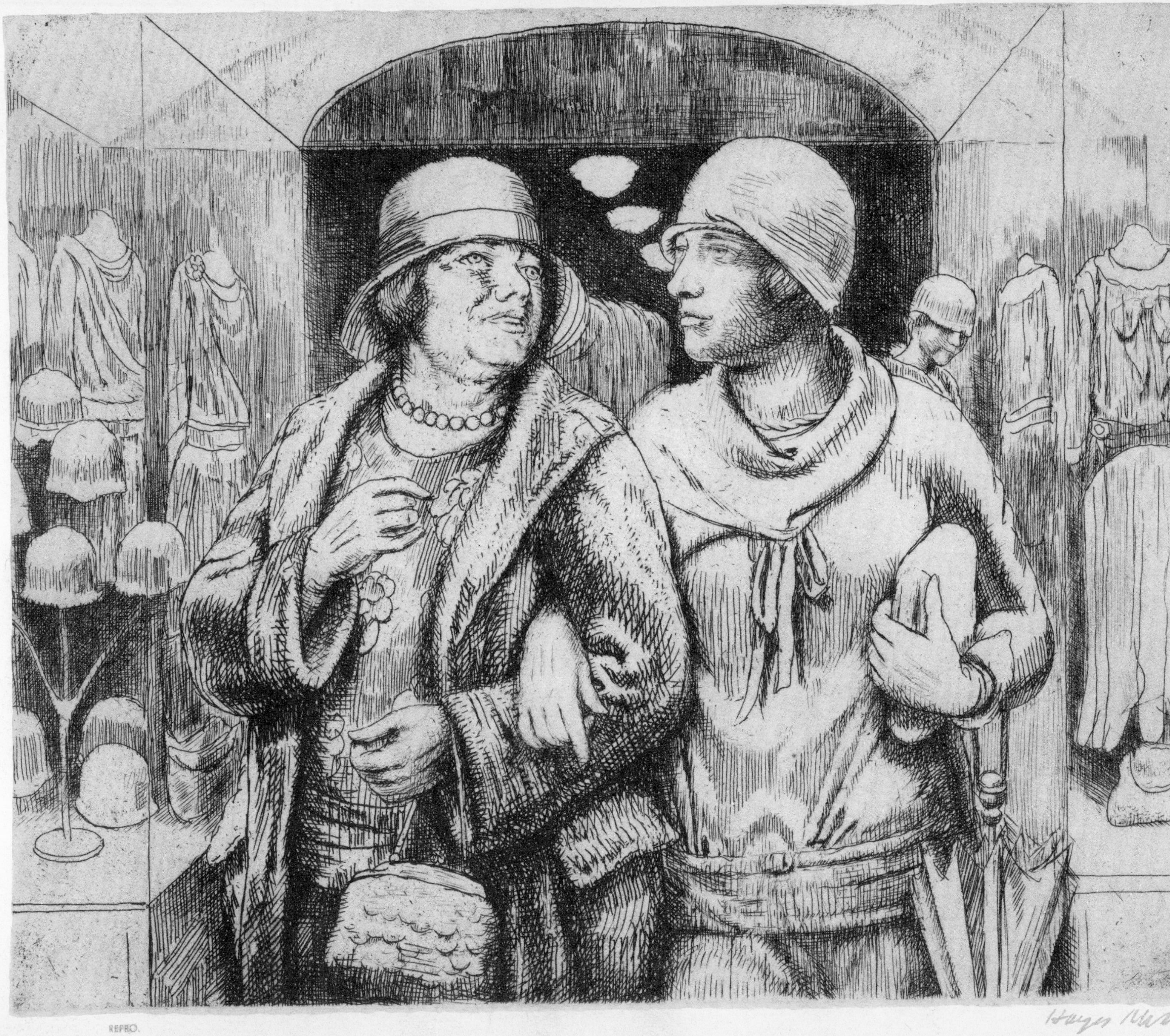

REPRO.

Hayes Miller

PLATE NUMBER SEVENTY-FIVE

Women Shopping

BY KENNETH HAYES MILLER

(*See reverse side for plate*)

KENNETH HAYES MILLER, one of America's most distinguished artists and teachers of the elder generation, was born at the Oneida Community, Kenwood, New York, on March 11, 1876. This strange "perfectionist" community was forced to disband in 1880, and young Miller was educated at the Horace Mann School in New York. His interest in art was generously fostered, and after graduate study with Kenyon Cox and William M. Chase, he spent some time in the great European galleries. He came back with a reverence for tradition that he has stanchly clung to. He has worked through several influences, notably those of the poles-apart Ryder and Renoir. Miller is possibly even more noted as a teacher than artist, and for over a quarter of a century has been conducting classes at the Art Students' League.

Women Shopping is an example of Miller's latest period. He is now fascinated by the rich variety of Fourteenth Street life, and most of his subjects are drawn from that locality. The types are treated with a frank, almost crude realism that could scarcely be deduced from Miller's early works.

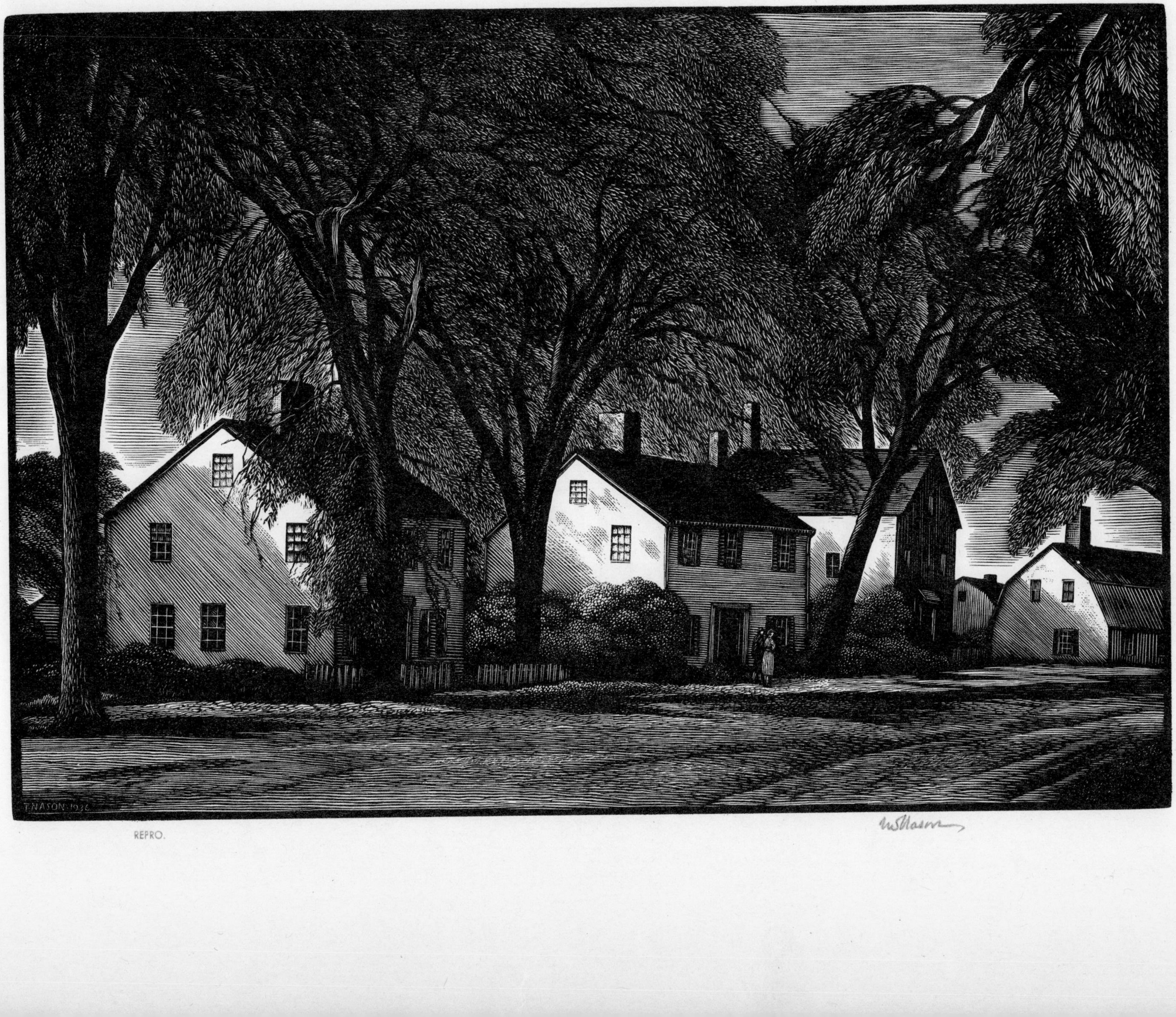
T. NASON 1936

REPRO.

PLATE NUMBER SEVENTY-SIX

Village Street

BY THOMAS W. NASON

(*See reverse side for plate*)

WHILE MOST WOODCUTS are transparently ephemeral in quality, at best fitted as book tailpieces or colophons, one occasionally turns up that transcends the seeming limitations of the art. Such is Thomas Willoughby Nason's *Village Street*, which captures the sleepy serenity of a small-town residential street as even few paintings have. Nason is one of the most distinguished practitioners of wood engraving. Born at Dracut, Massachusetts, fifty years ago, he has won many awards, including the City of Warsaw Prize and *diplôme d'honneur* at the International Exhibition of Wood Engravers at Warsaw, in 1933. His work is in many collections both here and abroad, and has often been reproduced in *Fifty Prints of the Year*.

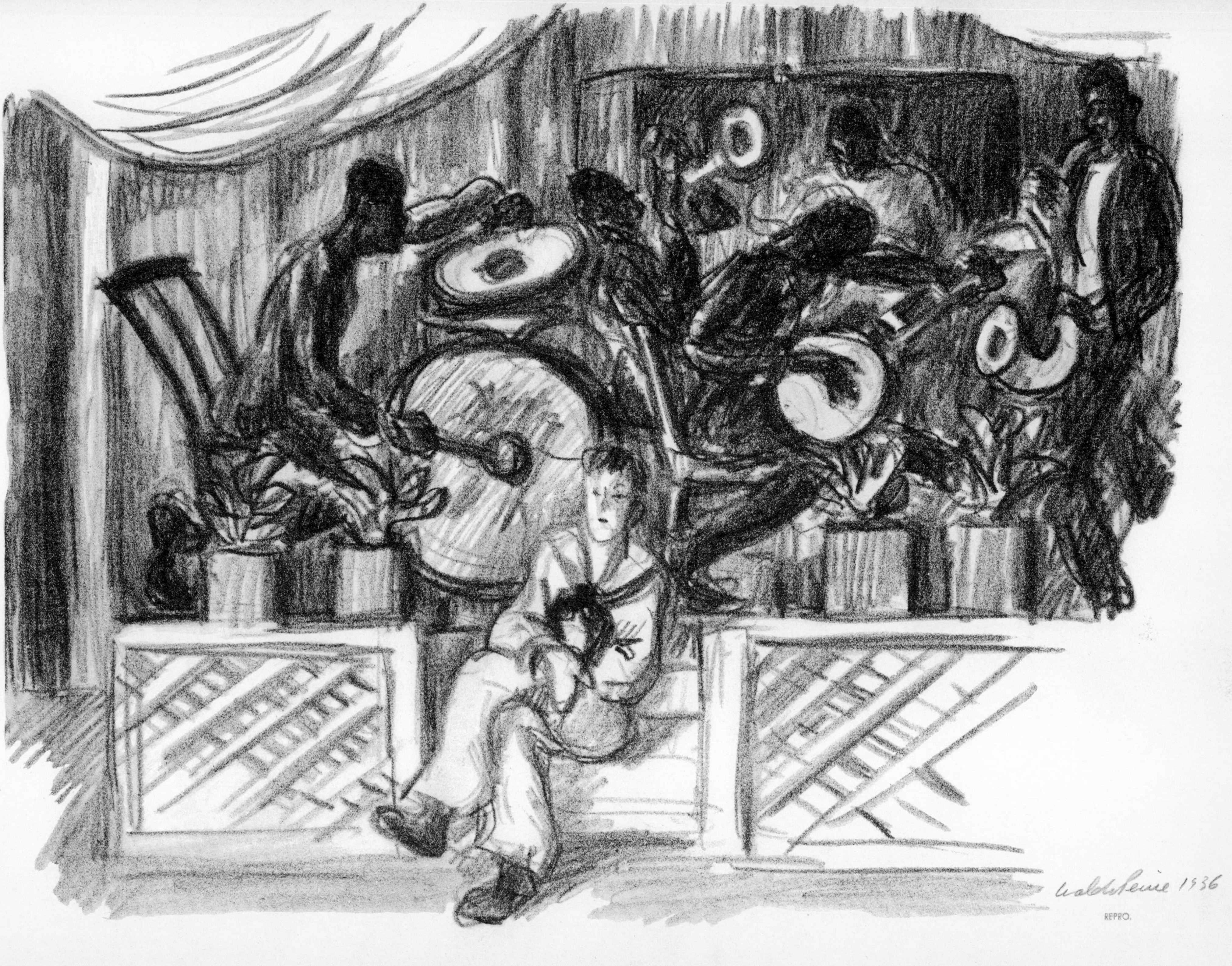
REPRO.

PLATE NUMBER SEVENTY-SEVEN

Negro Band

BY WALDO PEIRCE

(See reverse side for plate)

AFTER BANGING AROUND quite a bit, getting an education, making the Grand Tour, and living in all sorts of strange places, Waldo Peirce says that he is "well content to return to his native Maine," where he was born fifty-five years ago. "I think it's a fortunate artist," Peirce declares, "who has a birthplace and environment he is happy to return to after the Grand Tour, etc., and he should do his best in his home country . . . not as a regional purveyor of small beer, etc., but cosmically in harmony with what is about him—land, sea, sky, people, etc., whereby his art, if any good, becomes international, and not local."

Negro Band blares out hot rhythms at the Silver Slipper, a Key West dance hall.

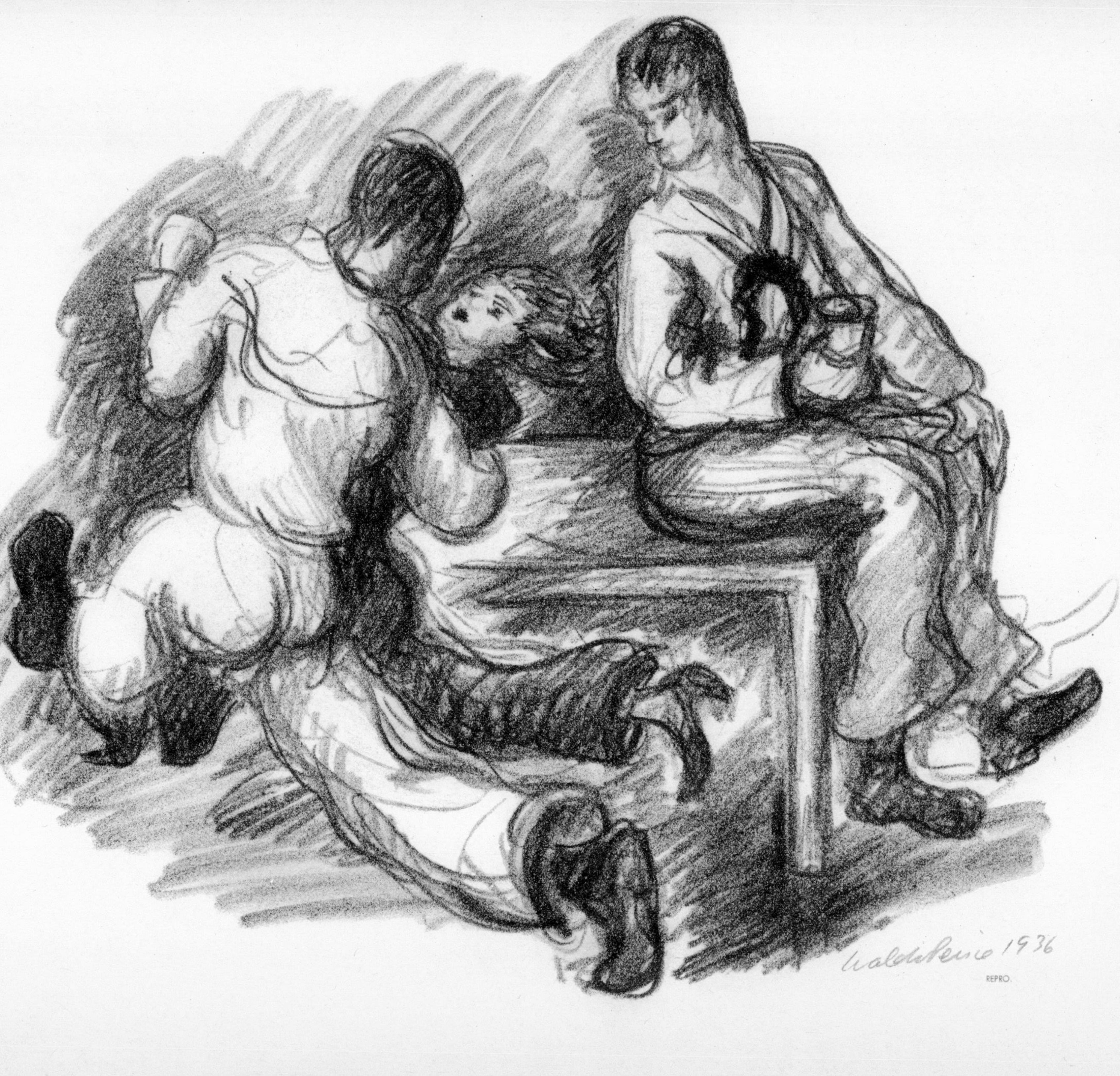
REPRO.

PLATE NUMBER SEVENTY-EIGHT

Sailors Dancing

BY WALDO PEIRCE

(See reverse side for plate)

PEIRCE'S KEY WEST lithographs are done with bold, slashing strokes, used with economy and telling vigor. The furious tempo of *Sailors Dancing* is a triumph of linear rhythms, and indicates long, thoughtful assimilations of Rubens and Delacroix.

Speaking of this lithograph and *Negro Band,* the artist says, "I was merely registering the life and movement that was going on about me for the moment . . . the blare of the Negro orchestra and the robustious rumbas of the Coast Guard with the ladies of Key West. I hope I am not belittling Sloppy Joe's by confessing it was a most decorous joint, as fitting and proper for women and children as for sailors and beachcombers. As I remember the opening of the Silver Slipper, the dance hall adjacent to the bar, there was a sign above the entrance: NO VULGAR DANCING. I almost looked for a pendent sign on the opposite wall taken from *Pinafore:* SAILORS NEVER SHOULD BE SHY. This last was apparently superfluous."

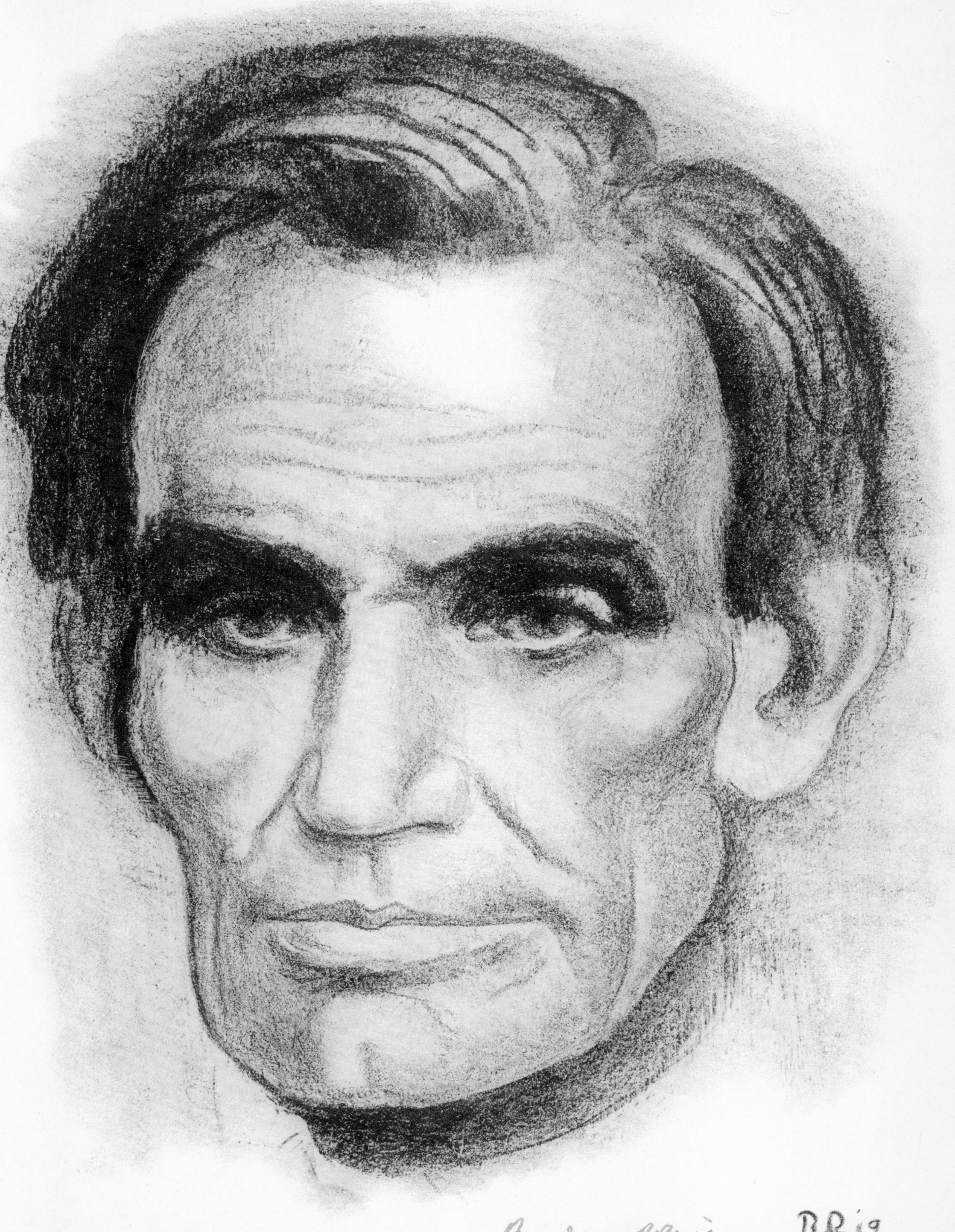

REPRO Boardman Robinson B.R.19

PLATE NUMBER SEVENTY-NINE

Lincoln

BY BOARDMAN ROBINSON

(*See reverse side for plate*)

BOARDMAN ROBINSON is pre-eminent among American artists not only because his work is distinguished artistically, but it throbs with a sincerity and searching truthfulness that are rare among many modern artists. Robinson's career has been long and varied. Born in Nova Scotia sixty-three years ago, he was educated in Canada and England. While studying art in Paris, he came under the influence of Forain, whose savage brush was powerfully suggestive to this young artist who was trying to find the right instrument for his radical ideas. His life and his art have been given to the championing of liberal causes, as illustrator, painter, and, in recent years, as a mural painter. The boldness of his mural technique both in Kaufman's Department Store in Pittsburgh and in Radio City, New York, emphasizes Robinson's adroitness, for he did not do his first murals until he was over fifty years old.

The sobriety, depth, and vigor of Robinson at his best is epitomized in this superb head of Lincoln. It is the conception of a thoughtful, sincere thinker and artist pondering the essential personality of one of America's greatest leaders.

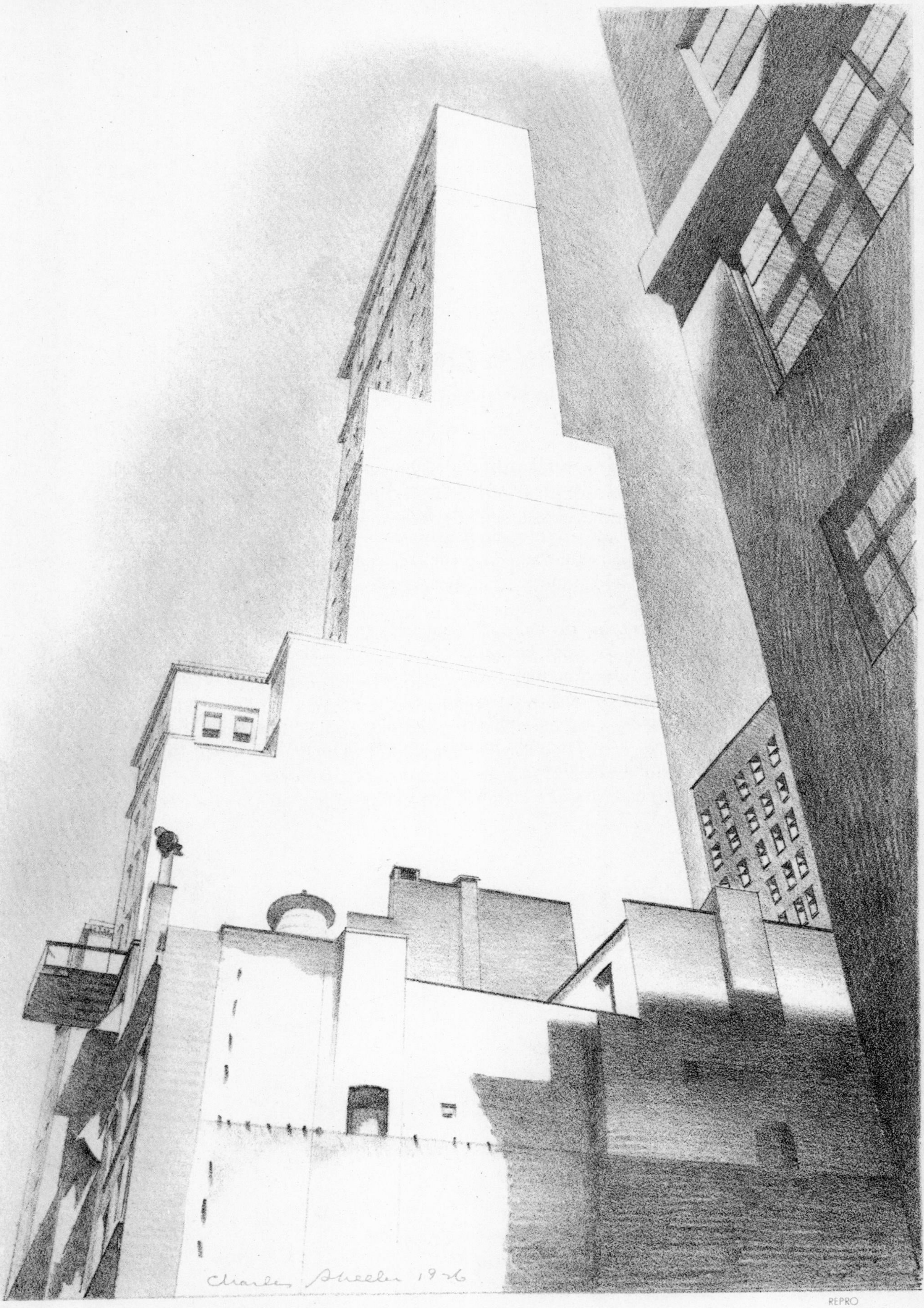
Charles Sheeler 1926

Delmonico Building

BY CHARLES SHEELER

(See reverse side for plate)

CHARLES SHEELER was born in Philadelphia in July, 1883, of Welsh and Irish ancestry, though his parents were born in America. He studied applied design at the Pennsylvania Museum and the School of Industrial Art in Philadelphia. William M. Chase was his painting instructor at the Pennsylvania Academy of Fine Arts, and with Chase he made two gallery-touring trips to Europe. In 1913 he exhibited at the epochal Armory Show, and since then has exhibited every year.

Sheeler is primarily an intellectual and experimentalist. He does not rule out emotion in his work, but rather, it rarely has a cogent place in his special approach to subject matter. *Delmonico Building* not only reveals his interest in the relationship of planes to one another but also his profound absorption in photographic effects—he is one of the best of living photographers. The formal loveliness of this lithograph, its taste and restraint, are characteristic of his modern-building studies.

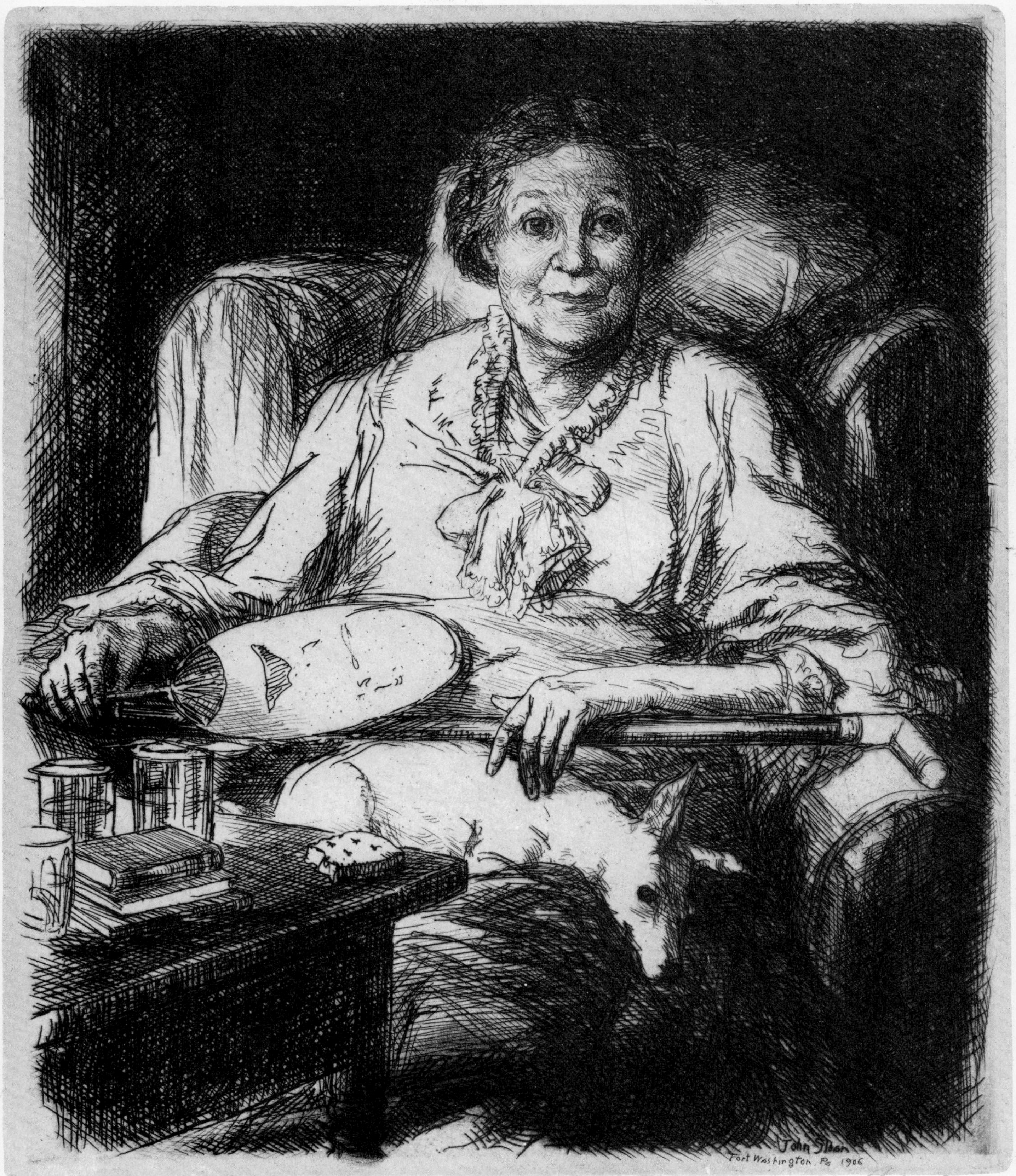
John Sloan
Fort Washington, Pa 1906

REPRO

John Sloan

PLATE NUMBER EIGHTY-ONE

Mother

BY JOHN SLOAN

(*See reverse side for plate*)

JOHN SLOAN was born at Lock Haven, Pennsylvania, sixty-eight years ago. Since then he has led as active a life as any Renaissance artist, and today, though the dean of American artists, he is vigorous, interested, and a hard worker. Ever since his newspaper days, John Sloan has had a finger in many an artists' pie, has fought many a battle for human rights. In 1908, as one of The Eight—Arthur B. Davies, Glackens, Ernest Lawson, Luks, Henri, Shinn, and Prendergast were the others—he helped organize several revolutionary exhibitions. Five years later, he was one of the leading spirits behind the famous Armory Show, which eventually led to the founding of the Society of Independent Artists. Sloan was its first president, and has been active in its councils ever since. Fifteen years ago, when he first began to go to Santa Fe for the summers, he became intensely interested in the American Indian, and has worked tirelessly keeping their art before the American public. Besides all this, Sloan is a teacher of art—and a great teacher. He taught for fourteen years at the Art Students' League, and in 1930 became its president.

Mother reminds us that John Sloan, amid his multifarious activities, is essentially a family man. His boyhood was singularly happy, his married life no less so. *Mother* is one of those rare compositions that speak so eloquently for themselves that any except formal comment would be superfluous. The composition is simply effective, the draftsmanship vigorous, the entire work animated by sympathy and shrewd insight. Sloan's *Mother* is one of the most dignified conceptions of the subject in the entire realm of etching.

John Sloan 1926

John Sloan

The Subway Stairs.

PLATE NUMBER EIGHTY-TWO

Subway Stairs

BY JOHN SLOAN

(See reverse side for plate)

JOHN SLOAN received part of his early education in the vigorous school of the American newspaper. After courses at the Spring Garden Institute and the Pennsylvania Academy of Fine Arts, both in Philadelphia, he worked on the illustrating staff of several local newspapers. The power of the press was expressed far more by cartoons in those days than in this, and high standards were demanded of newspaper illustrators. It was by no means unusual for one of them to graduate into a first-rate artist. Certain it is that John Sloan's line acquired subtlety and eloquence during his career as a newspaperman. He learned that there could be no paucity of subject matter in the many-sided life of a great city.

Subway Stairs tells its own story. It is just a snippet of New York life, certainly with no arresting quality of its own. But here the artist's selective eye lifts the scene to distinction. As is a commonplace with Sloan, every fact is tempered with sympathy and insight. The main figure is wholly gracious: the touch of satire is reserved for a male back. Surely, it is the back of a man with a weak, querulous face. It is no small triumph that this master of the facts of life is also subtly suggestive as well.

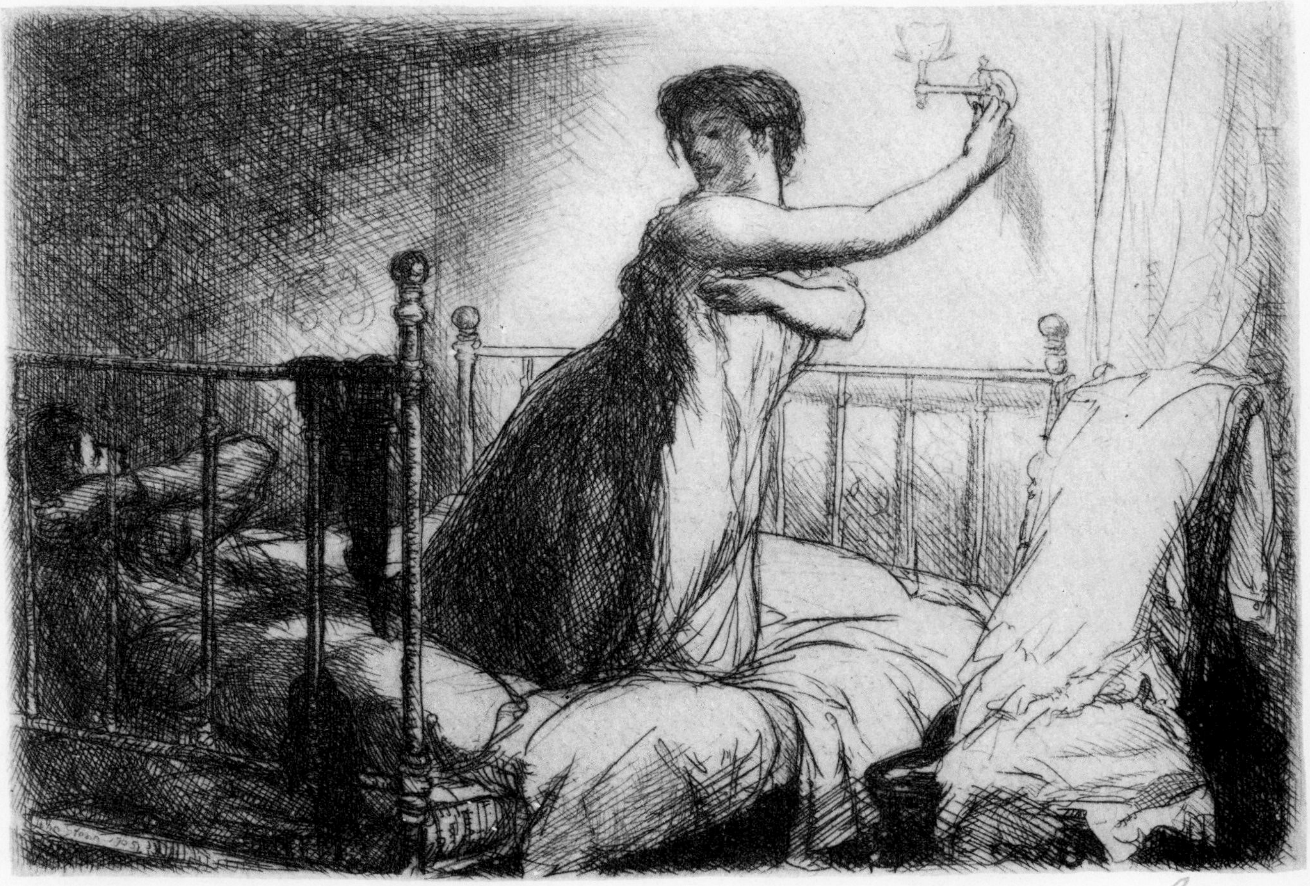

REPRO.

John Sloan

Turning out the Light

PLATE NUMBER EIGHTY-THREE

Turning Out the Light

BY JOHN SLOAN

(See reverse side for plate)

JOHN SLOAN is New York's Hogarth. For years, his studio was near Seventh Avenue, with front windows facing Twenty-third Street, and the back ones looking toward Twenty-fourth Street. In those days—the first decade of the twentieth century—this was in the very heart of New York's wicked Tenderloin district. Sloan used to pass hours at his windows watching all aspects of city life, from the sensational to the commonplace. In this way, from a student of the genre scene he evolved progressively into connoisseur and master. What he saw was transferred to his plate from memory, for John Sloan thinks memory's eye is more trustworthy, more imaginatively selective, than the physical eye.

Turning Out the Light is a typical scene from the homely drama of a great city's life. As John Sloan himself said of one of his early paintings, *Three A.M.,* "Night vigils at the back window of a Twenty-third Street studio were rewarded by motifs of this sort; many of them were used in my etchings." Like the same picture, *Turning Out the Light* "is redolent with the atmosphere of a poor, back, gas-lit room." Furthermore, it is one of Sloan's most impressively designed etchings, with the balance of blacks and whites finely calculated.

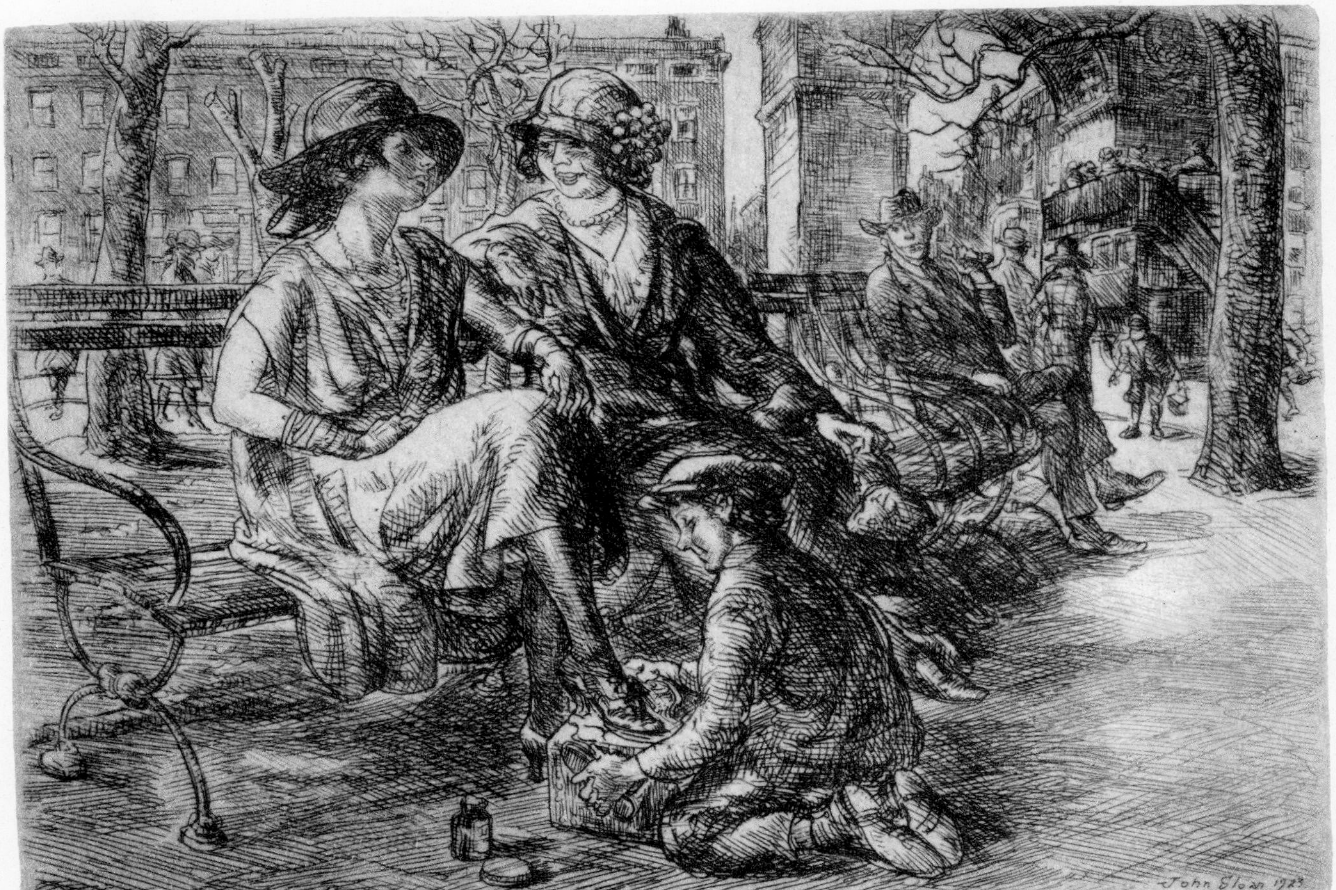
John Sloan 1923

REPRO.

John Sloan

Shine, Washington Square

PLATE NUMBER EIGHTY-FOUR

Shine, Washington Square

BY JOHN SLOAN

(See reverse side for plate)

WHEN JOHN SLOAN moved over to Washington Square in 1927, he had, as he expresses it, "no good windows": that is, his windows afforded none of that rich peepshow life that had endowed his pen and brush with so much vitality when he was living on Twenty-third Street. To get subject matter, he had to go outdoors, and soon the Square became the scene of many of his compositions. He did not lurk with sketching pad in hand and poised pencil, for except when doing nudes or portraits, Sloan composes from memory.

Shine, Washington Square, is a realistic scene, but it has a certain lyric quality that Sloan does not always allow to creep into his work. Possibly he had spring fever the day he did it. Anyway, the effect is stunning. For those who do not know Greenwich Village, be it said that the Washington Arch, seen in the background, was erected in honor of Admiral Dewey early in this century, and commands the southern end of Fifth Avenue.

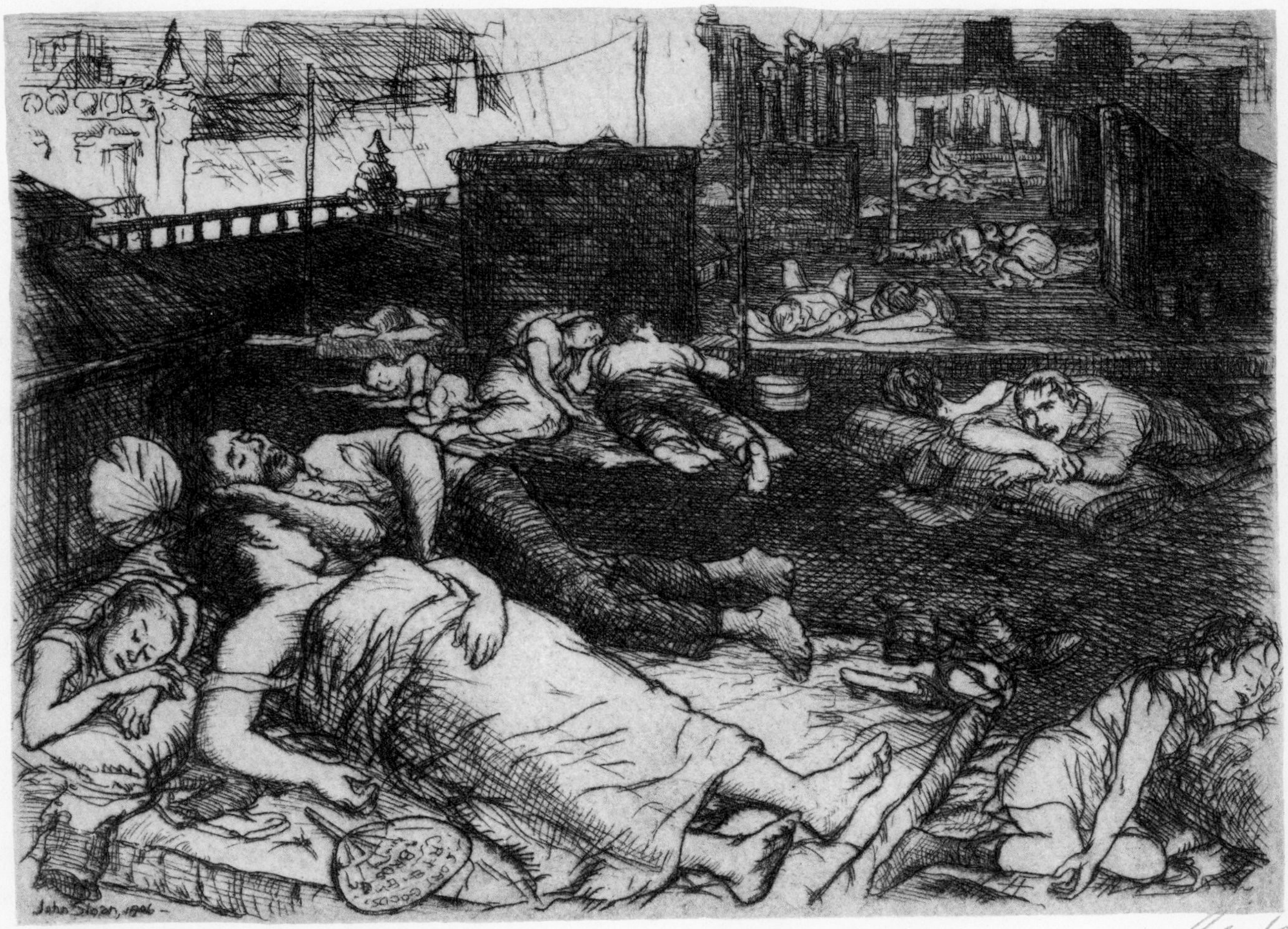
John Sloan, 1906 -

REPRO.

John Sloan

Roofs Summer Night

PLATE NUMBER EIGHTY-FIVE

Roofs, Summer Night

BY JOHN SLOAN

(See reverse side for plate)

THIS IS SLOAN in his bitterest mood, and though it is far from being a mere illustration, *Roofs, Summer Night,* reminds us that Sloan is a great illustrator. Early in the century, he did some wonderful cartoons for *Collier's*, *Everybody's,* and *Harper's Weekly,* but perhaps the best were in *Masses*. *Roofs* comes from a crusader, and it seems all the more powerful because it presents the facts calmly, without the slightest exaggeration—perhaps with some understatement. One of the most admirable things about Sloan's art is that despite his preoccupation with facts, he never overdocuments.

Roofs belongs to Sloan's early Twenty-third Street period. The sweltering men and women are, perhaps, the rank and file of the Tenderloin, one of New York's most vicious districts about thirty years ago. They do not seem vicious, however—merely exhausted, bedraggled, pitiable, and terribly, terribly warm. The glow from the street lights that penetrates beyond the roof ledge has a tropical suggestiveness.

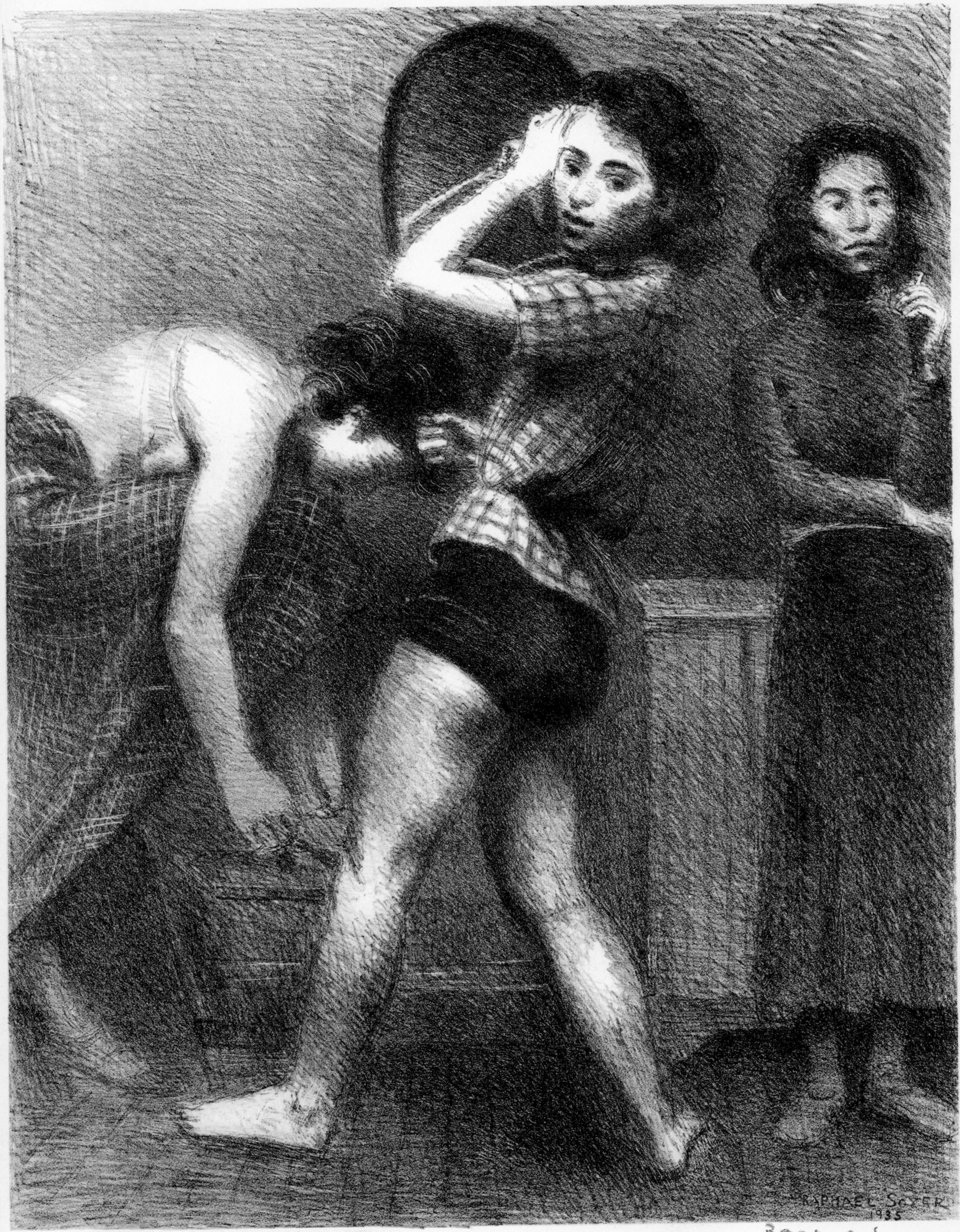
RAPHAEL SOYER
1935

Backstage REPRO. Raphael Soyer

PLATE NUMBER EIGHTY-SIX

Backstage

BY RAPHAEL SOYER

(*See reverse side for plate*)

RAPHAEL SOYER came to the United States when he was ten years old, having been born in Tombov, Russia, in 1899. The lad was gifted, and when he was old enough went to the Art Students' League for instruction, meanwhile supporting himself by selling newspapers and working in factories. Recognition came to him early, and a number of his paintings hang in important American galleries, including the Metropolitan and Whitney, in New York, as well as in various private collections. His two brothers, Isaac and Moses, are also talented artists. Soyer illustrates phases of New York life, and maintains his studio in the heart of the colorful Fourteenth Street district.

Backstage is one of several lithographs Soyer has devoted to the stage. Though a pleasing enough composition, and interesting for the artist's dramatic disposition of light and shadow, it is notable primarily for the intense emotion that permeates it.

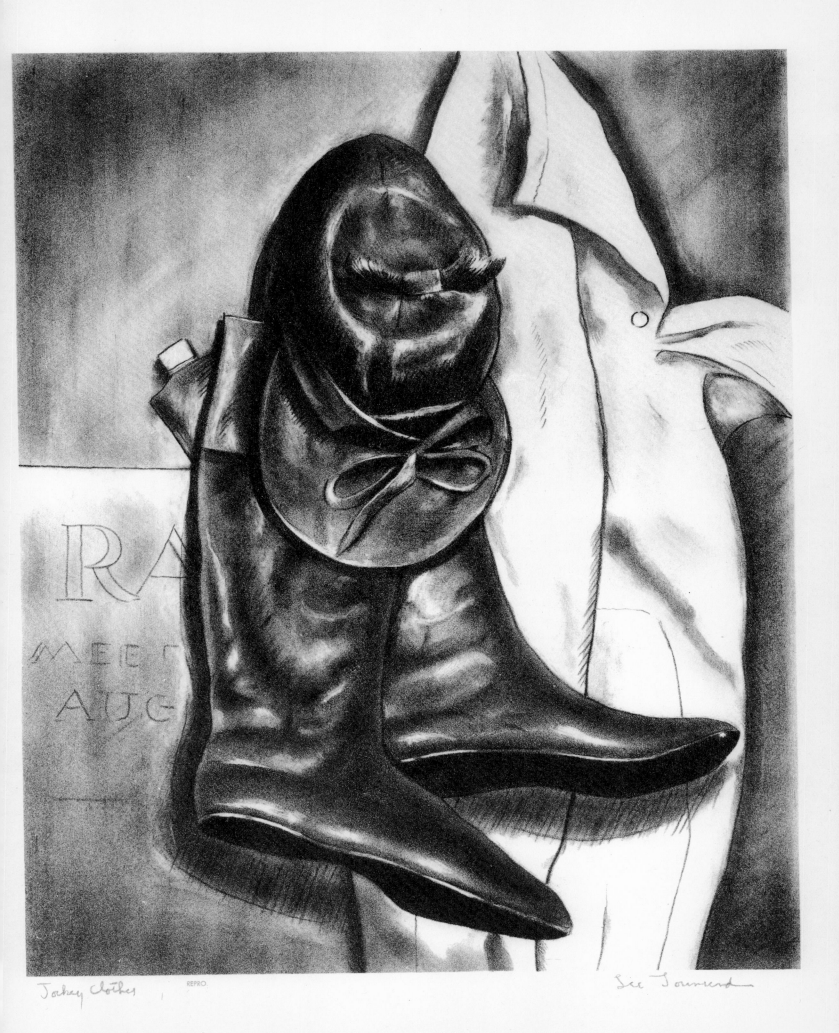

Jockey Clothes   REPRO.   Lee Townsend

PLATE NUMBER EIGHTY-SEVEN

Jockey Clothes

BY LEE TOWNSEND

(*See reverse side for plate*)

THE LITHOGRAPHER OF *Jockey Clothes* is probably the only artist in this country who is also a professional horse trainer. He has worked with horses all his life, which is reasonable enough, considering that he was born right next to a county fairgrounds. The place was Wyoming, Illinois, the date 1895. He bought his first race horse at the age of seventeen, and raced her at near-by fairs. He rode as a jockey for a few years, until he smashed his left foot in a spill. Every summer he races either his own, or takes horses on shares, through the county-fair or half-mile circuit in Pennsylvania, Ohio, and New York. There he gets his material for drawings and paintings. His career as an artist began almost as early as that in the paddock. At first he confined his efforts to decorating horsemen's trunks and water buckets at the Wyoming fairgrounds. After his accident he went to Chicago, and studied at the school of the Art Institute. He later had a year in Paris.

Townsend made the drawing for *Jockey Clothes* during a county fair. The owner of the boots and pants had won two races in the day's card, and the artist made the drawing after the jockey had hung them up in his stall.

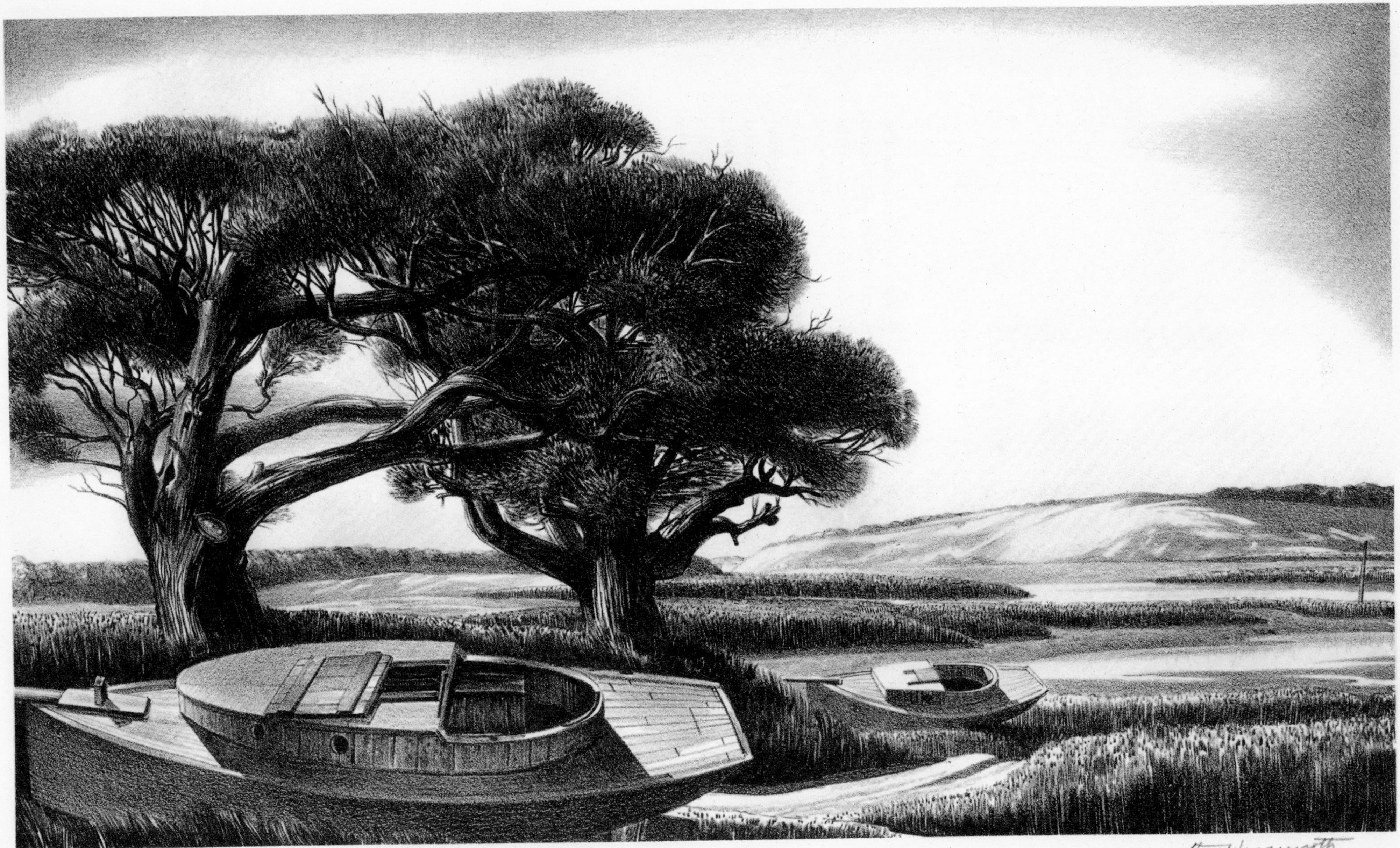

REPRO.

Stow Wengenroth

PLATE NUMBER EIGHTY-EIGHT

Quiet Day

BY STOW WENGENROTH

(*See reverse side for plate*)

ALL OF STOW WENGENROTH'S WORK is colored by a powerful and thoughtful personality. This young artist has a lively interest in the drama of light and shade, and in a certain sense most of his compositions, though in no sense overwrought, are gently theatrical. The locale of *Quiet Day* is Wellsleet, on Cape Cod. The elements of the scene are of the simplest: the dunes in the distance, in the foreground two somber willows standing guard over the small boats grounded amid the bulrushes.

Wengenroth was born in Brooklyn on July 25, 1906. He studied with Wayman Adams, George Bridgman, John Carlson, and George Pearse Ennis, and at an early age asserted his own unmistakable individuality. Most of his lithographs are devoted to architectural subjects and New England scenes.

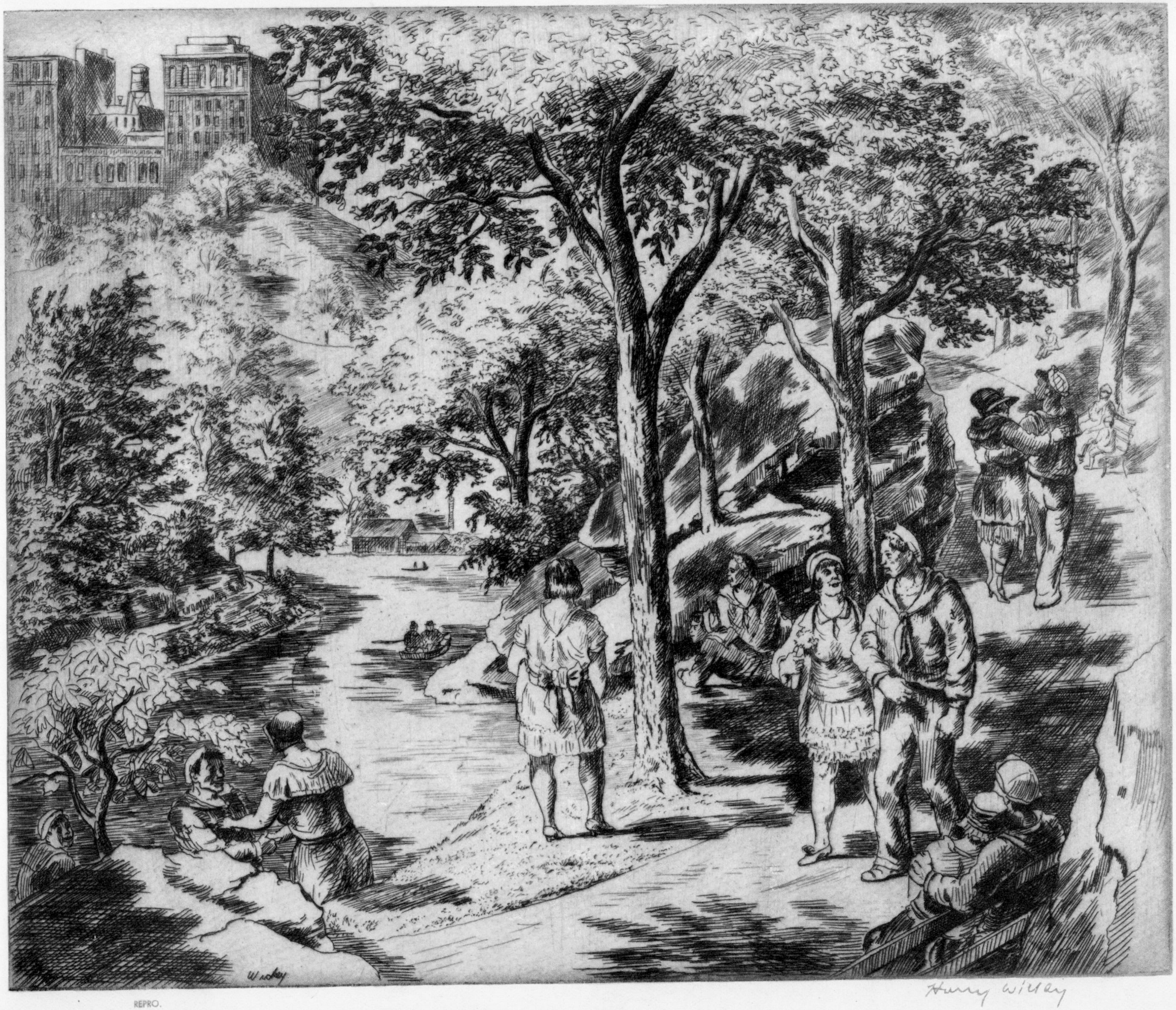

REPRO.

Harry Wickey

PLATE NUMBER EIGHTY-NINE

Central Park

BY HARRY WICKEY

(*See reverse side for plate*)

UNTIL HARRY WICKEY, at the age of twenty-two, arrived in New York in 1914, his life had been as full of incident as Sinbad the Sailor's. He came from a family of pioneers who believed that labor is a salutary thing, and young Harry was allowed to work the theory to death. Fortunately, all this agreed with him, and his desire to be an artist was not to be smothered. He tried art schools in Detroit and Chicago, but they did not like him—and he did not like them. In New York, he got his first real break from Robert Henri, who said of some of his drawings, "I would be very proud if I were the author of this work." Finally he met Harvey Dunn, who encouraged him to become an illustrator. But the editors did not like his illustrations—he confesses that Dunn occasionally touched up one of his drawings to make it salable.

The World War intervened. Harry Wickey went overseas, put in a lot of time thinking, and came back determined not to kowtow to the editors. The result was that his own standards forced him out of the illustrating field. He began to teach, and was so successful that it was the main source of his livelihood from 1919 to 1933. In 1920 he began to get interested in etching—a medium he reluctantly abandoned in 1935, when his eyes began to go back on him. His latest passion is sculpture.

Central Park is one of several etchings Wickey has devoted to that subject. No special locality is intended, though the artist confesses that he had the lagoon near Fifty-ninth Street in mind. The incidents and forms are freely selected from that vicinity—their truth is obvious to anyone who knows the microcosm that is Central Park. The etching was made in 1931, at a time when the artist had matured his ideas about presenting the sculptural aspect of his material.

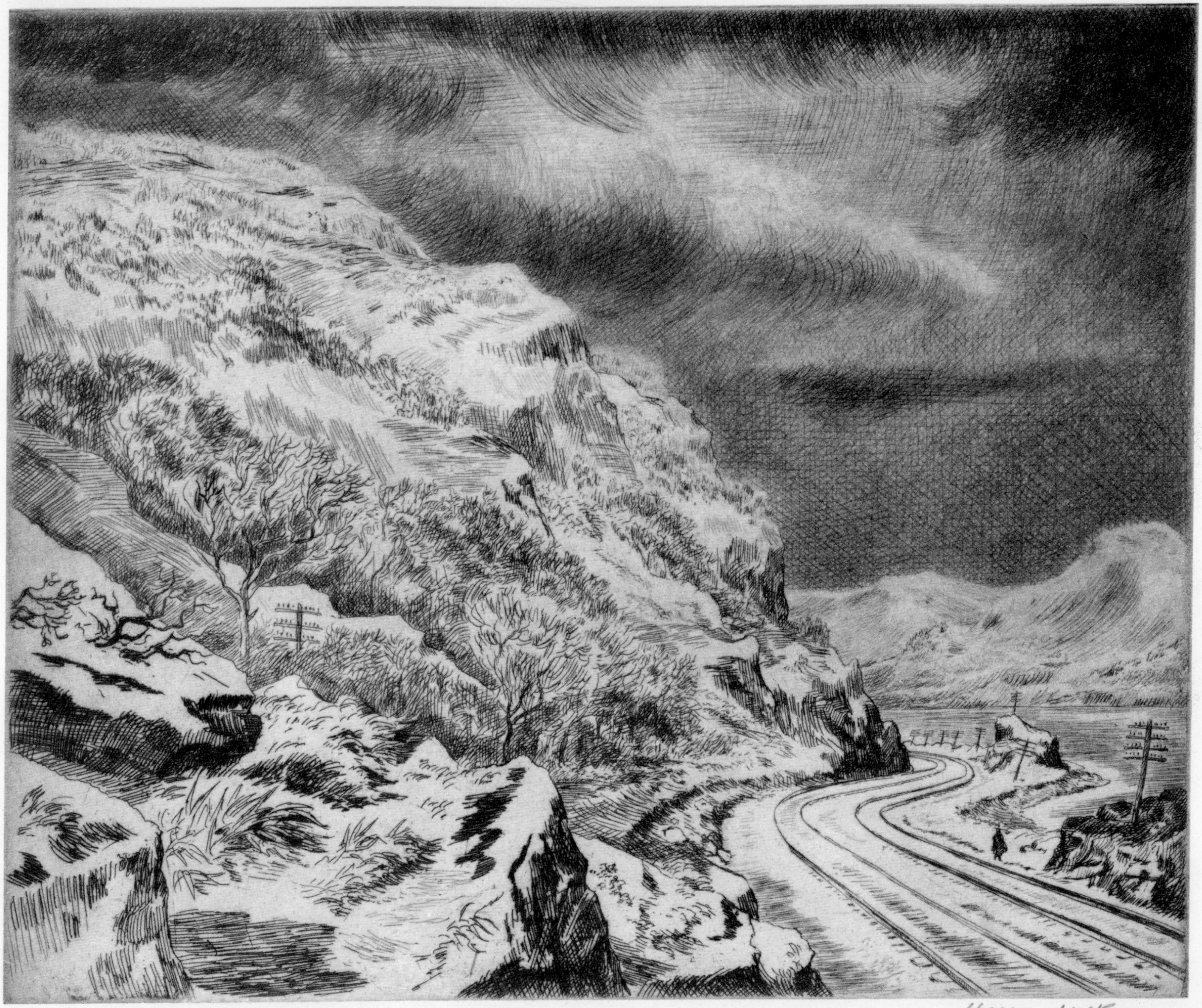

REPRO.

Harry Wickey

Hudson Highlands Under Snow

BY HARRY WICKEY

(*See reverse side for plate*)

IN 1929, THE ARTIST moved from New York City to Cornwall Landing, about fifty miles up the Hudson. Here his latent interest in landscape began to assert itself. He perched his studio on the riverbank, and was afforded splendid opportunities for studying the character of the river and mountains in all varieties of weather. For four years, from 1930 to 1934, Wickey did little else than concentrate on these ever fascinating views, studying rocky formation and mountain contour. A whole series of plates was devoted to this subject matter.

Some views were studied over and over again, often under approximately the same weather conditions. For instance, *Hudson Highlands Under Snow* is but one of some twenty etchings that the artist made of this segment of landscape. The cold, bleak beauty of the river and mountains under a heavy fall of snow has proved a very grateful subject for his etching needle: the thrilling quality of the country has been communicated to the plate.

"I wish to convey to those looking at my work a full sense of the actual," Mr. Wickey has written. "By actual I mean that each object within my space be so related that the individual color, texture, weight, volume, and movement become a definite entity in relation to its neighboring entities. These qualities must be unified by the spirit of life." A better illustration of this credo, or a better introduction to the artist's later graphic work, could not be found than *Hudson Highlands Under Snow*.

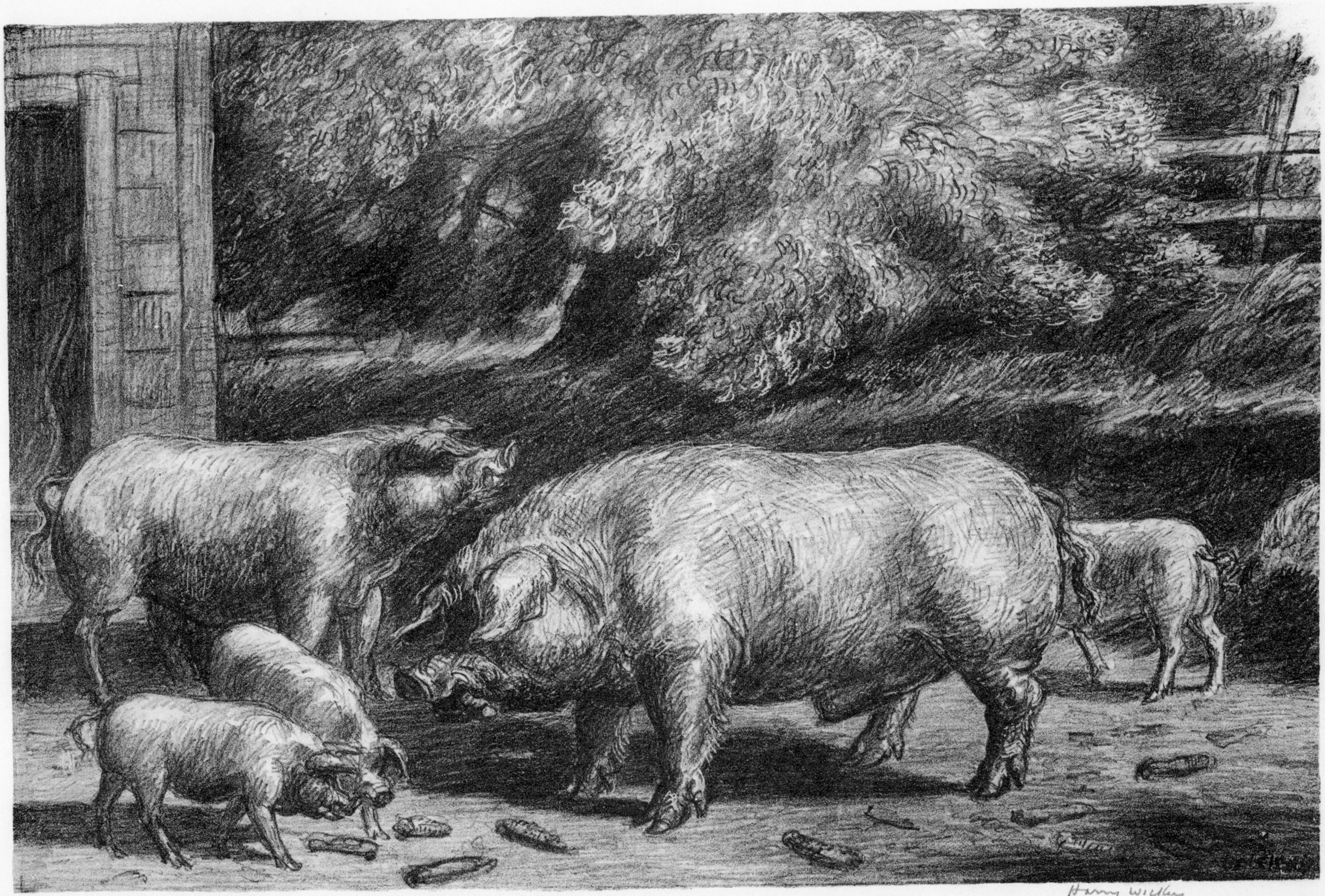

REPRO.

Harry Wickey

PLATE NUMBER NINETY-ONE

Hogs Near a Corncrib

BY HARRY WICKEY

(*See reverse side for plate*)

IN 1935, WICKEY began to have difficulties with his sight, and thus had practically to abandon etching, for which extremely close work is required. He turned to freer and less eye-taxing media. That year he made a trip to the home farm in Ohio, and went again the following summer. Both trips were extraordinarily rich in results: some of the material went into drawings and water colors, and some found a fuller expression in lithography and sculpture.

Hogs Near a Corncrib, a lithograph done in 1936, is one of a large number of studies Wickey made of farm animals that year. Needless to say, although the actual locale of the scene is northwestern Ohio, this is true to farm life anywhere, at any time. The artist has caught the very essence of swinishness: each of these porkers is Very Hog of Very Hog.

"What I learned about hogs is to be found in this picture," Mr. Wickey says. "I tried to realize the form, color, weight, and texture of the objects in my space, and present without exaggeration the mood of this particular incident."

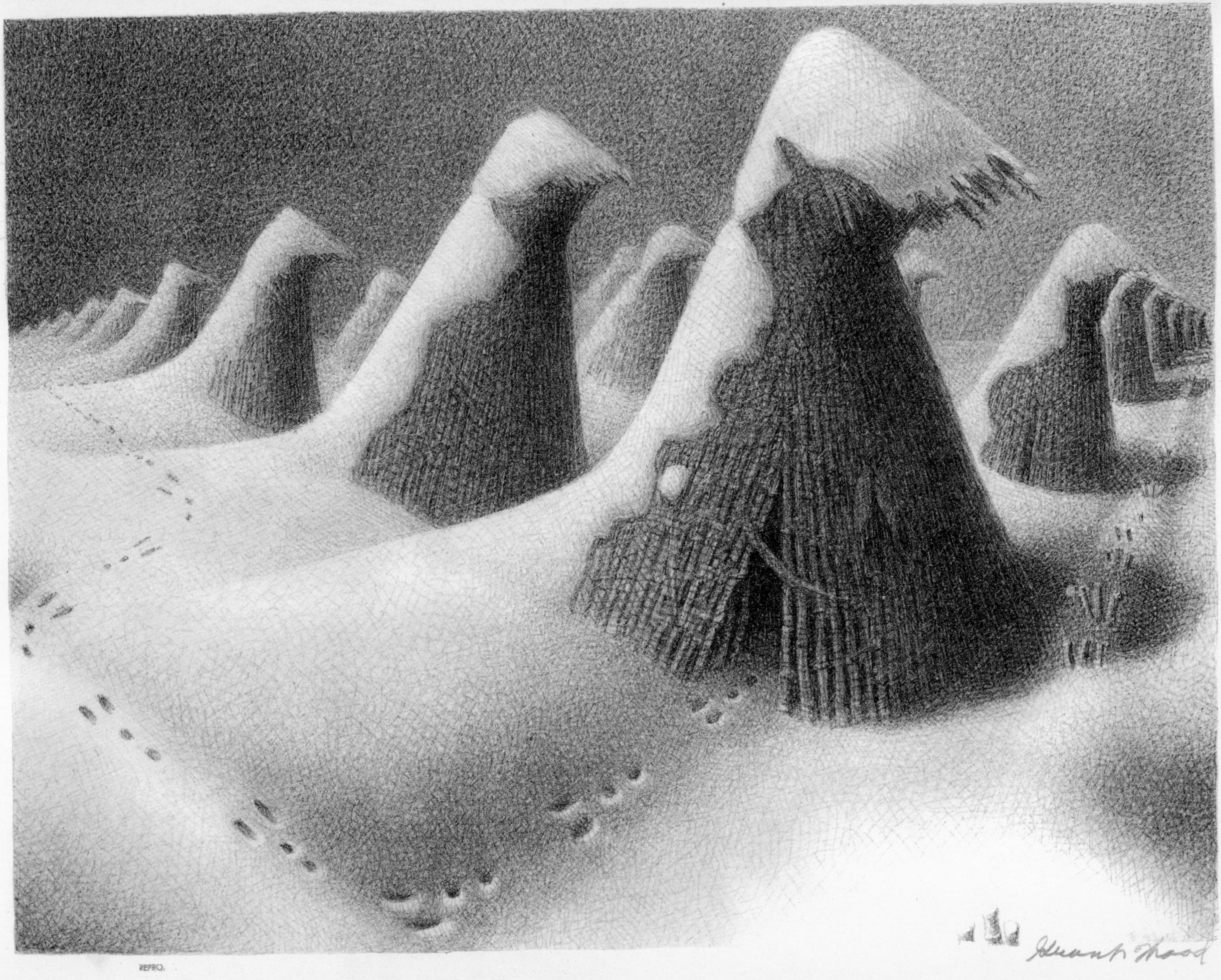
Grant Wood

REPRO.

PLATE NUMBER NINETY-TWO

January

BY GRANT WOOD

(See reverse side for plate)

GRANT WOOD leapt into nation-wide fame in 1933, when his painting, *American Gothic,* won tremendous critical and popular acclaim at the Century of Progress Exhibition of Paintings and Sculpture at the Chicago Art Institute. Since then, he has gained a growing recognition that has put him well in the van of America's most distinguished artists. Born in Iowa in 1892, he was first interested in metalwork and handmade jewelry before turning to the graphic arts. He studied at the Chicago Art Institute and the Académie Julian in Paris. Quite as important as his academic training was his study of the German primitives: they may be said to have given him a point of departure in his treatment of regional types.

The artist lives in Iowa City, whence he draws upon the rich hinterland of the Middle West. Long before the Federal Arts Project, Grant Wood founded a school in Stone City, Iowa, for fostering local talent. He now teaches at the University of Iowa. A graceful raconteur, a superb conversationalist, and something of an authority on a variety of things besides art, this stocky, blond, blue-eyed man looks like anything but a conventional artist.

January, a snow scene with stacked-up cornshocks, shows Wood's strong interest in recurrent pattern—an interest that is almost Oriental in its intensity.

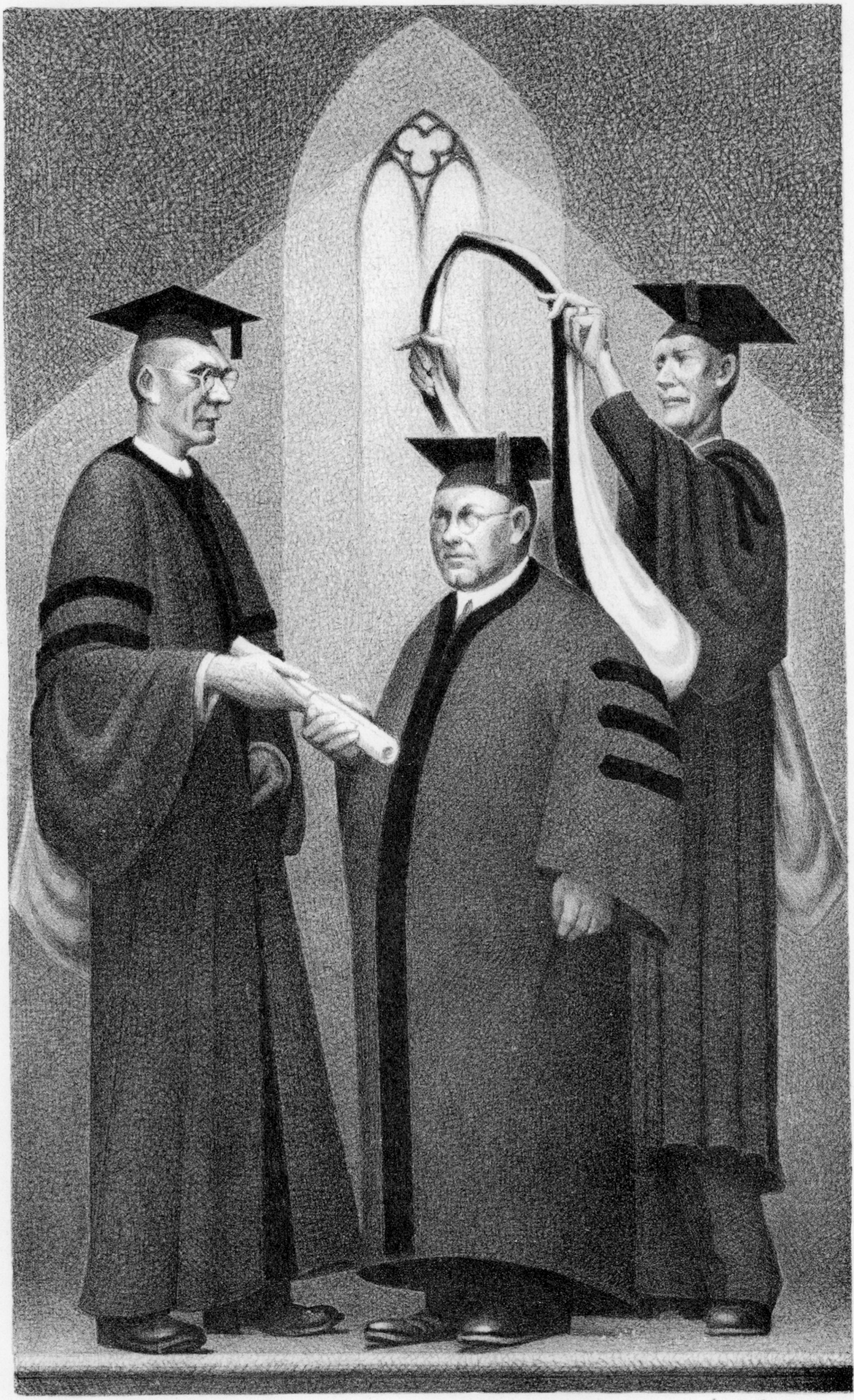

Grant Wood - 1937

PLATE NUMBER NINETY-THREE

Honorary Degree

BY GRANT WOOD

(*See reverse side for plate*)

AN ALTERNATE TITLE for this trenchant satire might have been *Apotheosis of Nonentity*. For here, in what might at first glance look like a surgical operation in a cathedral, Grant Wood has caricatured a disagreeable American vice: glorification of the second-rate by mumbo jumbo. The squat, paunchy, mindless, and self-satisfied center of academic attention in this mysterious ceremony has just presented the old alma mater with a new, if slightly reduced, replica of the Yale Bowl. In return for this support of enlightenment and culture, he is becoming an honorary doctor of law. From their well-shod feet, which give the three figures a little the appearance of magnified penguins, to their extremely unbecoming mortarboards, these celebrants of a now meaningless rite are unconscious that they border on the obscene.

The healthy, laughing hatred of sham that motivates a lithograph of this sort is apt to make the observer underrate the artistry with which it is projected. Notice the stance of the magnifico who is handing Mr. Dope his diploma. Is it not the very essence of petty importance? And is not the entire vacuity of Dope himself expressed in his flat-footed, well-fed posture? It leaves no doubt that he is one of the characters in *Who's Who,* and will be mourned by many when he dies—particularly after the reading of his will.

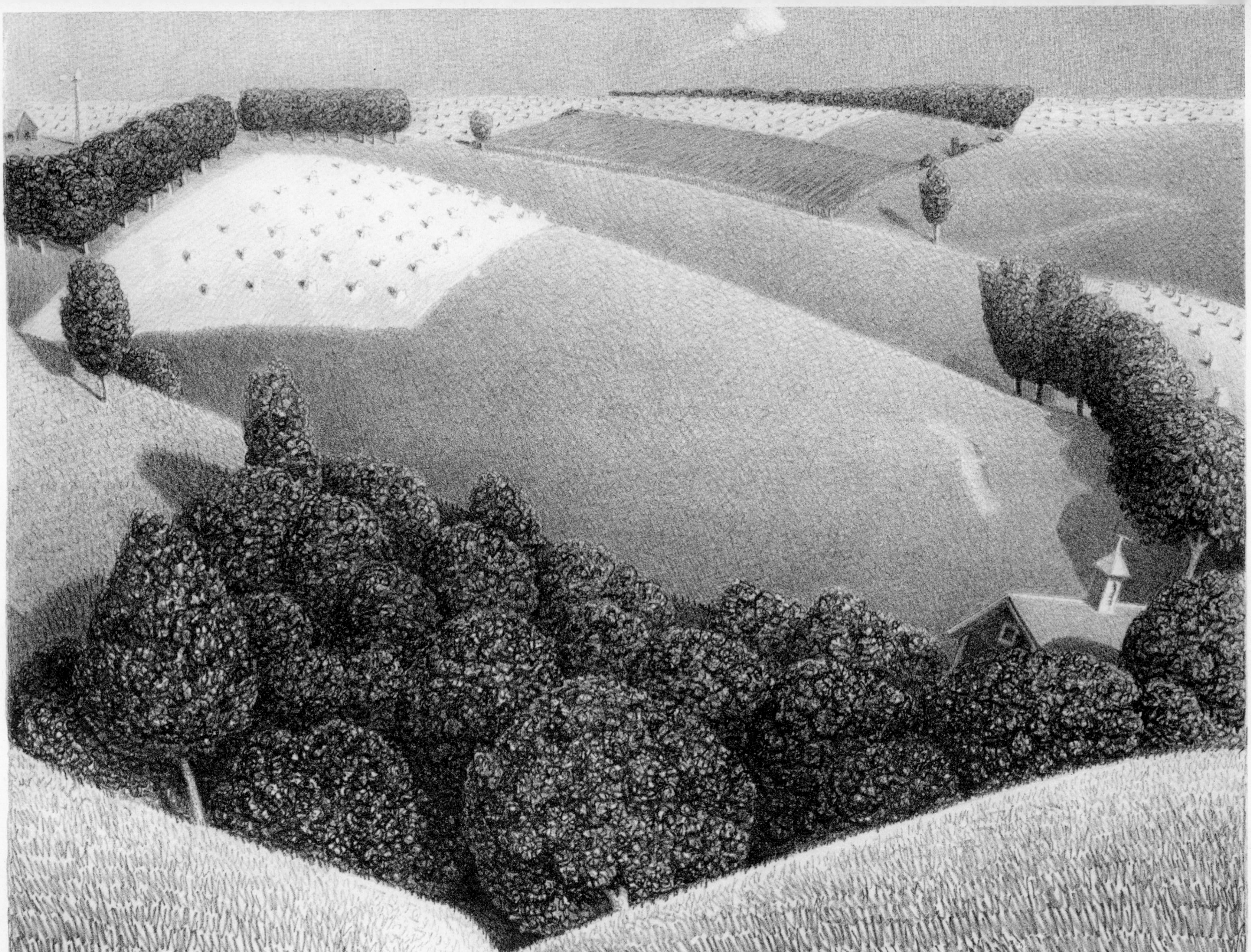

PLATE NUMBER NINETY-FOUR

July Fifteenth

BY GRANT WOOD

(*See reverse side for plate*)

UNDER A BLAZING SUN, caught in the very fullness of summer, this Iowa landscape projects the very essence of fertility. Trees at full foliage, seeming to rock in an excess of honeyed sap, burgeoning fields, an unmistakable, if invisible, cloudless sky, a building all but swallowed up by the richness of nature—these are the portrait of America's most valuable wealth. No dust bowl here, no starved cattle or skulls bleaching on cracked surfaces!

Hardly likely to give the most ardent devotee of photographic realism even a passing twinge, Mr. Wood's portrait of Iowa in rich blossom is, in reality, a highly unrealistic picture. Not only are all forms simplified beyond the usual way of unaided nature, but the laws of gravity and perspective are flouted in the interest of the decorative scheme. It would, one can hardly doubt, have been possible to anyone so wishing to give a more accurate likeness of the scene Mr. Wood had in mind. But there can be no question that his perfectly legitimate artistic liberties with actuality are exactly the agents that have produced the quality—the essence of summer at the crest—at which he was aiming, and which he has so perfectly achieved.

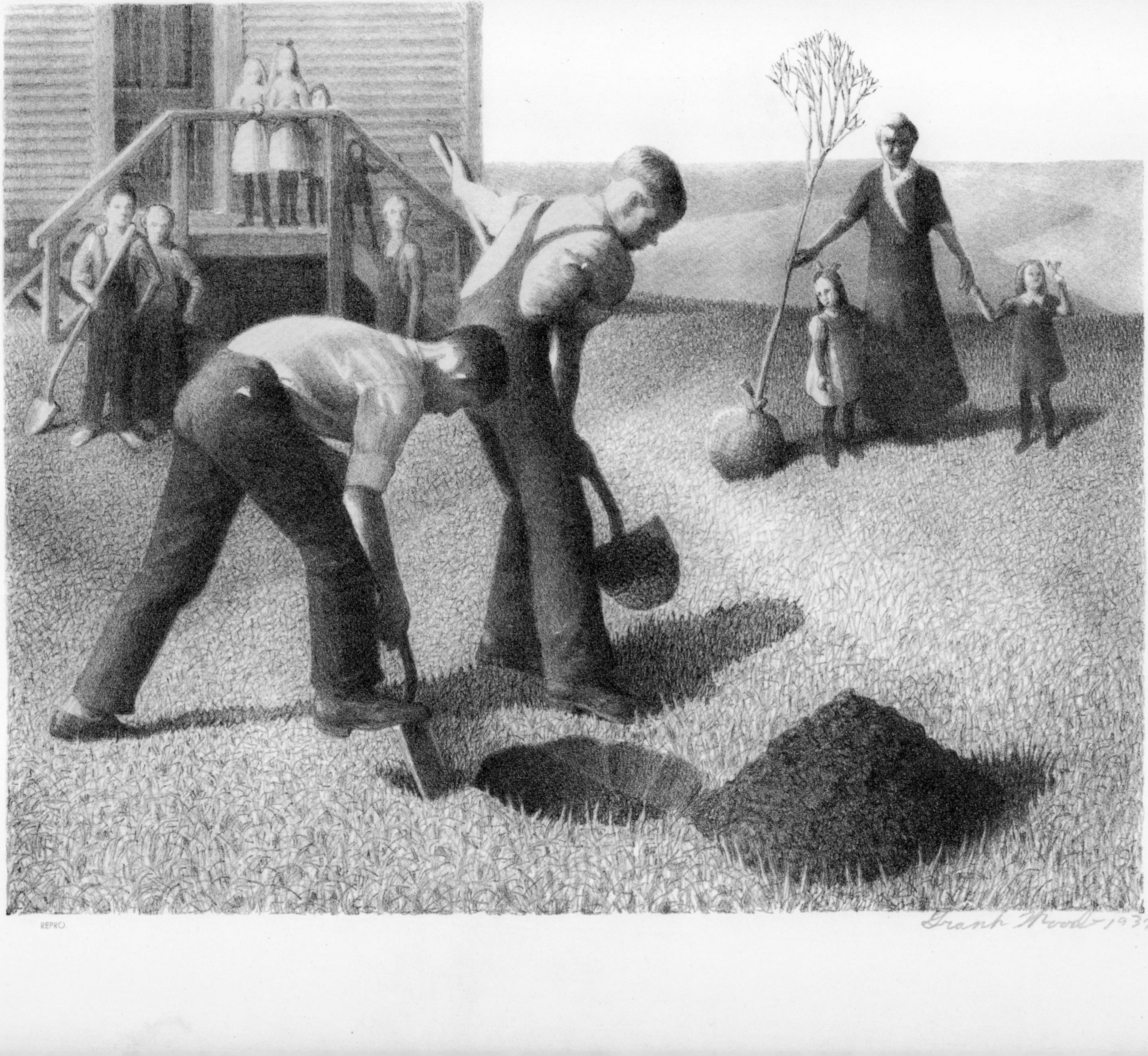
Grant Wood 1937

PLATE NUMBER NINETY-FIVE

Tree-Planting Group

BY GRANT WOOD

(*See reverse side for plate*)

IN 1872, the state of Nebraska set aside one day a year for the planting of trees, and since then most of the states of the Union have followed suit. Thus, Arbor Day came into existence. Probably its very existence is unknown to many dwellers in large cities, but out in the Middle West, where agriculture is king, Arbor Day is an occasion of importance, marked by ceremonies of various sorts, especially in the farm belt.

Grant Wood has caught the solemnity of this modern Ceralia in his *Tree-Planting Group*. The importance of forestation is inculcated in the schools of the Middle West through thousands of annual rites such as we see in this lithograph. The composition has humor, a rich appreciation of local types, and yet a sincere reverence and real understanding of the seriousness of the occasion. The schoolteacher, flanked by two small girls, advances with the sapling. Two of the older boys are busy preparing its bed, one of them wielding the spade. The careful haircuts of these solemn young chaps constitute a characteristic Grant Wood touch of observation.

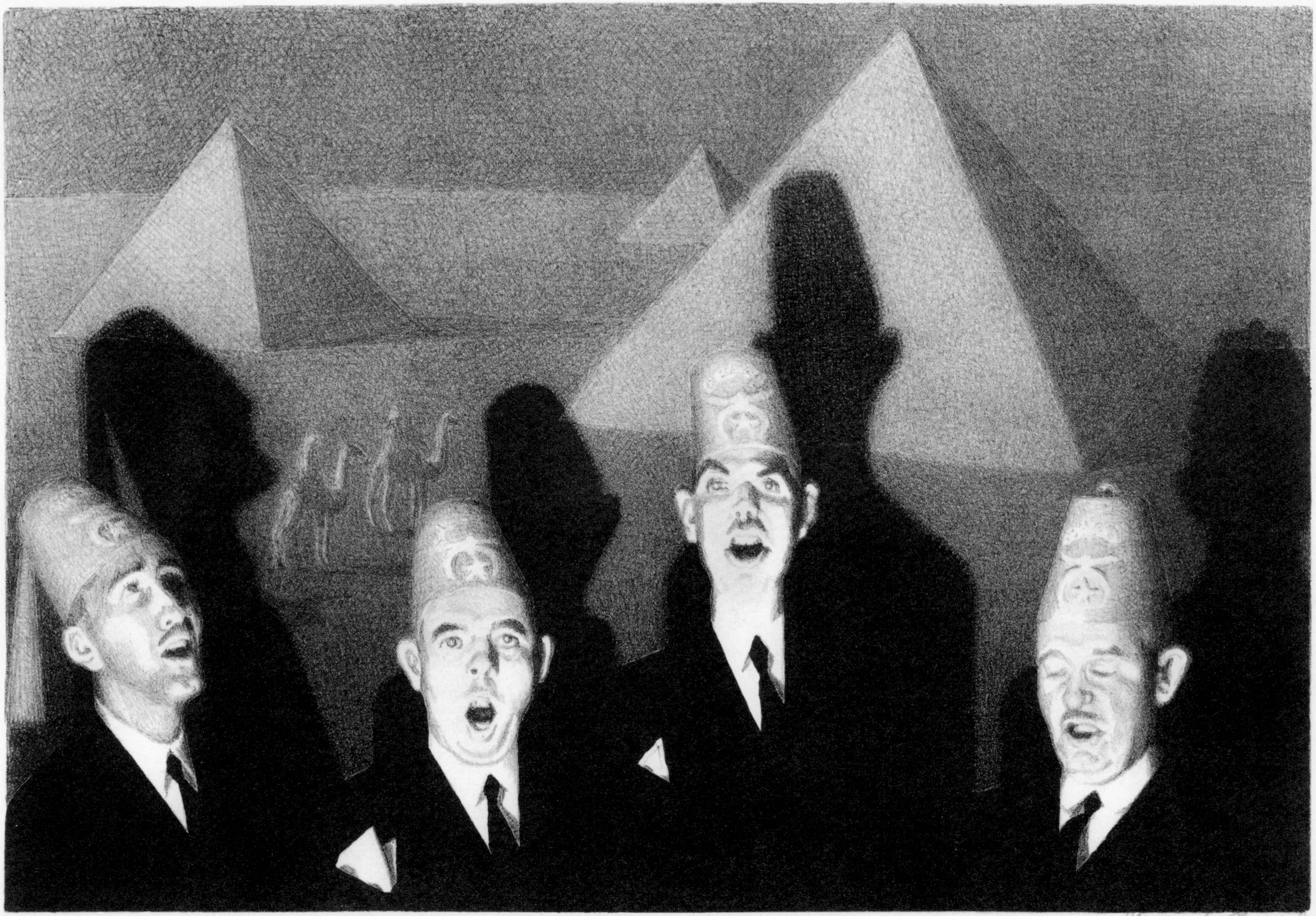

REPRO.

Grant Wood

PLATE NUMBER NINETY-SIX

Shriners' Quartet

BY GRANT WOOD

(See reverse side for plate)

THE ANCIENT ARABIC ORDER OF NOBLES OF THE MYSTIC SHRINE was founded in the United States in 1872. It makes claim to traditions of great antiquity, and is, in its make-up, among the swankiest of fraternal organizations. Although not actually a Masonic order, only thirty-second-degree Masons, or Knights Templar, can belong to it. While many Shriners do not take their seventh-century origins too seriously, others do, at least to the extent of occasionally luxuriating in the land of the Nile. Here are four Shriners, with the pyramids of Gizeh behind them. It would be interesting to know what they are singing. Is it some esoteric Shrine hymn? Or is it—could it possibly be—"Sweet Adeline"?

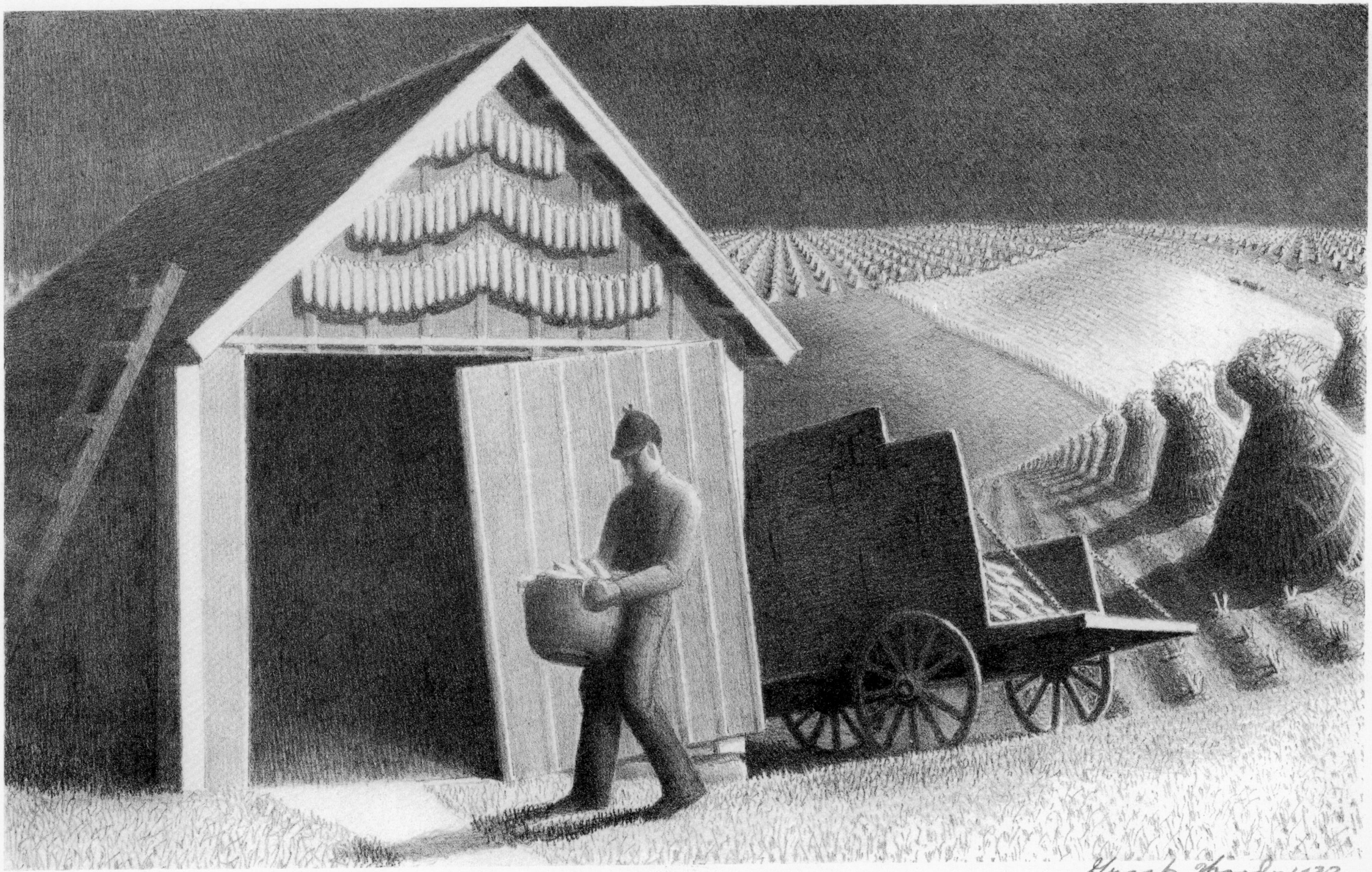

Grant Wood - 1937

PLATE NUMBER NINETY-SEVEN

Seedtime and Harvest

BY GRANT WOOD

(See reverse side for plate)

NEVER, PERHAPS, has the opulence of the agricultural Middle West been more lavishly portrayed than in Grant Wood's *Seedtime and Harvest.* In the state of Iowa, there are over two hundred and twenty thousand farms. It is the greatest corn-producing state in the Union, and leads also in the production of oats. These are pertinent facts to remember when looking at *Seedtime and Harvest.* It seems that the broad, rich acres stretch to infinity, and yet that the bursting produce of these fields is but a tithe of what this fabulously fertile country gives from its soil. Wood is pre-eminent in suggesting the bounteousness of nature.

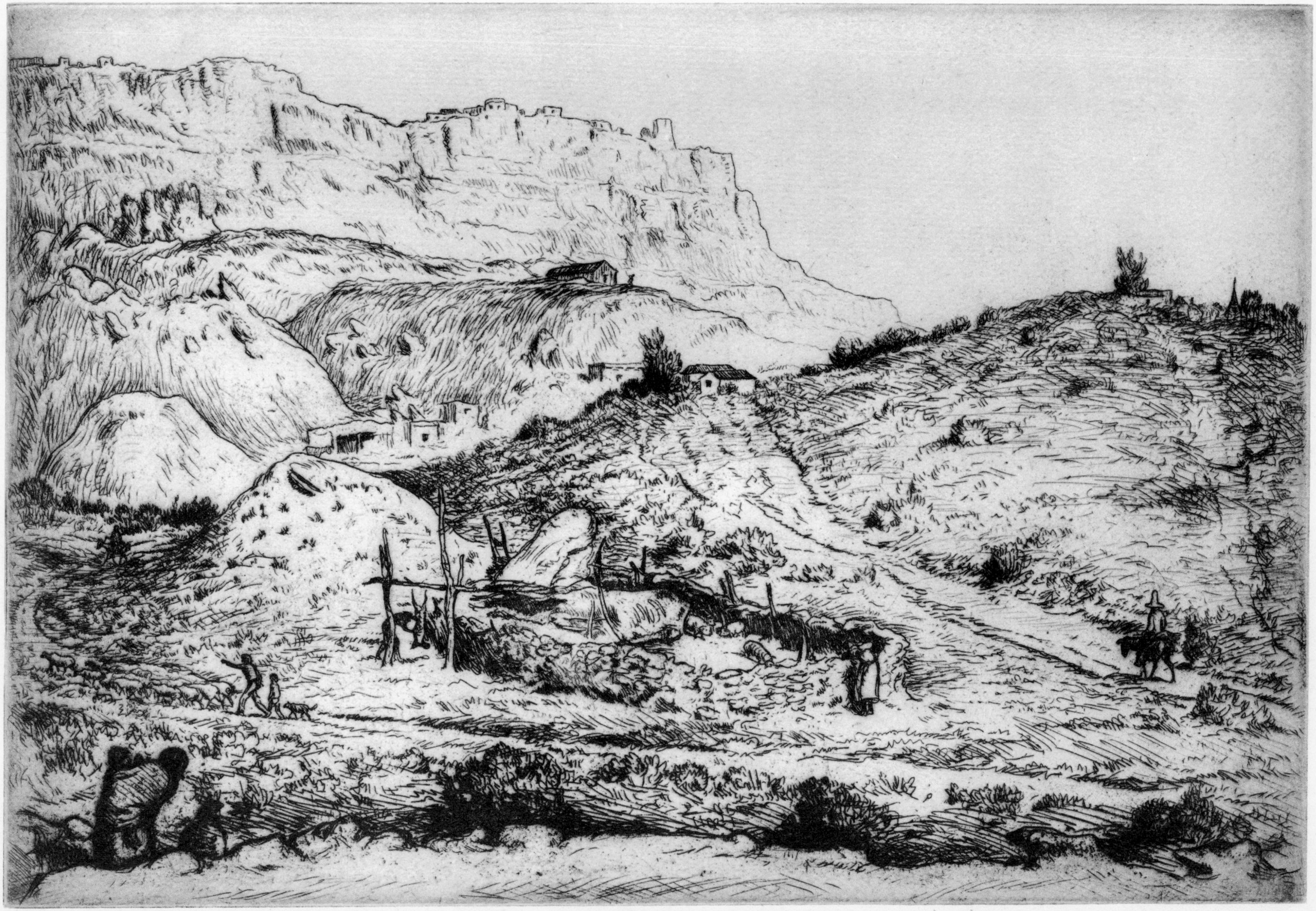

PLATE NUMBER NINETY-EIGHT

Walpi in Sunlight

BY MAHONRI YOUNG

(*See reverse side for plate*)

MAHONRI YOUNG has had an exciting and varied career. Born in Salt Lake City, Utah, on August 9, 1877, he is a grandson of Brigham Young, the Mormon leader. He lived out West until he was twenty, modeling in clay and adobe. He then came East to study painting at the Art Students' League, later going to Paris to study at the Académie Julian. In 1912, he first began his now famous studies of the picturesque Navajo Indians, whom he delineated in bronze bas-reliefs, etchings, and pastels. He returned to New York, drawn by the varied subject matter of the town, particularly by his interest in the laboring classes. This was expressed in bronzes of workingmen and by vigorous etchings of New York construction. He has taught at both the Art Students' League and the American School of Sculpture, and is still an instructor at the former institution. Young makes his home in New York. He has a summer place at Ridgefield, Connecticut, and is married to a daughter of the late J. Alden Weir, a distinguished painter.

Walpi in Sunlight was done over a long period of time—it was actually ten years in the making. It represents a Navajo locality in northern Arizona. Young's profound understanding of landscape values is expressed through a conventional but perfectly mastered technique.

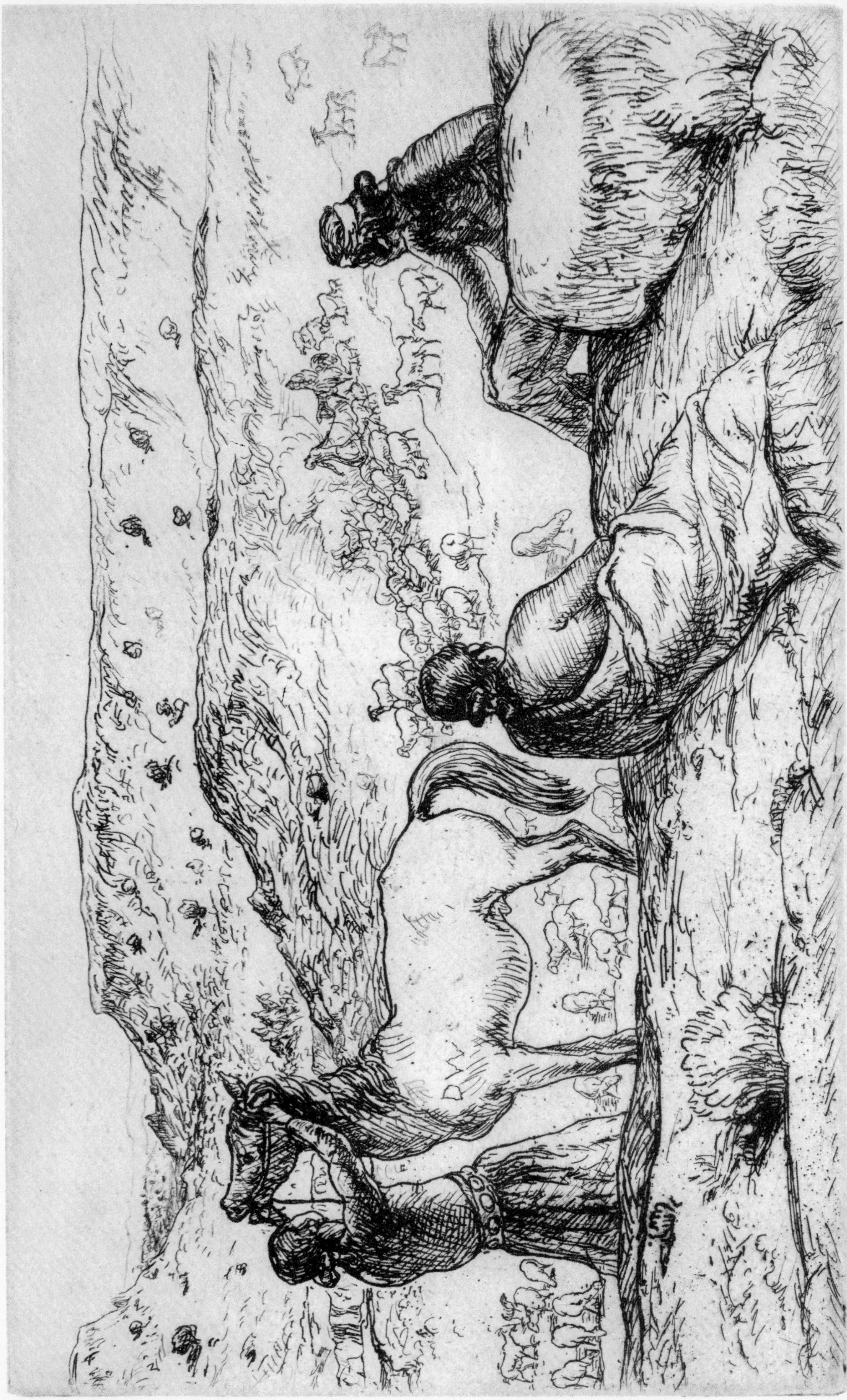

PLATE NUMBER NINETY-NINE

Three Navajos

BY MAHONRI YOUNG

(*See reverse side for plate*)

ARIZONA HAS, outside of Oklahoma, the largest Indian population in the United States. Of the forty-five thousand redskins in the state, a large percentage are Navajos, a seminomadic tribe of the great Athapascan stock that stretches from the region of Hudson Bay to the state of Chihuahua, in northern Mexico. The Navajos are herders, weavers, and picturesque scenic accessories —mainly the latter to the tourists who scour their once-happy hunting grounds in streamlined cars. But Mahonri Young knows the Indians as human beings. After all, he has been studying them for a quarter of a century and more.

Three Navajos is a handsome, atmospheric etching, extraordinary in its sympathetic treatment of the Indian women and painstakingly accurate in its rendering of the difficult Arizona terrain.

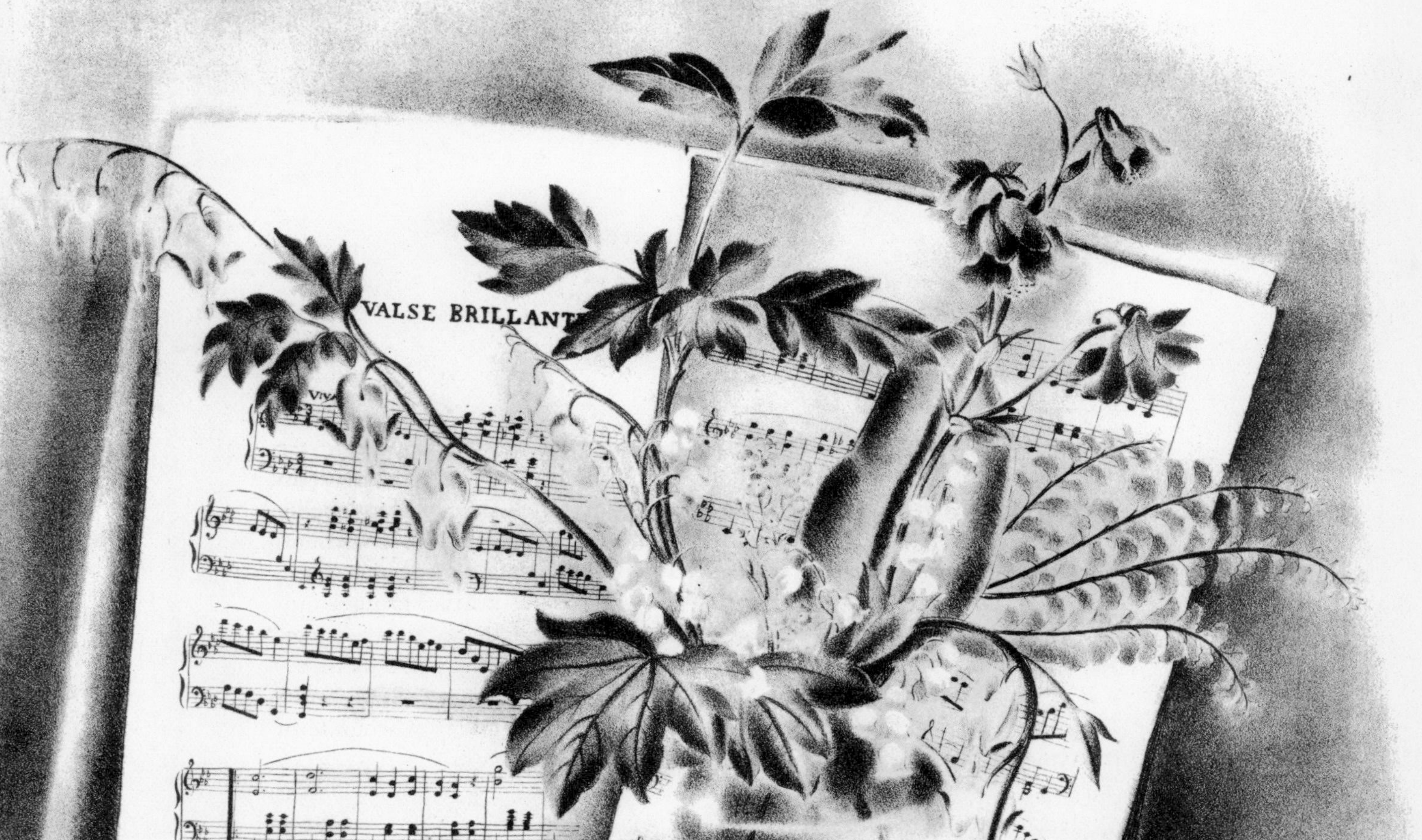
VALSE BRILLANTE

REPRO

"Valse Brillante"

Minnetta Good

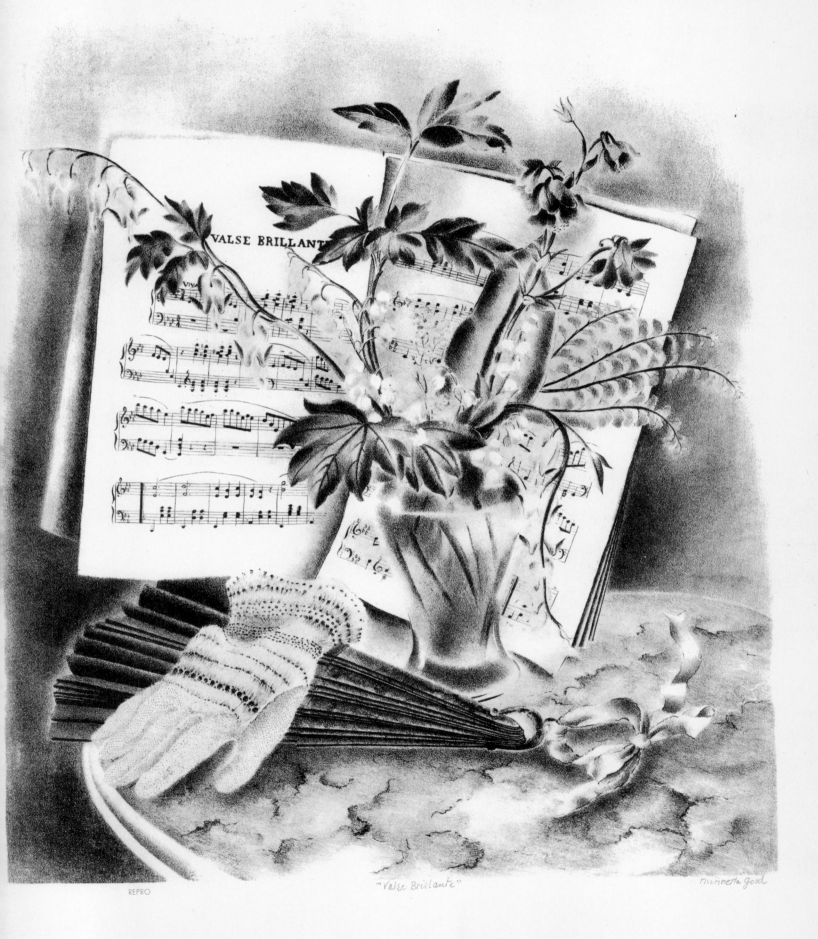

PLATE NUMBER ONE HUNDRED

Valse Brillante

BY MINNETTA GOOD

(See reverse side for plate)

PURPOSELY out of alphabetical order is *Valse Brillante,* which literally cries
out to be a tailpiece. It is the bravura composition of a young California artist,
who is absolutely self-taught, despite the fact that she works in many media.
Those who have gone through ninety-nine prints to come to this cool, frivolous,
and yet nostalgic hundredth will not go unrewarded even if they see in it only
a skillful arrangement, with a favorite Chopin valse as the background.